Conceptual Harmonies

Conceptual Harmonies

The Origins and Relevance of Hegel's Logic

PAUL REDDING

The University of Chicago Press
Chicago and London

The University of Chicago Press, Chicago 60637
The University of Chicago Press, Ltd., London
© 2023 by The University of Chicago
All rights reserved. No part of this book may be used or reproduced in any manner whatsoever without written permission, except in the case of brief quotations in critical articles and reviews. For more information, contact the University of Chicago Press, 1427 E. 60th St., Chicago, IL 60637.
Published 2023
Printed in the United States of America

32 31 30 29 28 27 26 25 24 23   1 2 3 4 5

ISBN-13: 978-0-226-82605-9 (cloth)
ISBN-13: 978-0-226-82607-3 (paper)
ISBN-13: 978-0-226-82606-6 (e-book)
DOI: https://doi.org/10.7208/chicago/9780226826066.001.0001

Library of Congress Cataloging-in-Publication Data

Names: Redding, Paul, 1948– author.
Title: Conceptual harmonies : the origins and relevance of Hegel's logic / Paul Redding.
Other titles: Origins and relevance of Hegel's logic
Description: Chicago : The University of Chicago Press, 2023. | Includes bibliographical references and index.
Identifiers: LCCN 2022043822 | ISBN 9780226826059 (cloth) | ISBN 9780226826073 (paperback) | ISBN 9780226826066 (ebook)
Subjects: LCSH: Hegel, Georg Wilhelm Friedrich, 1770–1831. | Hegel, Georg Wilhelm Friedrich, 1770–1831—Sources. | Logic. | Logic—History. | Mathematics, Greek.
Classification: LCC B2949.L8 R39 2023 | DDC 193—dc23/eng/20221207
LC record available at https://lccn.loc.gov/2022043822

Contents

Hegel's Texts: Translations and Abbreviations vii
Preface ix

Introduction 1

Beginning: Hegel's Classicism

1 Logic, Mathematics, and Philosophy in Fourth-Century Athens 21
2 Hegel and the Platonic Origins of Aristotle's Syllogistic 42
3 The General Significance of Neoplatonic Harmonic Theory for Hegel's Account of Magnitude 57

Middle: Classical Meets Modern

4 Geometry and Philosophy in Hegel, Schelling, Carnot, and Grassmann 87
5 The Role of *Analysis Situs* in Leibniz's Modernization of Logic 108
6 Hegel's Supersession of Leibniz and Newton: The Limitations of Calculus and Logical Calculus 126

End: The Modern as Redetermined Classical

7 Exploiting Resources within Aristotle for the Rehabilitation of the Syllogism 147
8 The Return of Leibnizian Logic in the Nineteenth Century: From Boole to Heyting 169

9	Hegel among the New Leibnizians: Judgments	191
10	Hegel beyond the New Leibnizians: Syllogisms	213
	Conclusion: The God at the Terminus of Hegel's Logic	228

Acknowledgments 233
Notes 235
Bibliography 261
Index 277

Hegel's Texts:
Translations and Abbreviations

The following translations have been used, although sometimes modified. Except where Hegel's texts have numbered paragraphs, page numbers in the English translations are followed by volume and page numbers from G. W. F. Hegel, *Gesammelte Werke* (Hamburg: Felix Meiner, 1968–) or *Vorlesungen: Ausgewählte Nachschriften und Manuskripte* (Hamburg: Felix Meiner, 1983–).

BRF: *Briefe von und an Hegel*. Vol. 1, *1785–1812*. Edited by Johannes Hoffmeister. Hamburg: Meiner Verlag, 1969.

DIFF: *The Difference between Fichte's and Schelling's System of Philosophy*. Translated and edited by H. S. Harris and Walter Cerf. Albany: State University of New York Press, 1977.

E:L: *Encyclopedia of the Philosophical Sciences in Basic Outline. Part 1, Science of Logic*. Translated and edited by Klaus Brinkmann and Daniel O. Dahlstrom. Cambridge: Cambridge University Press, 2010.

E:PN: *Hegel's Philosophy of Nature*. Edited and translated with an introduction and explanatory notes by M. J. Petry. 3 vols. London: George Allen and Unwin, 1970.

E:PS: *Hegel's Philosophy of Mind*. Translated from the 1830 edition, together with the *Zusätze*, by W. Wallace and A. V. Miller, with revisions and commentary by M. J. Inwood. Oxford: Clarendon Press, 2007.

LHP: *Lectures on the History of Philosophy, 1825–6*. Edited by Robert F. Brown. Translated by R. F. Brown and J. M. Stewart, with the assistance of H. S. Harris. 3 vols. Oxford: Clarendon Press, 2006–9.

MISC: *Miscellaneous Writings of G. W. F. Hegel*. Edited by Jon Stewart. Evanston, IL: Northwestern University Press, 2002.

PHEN: *The Phenomenology of Spirit*. Translated and edited by Terry Pinkard. Cambridge: Cambridge University Press, 2018.

PR: *Elements of the Philosophy of Right*. Edited by Allen W. Wood. Translated by H. B. Nisbet. Cambridge: Cambridge University Press, 1991.

SEL: *System of Ethical Life* (1802/3). In *System of Ethical Life and First Philosophy of Spirit*, edited and translated by H. S. Harris and T. M. Knox. Albany: State University of New York Press, 1979.

SL: *The Science of Logic*. Edited and translated by George di Giovanni. Cambridge: Cambridge University Press, 2010.

Preface

At the outset of his pathbreaking interpretation of Hegel's *Science of Logic*, the work that Hegel described as containing that on which all the rest of his work depended, Robert Pippin comments: "To understate the matter in the extreme: this book still awaits its full contemporary reception. . . . It has not inspired the kind of engagement found in work on Kant's *Critiques* or Hegel's own *Phenomenology of Spirit* or *Philosophy of Right*" (Pippin 2019, 4). Such comments apply particularly to the first half of "Subjective Logic," the second volume of *The Science of Logic*, and the place in which Hegel comes closest to the style of work that the term "logic" usually brings to mind—the systematic treatment of forms of judgment and inference.

In general, interpreters coming from the direction of Hegel studies, on the one hand, and logic itself, on the other, have been reluctant to engage with the details of Hegel's subjective logic. For many orthodox Hegelians it is routinely repeated that Hegel's logic has precious little if anything to do with "logic" as standardly understood and especially "formal" or "mathematical" logic. For logicians, the source of the reluctance has had more to do with the belief that Hegel stands on the wrong side of those "foundational" works that, in relation to logic, might be considered to have established its modern paradigm. Even where some nonclassical logicians show sympathy with the dialectical spirit of Hegel (e.g., Priest 1989/1990), they rarely engage closely with "the letter" of his "Subjective Logic."[1]

Although with a focus on Hegel's *Phenomenology of Spirit* rather than his *Logic*, Robert Brandom has, over the last three decades, confronted this reluctance. Inspired by the work of Wilfrid Sellars and Richard Rorty, Brandom has attempted to establish a place for Hegelian thinking within contemporary analytic philosophy in a way that does not flinch from the fact of the latter's origins in the logical revolution sparked by the work of the German mathematician Gottlob Frege in the latter decades of the nineteenth century. Rorty had pointed to the holistic and pragmatic approaches to reasoning that had emerged among Frege's successors during the "linguistic turn" of the 1930s, 1940s, and 1950s (Rorty 1967), undermining analysis's commitment to the idea of the mind's "mirroring" of the world in thought (Rorty 1979). Progressive post-Fregeans, such as Carnap, Quine, and, especially, Sellars, he thought, had liberated philosophy from this mythical view leading to ideas that had "been a commonplace of our culture since Hegel. Hegel's historicism gave us a sense of how there might be genuine novelty in the development of thought and of society" (Rorty 1982, 3). But while Rorty's appeal to Hegel had the purpose of *freeing* philosophy from the framework of analysis as originally conceived, Brandom's has been more in the service of "extending" the project of analytic philosophy in a way that rescues its original spirit (Brandom 2008, ch. 1). With the help of Hegel, analytic philosophy could be freed from the imagery of the mind as a mirror of nature with its implicit understanding of representation as resemblance, and so be rehabilitated as a meaningful project.

On Brandom's account, both Hegel and analytic philosophy are compatible participants within that extended modern "Copernican revolution" that Kant had declared in philosophy and in which he challenged the idea of the mind's representations as resembling the world "in itself." But prior to Kant, Brandom points to the significance of Descartes's innovative application of algebra to geometry in the seventeenth century. According to Brandom, Descartes's "analytic geometry" had freed the concept of representation from resemblance: "Treating something in linear, discursive form, such as '$ax + by = c$' as an appearance of a Euclidean line, and '$x^2 + y^2 = d$' as an appearance of a circle, allows one to calculate how many points of intersection they *can* have and what points of intersection they *do* have, and lots more besides. These sequences of symbols do not at all *resemble* lines and circles. Yet his mathematical results . . . showed that algebraic symbols present geometric facts in a form that is not only (potentially and reliably) *veridical*, but conceptually *tractable*. . . . He saw that what made algebraic understanding of geometric figures possible was a global *isomorphism* between the whole system of algebraic symbols and the whole system of geometric figures" (Brandom 2019, 39; cf. 2009, 28).

While Brandom has distanced himself from the details of Hegel's own ideas about his logic and its ancestry, Descartes's analytic geometry nevertheless can seem a singularly unhappy choice. Hegel had a lifelong interest in mathematics and, especially, Greek geometry and modern celestial mechanics, and in relation to the latter he had unequivocally championed the role of Kepler over Newton. Hegel's support of Kepler has often been dismissed because it involved the latter's appeal to Plato's cosmology, with that aspect of Kepler's work typically seen as unconnected with the advances he made in empirical astronomy. While this is the type of dimension from which Brandom is happy to abstract, in this work it will be argued that Hegel was in fact on much sturdier ground in his appeals to Plato and Kepler than is usually assumed. Independently of these considerations, however, are ones that are much closer to the issue of Descartes's analytic geometry. Hegel praised Kepler's reliance on Apollonius's synthetic geometry of conic sections over Newton's new "analytic" point of view that was linked to the infinitesimal calculus that he helped shape, an innovation that itself had relied on Descartes's analytic geometry. "It is well known that the immortal honour of having discovered the laws of absolutely free motion belongs to *Kepler. Kepler proved* them in that he discovered the *universal* expression of the empirical data. It has subsequently become customary to speak as if *Newton* were the first to have discovered the proof of these laws. The credit for a discovery has seldom been denied a man with more unjustness" (*E:PN*, §270, remark).

In the context of this remark Hegel appeals to a recent work in mechanics (Francoeur 1807) done in the style of the type of geometry being practiced in Paris in the newly formed École Polytechnique—a style of geometry that had been self-consciously proposed as an alternative to Descartes's analytic geometry. This rival geometrical tradition of projective geometry, to which Kepler is regarded as a precursor, had been introduced in the seventeenth century by Girard Desargues just two years after Descartes's *Géométrie* of 1637. However, it had fallen on deaf ears and lain dormant for almost two centuries before being revived in France in the last decades of the eighteenth century by Gaspard Monge and by one of his former students, Lazare Carnot. The remarkable Carnot had become a major figure in the French Revolution and Revolutionary Wars and among his achievements had been the establishment of a new educational institution meant to serve the ends of the revolution, the École Polytechnique, at the head of which he had appointed Monge. Hegel's strong feelings about the "unjustness" of the treatment of Kepler had sources deep within his views about the relation of modernity to antiquity that would be expressed toward topics that ranged from the French Revolution to the disciplines of geometry, algebra, and logic. All of these happened to converge in the revolutionary new institution, the École Polytechnique (Gray 2007, ch. 1).

Elsewhere I have objected to elements of Brandom's "strong inferentialist" interpretation of Hegel (Redding 2015), but more recently I have come to see Brandom's broader narrative locating of Hegel as the source of these problems. Hegel should not be regarded as a somewhat eccentric figure within the tradition running from analytic geometry to analytic philosophy via the logics of Kant and Frege; rather, he should be regarded as one of its most powerful critics. Moreover, his critique of analytic geometry, I believe, holds the key to his critique of analytic philosophy and its favored logic. Hegel, I will argue, had identified with this different geometrical tradition, which had been revived around the turn of the nineteenth century and of which he was certainly aware. He possessed the book by Carnot in which the Frenchman had first reintroduced projective geometry to the world (Carnot 1801; Mense 1993, 673).

While the framework of analytic geometry was, as Brandom astutely points out, later presupposed by Frege's logic and the analytic philosophy to which it gave rise, projective geometry would be implicated in the structure of the second wave of Leibnizian logic in the nineteenth century associated with the English mathematician George Boole and followers such as Charles Sanders Peirce. The original version of this algebraic Aristotelian logic had stemmed from Leibniz himself and, while generally thought to have had little impact in European philosophy before its discovery at the end of the nineteenth century, had deeply influenced the form of logic taught at the Tübingen Seminary during Hegel's years there. Moreover, despite being inspired by Descartes's application of algebra to geometry, Leibniz had tempered this with a criticism of Descartes's analytic geometry similar to that of the projective geometers. Leibniz had thus advocated a nonmetrical approach to geometry he called *analysis situs*, the analysis of situation. In one of the books in which Carnot reintroduced projective geometry to the world (Carnot 1803a), he presented his own "geometry of position" as a realization of Leibniz's *analysis situs*.[2]

A distinguishing feature of the nineteenth-century version of Leibnizian logic would be the presence of a principle directly inherited from projective geometry, usually referred to as the principle of "duality." In fact, at the end of the nineteenth century, a young Bertrand Russell, prior to his conversion to Fregeanism and "analysis" more generally, would point to this feature as characterizing Hegel's account of space (Russell 1897). I will argue, however, for its centrality to Hegel's logic as a whole, in much the same way that it was central for Boole and the post-Booleans but not for Frege, Russell, or Brandom.

The presence of this principle of duality in Hegel, in the form of two irreducibly different forms of judgment, disrupts Brandom's idea of a logical analogue of the "universal isomorphism" between geometric and algebraic forms of expression. Nevertheless, with it Hegel expresses a type of equivalence between different judgment forms similar to the difference between the discrete and continuous magnitudes of algebra and geometry to which Brandom alludes. Rather than a global equivalence, however, Hegel's logic will exhibit a local form of equivalence between logical forms that differ in the way that algebraic and geometric expressions differ. And rather than an "isomorphism," Hegel's logic will demonstrate that weaker form of equivalence that mathematicians call "homomorphism"—a form of equivalence closer to that of what in the nineteenth century came to be called "homology" in the science of comparative anatomy in which the arm of a human was regarded as in certain ways equivalent to the wing of a bird, despite their functional differences. The linked ideas of duality, homomorphism, and homology, I will argue, better capture what Hegel describes as an "identity in difference" or an "identity of identity *and* difference,"[3] formulations that escape the analytic framework of Brandom's interpretations. Hegel's appeal to a form of homomorphic equivalence between different logical forms will be shown to be a central feature of his logic.

The fact of the presence of a small book on geometry in Hegel's library is not being proposed as evidence of some specific influence traceable from Carnot to Hegel. Rather, the tradition of projective geometry, as signaled by its anticipation by Kepler, had its roots deep in the mathematical culture of Plato's Academy in its early decades. This was a culture focused on the notion of "measure" because confidence had been shaken in the capacity of the mind to take the measure of the world in a literal sense by the discovery of the phenomenon of incommensurability between the discrete magnitudes of arithmetic and the continuous magnitudes of geometry—a discovery now usually described as the discovery of the "irrational numbers." This is usually discussed as a consequence of the discovery of one of the founding theorems of Greek geometry, Pythagoras's theorem, but it had also been linked to the Pythagorean interest in music and the generalization of its organizational principles to the cosmos. Hegel locates the principle of local homomorphism, as we will see, in Plato, but a more familiar sense of what it might amount to for logic will perhaps be gained from the role played by analogy in Aristotle and his use of the notion of "mean" in the *Nicomachean Ethics*, where he invokes two different types of mean or middle terms drawn from contemporary music theory to differentiate two different types of justice (Aristotle 1984, *Nicomachean Ethics*, 1131a28–32b20). As we will see, in his discussion of Plato's *Timaeus*, Hegel would stress that what typically distinguishes Plato's "syllogism" from Aristotle's is that Plato's has a "doubled" or "broken" middle term. From Hegel's perspective Aristotle's discussion of justice would have been one of the few places in Aristotle's texts in which Plato's approach, with its dual means or middle terms, could be recognized. But it is not just a question of whether one or two "means" are employed. The two means employed by Aristotle here were in fact two of three—the geometric, the arithmetic, and the harmonic—and the "principle of local homomorphism" would turn out to rest upon the type of unity meant to be achieved among them.

It was a conception of syllogism modeled upon this type of unity among the three otherwise incommensurable means that, I will argue, had been behind Hegel's widely misunderstood support for Kepler's cosmology with its strange association with the ancient doctrine of the "music of the spheres." Hegel's appeal to Kepler's geometric approach to cosmology, in contrast with the predominantly "analytic" approach originating from Descartes and Newton, was actually in accord with the reemergence of nonmetrical forms of geometry that would go on to play important roles within not only the development of nineteenth-century science but also that century's rehabilitation of logic.

The work that follows has grown out of what was first planned as an introductory chapter to an interpretation of Hegel's metaphysics and the consequences that this metaphysics held for his *Realphilosophie*. However, the chapter then grew into the first half of a planned book aimed at grounding Hegel's metaphysics in this reconstruction of his logic. This ambition also soon proved wildly unrealistic, however, and this reading of Hegel's logic was reconceived as the subject of a stand-alone work. Making a case for this unusual and counterintuitive reading of Hegel involves appeals to episodes from the history of mathematics that are not typically seen as relevant for either logic or philosophy and with which many readers will be unfamiliar—on the one hand, the ancient Pythagorean theory of the musical "means," and on the other, modern projective geometry and other forms of nineteenth-century "geometrical algebra" that revived these ancient approaches. I have therefore tried to supply enough of this historical background as necessary for conveying how Hegel could make use of *it* and how it might make sense of *him*. Given this need, together with that of keeping the presentation as uncluttered and as clear as possible, I have maintained a focus entirely on the relevance of these issues for Hegel's logic and have resisted the temptation to draw consequences for his philosophy more broadly. There is no attempt, then, to locate my interpretation of Hegel within the burgeoning context of the many contemporary interpretations of his work. I have had to ignore even those recent accounts of Hegel's *Science of Logic*, such as that of Robert Pippin referred to above, in which the focus is not predominantly on these narrowly "logical" issues, in the usual understanding of this term.

For the same reason I make no attempt to engage directly with Brandom's contrasting account of the logic structuring Hegel's *Phenomenology of Spirit*.

I know that Bob advises young philosophers that have come into his orbit to work out their own "big idea." My hope is that this advice works not only for the young. While reference to Brandom's own powerful reading of Hegel only very occasionally appears in these pages, my debts to his work, stretching over more than three decades, will be obvious.

Introduction

> Had I more space, I now ought to show how important for philosophy is the mathematical conception of continuity. Most of what is true in Hegel is a darkling glimmer of a conception which the mathematicians had long before made pretty clear, and which recent researchers have still further illustrated.
>
> C. S. PEIRCE, "The Architecture of Theories"

0.1 Greek Geometry, Pythagorean Harmonics, and Hegel's Syllogism: An Initial Sketch

In his 1825–26 *Lectures on the History of Philosophy* at the University of Berlin, Hegel discussed Plato's natural philosophy as given mythical expression by the apparently fictional Pythagorean mathematician-cosmologist, Timaeus of Locri. Following Plato, Hegel identifies the organizing principle giving structure to the body of the cosmic animal as "the most beautiful bond [*der Bande schönstes*]," and then (loosely) quotes Plato himself: " 'This brings into play in the most beautiful way the proportion [*die Analogie*] or the continuing geometric ratio [*das stetige geometrische Verhältnis*]. If the middle one of three numbers, masses or forces is related to the third as the first is to it and, conversely, it is related to the first as the third is to it (*a* is to *b* as *b* is to *c*), then, since the middle term has become first and last and, conversely, the last and the first have become the middle term, they have then all become one.' " Hegel then adds in his own words: "With this the absolute identity is established. This is the syllogism [*der Schluss*] known to us from logic. It retains the form in which it appears in the familiar syllogistic [*im gewöhnlichen Syllogismus*], but here it is the rational" (*LHP* 2:209–210; 3:39).[1] The peculiar unity among the two extremes and the middle term alluded to here will be expressed in the idea that Plato's syllogism demands a middle term that is simultaneously *two*, a middle term that is "broken" or "doubled" (211; 3:41), a feature that will be seen to be lacking in the "familiar syllogistic" of Aristotle.

This fixation on the most beautiful bond of Timaeus's cosmology had been central to Hegel's thinking from his earliest philosophical period and has posed challenges to attempts to portray him as a serious *modern* philosopher—indeed, from the point of view of many, as a philosopher at all. It is known from Karl Rosenkranz, the editor who had access to Hegel's

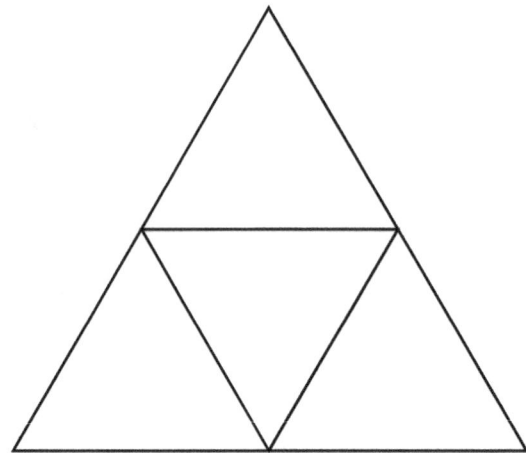

FIGURE 0.1 Hegel's "triangle of triangles" (adapted from Schneider 1975, 149).

manuscripts and papers after his death, that Hegel had written a now-lost fragment, seemingly sometime in 1800–1801, in which he had experimented with a diagram to represent this same *Analogie* from Plato's *Timaeus* (Schneider 1975). Rosenkranz dated the diagram roughly around the time at which Hegel had left his position as house tutor to a wealthy family in Frankfurt to embark on an academic career at the University of Jena. The diagram depicts a "triangle of triangles" showing the inverted embedding of one equilateral triangle within another, the embedded triangle having sides half the length of the larger triangle such that a further three smaller triangles are produced inside the first with the same orientation as it, as in figure 0.1.

In the generation of such a diagram, the division of the initial figure produces further instances of the same figure that can each be further divided, the process being able to be iterated indefinitely in a way now referred to as "fractal."[2] It is often noted that during the earlier years of his stay in Frankfurt from 1797 to 1800, Hegel had been attracted to "mystical" (Lukács 1975, 121–123) or "theosophical" (Harris 1983, 184) elements within medieval Christianity that, Lukács and Harris argue, he soon moved beyond. The triangle was a commonly used representation of the Christian doctrine of the Trinity, and Hegel would probably have been aware that this motif was to be found in tiling patterns in cathedrals, such that the iteration of the division of the initial triangle within the smaller similarly aligned triangles was meant to induce a sense of infinity in the viewer. Hegel would soon abandon the project of finding diagrams that were adequate to what he thought of as fundamentally conceptual relations, and so the proper concept of infinity. But Hegel's diagram nevertheless conveys the particular importance the ancient science of geometry would continue to hold in relation to his conception of logic. It is known, for example, that he embarked upon an intensive reading of Euclid's *Elements* around 1800 (Paterson 2005), and it has been suggested that his triangle of triangles had represented an interest in a type of "geometric logic" (Schneider 1975, 139).[3] Moreover, as we will see, the "triangle of triangles" involved had connotations other than Christian ones, linking it to ancient Pythagorean mathematics and in turn to Timaeus's most beautiful bond.

In the 1825–26 *Lectures*, addressing Timaeus's account of the structure of the cosmic mind, Hegel touches upon a number series found in Plato's text that had got him into hot water in his dissertation, "On the Orbits of the Planets" (*Misc*, 170–206), written in 1801 at the University of Jena to satisfy the conditions allowing him to teach there. The dissertation, roughly contemporaneous with the "triangle of triangles," is infamous for Hegel's having invoked a sequence of seven numbers in an apparent explanation of the comparative distances of the (then-known) seven planets from the sun. Hegel had become, and still is, roundly mocked for what has been seen as an attempt to preempt any empirically based cosmology by some type of ancient number mysticism, but what Hegel was actually attempting, I will argue, was of an entirely different nature. Defenders have pointed to the exaggerations involved in his critics' descriptions of his claims, confined to the last page or so of the dissertation (e.g., Harris 1983, 96; Craig and Hoskin 1992). Moreover, the bulk of the dissertation had been devoted to a topic much more expected of a modern philosopher—a critique of the idea that Newton's laws could be said to explain the laws of planetary motion that Kepler had arrived at empirically and expressed geometrically—a critique that Hegel would continue in his later systematic philosophy of nature (*E:PN*, §270, remark and addition). That is, rather than attempt to usurp empirical observation by a priori reasoning, Hegel actually seems to have been defending the role of observation in astronomy, denying that Newton's methods could properly be described as empirical. That is, absent the last few pages, Hegel's dissertation was devoted to a type of philosophy of science that would be unlikely to raise eyebrows even today. Let's remain for the moment, however, with this troubling number series itself.

In his suggested series—1, 2, 3, 4, 9, 16, 27—Hegel had altered Plato's original series of 1, 2, 3, 4, 9, 8, 27 (Plato, *Timaeus*, 35b), which itself had drawn upon the *tetraktys*, a type of triangular figurative number used by contemporary Pythagorean mathematicians consisting of an array of ten elements arranged like the pins in ten-pin bowling (as pictured in fig. 0.2)—that is, in four rows of one, two, three, and four units, respectively.

We will later explore some of the various levels of significance this figure held for the Pythagoreans, but two points are worth noting here. The first is obvious: this is the similarity of the Pythagorean *tetraktys* to the triangle of triangles. Hegel's diagram would result from simply "joining the dots" within any of the component triads. The second concerns the meanings the *tetraktys* held for the Pythagoreans and, following them, Plato. It will be argued that these could have a significance for Hegel beyond the "number mysticism" with which his interest in Plato is usually associated.

Concern with such arcane matters was not peculiar to Hegel. In 1794, during the time of his close association with Hegel at the Tübingen Seminary, Friedrich Schelling wrote a commentary on Plato's *Timaeus* (Schelling 1994) that would feed into the philosophy of nature that he pursued at Jena when working collaboratively with Hegel in the early years of the new century. These interests caught the attention of the romantic *Naturphilosoph* Franz von Baader, who, in 1798, published a work, entitled *On the Pythagorean Tetrad in Nature, or The Four Regions of the World* (Baader 1798; Förster 2012, 240–242).[4] Baader's *pythagoräische Quadrat*, a figure meant to express his criticism of Schelling's acceptance of aspects of Kant's natural philosophy (Förster 2012, 241), was, in fact, the *tetraktys*, which he represented as an equilateral triangle within which he placed a single point, as in figure 0.3 (Baader 1798, 49 note).[5]

In the early 1790s, Baader seems to have shared political as well as scientific and theosophical interests with Schelling and Hegel. Having spent time in England, Baader had become an admirer of Mary Wollstonecraft and William Godwin, as well as Jean-Jacques Rousseau, although his views remained predominantly religious (Betanzos 1998, 63–64).[6] In accord with his Catholicism, however, he would be critical of the Spinozist pantheism that he attributed to both Schelling and Hegel, but to which he nevertheless came close.

Such combinations of scientific, theosophical, and political interests were in no way restricted to these three, Pythagoreanism having come to have widespread contemporary relevance via the French Revolution. According

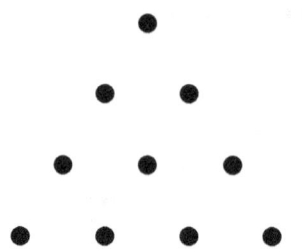

FIGURE 0.2 The Pythagorean *tetraktys*.

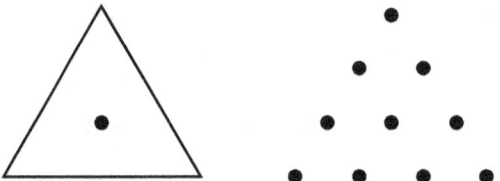

FIGURE 0.3 Baader's *Quadrat* and the Pythagorean *tetraktys*.

to historian James Billington, "the image of the revolutionary as a modern Pythagoras and of his social ideal as Philadelphia" distilled "the high fraternal ideals common both to the occult brotherhoods of Masonry and Illuminism and to the idealistic youthful mobilization to defend the revolution in 1792–94" (Billington 1980, 99–100). As Terry Pinkard has described the situation, while the much-repeated story of the three fellow seminarians, Hölderlin, Schelling, and Hegel, planting a "freedom tree" on July 14, 1793, may well be a myth, it nevertheless captures "the spirit that was undoubtedly animating the three friends. A political club had formed in the 1790s at Tübingen to discuss the Revolution, to read various revolutionary tracts, and in general to raise the spirits of the seminarians who were inspired by the events of the Revolution; Hegel was a member of the club" (Pinkard 2000, 24). There is evidence that Hegel, when employed as a house tutor in Bern and, especially, Frankfurt, remained involved in a secretive way with Masonic groups and, in particular, with a former student and club member from Tübingen, J. K. F. Hauff (d'Hondt 1968, chs. 1 and 2). Hegel's links to Hauff, whether direct or indirect, suggest an attraction to Pythagorean ideas quite different from the more theosophical/nature-philosophical attitudes of Schelling and Baader.

Clearly during these early years Baader, Schelling, and Hegel had all been concerned with construing the god of Christianity in ways that suggested a type of pantheism—itself a somewhat revolutionary and dangerous stance—a position that Baader would explicitly come to oppose.[7] As part of this, inspired by Plato's conception of a world-soul in the *Timaeus*, all three were also concerned with combating the type of mechanistic view of the world that could be understood as the complement to an entirely extramundane concept of God. In the service of this idea of reanimating the extended physical world, both Schelling and Baader believed that more recent sciences such as chemistry testified to the pervasion of the world by some mind-like substance, Baader, for example, pursuing the idea of heat as a quasi-mind-like *Wärmestoff* (Betanzos 1998, 62). Along with this went a fascination with symbolic ways of presenting such an animated conception of the world to combat what were seen as the lifeless abstractions of modern rational thought. However, in line with the assessments of Harris and Lukács, Helmut Schneider has attributed a quite distinct attitude to Hegel: "The 'triangle fragment' does not rest on mystical experience. It is about rational construction and geometrical logic" (Schneider 1975, 139).

Interest in such a "geometrical logic," I will argue, is evidenced by the science books in Hegel's library, and in particular, the combination of works on Greek mathematics and recent and contemporary developments in that discipline (Mense 1993, 670). In relation to the latter might be noted two books by the French mathematician Lazare Carnot (Mense 1993, 673 and 682), who would revive a form of geometry that would become central to advances in mathematics and physics through the nineteenth century and beyond. In one, Carnot's *De la corrélation des figures de géométrie*, first published in 1801, would be found a peculiar type of "double ratio" that linked back to the Pythagorean *tetraktys*, or more specifically, to another, related Pythagorean *tetraktys* called the "musical *tetraktys*." The musical *tetraktys* was also called *harmonia*, and this name was reflected in the name "harmonic cross-ratio" that would later be given to this important geometrical structure introduced in Carnot's book. Moreover, in one of the books on Greek mathematics in Hegel's library, Nicomachus of Gerasa's *Introduction to Arithmetic* (Mense 1993, 672), this musical *tetraktys* was identified as the most beautiful bond of Plato's *Timaeus* that, as we have seen, Hegel would identify as the "rational form" of the "syllogism known to us in logic." Given this spread of Hegel's interests, it is hard to see how he could *not* have been interested in the contents of Carnot's book, but there would have been many more reasons for Hegel's interest in this particular mathematician.

Count Lazare Nicolas Marguerite Carnot is now entombed in the Pantheon in Paris and regarded as one of the heroes of the French Revolution and Revolutionary Wars (Gueniffey 1989). Trained as a military engineer, Carnot had been elected a member of the National Assembly in 1791 and by 1794 "had achieved his objective of virtual total control of military affairs" (Gueniffey 1989, 199). In the same year, in his capacity as a member of the Committee for Public Safety, he was involved in the overthrow of Robespierre and the ending of the Terror. Hegel's five-year stay at the Tübingen Seminary between October 1788 and June 1793 broadly overlapped with the period from the formation of the National Assembly (June 1789) to Robespierre's fall (July 1794),[8] and we know he followed these events with intense interest. Besides the small book on geometry, Hegel also possessed an earlier work of Carnot's, *Réflexions sur la métaphysique du calcul infinitésimal*, published in French in 1797. While proficient in French, Hegel possessed both books in

German translation, *Réflexions* having been translated by a former seminarian at Tübingen, J. K. F. Hauff, whose period there overlapped with Hegel's. Four years Hegel's senior, Hauff was, like Hegel, from Stuttgart and in 1790 had effectively been expelled from the seminary for his revolutionary activities. Even had they not been acquainted, Hegel surely would have been aware of his older fellow student. After Tübingen, Hauff had gone on to become a mathematician and political activist and, having translated a number of books published by the revolutionary Parisian publishing house Imprimerie du Cercle Social, seems to have been associated with the moderate Girondist wing of the Revolution.

In his study of Hegel's "secret" revolutionary associations in the 1790s, Jacques d'Hondt has postulated that Hegel and Hauff may have been associated during the time both lived in Frankfurt, especially in relation to Masonic clubs (d'Hondt 1968, 46–50). Besides Hauff's translation of Carnot, Hegel also possessed his translation of Pierre-Simon Laplace's *Exposition du système du monde*, first published by the Cercle Social (45). This influential publishing house, associated with the Girondist party (Kates 1985), had also published a work by the Swiss lawyer Jean-Jacques Cart, on the oppression of the French-speaking Vaudois by their neighboring German-speaking Bernese, which Hegel had translated while in Berne. Later, while living in Frankfurt in 1798, Hegel would publish this translation and a commentary with the same publishers who had published both of Hauff's scientific translations. As suited the justifiable secretness that accompanied Hegel's associations with the revolutionary movement, he had published this anonymously.

The results of d'Hondt's sleuthing suggest links between Hegel and Hauff that were both political *and* scientific. Hegel's political allegiances during this period were definitely toward the type of anti-Jacobin position associated with the Cercle Social, but his links to contemporary mathematical science, as mediated by Hauff's translations, also suggest interests different from those of Schelling and Baader. For his part, Hauff's association with Carnot seems to have exceeded that of simple translator, as studies of the young German's correspondence with Carnot during the translation of *Réflexions* suggest that he had in fact been influencing the direction that Carnot's mathematical work was taking at the time (Schubring 2005, 349). Hauff went on to become the first professor of mathematics at the University of Marburg and is occasionally mentioned in histories of the genesis of non-Euclidean geometry in the nineteenth century via his influence on the "astral geometry" of Ferdinand Karl Schwikardt.[9]

Hegel's interest in what Helmut Schneider calls "rational construction and geometrical logic" (Schneider 1975, 139) would have attracted him to Carnot, given that the latter was taking mathematics in a direction that was to provide a type of logical framework for the sorts of nonreductionistic approaches to science favored by Schelling and Baader but largely free of the mystical symbolism found in *Naturphilosophie*. Within the history of science, Carnot is now best known for two aspects of his work: his early role in the flowering of modern projective geometry, on the one hand, and, on the other, within the development of mechanics (Carnot 1803b; Gillispie and Pisano 2013, chs. 2–4) and, indirectly, thermodynamics.[10] Both aspects were linked and reveal the deeply practical nature of his outlook.

At a time during which the modern distinction between "pure" and "applied" mathematics was only just emerging, Carnot conceived of geometry as *essentially* "applied"—a view that, as we will see, Hegel shared but Schelling did not. In this, Carnot's attitude was similar to that of his former teacher, Gaspard Monge. Monge had developed a "descriptive geometry" (Monge 1799),[11] dedicated to representing three-dimensional objects on differently oriented two-dimensional planes, so to meet the needs of the modern engineer. In turn, the École Polytechnique established by Carnot in his capacity of minister of war was meant to provide this training, and this type of institution would proliferate throughout the nineteenth century (Barbin, Menghini, and Volkert 2019). Thus, both worked on developing a form of mathematics better suited to worldly application than either traditional Euclidean geometry or the algebraic mechanics recently developed by Joseph-Louis Lagrange. To this end they resurrected a then-forgotten form of geometry from the seventeenth century—projective geometry—which in turn had roots in ancient Greece and was concerned with calculating relations among different two-dimensional projections of three-dimensional objects or arrangements of objects. The harmonic cross-ratio introduced by Carnot in *De la corrélation* was central to this task, as a generalization of it (later called the "*anharmonic cross-ratio*") would turn out to be the main device for calculating distances between locations in three-dimensional space on the basis of distances represented in two-dimensional maps—an invaluable resource for military engineers like Carnot and Monge.

The earlier of the two books by Carnot in Hegel's possession, *Réflexions sur la métaphysique du calcul infinitésimal*, was representative of the "heavy investment in standard works on the calculus and mechanics" evidenced by Hegel's library (Mense 1993, 670). In *The Science of Logic* Hegel would make extensive use of the way Carnot had there treated infinitesimal magnitudes as found in the modern differential and integral calculus of Leibniz and Newton—an issue at the heart of the main section of his 1801 treatise at Jena. Hegel was clearly aware that modern calculus also had roots in ancient geometry, specifically in Archimedes's efforts to calculate the circumferences and areas of circles,[12] and this was related to his championing of Kepler's approach to celestial mechanics over Newton's analytic approach, and Carnot's geometrical mechanics over Lagrange's purely algebraic account.[13] Here there were parallels with the way projective geometry was concerned with relations between three- and two-dimensional geometric objects, because modern calculus, Hegel believed, had effectively reduced *two*-dimensional geometrical objects (circles and other conic sections) to *one*-dimensional ones (straight lines) without acknowledging that a different conception of magnitude had been invoked—an idea he had found in Greek geometry.

This issue in turn linked to another aspect of Greek mathematics that was crucial for Hegel, the status of ratios and proportions in relation to theories of number and magnitude, a topic to which he would dedicate almost two hundred pages in book 1 of *The Science of Logic*. Two years after *De la corrélation* Carnot would expand on its results in *Géométrie de position*, the name for which he self-consciously chose to echo a project earlier suggested by Leibniz from his own encounter with seventeenth-century projective geometry and that he had called *analysis situs*, or "situational analysis." Rebelling against the way that Descartes and Fermat had arithmetized geometry, Leibniz had proposed a nonmetric form of geometry based on the idea of "congruence" between geometric figures. For example, two triangles ABC and DEF were considered congruent if one could be superimposed on the other.[14] Eliding the actual numerical quantities involved was meant to counter the "analytic geometry" of Descartes and Fermat, in which geometric objects were conceived as equations with numerical values. In doing so, Leibniz revived an approach that the late nineteenth-century Danish historian of mathematics Hans Georg Zeuthen would describe as the "geometric algebra" of the Greeks—a form of mathematics that was like algebra because it "dealt with general magnitudes, irrational as well as rational," while using geometric diagrams to "visualize its procedures and impress them in memory" (quoted in Høyrup 2017, 133).[15]

Projective geometry would be developed throughout the nineteenth century and would become closely linked to other developments in the nonmetrical treatment of space, including the geometric vector analysis of Hermann Grassmann from the 1840s (Crowe 1967), that he called "linear extension theory" and that is widely known as "linear algebra." Grassmann's work, like Carnot's, had been inspired by Leibniz's *analysis situs* and, again like Carnot's, related back to post-Euclidean elements of Greek mathematics that had been utilized by Newton in his celestial mechanics. While Euclid's geometry is most known for the geometry of plane figures, certain books of his *Elements* had considered three-dimensional figures such as the "Platonic solids"—tetrahedron, cube, octahedron, dodecahedron, and icosahedron. Three-dimensional geometry (or "stereometry"), however, would come to flourish only in the *post*-Euclidean phase of Greek mathematics, with the likes of Archimedes of Syracuse and Apollonius of Perga. With Apollonius in particular, the phase of Greek geometric algebra would deal with analogues of quadratic equations via the examination of two-dimensional sections through the three-dimensional cone (Heath 1896). Grassmann, who called vectors *Strecken* (stretches) would "add" vectors in two-dimensional space in the way treated in the parallelogram of forces but would also "multiply" such vectors within three-dimensional space. One wonders just how close together one might have found the works of Carnot, Archimedes, and Nicomachus on Hegel's bookshelves.

0.2 Hegel, Logic, and Mathematics: Some Potential Misunderstandings Countered

The span of the history of some of the fundamental notions of this type of mathematics and its associated logic from ancient philosophy to the nineteenth century will be the broad context within which Hegel's logic will be discussed in this work. With few exceptions, such an approach goes against the grain of contemporary Hegel scholarship. Here, the Hegelian orthodoxy, from late nineteenth-century British Hegelianism to the present, is likely to dismiss the idea that Hegel's logic was in any way "mathematical" (e.g., Beiser 2005, 161). I suggest, however, that this is based upon fundamental misunderstandings of the nature of mathematics and its history. For far too long, this misunderstanding has obscured the relevance of this history for understanding Hegel.

Signs of change can be noted here, however. Alan Paterson, for example, has argued that while Hegel would be critical of the *degree* to which modern logic is identified with mathematics, "the importance of mathematics in Hegel's logical investigations prefigures the dominant role that mathematics plays in present day logic" (Paterson 2005, 64). In a similar spirit, Brady Bowman (Bowman 2013, ch. 5.4) has pointed out that in *The Science of Logic* Hegel treats geometry as the "highest form of finite theoretical cognition" that has an "inner identity" with the methodology of philosophy itself (170), and, following Paterson, argues for the importance for Hegel's logic of ancient Greek geometry, especially as transmitted by Proclus (171n18; cf. Paterson 2005, section 2). While Bowman locates Hegel within the framework of the critique by Friedrich Heinrich Jacobi of the adoption within German circles of a Spinozist-inflected form of modern "methodicalism," reflected in Spinoza's use of the Euclidean axiomatic method, I will argue that the significance of geometry for Hegel was more focused on the different form of ancient geometric algebra that went beyond the scope of Euclid's approach.[16]

In relation to the approach developed here, of particular importance is the suggestion by Hegel scholar Michael Wolff of deep connections between Hegel's logic and Grassmann's geometric linear algebra (Wolff 1999).[17] Wolff stresses the connections of both to an essay by Immanuel Kant from the transitional phase of his precritical years on the problem of the role in mathematics of negative numbers (Kant 1992a). But rather than rely simply on the idea of a mere convergence or coincidence of the views involved, I will endeavor to show how underlying these are connections that go back to the earliest years of interactions between mathematics and philosophy in Plato's Academy. This will in turn raise another questionable aspect of the conventional denial of the relevance of mathematics to Hegel's logic.

It is agreed by all that Hegel's conception of logic and its dialectic relates back to what Hegel describes as the "speculative" thought of Plato and Aristotle. Indeed, there are ample examples of quotes from Hegel in which he denounces the "formalism" of existing logic and specifically the type of turn to mathematics in the likes of Leibniz and the logic authority at Tübingen, Gottfried Ploucquet, as adequate to the speculative logic of the classical age. But the unquestioned assumption behind the conventional view is that the speculative thought of Plato and Aristotle was itself in no way mathematical, an assumption that, in relation to Plato, has been deeply questioned by scholars from Aristotle himself to the present. Among the more recent of these, the view that Plato had in fact been very influenced by Pythagorean mathematicians such that mathematical objects were grasped as intermediaries between the empirical world and the world of ideas has been generally known as the "unwritten doctrines" view of Plato. Although this thesis will here be accepted as a plausible interpretation, it is not part of the scope of this work to argue for it. All that is needed here is that it was in fact Hegel's view, and the passage from the *Timaeus* with which this introduction started can be taken as evidence in this regard. The mathematics bound up with Plato's "syllogism" was a form of mathematics based in ratios and proportions and that had been grounded in earlier theories of music. It may be different from modern mathematics, but it was mathematics, all the same, and its relevance would stretch well beyond the domain of music. Moreover, it could be appealed to in the context of criticisms of the abstractions of modern rational thought.

Modern mathematics and its application in the physical sciences had emerged after the assimilation of a distinctly non-Greek form of mathematics in the sixteenth and seventeenth centuries: algebra, as transmitted to the

European sciences from Arabic, and ultimately Indian, sources. Algebra is usually accredited with the introduction of generality into arithmetical procedures, most obviously associated with the introduction of variables that would allow the formulation of various equations such as linear equations (e.g., $4x + 2 = 18$), quadratic equations (e.g., $x^2 + 3x + 2 = 0$), and so on, such that "x" is immediately understood indefinitely as whatever number or numbers "satisfy" such equations.[18] Greek algebra was, however, poorly developed and did not utilize symbols as variables in this way, and numbers were correspondingly conceived by the early Pythagoreans as meaning "*a definite number of definite things . . . five chairs, seven people, ten cows*" (Klein 1985, 45). Even Diophantus of Alexandria, living in the third century CE and regarded as the most advanced of Greek algebraists (Heath 1910), had been limited to formulating simple linear equations with phrases concerning the addition of "unknown quantities" to others to get a number equal to some third.[19] Individual letters had been used in Greek mathematics to represent specific integers (that is, used as constants), but Arabic mathematicians had used letters as variables—symbols of those "unknown quantities" as referred to by Diophantus above. It would be this type of algebra utilizing the letters "x" and "y" as variables that would allow Descartes to link geometric figures such as straight lines and curves to polynomial equations via the use of orthogonal coordinates. In turn, this algebraic approach would be generalized by Leibniz from geometry so as to apply to Aristotle's syllogistic logic to produce the first form of genuinely "modern" logic.

However, it would come to be argued in the late nineteenth century that the algebra-geometry distinction was not as rigid as it may seem. Greeks had actually utilized a "geometric" form of algebra, in which the use of diagrams had allowed the type of abstraction and generalization otherwise achieved with algebraic symbols (Høyrup 2017). Moreover, and seemingly independently, toward the end of the nineteenth century developments in these new forms of geometry would themselves come to be described as "geometric algebra,"[20] and it had become clear that this *modern* geometric algebra had its roots more in post-Euclidean developments within ancient geometry and, in particular, the tradition of geometric "problems" not reducible to the more familiar axiomatic method of Euclid's *Elements* (Knorr 1986). But modern geometric algebra also had more recent roots as well, and in this regard, Grassmann seems to have been influenced by an essay published by Kant in the 1760s addressing the question of "negative magnitudes" and bearing on Leibniz's conception of number.

In "Attempt to Introduce the Concept of Negative Magnitudes into Philosophy" (Kant 1992a), Kant had employed the idea of directed line segments

INTRODUCTION

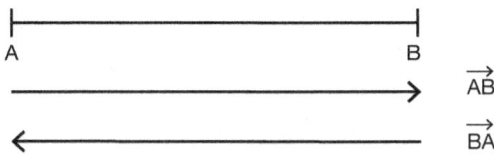

FIGURE 0.4 Oppositely directed segments of a single line segment such that $\overrightarrow{AB} = -\overrightarrow{BA}$.

in an attempt to explain the ontology of negative numbers. In the course of a sea voyage from Lisbon to Brazil, distances traveled in an east–west direction will be recorded in the ship's log in positive numbers, while those distances traveled in a west–east direction, in the hands of countervailing winds, say, will be recorded as negative. Here, the actual miles traveled in one direction will, of course, be no different from those traveled in the other. Positive and negative values have meaning only in relation to the intended destination of the journey.

It was just this type of quasi-mechanical analysis that Leibniz had thought could be directly captured in his geometrically conceived *analysis situs*, while his eighteenth-century follower (and correspondent of Kant), Johann Heinrich Lambert, had similarly appealed to a type of universal language of such diagrammatic representations. Kant would introduce his own approach as a critique of Leibniz's *analysis situs*, and after his transition to "critical philosophy" would continue to employ the vector-like "phorometric" treatment of space in his *Metaphysical Foundations of Natural Science* of 1786 (Kant 1985, pt. 2, ch. 1), which would be adopted by *Naturphilosophen* such as Baader and Schelling.

For their parts, both Carnot and Grassmann would, like Kant, distinguish an absolute or real magnitude, the length of the vector, from the "signed" magnitudes with positive or negative values indicating opposed directions. This meant a type of nonmetrical "algebra" could be applied. For example, a simple line segment extending between points A and B can, when designated as '$\overrightarrow{AB}$' be thought as directed from A to B and, when designated '$\overrightarrow{BA}$' be thought of as directed in the opposite direction from B to A, and thereby given a negative value in relation to the former (fig. 0.4). With this, the expressions '$\overrightarrow{AB}$' and '$\overrightarrow{BA}$' can be understood as able to be related by the equation '$\overrightarrow{AB} = -\overrightarrow{BA}$'

Grassmann would treat vectors as, like numbers, able to be added and subtracted, multiplied by numbers, called "scalars," and even multiplied by each other. Peculiarities of these quasi-algebraic operations would, however, link his vector analysis back to an idea from Greek geometry that Hegel had taken very seriously—the idea that magnitudes relating to objects with different spatial dimensions were incommensurable and that thought needed to deal with different kinds of magnitudes just as it needed to deal with different kinds of things.

The discovery of incommensurability among magnitudes had formed an important part of the intellectual context within which Plato's Academy had been established in ancient Athens and had occupied the activities of many of its members, including Plato himself. In fact, it will be argued that Plato's most beautiful bond, which Hegel had grasped as at the heart of his "syllogism," can be seen as an attempt to reestablish a type of unity among what had become understood as incommensurable magnitudes. But this incommensurability had not been only manifest within geometry, where it is typically seen as having been a consequence of one of Greece's greatest geometric achievements, Pythagoras's theorem. It had also had significance for the activity that today we see as having little to do with geometry—the musical theory distinguishing consonant from dissonant intervals. In fact, some have argued that its significance had originally been predominantly in relation to that domain (Szabó 1978; Borzacchini 2007).

Central to the claims of this book will be that Hegel had followed Plato in modeling his syllogism on the type of unity achievable among the three ways of dividing musical intervals that were encoded within the musical *tetraktys*: division according to what were known as "geometric," "arithmetic," and "harmonic" means. We have already seen mention of the first of these in the "proportion [*Analogie*] or the continuing geometric ratio [*das stetige geometrische Verhältnis*]" that Hegel quotes from Plato concerning the syllogism behind the "familiar syllogistic" of Aristotle.[21] We will later explore the roles played by these three means within Pythagorean music theory and their greater relevance for Plato, but here it may be helpful to point to one place in Aristotle's corpus where he actually employs the distinction between geometric and arithmetic means—his account of justice in the *Nicomachean Ethics* in terms of the much misunderstood doctrine of "the mean."

Aristotle's ethical doctrine of the mean is often interpreted as a somewhat bland call for moderation in all things, but this ignores the fact that he had pointed to the use of two *different* "means," one that "mathematicians call ... geometrical" and another that had been called "arithmetical" (Aristotle 1984, *Nicomachean Ethics*, 1131a 28–32b20). The former was appropriate for cases of distributive justice, and the latter for the quite different cases of rectificatory justice. Were it the case that the measures appropriately applied in rectificatory contexts were applied to distributive ones, a definite injustice would result. Nevertheless, what this situation called for was not simply the differentiation of two different species of a single genus, justice.

In his wide-ranging studies Aristotle had applied the device of analogy in ways that can be thought of as modeled on what music theorists called the "geometric proportion," which entailed a ratio between two ratios. Thus for ratios standing between two entities, a and b, on the one hand, and two others, c and d, on the other, it would be said that a stands to b as c stands to d ($a : b :: c : d$). Probably the most familiar example of this is his linguistic theory of metaphor (Aristotle 1984, *Poetics*, ch. 21), although Aristotle contrasted metaphor in which analogies are posited across different kinds with a more scientific application *within* kinds. In the case of justice, however, the situation is quite complex. The principle behind the application of these different means in these different contexts itself appears to involve a geometric proportion: the arithmetic ratio is meant to stand to cases of rectificatory justice as the geometric ratio itself stands to cases of distributive justice. Hegel, I suggest, would treat this as a distorted application of Plato's most beautiful bond, which unified these two means in a more symmetrical way.

It was this three-in-one structure that was expressed in the peculiar double ratio reanimated by Carnot and that provides a striking model for the relations among the two incommensurable judgments that make up Hegel's own syllogism—judgments that can be deemed equivalent in a homologous way that involves similar structures supporting different functions. Such homologous pairs expressing a local homomorphic equivalence within Hegel's logic are recognizable in Aristotle's conception of the relation between the appropriate rules for distributive and rectificatory justice but are freed from an asymmetry present there. In short, rather than being driven by any literal idea that the cosmos emitted harmonious sounds beautiful to the ear of God, Hegel took the ancient "harmony of the spheres" doctrine to encode a logical structure that, he thought, governed thoughtful forms of human life. Aristotle's syllogistic was a two-dimensional deformed expression of Plato's original three-dimensional syllogism, the two (geometric and arithmetic) middle terms of the latter having been reduced to a single middle term in the former. Consequently, Hegel would, in his "Subjective Logic," aim to restore to the Aristotelian syllogism its three-dimensional completeness.

The subsequent history of logic is usually taken to have simply refuted Hegel's efforts in this area, but this assumption will be challenged. Many of Hegel's ideas, it will be argued, have resonated within the work of logicians working within the "nonclassical" alternative to the modern equivalent of Aristotle's formalism, the "classical" quantified predicate calculus stemming from the work of Gottlob Frege and Bertrand Russell. In this classical approach, logic was considered as providing a universal language within which the truths of other disciplines—in the first instance, arithmetic—were to be grounded, a doctrine known as "logicism."

0.3 How the Argument of This Book Progresses

In the first part of this work, "Beginning: Hegel's Classicism," the Greek musico-mathematical background to Plato's syllogism as presented in the dialogue *Timaeus* will be set out in a way so as to enable an understanding of how it could provide a model for Hegel's idea of a syllogism in *The Science of Logic*. In chapter 1, after an initial look at the Pythagorean number-theoretic background to Plato's philosophical arithmetic and its notion of "measure," we review some of the features of Aristotle's logical doctrines, showing their dependence on Plato's notion of "division" or *diaresis*. Chapter 2 then moves to examine the claim made in the early twentieth century by classicist Benedict Einarson showing Aristotle's terminological borrowings from the music theory of contemporary Pythagorean mathematicians, a feature that brings Aristotle's formal logic into a relation with Plato's mythological account of the "syllogistic" structure of the cosmos in the dialogue *Timaeus*. In chapter 3, it is argued that Hegel's account of the category of magnitude in book 1 of the *Logic* leading to the concept of a ratio of powers shows how this puzzling mathematical object could have been understood by Hegel as a manifestation of the unity of the three musical means at the heart of Plato's syllogism, and how this could come to be associated with the major invariant to be found in the revived science of projective geometry, the "harmonic cross-ratio."

The second part, "Middle: Classical Meets Modern," commences in chapter 4 with a comparison of the attitudes held toward geometry by Hegel and Schelling around the turn of the nineteenth century. Of the two, Schelling's is the more conventional in that it presupposes the certainty of Euclidean geometry and, while critical of aspects of Kant's understanding of mathematics, is still largely indebted to Kant. In contrast, Hegel is moving in directions like those found in various revivals of geometric algebra in the nineteenth century; in particular Hegel's has features that reflect the type of projective geometry being introduced around that time by Lazare Carnot, as well as features of the later "linear extension theory" introduced in the 1840s by Hermann Grassmann. Both Carnot and Grassmann had styled their approaches on a project announced but never developed by Leibniz called *analysis situs*. Leibniz had also experimented with an algebraic form of logic that had anticipated the form in which logic would be rejuvenated in the nineteenth century by the work of the mathematician George Boole, and in chapter 5 we consider key features of this logic, with an eye to the more "geometric" interpretation of its form as suggested by the approach of an *analysis situs*.

While Leibniz had made no real progress toward the realization of his *analysis situs*, his eighteenth-century follower, the Swiss mathematician Johann Heinrich Lambert, had. Moreover, Lambert would become involved in disputes over how to develop this aspect of Leibniz's thought, as well as over the diagrammatic representation of logic, with the philosopher Gottfried Ploucquet (Pozzo 2010), whose approach to logic was what Hegel had been taught as a student at the Tübingen Seminary. This all provides the context in which Hegel's attitude to Leibniz's advances, both in logic and in calculus, can be examined, which is undertaken in chapter 6. This prepares us for the topics to be pursued in the final part, "End: The Modern as Redetermined Classical."

This commences with an overview, in chapter 7, of what, from Hegel's viewpoint, constitutes the features of Aristotle's syllogism that might enable its rehabilitation as a more genuinely rational logic like that of Plato. Greek geometric algebra had allowed Aristotle to achieve within logic the type of generality needed for it to be a science. This, however, had come with limits. The great reformer of Greek geometry and associate of Plato, Eudoxus of Cnidus, had seemed to have banished numbers from geometry, and, akin to this, Aristotle seemed to have banished singular terms from logic. On this, however, he was not entirely consistent, blurring a distinction that would become explicit only later with the work of medieval nominalists, between definite singular terms and indefinite common names. Hegel's logic is treated as involving a systematic disambiguation of this singular-particular conflation found in Aristotle. This in turn is shown to underlie certain commonalities between Hegel's logic and nineteenth-century developments in logic in which similar theoretical issues were being argued out.

Chapter 8 examines the path taken by algebraic logicians from the mid-nineteenth to the early twentieth century, from Boole himself to the alternative presented by the "intuitionist" logician Arend Heyting. This is a path that passes through a number of logical thinkers who share features found in Hegel's thought, which are perhaps most recognizable in the work of Charles Sanders Peirce, especially when his work in contrasted with the inventor of modern twentieth-century "classical" logic, Gottlob Frege. Other thinkers besides Peirce, however, such as Hugh MacColl and W. E. Johnson, help in bringing features of Hegel's logic into focus.

Chapters 9 and 10 reexamine Hegel's theories of the judgment and syllogism, now with the help of resources drawn from the "neo-Leibnizian" logicians examined in chapter 8. Chapter 9 focuses in particular on the "cycles of conceptual redetermination" that make up Hegel's evolving and self-correcting account of judgment structure, in particular drawing upon resources found in the logic of the Cambridge logician W. E. Johnson, especially in relation to the logic of inductive inference. In turn, Johnson's analysis of induction shows the dependence of induction on what Peirce had called "abduction," which takes us from the realm of individual judgments to that of the inferential relations among judgments in syllogisms.

In chapter 10, in line with the project of a geometrical logic, conceptions of inference are clarified by the use of diagrams, starting with a comparison between the ways that Hegel and Peirce had attempted to utilize Aristotle's three syllogistic "figures" to differentiate the types of logic appropriate to different phases of rational inquiry: deduction, induction, and abduction as the phases of logical life. This in turn leads to recent experiments within diagrammatic logic involving the expansion of the traditional "square of opposition" into a logical hexagon that again show parallels with Hegel's treatment of the relation among the syllogism's three figures. When understood as mapping possible alternative paths through inferential processes, such diagrams suggest being read in a three-dimensional way that returns us to Hegel's initial affirmation of Plato's syllogism over Aristotle's—its split middle term making it the appropriate logic for a three-dimensional world.

BEGINNING

Hegel's Classicism

1

Logic, Mathematics, and Philosophy in Fourth-Century Athens

> Now, the part that puts its trust in measurement and calculation is the best part of the soul.
>
> PLATO, *Republic*

Leibniz is often nominated as the person who made logic mathematical, implying that logic before him, essentially the Aristotelian syllogistic, was in no sense mathematical. In this work it will be argued that this common assumption is misleading and distorts not only our understanding of the origins of logic in the ancient world but also how this was understood and appropriated by Hegel. From Proclus to more recent commentators (e.g., McKirahan 1992, chs. 11–13), attention has been directed to the influence of the proof structures that broadly differentiated Greek geometry from the mathematics of the Egyptians and Babylonians from whom the Greeks borrowed. We are most familiar with these proofs as they appear in Euclid's *Elements*, and while Euclid postdated Aristotle, it is generally acknowledged that many of the proofs found in this most famous of mathematical texts had originated in work done by members of Plato's Academy in its early years.[1] It is in this sense that one leading interpreter of Aristotle's logic has described it as "unthinkable without the emphasis on deductive reasoning in geometry that he had found in Plato's Academy" (Corcoran 2003, 284). Not that we can think of Aristotle's syllogistic as simply some kind of "applied mathematics." The external medium for rational thought for Aristotle was language, and, moreover, he thought of his own linguistic syllogisms as providing the logic underlying geometric proofs. Mathematics effectively provided paradigmatic instances of the types of proofs for which he sought to give to logic, and so logic could not simply be mathematics.

Two influences in particular had come together in relation to Aristotle's "invention" of logic, both via the influence of Plato—the linguistic practices of Socratic dialectic, as presented by Plato in his dialogues, and issues from contemporary mathematics. According to Paul Shorey, Plato had anticipated "nearly everything in the Aristotelian logic" (Shorey 1924, 1). Prior to Shorey, and for some interpreters after him (e.g., Bochenski 1961, 66; Rose 1968), it had been common to trace the origins of Aristotle's syllogistic to the method of *diairesis* or "division" discussed by Plato within the *Phaedrus* and, especially, the "late" dialogues, the *Sophist*, the *Statesman*, and *Philebus*. Shorey contested this, however, suggesting that as Aristotle's syllogistic was also a "doctrine of causality," a more appropriate source for it would be Plato's account of ideas in the *Phaedo*, an account more ontologically than methodologically focused, and relevant to the issue of final causes as presented in a mythological way in Plato's *Timaeus* (Shorey 1924, 6).

We will be examining both of these methodological and ontological dimensions, which, as we will see, would be central for Hegel. Aristotle himself criticized Plato's *diairesis* as a method (Aristotle 1989, *Prior Analytics*, book 1, ch. 31), mainly on the grounds that by itself it could not lead to the *discovery* of kinds, but rather, simply presupposed them. However, it could be argued that it was Plato's relative indifference to such epistemological concerns that allowed *diairesis* to provide a model for a general conception of deductive inference appropriate for Aristotle's logic.[2] For the moment, however, let us focus on in what sense Plato's method of *diairesis* might have drawn upon the practices of mathematicians.

1.1 The Logic of Platonic *Diairesis* and the Notion of "Measure"

It is in the second half of Plato's dialogue *Phaedrus* that one finds possibly the most familiar reference to the "systematic art" of division (*diairesis*). Strictly, there are two stages to this art: the first, collection (*synagoge*), "consists in seeing together things that are scattered about everywhere and collecting them into one kind, so that by defining each thing, we can make clear the subject of any instruction we wish to give" (Plato 1997, *Phaedrus*, 265d). It is in relation to the second diairetic dimension that we encounter one of Socrates's best-known metaphors: one must "be able to cut up each kind according to its species along its natural joints" (Plato 1997, *Phaedrus*, 265e). Socrates suggests a method that arranges elements in a type of pyramidal or inverted treelike structure, whose "branches" progressively split as one passes down from the top, in a pattern that clearly alludes to the type of conceptual "tree" that Porphyry would later attribute to Aristotle (Porphyry 2006). But Plato's version, in contrast to Aristotle's, should not be thought of as primarily a classification of *kinds of things*—it was a system of classification of separate *ideas* that only with Aristotle would be located *within* things as the essences or natures that make those things the kinds of things they are. Moreover, besides this parallel, we can see in Plato's diairetic hierarchy something of the conceptual organization that will be manifest in Aristotle's syllogisms. It would be the type of organization that would be expressed in the capacity to make inferences: if we know that the idea <Greek> is situated at a node below that of <human>, and <human> at a node below <animal>, we thereby know that to be a Greek is not only to be human but also to be an animal.[3]

In the *Sophist* and the *Statesman*, Plato has the main speaker, the so-called Eleatic Stranger, describe in more detail the process of dividing terms in search of a definition so as to avoid false classifications. In the *Statesman* especially, the Stranger appeals to a notion of measurement and focuses upon the need for the objective classification of a thing in terms of its proper or due "measure"—its *metron*, which is sometimes also translated as "mean."[4] This latter sense seems to come into focus when objective measure or classification is contrasted with its opposite, a type of merely comparative judgment involving excess or deficit, a polarity between "the greater and the smaller" rather than the invocation of the proper measure (Plato 1997, *Statesman*, 283c–285c). Like the modern English word *measure*, *metron* had, besides the sense of a standard or rule, the connotations of moderation, as when one says of a person that their reaction was "measured"—hence the verb *metriaso*, "to be moderate" (Liddell and Scott 1882). Here there is an obvious connection to Aristotle's appeal to moderation in action, in his well-known ethical account of virtue as the "mean" between two vices in the *Nicomachean Ethics* (1106b36–1107a8), although Aristotle will use a different term—*meson* (and the related *mesotis*), literally meaning "a middle," and having the connotations of "middling" or "moderate" (Liddell and Scott 1882). This variant, we will see, will be of particular significance.

In the *Sophist* Plato points to the philosopher's method of *diairesis* to distinguish philosophy from its sophistic facsimile, and the appeal to an objective measure in the *Statesman* is surely meant to counter the type of relativistic thinking summed up by Socrates in the *Theaetetus*, when he recalls the Protagorean doctrine that it is man who is "the measure of all things: of the things which are, that they are, and of the things which are not, that they are not" (Plato 1997, *Theaetetus*, 152a). Consonant with the theme of measure, Plato has Socrates discuss "the calculations practiced by philosophers" as the "philosophers' arithmetic" (Plato 1997, *Philebus*, 56d–57a). But how, exactly, might this classification be linked to mathematics? That it *is* so linked, however, is surely suggested by Plato via the setting he gives to the dialogue.

Both the *Sophist* and the *Statesman* take place on the same day (the day following that on which the dialogue of the *Theaetetus* had supposedly taken place) and involve the same participants. Furthermore, both start with an interchange between Socrates and Theodorus, whom Socrates describes as the "best arithmetician and geometer" (Plato 1997, *Statesman*, 257a). We have already met Theodorus in the *Theaetetus*, where he was portrayed as introducing two young Athenians, Theaetetus and "Young Socrates" (that is, not Socrates but a younger man sharing the same name), to the idea of the irrationality of the square roots of non-square numbers between 3 and 17. In fact, this scene is often taken as broadly historically based (e.g., von Fritz 1945, 243), the mathematician Theodorus of Cyrene being thought to have introduced the problem of irrational or "incommensurable" magnitudes into Athenian cultural life in 399, the year of the death of Socrates.

The discovery of incommensurable magnitudes, taken by many historians of mathematics as particularly significant for the subsequent development of the "golden age" of Greek geometry starting with Euclid's *Elements*, was traditionally attributed to Hippasus of Metapontum, in the fifth century BCE, and undermined the relationship between arithmetic and geometry that had been dominant in Greece up to that time. This had been the approach of the early Pythagorean mathematicians, who had conceived of all magnitudes as generated from the *monas* or "unit" (from *monos*, "alone"), making the *monas* fundamental to the structure of the world. Legend has it that Hippasus was drowned at sea by other members of the Pythagorean sect for having made this truth about the irrationality of the world known beyond the circle of the sect itself. Ironically it had been "Pythagoras's theorem," showing the area of a square built on the hypotenuse of a right-angle triangle to be equal to the sum of the squares built on the other two sides,[5] that had contained the seeds for the destruction of the Pythagorean arithmetical worldview. From Pythagoras's theorem it could be shown reasonably easily that in the case of the right-angle triangle formed by the diagonal of a unit square, no common measure could be found for the ratio formed by the diagonal with the other sides—that is, they were incommensurable magnitudes.[6]

This familiar story has been contested over recent decades, however. In the late 1970s, the historian Árpád Szabó argued for a much earlier date for the discovery of incommensurability and, moreover, contextualized the discovery as initially occurring within Pythagorean musical theory rather than geometry (Szabó 1978, intro. and ch. 1). Building on and modifying Szabó's account, more recently Luigi Borzacchini (Borzacchini 2007) has argued that the idea of incommensurability had been long familiar to the Pythagoreans, but not under such a description that implies some expected comparability of magnitudes. Rather, the Pythagoreans had recognized a fundamental opposition between continuous and discrete magnitudes, reflecting a cosmological opposition famously expressed by the mathematician and cosmologist Philolaus between the limited and the unlimited. This was reflected in various ways in their harmonic theory, such that when the geometric discovery was shown it came more as "confirmation" of something intuitively known (Borzacchini 2007, 287). The idea of a fundamentally musical locus for the emergence of the notion of "incommensurability" has likewise been suggested by the historian of Greek music Andrew Barker, who links the idea to the opposition between consonant and dissonant intervals (Barker 2007, 291–292).

In Plato's *Statesman*, the issue of incommensurability is brought up in an indirect way in the dialogue when Plato has the visitor make a pun linking the fact that humans walk on "two feet"—which distinguishes humans from four-footed animals—to the incommensurability of the diagonal of a unit square with its "two feet," the two sides of the square that together with the opposite diagonal form the right-angle triangle (Plato 1997, *Statesman*, 266b; see also translator's note 23).[7] In recent times, debates over the issue of whether or not in science differing theories might be "incommensurable," and so unable to be rationally compared, have invoked the thought of a type of conceptual incommensurability threatening rational decision (e.g., Kuhn 1962). Given that mathematics was the science in which the Greeks were most advanced, one can get a sense of how this issue might have loomed large for members of Plato's Academy.

Despite the broad hints about the significance of mathematics for the diairetic method, for the most part conventional interpretations of this section of the *Statesman* construe Plato's meaning in a particularly counterintuitive way. Plato had encouraged mathematical research among his colleagues in the Academy and, as reflected in Socrates's account of the proper education of future leaders in *Republic* book 7, young men at the Academy had to study mathematics for ten years before being allowed to progress to the study of dialectic. And yet, as has been recently pointed out (Fisher 2018), it has been usual for interpreters of the *Statesman* to treat it as expressing an attitude critical of the relevance of mathematical thought for the philosophical method, associating mathematics with the merely comparative form of "measurement" between "the greater and the smaller," which the Stranger challenges with the need to find the "due measure." Jeffrey Fisher questions the appropriateness of the standard interpretation on both textual and contextual grounds but does not consider the dialogue in the broader context of the mathematical issues occupying Academicians at the time. However, rather than being an argument *against* the relevance of mathematics in philosophy, might it not be that the issue of "due measure" has more to do with attempts to face the threat of a conceptual incommensurability within mathematics that was threatening to spread beyond it?

What Hippasus had shown was that continuous magnitudes such as the diagonal of a unit square could not find their "measures" in terms of the arithmetic supported by the Pythagoreans—an arithmetic limited to the positive natural numbers and to the ratios holding among them. And if certain continuous magnitudes such as geometric line segments could not be so measured, then it would appear that they could be made no more determinate than being said to be larger or smaller than each other. Here the issue quickly spirals from being about mathematics itself to what we would now consider the philosophy of mathematics. Ways forward would seem to involve nothing short of a reconceptualization of the very notion of magnitude. This indeed did happen and represents the first of a series of such reconceptualizations that would continue in the early modern period and eventually find its apparently ultimate solution in the formalization of the "real" numbers at the end of the nineteenth century. In short, here questions about numbers become quickly bound up with questions concerning the concept of number and the nature of concepts more generally.

In linking the idea of comparative measure of larger and smaller to the skeptical doctrines of the Sophists, Plato brings into question the context-limited nature of judgments typically exploited by Sophists. Thus, in the *Phaedo*, for example, Simmias is said to be large when compared to Socrates but small when compared to Phaedo. Surely there is something amiss with accounts of the world in which, as Socrates points out, "Simmias is called both short and tall, being between the two, presenting his shortness to be overcome by the tallness of one, and his tallness to overcome the shortness of the other" (Plato 1997, *Phaedo*, 102d). Is it not possible to talk about things in terms of characteristics that they simply possess or do not possess? Is it not possible to talk about things as they are "anyway," independent of comparative assessments? In order to talk and think in this way, one needs some notion of "measure" akin to that with which one can give Simmias's height in a clear and non-self-contradictory way, such as with a rule. These contextual or relational judgments had been exactly the types of judgments seized upon by the Sophists in their denials that reality could be cut "at the joints." If there are no "due" measures, then in all cases man is the measure, and each man can seemingly choose the units in which he measures to suit the occasion.

In the first part of the twentieth century, the Husserlian philosopher Jacob Klein had taken this crisis in mathematics as having great significance for the philosophical outlook of the Old Academy as reflected in the stances of Plato and Aristotle, and in stressing the importance of this mathematical context he was far from alone. Klein notes the earlier work of the interpreters Julius Stenzel, Oskar Becker, and J. Cook Wilson (Klein 1968, 76), and to this list could be added French scholars such as Léon Robin (Robin 1908). In fact, this view has a long history stretching back to Aristotle himself.[8] In particular, it had been central to Neoplatonic readers of Plato such as Proclus, who was an especially influential authority on Plato for Hegel and his contemporaries. More recently, a view concerning the mathematical basis of Plato's philosophy, interpreted with an emphasis on the "unwritten doctrines" ascribed to Plato by Aristotle and others, was put forward in the second half of the twentieth century by members of the "Tübingen School,"[9] by Kenneth Sayre (Sayre 2005),[10] and John Findlay (Findlay 1970, 1974b), as well as a number of Italian and French scholars.[11]

On this interpretation, Plato's dialogues of the late period increasingly express the metaphysical beliefs attributed to him in the doxographic tradition. It is in the dialogues of the middle period that is found the familiar "Platonic" theory of forms, as classically represented in the *Republic*, in which the forms are primary and simple and belong to a radically transcendent realm. In the later period, and especially in the *Philebus*, so these interpreters argue, Plato's metaphysics would become increasingly based on the primacy of two principles that had come from the Pythagorean tradition—the principles of the determinate one and the "indeterminate dyad" of the "greater and the smaller," effectively Plato's version of the distinction between the limited and the unlimited expressed by Philolaus. The forms were now understood as generated from these two principles and as reflecting the antithetical structures of each. Moreover, the conceptual schemes revealed by the diairetic method in late works like the *Sophist, Theaetetus*, and *Philebus* are regarded as being meant to show the reconciliation of these two principles at work in both thought and the world. Findlay in particular would stress the parallels here with Hegel: "The expansion of the Eide into the realm of instantiation is seen not to be an inexplicable fall, but a carrying further of the domination of multiplicity and detail which is already present at the eidetic level. A Neoplatonist like Proclus worked the whole mystery out: the One must go forth from itself into endless specification and instantiation in order to return to itself eternally and, so to be the One. And these thoughts also underlie the Dialectic of Hegel, for whom the Absolute Idea is the eternal vision of itself in its Other" (Findlay 1983, 18).[12]

Not all these authors agree on all the details, but all recognize the phenomenon on which Aristotle had commented concerning the importance given by Plato to Pythagorean number theory and his associated construal of the forms as measures, at the same time as generally rejecting Aristotle's criticisms of Plato in this regard. As representative we might consider the view of Kenneth Sayre. Sayre describes Plato as having realized by the time of the *Parmenides* the problem of the "radical separation between Forms and objects" and "in the second part of the *Parmenides* we find a lavish defense of Pythagorean ontology against the Eleatic attack, and at the same time an exploration of the conditions of a more adequate theory" (Sayre 2005, 174–175). This development would lead to a narrowing of the separation of worldly objects and transcendent forms:

> In the earlier theory . . . the Forms are absolute, both in the sense of being themselves incomposite and in the sense of not depending for what they are upon other things. . . . By the time of the *Philebus*, however, Plato's thinking in this regard has so changed that the Forms are no longer conceived even to be ontologically basic. Like sensible things, Forms in this later context are conceived as being constituted from two more fundamental ontological principles—in the case of the Forms, the Great and (the) Small and Unity. . . . The fact that both Forms and sensible things are constituted from the Great and (the) Small bespeaks the second fundamental deviation of the later from the earlier theory. Since both Forms and sensible things come to be by the imposition of measure upon the same basic ontological principle, their respective modes of being can no longer be conceived as radically distinct. (183–184)

What will be significant for Hegel's *Logic* is the idea that the changed theory of forms had transformed Plato's understanding of the forms as paradigms (*paradigmata*) against which worldly phenomena could be measured. "According to the theory of the *Phaedo* and the *Republic*, Forms are standards or paradigms by which sensible objects are given names and identified, inasmuch as objects share the names of the Forms in which they participate" (184). However, the problem pointed out by Parmenides concerned how to conceive of comparison across such an incommensurable divide, and because of this, the notion "never amounted to much more than a metaphor." With the transformed account of forms in the *Philebus*, however, the idea of forms as paradigms "is given a literal and relatively unproblematic sense" (184).

Those familiar with the opening sections of Hegel's *Science of Logic* might recognize a certain structural similarity to Plato's attempts to close the initial seemingly incommensurable gap between the forms and worldly objects and the dynamics consequent to Hegel's similarly "incommensurable" initial categories of "Being" and "Nothing," categories that eventually are interrelated within the "Actuality" (*Wirklichkeit*) in which the "Objective Logic" terminates.[13] However, this is not sufficient to place Hegel on the side of Plato over against Aristotle, as Hegel will side with Aristotle's epistemological privileging of sensible worldly objects in the generation of knowledge. In contrast, in Plato's late ontology according to Sayre the suprasensible is still favored epistemologically over the sensible, retaining the earlier idea that the forms could be cognized directly without the need to consult the objects of the empirical realm (Sayre 2005, appendix A).

The unwritten-doctrines interpretation, with its reliance on the view of Plato found in the Greek "doxographic" tradition, has remained controversial among Plato scholars. Here, I will simply accept the plausibility of this thesis for our purposes rather than attempt to argue for it; after all, it is not Plato's actual views that are in question but Hegel's views of Plato in relation to the origins of Aristotle's logic. And as acknowledged by both Hans Krämer of the Tübingen School (Krämer 1990, ch. 11) and John Findlay (Findlay 1974a), Hegel's interpretation of Plato had been along the general lines of the unwritten-doctrines interpretation. I will take the view of Sayre sketched above in which Plato retains his earlier epistemological privileging of the forms even when the gap between them and the world is narrowed as broadly corresponding to how Hegel understood Plato.

Aristotle sets out this view of Plato in *Metaphysics* book 1. Plato, he writes, "agreed with the Pythagoreans in saying that the One is substance and not a predicate of something else; and in saying that the numbers are the causes of the substance of other things, he also agreed with them; but positing a dyad and constructing the infinite out of great and small, instead of treating the infinite as one, is peculiar to him" (Aristotle 1984, *Metaphysics*, 987b23–27). Plato also, he continues, diverged from the Pythagoreans in introducing the forms in the context of "his inquiries in the region of definitory formulae." Moreover, this was bound up with "his belief that the numbers, except those which were prime [*proton*], could be neatly produced out of the dyad as out of a plastic material" (987b30–35).[14]

In the 1920s, Julius Stenzel argued that Plato's method of *diairesis* had drawn on the Pythagorean mathematics of his contemporaries in virtue of the fact that the pattern of ideational division was modeled on a "figured number" that had a special relevance for the Pythagoreans, the *tetraktys*, but to understand the connection we need to understand something about how the Pythagoreans connected the two branches of mathematics, arithmetic and geometry. For the earliest Pythagoreans, geometric structures were understood on the basis of arithmetic.[15] First, a spatial point was conceived as the monadic unit when considered "in position," with a line then being conceived as composed of such units, said to be typically represented by sequences of pebbles. In turn, figures in the two-dimensional plane such as squares and rectangles could be conceived as composed of arrays of two-dimensional lines. That is, what *we* know as "square numbers" (numbers multiplied by themselves) were, for the Pythagoreans, *literally* square, measuring areas rather than lengths. To these could be added triangular and oblong numbers as well as the peculiar L-shaped *gnomon*.[16] Finally, a three-dimensional solid could be thought of as assembled from planar figures—for example, arraying three square numbers of nine units each formed a cubic number of volume of twenty-seven units.[17] Of the two-dimensional numbers, a triangular number of great significance was, as we have seen, the *tetraktys* or tetrad in which the unit/points were arranged in four rows consisting of one, two, three, and four elements (fig. 0.2). This arrangement encoded relationships that were particularly significant within the Pythagorean worldview.

Among the meanings attributed to this figure was that the four rows stood for the ways in which space was conceived. The first row represented a point in space, understood as the fundamental numerical unit, the *monas*, "in position," while the second represented the one-dimensional line, the third a two-dimensional area, and the fourth a three-dimensional solid. The *tetraktys* is thus the source of Plato's number series that Hegel had appealed to in his 1801 thesis at Jena, 1, 2, 3, 4, 9, 8, 27, since it is obvious on a moment's reflection that this series (as Hegel notes [*LHP* 2:213; 3:44]) is generated by simply raising the numbers 1, 2, and 3 to the first, second, and third powers: 1^1, 2^1, 3^1, 2^2 (4), 3^2 (9), 2^3 (8), 3^3 (27). It would seem, then, that Plato's sequence, following Pythagorean number theory, somehow alludes to the necessary three-dimensionality of the cosmic body pervaded by the cosmic mind. That thought about the three-dimensional world needed somehow to reflect its tridimensionality would, I suggest, become a central imperative for Hegel's logic.

Importantly, the *tetraktys* testifies to the way that the Pythagoreans had conceived of numbers in a very different way from the way in which they are now thought of—that is, it testifies to their very different *concept* of number. It is important to remember that numbers for the Greeks were limited to the natural numbers. What are now thought of as "rational numbers," that is, fractions of whole numbers, were then not considered as numbers per se but as ratios *composed of* whole numbers. Importantly, the Greeks also lacked the concepts of negative numbers as well as the number zero. Without the latter in particular, the resources for the development of algebra as conventionally conceived were limited. But neither did the Pythagoreans consider the numbers 1 and 2 as numbers as such. They were rather the principles (*archai*) from which the rest of the number series could be generated, as reflected in Plato's idea expressed in the *Statesman* of the unit and the indeterminate dyad of the greater and the smaller as opposed measures for all things. Aristotle gives this more general background to Pythagorean number theory in *Metaphysics* book 1 (Aristotle 1984, *Metaphysics*, 986a13–26), starting with two pairs of contrarily opposed principles: limited and unlimited and odd and even. The list continues on to include the one and many; right and left; male and female; resting and moving; straight and curved; light and darkness; good and bad; and square and oblong. In this style of thought, all of these oppositions are meant to be understood as in some sense analogous to each other: odd is to even just as one is to many just as right is to left, and so on. The inclusion of "good" and "bad" here signals that there is a sense in which in all these pairs, the first is evaluated as good, the second as bad. Such a series of analogous ratios would have a lasting significance for Hegel.

The list of Pythagorean contrary pairs totals 10, but it is to be remembered that a special place was given to the numbers 1 to 4 from which 10 could be generated as four rows of one, two, three, and four units. We have seen how with square and oblong numbers, numbers were given geometric significance. In the *tetraktys* this is generalized as the four successive rows, and hence the numbers 1 to 4, besides relating to the dimensionality of space, also represent the exponential powers of numbers: zeroth, first, square, cube.[18] As will be seen (in chapter 2), in the harmonic theory of the contemporary of Plato, Archytas of Tarentum, the musical scale would be divided in ways restricted to ratios of the numbers 1 to 4.

Stenzel proposed that Plato's diairetic pyramid had been conceived on the analogy of the *tetraktys*, such that the monad at the summit divided into the two lower nodes, which each then divided into further lower nodes, and so on (Stenzel 1924, 30–32). Aristotle had pointed out that the Pythagoreans held the *monas* to be both odd and even (Aristotle 1984, *Metaphysics*, 986a20), and so able to divide into the first even and odd numbers, 2 and 3, this division being repeated at each subsequent node so as to generate all the natural numbers. Stenzel then compares this branching division of numbers with a Platonic diairetic pyramid as reconstructed from a passage from Plato's *Sophist*. Analogous to the way the node 2, say, divides into even and odd numbers, 4 and 5, a node on the diairetic pyramid, animate things, divides into animate things living in herds and those living alone. In fact, as Jacob Klein would later note, the distinction between genus and species had first been used by the Greeks in relation to numbers (Klein 1968, ch. 7B) and, as alluded to earlier, to distinguish numbers themselves from continuous magnitudes.[19] Thus, after the discovery of incommensurability, "linear" and "square" numbers would come to be conceived as belonging to different genera—that is, as heterogeneous. Aristotle would insist on not crossing such generic boundaries, meaning that areas could be added to areas and lengths to lengths, but not lengths to areas. Hegel would effectively appeal to this principle in his criticism of Newton's use of differential calculus in his mechanics in which a square numerical value was reduced to a linear one in the process of "differentiation" (see below, chapter 4.3).[20]

What Plato was searching for with the diairetic pyramid was a comprehensible structure conceived as able to unify the extended world of becoming, without which it would be an unstable multiplicity—unity being represented at the top of the pyramid, with the multiplicity of unstable items of becoming represented at the lowest termini. The most explicit account of this structure would be found in the dialogue *Timaeus*, with Timaeus's story of the way the demiurge had fashioned the cosmos as simultaneously bodily and intelligent, with the parts of each unified into a whole. Let us here, however, concentrate on the ways in which the ideational branching structure of kinds as found later in Porphyry's tree might be seen as analogous to the structure of the *tetraktys*.

The distinctively tetradic dimension of Plato's ideational structure will come into focus when we remember that the four levels of the tetrad represent zero-, one-, two-, and three-dimensional spaces, which in turn are correlated with numbers raised to the zeroth, first, second, and third powers. Later, Leibniz would, in his own way, suggest that numbers could be assigned to concepts to capture their internal conceptual structure as a type of "product" of component concepts. "For example, since man is a rational animal, if the number of animal, a, is 2, and of rational, r is 3, then the number of man, h, will be the same as ar: in this example, 2×3 or 6" (Leibniz 1966, 17). This in turn would capture their external inferential relations. Just as if 3 divides 6 and 6 divides 12, then 3 divides 12, if a (the concept <animal>) divides h (the concept <human>) and h divides p (the concept <philosopher>), then a divides p. That is, if all humans are animals, and all philosophers are human, then all philosophers are animals. Leibniz's numerical modeling of inferential relations was not new, however, and this pattern of iterated divisibility is found, as we will see, in Aristotle's conception of the "perfect" or "complete" syllogism, which he seems to have borrowed from contemporary mathematical theories of proportion to schematize syllogistic inferences. However, it seems that the pattern of mere divisibility had not provided the whole answer for Plato, who had suggested more complex patterns among ratios that came ultimately from the three "means" of Pythagorean harmonic theory. For the moment, however, let us look in more detail at the way in which the repetition of numerical division fits Aristotle's idea of syllogistic inference.

1.2 Aristotle's Logical *Organon*: An Initial Look

Aristotle's explicit logical doctrines would be collected into the five books making up the *Organon*, and what is now seen as central to formal logic, as we understand it, is to be mainly found in the account of syllogisms in book 1 of the volume *Prior Analytics*, while the more general applications of syllogisms within scientific demonstration are treated in the *Posterior Analytics*. A syllogism, Aristotle tells us at the start of the *Prior Analytics*, is "a discourse [*logos*] in which, certain things being supposed, something different from the thing supposed results of necessity because these things are so" (Aristotle 1989, *Prior Analytics*, 24b19–20). Thus, a syllogism is a deduction of some verbal conclusion from "certain things being supposed," but Aristotle was interested in deductions that take a very particular form, with a conclusion being deduced from specifically two premises (*protases*) "affirming or denying something about something" (24a16). Traditionally, syllogisms have been considered as fundamentally linguistic structures—three sentences connected by patterns of inference—but more recently attention has been drawn to the underlying mathematical patterns within these linguistic structures, patterns whose presence are signaled by Aristotle's use of "figures" (*schemata*), the term used by Greek geometers for the diagrams that accompanied their symbolically articulated proofs (e.g., Corcoran 2003).[21]

For some syllogisms—those described as "perfect"—it can be grasped immediately that the conclusion follows from the premises. Consider, for example, the perfect syllogism type that would later be described as in the mode "Barbara" of syllogisms of the first figure (*schema*):

> All As are B
> All Bs are C,
> Therefore, All As are C.

By contrast, syllogisms in the third figure, such as the mode "Felapton," are generally not so obvious on first encounter and require a degree of at least psychological manipulation:

> No As are B
> All As are C,
> Therefore, Some Cs are not Bs.

For Aristotle, proofs of syllogisms such as that of Felapton proceeded by "conversion," a type of translation, into a "perfect" or "complete" syllogism in the first figure such as that of Barbara, which in turn did not require further proof because one could simply immediately "see" that it was the case. This intuitive validity of syllogisms such as Barbara was effectively understood as following from the fact that one can "see" how there is an iteration of the type of containment relation captured by the iteration of divisibility in Plato's diairetic pyramid. As Aristotle puts it in a passage in the *Prior Analytics* to which we will have occasion to return,

> Whenever, then, three terms are so related to each other that the last is in the middle as a whole and the middle is either in or is not in the first as a whole, it is necessary for there to be a complete deduction [*syllogismon telion*] of the extremes. (I call the *middle* [*meson*] which both is itself in another and has another in it—this is also middle in position—and call both that which is itself in another and that which has another in its *extremes* [*akron*]. (Aristotle 1989, *Prior Analytics*, 25a32–38)

However, in order to bring out clearly the transitive nature of the predicative relation, Aristotle commonly chooses to reorder the words within the component statements of such syllogisms so that the predicate term precedes the subject term, a structure that was in fact unnatural to the Greek language. This change allows the iteration of the predicate as said or predicated of the subject to be shown more perspicuously:

> For if A is predicated of every B and B of every C, it is necessary for A to be predicated of every C.... Similarly, if A is predicated of no B and B of every C, it is necessary that A will belong to no C. (25b38–26a3)

It is clear that the underlying relations between the terms in such inferences are just those found in Plato's diairetic hierarchy—in fact, Plato also employs two ways of talking about the relations holding among the nodes. It would also appear that Aristotle's second form of expression employing the "said of" rather than "is in" relation more neatly fits the model of the dividing pyramid of numbers. For example, if a node A divided into left- and right-hand branches B and B' and is B similarly divided into C and C', it could be said that the fact of A being predicated of B (as, say, animal of human) and B of C (as in human of Greek) directly shows that A (animal) is predicated of C (Greek). We will see, however, that Aristotle's model of the middle term as "that which is itself in another and that which has another in it" does not, in fact, do justice to what Plato (and later Hegel and also Peirce) will say of the role of a "mean," and that this feature of Aristotle's perfect syllogism will be bound to another feature of the way Aristotle describes the linguistic form of the component statements.

Aristotle further specifies something about the statements that they are to be "either universal, or particular, or indeterminate" (Aristotle 1989, *Prior Analytics*, 24a16–17). That is, they are to be statements about, say, all Greeks, some Greeks, or just Greeks without further specification. What seems omitted are individuals—the referents of singular statements; for example, statements say, about Socrates or Plato—a category that Aristotle captures with the term *kath ekaston*, a category that is still distinct from some particular (*merikos*), even when this latter determination is limited to one.[22] This omission, which is explicit in the account of judgment types given in *De Interpretatione*, had become a focus of comment over the last century, given that, it would seem, the "syllogism" that for many is the first to come to mind—"All men are mortal; Socrates is a man; and therefore, Socrates is mortal"—is, in fact, strictly in question as to its status *as* a syllogism at all (Łukasiewicz 1957, 1; Patzig 1968, 4–5). On the other hand, as Günther Patzig points out (4–5), Aristotle does give a number of examples of syllogisms involving singular subjects, and it could be argued that other aspects of his accounts of judgments suggest that the meanings of particular and universal judgments are themselves dependent in some way on the existence of properly singular judgments about specifiable individuals like Socrates rather than just "some or other" person.[23]

I will argue that Aristotle's omission of specific individuals here reflects transformations going on in the mathematics being practiced in the Academy at the time—changes leading from the more arithmetically based conceptions of geometry characteristic of the early Pythagoreans toward a more abstract type of thought, enabling the development of Greek geometric algebra. A mathematician associated with Plato's Academy, Eudoxus of Cnidus, seems to have been particularly influential in this innovation that has been described as the reverse of Descartes's later analytic geometry (Dieudonné 1985, 1–3). That is, in contrast to the way that Descartes's analytic geometry would come to be based on the reduction of the continua of geometric magnitudes—determinate lines, planes, and volumes—to determinate patterns of discrete numbers, Greek geometry was in the process of liberating geometry *from* reduction to numbers as then understood. This move was necessitated by the inadequacy not only of the number system employed by the Pythagoreans, but of their very conception of number. They had found that their numbers—the positive "natural" or "counting" numbers—could not in fact give the measure of certain continuous magnitudes, such as the diagonal of the unit square. But, in virtue of the innovations of Eudoxus, continuous magnitudes would come to be understood as themselves determinate mathematical objects capable of determinate relations with other such objects without the need for numerical specification, and this in turn would be understood as demanding a new concept of number.

Thus, the numbers invoked by Descartes and others in the early modern period would simply not be the same kinds of things as those to which the Pythagoreans had appealed. Descartes's "real" numbers, as he called them, had to include irrational numbers (equivalent to those continuous magnitudes that were for the Greeks not numbers at all), because the solutions of the complex equations required in the developing sciences depended upon them. Moreover, Descartes's numbers would crucially include a number that was not part of the Greek number system, the number 0 (zero), which had come into European mathematics from Indian sources via Arabic mathematics, from which was taken the modern notion (and name) of algebra. Significantly, the Dutch mathematician Simon Stevin, who introduced the modern decimal system of numbers, would identify the spatial point with the number zero (Klein 1968, 200–211).

The Cartesian re-arithmetization of geometry would lead to a new form of "monadology" as famously advocated by Leibniz. Leibniz's new "monad" would have some of the feel of the original *monas* of the Pythagoreans, but it would be transformed in its new arithmetical environment to become radically abstract rather than concrete. This transformation would allow Leibniz to reintroduce numbers explicitly into the conception of logical processes, becoming the "official" inventor of "mathematical logic" (see below, chapter 7). In fact, he would, as George Boole would in the nineteenth century, reduce the numbers involved to only two, 0 and 1, which he could equate with the (what would later be called) "truth-values" of true and false for the purposes of a calculus for a "propositional logic."

In contrast to many philosophers in the first half of the nineteenth century, Hegel would be acutely aware of the new algebraic features of Leibniz's logic, and, unlike many present-day philosophers, he would be similarly aware of the peculiarities of the still distinctly Greek sense of mathematics and its reflections in the "syllogisms" of both Plato and Aristotle. Hegel would be particularly concerned with what in Aristotle's logic compromised its application to empirical entities in the actual world. To use the language of Plato's *Statesman*, Aristotle wanted to find some type of measure in the empirical world that could be brought as the appropriate "due measure" to our judgments and thoughts, but something about his logic prevented this—something linked to the problematic way that empirically given individual things would be represented within his syllogistic. Ironically, while it was Plato's rejection of the empirical that was the problem for which Aristotle attempted to provide the solution, it was Plato's own conception of unity, within which was preserved the opposition between the discrete monad and the indeterminate dyad of the greater and lesser, that would turn out to provide a solution to the ratiocinative limitations of Aristotle's logic.

It has been argued by Alan Paterson that "throughout his life, Hegel maintained a deep and sustained interest in geometry and its philosophical basis" (Paterson 2005, 61).[24] In 1800, and so around the time he had played with the idea of a "triangle of triangles," Hegel had devoted himself to a systematic and thorough study of Euclid's *Elements*, seemingly taking Proclus's commentary as his guide (Paterson 2005, section 2), and the normativity of Greek geometry over the modern approach would be proclaimed by F. W. J. Schelling around the same time. Like Schelling, Hegel resisted the early modern impulse to see geometry as reducible to arithmetic, but, in contrast to Schelling, he did not simply deny the need to translate continuous magnitudes into the language of discrete arithmetical quantities.[25] For Hegel, geometry was implicitly reliant on arithmetic for making determinate its distinctive objects,[26] just as arithmetic was itself reliant on the relations among geometric objects (see below, chapter 4.3). This attitude gave expression to Plato's late Philolaic idea that discrete unit- or monad-based arithmetical relations were dependent on the opposing relations of greater or smaller, or more or less, applicable to continuous magnitudes, just as the latter were dependent on the former.

We will see this same reciprocal structure repeated in Hegel's account of the interactive duality of qualitative and quantitative judgment types that he would later explore in "Subjective Logic," volume 2 of *The Science of Logic*—opposed judgment types that could be understood as nevertheless somehow equivalent across the divide of incommensurability in a way analogous to the way discrete numbers and continuous magnitudes could be brought together for the purposes of measuring the world (see below, chapter 2.5).[27] For Hegel, Aristotle's attempt to find an empirical measure for judgments that had an ideational structure could not be conceived in terms of some direct matching of judgments to the world but would take place within a structure in which opposed judgments confronted each other with their own distinct measures, with each taking "the measure" of the adequacy of the other's measure. Moreover, the underlying mathematical model for Hegel's *Logic* with its opposed forms of measure will help us to understand his account of the otherwise puzzling "moments" of the concept—the moments of "singularity," "particularity," and "universality"—moments linked according to the pattern linking the three musical means.

With their respective ideas of *monas* or "monad," the Pythagoreans, on the one hand, and Leibniz, on the other, both conceived of the individual as a type of indivisible, determinate, and ineliminable unit that Aristotle had seemed willing to sacrifice in the rigorous deductions of his logic. This issue of the role of "singularity" (*Einzelheit*) in syllogistic structures will be central to our treatment of Hegel's relation to Aristotle's syllogistic and his appeal to Plato in this regard. It is often said that Aristotle did not have the conceptual resources to distinguish between "intensional" and "extensional" interpretations of logical features, and the unclarity of Aristotle's syllogistic in this regard is bound up, it seems, with his vagueness or ambiguity about the relevance of syllogistic reasoning about individuals. On the one hand, it is clear that Aristotle thought that scientific demonstrations are necessarily about kinds of things rather than individual things per se, and that he links his inquiry into syllogisms to demonstrative science in the very first sentence of the *Prior Analytics* (24a10–12). And yet, if one wants to bring the empirical world to bear on one's judgments, the relevant units here are surely individuals: kinds are not objects of which one has direct experience. Aristotle's compromise here would be to treat the individuals of which one does have experience as nonspecific instances of the kinds they instantiate. As he puts it in the *Posterior Analytics*, while one may be looking at Callias, what perception is of is strictly the universal "man"; it is not of "Callias the man" (Aristotle 1984, *Posterior Analytics*, 100a15–b1).

However, scientific demonstration was not the only use to which syllogistic reasoning was meant to be put. Importantly, the theory of syllogisms was meant also to be applied to the nondemonstrative context of dialectic—an application deriving from the approach of Socrates, which Aristotle treats as particularly relevant to philosophy because "the ability to puzzle on both sides of a subject will make us detect more easily the truth and error about the several points that arise" (Aristotle 1984, *Topics*, 101a35–7).[28] Moreover, Aristotle also discusses contexts of nondemonstrative forms of reasoning that are clearly meant to be about specific entities considered in their singularity rather than simply as indifferent instances of kinds, such as implied in his distinction between the two types of justice in the *Nicomachean Ethics*.

The medieval nominalists would attempt to clarify what was at stake with Aristotle's treatment of universals: What could a universal amount to, they asked, more than a collection of individuals? What could the phrase "a man" amount to beyond meaning some actual man—Callias or Socrates or Plato or . . . ? Aristotle's lack of clarity regarding the issue of the role of singular statements in syllogisms has long been commented upon, and for Hegel, the inability of Aristotle to do justice to determinate individuals per se within his forms of syllogistic reasoning would have a systematic explanation in the conception of the nature of social life in the ancient polis itself—it would be correlated with the nature of the Greek *Sittlichkeit*—the historically variable, conceptually mediated and expressed systems of customs (*Sitte*) making up Greek life, constituting its spirit (*Geist*) (see below, chapter 6). In this way, for Hegel, issues of the place of singular statements within patterns of reasoning and the use of "dialectical" nondemonstrative syllogistic reasoning would be related to the question of the relation of the apparently incommensurable continuous and discrete magnitudes. And all this in turn would bear directly upon the broader issue of the relation of logic to metaphysics.

1.3 The Formal/Ontological Issue

Mathematical approaches to logic are often seen as irrelevant to understanding Hegel's project of logic because, as it is often argued, Hegel's logic is deemed "metaphysical" or "ontological" rather than "formal" (see, for example, Beiser 2005, 161). This attitude, however, is based on a confusion. As a practice, mathematics in Hegel's time was not easily divided into "pure" and "applied" aspects, and this is reflected in Hegel's approach. Hegel's understanding of the status of mathematics was similar to that of Aristotle, who, with a focus more on Plato's middle-period position, contested Plato's separation of the realm of pure mathematical objects from the actual world in which those objects were manifest. The same could be said of the constitutive concepts of logic. And so, while it is true that for Hegel logical form could not be considered entirely in abstraction from the material that it was organizing, this did not itself preclude a study of logical form.[29] That is, Hegel's critique of "formalism" does not preclude the idea of a study of the logical form of thought, nor that of the "mathematical" dimensions of that form.

From the conventional perspective, Hegel's logic is understood as an articulation of "thought determinations" (*Denkbestimmungen*) that are regarded as something like the "categories" of Aristotle's *Categories*, a work traditionally included in the logical works although seemingly having more in common with Aristotle's metaphysical treatises (Cohen 2016, section 2). This is the view of the influential interpreter of Hegel's *Logic* Stephen Houlgate, for example. For Houlgate, what for others are paradigmatically logical words such as " 'concept,' 'judgment,' and 'syllogism' [for Hegel] name structures in nature, and so in *being itself*, not just forms of human understanding and reason. They are, therefore, ontological as well as logical structures—structures of being, as well as categories of thought" (Houlgate 2006, 116).

Houlgate's comments sit more easily with Hegel's "Objective Logic," which comprises the first two books of *The Science of Logic*, than they do with his "Subjective Logic," which comprises the final book. Read "materially," Hegel's "concepts" can be taken to be his equivalent of Aristotelian "natures" or "essences"—the view adopted by James Kreines, for example (Kreines 2015)— and on this model the "judgments" and "syllogisms" of the "Subjective Logic" are to be considered in turn as simply extending this to more complexly articulated material structures. However, the conceptual relations found in the first two books of *The Science of Logic* operate without a conceptual distinction that will, in book 3, be made explicit within the tripartite structure of "the concept." This is the distinction between "particularity" (*Besonderheit*) and "singularity" (*Einzelheit*) that comes into focus in the application of concepts in judgments. This is the distinction with which sense can be made of Hegel's insistence on Plato's syllogism, with its divided middle term, over Aristotle's.

It is clear that Hegel's *Logic* as a whole has an ontological dimension. As Robert Pippin puts it, logic is dually directed: it is directed to being in its intelligibility as well as to the intelligibility of that being.[30] However, it is far from clear that this ontological dimension should be understood on the model of the categories of Aristotle's logic to which books 1 and 2 are most approximate. First, such a conception flies in the face of Hegel's standard textual presentations in which he presents series of conceptual determinations as developing in such a way that at each stage a succeeding structure provides the "truth" of its antecedent—that is, provides the resources for a more adequate understanding of those antecedent structures than had been provided within the framework of their own determinations. The second half of book 3 of Hegel's *Logic* certainly shows a return to the "ontological" or "material" readings of conceptual structures found in the "Objective Logic," but this is crucially after Hegel has presented his own interpretation of the more formal approach of Aristotle's *Prior Analytics* that takes up approximately the first half of book 3. Moreover, this presentation is prefaced by an appeal to the approach of Kant, a philosopher for whom the primary role of concepts is that of organizing judgments that apply to the world but not because of any correspondence to the world as it is "in itself." This development surely cuts across the grain of Aristotelian category theory with its attempt to bring what was perceived as Plato's otherworldly ideas into the world.

Kant had made the categorial structure of appearance dependent upon the logical structures implicit in human judgment and inference, with this being usually seen as a mark of his "subjective" approach, enmeshed as it was, in Hegel's view, in the limitations of the "understanding" (*der Verstand*). And yet in the opening pages of the "Subjective Logic" Hegel describes as "one of the profoundest and truest insights to be found in the Critique of Reason that the *unity* which constitutes the *essence of the concept* is recognized as the *original synthetic* unity *of apperception*, the unity of the '*I think*,' or of self-consciousness" (*SL*, 515; 12:17–18).[31] This clearly signals a rupture with the more Aristotelian framework of the second book of the "Objective Logic," "The Logic of Essence," and it is only after Hegel's reconstruction of Aristotle's formal syllogistic that the ontological point of view with the section "Objectivity" is resumed. Moreover, for Hegel, Kant's formal logic was clearly predicated on the emergence of Leibniz's distinctly un-Greek algebraic logic, which cannot be ignored.

I will argue that viewed from the logical framework of the Greeks it becomes apparent that it is only in the modern context that "mathematical" and "formal" as standing opposed to the "metaphysical" or "ontological" can be so easily identified, but that the propensity for this division is already implicit in Aristotle's limited understanding of the syllogism. Hegel will identify the Platonic origins of the syllogism in the context of Plato's dialogue *Timaeus*, Plato's cosmological treatise that, because of its Pythagorean nature, can be regarded as both mathematical and material (see chapter 2). Moreover, it will be this paradigmatically material structure described in terms of ratios of numbers that provides the model for Hegel's reconstruction of Aristotle's paradigmatically formal syllogistic. Like most unmediated conceptual oppositions, Hegel will reject such a "dichotomous" distinction, showing Plato's syllogism to be implicitly formal and Aristotle's implicitly material. However, it will be only in the modern context, with its reintroduction of a distinctively modern abstract conception of the Pythagoreans' *monas*, and the elaboration of the determination of "singularity" and its distinction from "particularity," two notions that in much Hegel scholarship are not properly distinguished, that this integration of the formal and the material will be fully intelligible. It is in this sense that it is only in the light of modern approaches to logic, such as those of Leibniz and Kant, that we start to see what for Hegel a syllogism actually is.

2

Hegel and the Platonic Origins of Aristotle's Syllogistic

> It is evident from the things which have been said, then, what all demonstrations come from, and how. . . . But after these things, we must explain how we can lead deductions back into the figures stated previously. . . . For if we should study the origin of deductions, and also should have the power of finding them, and if, moreover, we could resolve those which have already been produced into the figures previously stated, then our initial project would have reached its goal.
>
> ARISTOTLE, *Prior Analytics*

In pursuit of the Platonic origins of the syllogism we are typically steered to Plato's account of the method of *diairesis* elaborated in the later dialogues (e.g., Bochenski 1961, 66; Rose 1968). Plato's account there, I have suggested, with its focus on the role of "due measure," calls out for an interpretation within the mathematical context of his time, a context in which the notion of "measure" was confounded by the discovery of the "incommensurable" nature of the magnitudes found in geometric objects when the measure invoked was the monadic unit from Pythagorean number theory. However, in stressing the Platonic origins of Aristotelian logic, Paul Shorey had in mind a more ontological than methodological Platonic model (Shorey 1924). This takes us into the mythically presented world of Plato's *Timaeus* with its Pythagorean doctrine of the most beautiful bond to which Hegel had been attracted—a structure that, according to Hegel, had a divided rather than a univocal "middle term." It is now time to start to fill out this general claim concerning the origins of the syllogism.

2.1 Pythagorean Harmonic Ratio Theory as Background to Plato's and Aristotle's Syllogisms

Aristotle had employed groups of three Greek letters—A, B, Γ; M, N, O; Π, P, Σ—seemingly as "schematic letters" for the representation of subject and predicate terms of syllogistically linked statements, in a manner that has appeared to many to have been borrowed from the practice of the geometers (e.g., Corcoran 2003, 268; Striker 2009, xiii).[1] Consonant with this, it has sometimes been claimed that Aristotle also employed labeled diagrams in his logic analogous to their use by geometers (e.g., Rose 1968; Netz 1999, 15; Bosley 2013).[2]

However, in the first half of the twentieth century a more radical thesis was put forward by the classicist Benedict Einarson, who argued that Aristotle had in particular drawn upon the mathematics of Pythagorean harmonic theory.

In a pair of papers Einarson showed that Aristotle's syllogistic was heavily indebted for its technical vocabulary to terms used in the theory of musical harmonics as well as in associated cosmological theories that had been developed within the Pythagorean tradition (Einarson 1936).[3] These claims would be repeated in 1978 by the Aristotle scholar Robin Smith (Smith 1978), but in the same year the historian of Greek mathematics Árpád Szabó (Szabó 1978) would independently argue for the broader influence of Pythagorean music theory on Euclidean geometry itself, especially those aspects having to do with ratios of magnitudes. I suggest that for Aristotle these musical origins may have been indirect and relatively insignificant, having been assimilated from the geometers. However, in the case of Plato they were clearly more important. Here, an apparent narrowing of the meaning of the term *logos* or ratio would distinguish Euclidean and Aristotelian usages of the term from earlier musical usages reflected in Plato. This difference would be relevant for the use of the notion of a "mean" or "middle term" employed in both music theory and geometry. Such a difference would be crucial for Hegel in distinguishing Plato's "rational" syllogism, with its ontological dimensions, from Aristotle's more limited "formal" syllogism, restricted as it was to the operations of the "understanding."[4]

In arguing for his radical thesis, Smith emphasized the points earlier raised by Einarson (Smith 1978, 202; Einarson 1936, 151) that the technical vocabulary used in *Prior Analytics* book 1, including the Greek words for "term" (*oros*) and "interval" (*diastema*) and the adjectives "extreme" (*akron*), "major" (*meixon*), "middle" (*meson*), and "minor" (*elatton*), all describing terms, had originally come from Pythagorean theorists of harmony, a mathematical discipline flourishing around the time of the founding of Plato's Academy.[5] Thus *oros* was a term designating the bounds of both geometric and musical intervals as well as a term in Aristotle's syllogism. The word *meson*, besides being a point dividing a musical interval, indicated the middle or "mean proportional" of peculiar double ratios of Greek mathematics, as when one says a is to b as b is to c ($a : b :: b : c$). It would play the role of "middle term" in Aristotle's syllogism—the term that was common to the two premises that was to be eliminated in the conclusion.[6] Aristotle also used the words *empiptein* and *katapyknosthai* to refer to the process by which a middle term is inserted into a syllogistic interval (Einarson 1936, 158; Smith 1978, 202)—again, both terms ultimately coming from harmonic theory to describe the division of musical intervals into smaller ones.

In addition to the borrowings described by Einarson and Smith, the term *diesis* could be mentioned, a technical term from harmonic theory, the so-called quarter-tone used in the measurement of musical intervals, that Aristotle compares to units of measure found in other sciences: "For everywhere we seek as the measure something one and indivisible; and this is that which is simple either in quality or in quantity. . . . And therefore in astronomy a 'one' of this sort is the starting-point and measure . . . and in music the quarter-tone (because it is the least interval) and in speech the letter [or simple sound, *stoicheion*]" (Aristotle 1984, *Metaphysics*, 1052b–1053a; see also 1016b).[7]

Such usage would not have been unconscious for a philosopher who, like Aristotle, had been trained in the Academy. Aristotle had apparently accepted the Pythagorean account of the musical intervals, although mistakes in his uses of technical vocabulary suggest limits to his understanding (Gibson 2005, 24–26).[8] However, while Aristotle seems to have been influenced by some areas of Pythagorean science (cf. Brumbaugh 1989, ch. 12), his cosmology as presented in his *On the Heavens* was largely independent of the Pythagorean "music of the spheres" approach found in Plato's *Timaeus*: "The theory that the movement of the stars produces a harmony, i.e., that the sounds they make are concordant, in spite of the grace and originality with which it has been stated, is nevertheless untrue" (Aristotle 1984, *On the Heavens*, 290b12–14). For Aristotle, such Pythagorean talk could be understood as mere metaphor, a topic on which he had a distinct theory (Aristotle 1984, *Poetics*, ch. 21). This, however, seems not to have been the case for Plato (e.g., Burnyeat 2000, 54–56). I suggest this holds also of their respective treatment of the "musical" dimensions of the syllogism.

Following Einarson, Smith notes how Aristotle's descriptions of syllogisms in *Prior Analytics* book 1, chapter 4, closely parallel formulae found in an important document from Greek mathematical music theory (Smith 1978, 202–205), the *katatomi kanonis*, usually known by its Latin name, *Sectio Canonis* (Barbera 1984b). This work, while often attributed to Euclid (Euclid 1975), is, like Euclid's *Elements*, said to compile material dating back to earlier mathematicians working in the Academy and elsewhere. In particular, some parts have been attributed to Archytas of Tarentum (Burkert 1972, 442), a contemporary and apparent friend of Plato and probably the major Pythagorean mathematician, harmonic theorist, and cosmologist of that period. In particular, the wording in Aristotle's account of the perfect syllogism in *Prior Analytics* book 1, chapter 4, closely follows a passage from the *Sectio Canonis* concerning a transitive relation of "measure." Aristotle writes that the terms of a syllogism are "so related to each other that the last is in the middle as a whole and the middle is either in or is not in the first as a whole," following this with a similar passage using schematic letters, "If A is predicated of every B, and B of every C, it is necessary for A to be predicated of every C" (Aristotle 1989, *Prior Analytics*, 25b32–26a3). In the *Sectio Canonis* a similar transitive relation is described with the notion of "measure": "Let there be an interval BC and let B be a multiple of C; and let it be that as C is to B, so B is to D. I say surely that D is a multiple of C. For since B is a multiple of C, C therefore measures B. Now as C was to B as B was to D, so C also measures D" (Euclid 1975, 239; cf. Einarson 1936, 155–156; Smith 1978, 203).

The *kanon* named in this work to be sectioned or cut (*tomi* or *katatomi*) was the ruler or measuring strip attached to the base of a monochord—a simple instrument on which a single string could be divided by a movable bridge, leaving a variable portion of its length to be plucked and sounded (Barker 1991, 50). The importance of such pairings of musical pitch of the sound with the lengths of a vibrating portion of the string should not be underestimated: they are thought to have given rise to "the first natural law ever formulated mathematically" (Ferguson 2010, 69). Szabó, following the fourth-century CE music theorist Gaudentius, claims the canon itself had come to be divided into twelve equal segments, accounting for the way the three musical means came to be exhibited in the "musical tetraktys" (Szabó 1978, ch. 2.7). A first cut would be made midway along the string at the point 6, such that the interval between 6 and 12 sounded with a tone an octave above that emitted by the freely vibrating string. This octaval interval 6 to 12 was now divided at the *diatessera* (perfect fourth) and *diapente* (perfect fifth) at points 8 and 9, respectively. Thus, within the octave between 6 and 12, the *diatessera* had a value (8) that was $\frac{4}{3}$ times that of the value of the whole octave (6), while the *diapente* had a value (9) that was $\frac{3}{2}$ times the value of the octave. As noted earlier, the three ratios involved, 2:1; 3:2, and 4:3, were all composed of numbers drawn from the *tetraktys*.[9]

This scale would be used by Plato in the *Timaeus*, but regardless of its formal elegance, the restriction of the ratios to the numbers 1 to 4 would later be contested by more empirically minded harmonic theorists. Compared to Plato, Aristotle was far more skeptical of the Pythagorean claims, and this attitude would be expressed by his student, the music theorist Aristoxenus (Aristoxenus 1902). Thus, Aristoxenus would later insist that an eleventh interval—(that is, the interval from C to the F of the next octave, an octave plus a perfect fourth)—sounded consonant, and so should simply be regarded as consonant. This, however, was rejected by the strict Pythagoreans on a priori grounds. Regardless of how it sounded to a listener, it was regarded as dissonant because its ratio, as 8:3, was not derivable from the *tetraktys* (Barbera 1984a). In sum, while on the basis of the lexical borrowing Smith describes

Aristotle's syllogistic as "a direct attempt . . . to develop a mathematical theory patterned after proportion theory and harmony" (Smith 1978, 202), we might think of this latter musical influence as less "direct" than is here suggested.[10] In the case of Plato, however, the Pythagorean links to what Hegel identifies as the syllogism at the heart of the cosmology of Plato's *Timaeus* are unmistakable.

2.2 Timaeus's Cosmic Animal and Its Relevance for Hegel

We have seen Plato's *Statesman* commencing with a clear signal of the relevance of mathematical issues. It is hard not to hear these being signaled as well in a jokey, playful way at the start of the *Timaeus* with the words with which Socrates starts the dialogue: "One, two, three . . . Where's number four . . . ?" (Plato 1997, *Timaeus*, 17a). The "number four" Socrates is referring to is the expected fourth participant of today's discussion that had been planned the day before, but we have noted the significance of the sequence 1, 2, 3, 4 would have held for this group of listeners. In any case, details of the Pythagorean complex of arithmetic, geometry, and harmony theory come into play when it becomes Timaeus's turn to speak on the topic of how the craftsman or demiurge brought order to the cosmos out of its initial state of disorder.

Timaeus describes how the demiurge wanted everything to be good and nothing bad, and so brought order to an "out of tune" (*plemmelos*) disorderly state (Plato 1997, *Timaeus*, 30a), creating the cosmos as a single living animal of which all other living things formed parts, both individually and as kinds. Because the best thing must be intelligent, he put intelligence in soul and soul in body, such that the living cosmos was itself endowed with intelligence. Noting that anything with bodily form must be both visible and tangible, he came to make the body of the cosmic animal out of the elements of fire and earth. That the ultimate elements of the cosmos were fire, air, water, and earth was a belief widely accepted by the pre-Socratic Greek philosophers, but the Pythagoreans had given the doctrine their peculiar twist in relation to the *tetraktys* in that these four elements were aligned with the numbers of the tetrad—fire with 1, air with 2, water with 3, and earth with 4. Timaeus introduces the idea of the needed bond with the claim we have earlier noted was quoted by Hegel:

> It isn't possible to combine two things well all by themselves, without a third; there has to be some bond between the two that unites them. Now the best bond [that is, Hegel's "most beautiful bond"] is one that really and truly makes a unity of itself together with the things bonded by it, and this in the nature of

things is best accomplished by proportion [*analogia*]. For whenever of three numbers which are either solids or squares the middle term between any two of them is such that what the first term is to it, it is to the last, and, conversely, what the last term is to the middle, it is to the first, then, since the middle term turns out to be both first and last, and the last and the first likewise both turn out to be middle terms, they will all of necessity turn out to have the same relationship to each other, and, given this, will all be unified. (Plato 1997, *Timaeus*, 31b–32a)

The multiple associations of the *tetraktys*'s number series 1, 2, 3, and 4 come into focus here: they align not only with the series of geometric objects, point, line, plane, and solid, and the cosmological elements, fire, air, water, and earth but also with the first four of the five "Platonic solids," tetrahedron, octahedron, icosahedron and cube, which provide the underlying physical structure of the respective cosmic elements.[11] Note, however, the main point concerning the need of these different levels to be linked by "means" or "middle terms." As Timaeus points out, were the cosmos planar rather than three-dimensional, only a single middle term (the equivalent of the number 2, standing between 1 and 3) would be needed, but as the cosmos is actually three-dimensional, two middle terms (as 2 and 3 stand between 1 and 4) are needed.[12] The demiurge made all these proportions

> as proportionate to one another as was possible, so that what fire is to air, air is to water, and what air is to water, water is to earth. He then bound them together and thus he constructed the visible and tangible universe. This is the reason why these four particular constituents were used to beget the body of the world, making it a symphony of proportion. (32b–c)

The need for two means in this context can be, and indeed has been,[13] interpreted as a requirement for two successive geometric means between the extremes. In fact, that two "mean proportionals" (geometric means) were so inserted between two extremes formed part of the solution to a famous mathematical problem of "doubling the cube"—that is, finding the increase in the length of the side of a cube needed to double its volume.[14] It soon appears, however, that two different types of mean, specifically, a harmonic and an arithmetic mean, are required. In discussing the division of the cosmic mind, which is clearly meant to be isomorphic to the cosmic body, Plato repeats the requirement for two middle terms: "one exceeding the first extreme by the same fraction of the extremes by which it was exceeded by the second, and the other exceeding the first extreme by a number equal to that by which it was exceeded by the second" (Plato 1997, *Timaeus*, 36a). These are the respective definitions of the harmonic and arithmetic means given by Plato's contemporary Archytas of Tarentum.

The first Pythagorean cosmological theorist about whom anything much is known is Philolaus of Croton, a rough contemporary of Socrates (Barker 2007, ch. 10). The cosmos, according to Philolaus, "was fitted together (*harmochthe*) out of unlimited things (*apeira*) and limiting things (*perainonta*). So there are two kinds of building blocks, for both the universe as a whole and the particular things in it, namely limiters and unlimiteds, which combine by a kind of fitting process" (Graham 2014, 49).[15] This mode of being fitted together (*harmochthe*) is a harmonia able to be described mathematically in terms of simple ratios among the natural numbers 1 to 4. Plato's late opposition of the "unit" and "indeterminate dyad" of the greater and the lesser would be a descendant of Philolaus's limit and unlimited. It is unclear whether the division of the musical scale that Plato refers to above originated with Philolaus (Barker 2007, 283–285), but it is known to have been used and developed by Plato's friend and student of Philolaus, Archytas of Tarentum (302–303).

The relevance of differing arithmetic and geometric series for natural philosophy had been raised by the physician and nature philosopher Adolf Karl August Eschenmayer in Hegel's own time, but not with the type of specificity found in Hegel.[16] Hegel was familiar with the Pythagorean background relevant to the thought of Plato and Aristotle. In the *Lectures on the History of Philosophy* he devotes considerable discussion to the Pythagoreans, drawing on authorities such as Aristotle and Sextus Empiricus (*LHP* 2:31–54; 2:23–49). He notes that Pythagoras was the first to call himself *philosophos* (*LHP* 2:33; 2:25) and in the *Encyclopedia Logic*, recognizes in his numericism "the first step towards metaphysics" (*E:L*, §104, addition 3). In terms of their natural philosophy, the Pythagoreans had gone beyond the more immediate approach of the other pre-Socratics, in that appealing to numbers in the constitution of the cosmos they appealed to something nonsensory and posited. Hegel thus comments on the "grandeur" of the idea of constructing a cosmos on a mathematical basis as a type of primitive Copernicanism in which theoretical argument is used to go beyond the immediacy and finitude of the senses. More particularly, he discusses the table of opposites as presented by Aristotle (*LHP* 2:42; 2:35), the role given to the privileged numbers of the *tetraktys* (44–45; 38), the role of ratios in the construction of the octave, and the perfect fourth and perfect fifth intervals (47; 41).

We have noted that the interval of the octave is represented by the ratio 2:1, that is, a vibrating string on a monochord that is divided at midpoint will produce a unison note one octave higher. Divided again, a length now one-quarter of the original will produce a note one octave higher again, generating the continuing geometrical series, 1, 2, 4, 8 . . . Here, for any three consecutive numbers a, b and c, a will stand to b as b stands to c ($a : b :: b : c$, or, expressed algebraically, $b = \sqrt{ac}$). But the geometric mean cannot be used to internally divide the octave:[17] internal division into consonant intervals requires either the arithmetic mean or the harmonic mean, which, as will be seen below, are complementary in two different ways. It is in this sense that two different but complementary means are, according to Plato, required to unify the cosmos.

The *arithmetic* mean had been traditionally described as holding when the second of three terms "exceeds the third by the same amount as that by which the first exceeds the second" (Barker 1989, 42). In algebraic terms, the arithmetic mean of two terms a and b is half their sum.[18] Archytas describes the complementary harmonic mean between two numbers as holding between three terms such that "the part of the third by which the middle term exceeds the third is the same as the part of the first by which the first exceeds the second" (42). In more modern terms, this can be expressed algebraically as twice the product of the numbers divided by their sum.[19] Applied within an octave, the arithmetic mean coincides with the perfect fifth or *diapente*, the harmonic mean with the perfect fourth or *diatessera*, these being the two consonant intervals within an octave recognized by the Pythagoreans. Moreover, as the author of the *Sectio Canonis* noted (Euclid 1975, §6), the octave is composed from these two "epimoric" intervals in the sense that, as can be appreciated by the layout of the keyboard of a modern piano or the fretboard of a guitar, the fourth and fifth added results in an octave. However, in terms of the relevant proportions of the vibrating string, the octave is the *product*, not the sum, of these two intervals. That is, $\frac{3}{2}$ multiplied by $\frac{4}{3}$ is equal to $\frac{2}{1}$. Here, this results from a systematic "homomorphism" involved between two different sequences of otherwise incommensurable magnitudes—those laid out in a continuing arithmetic sequence, on the one hand, and those laid out in a continuing geometric sequence, on the other. As we will see below (in chapter 3), the numerical relations involved here will be central to what Hegel takes to be the complete determination of the concept of number. A similar systematic homomorphism within Hegel's syllogism, I will argue, allows a syllogism to be understood as breaking down into two components that can be regarded as "homologues" of each other—judgments with opposed logical functions but equivalent structure. It will be such local homomorphisms rather than Brandom's "global isomorphism" that will provide a model for best understanding Hegel's inferentialist treatment of judgment.

The basic features of these interrelations had been demonstrated by Archytas in the "musical *tetraktys*" to be deployed by Plato and, later, Nicomachus, Iamblichus, and Proclus. This is achieved by expanding the series representing the division of the octave into perfect fourth and fifth (1:1, 4:3, 3:2, 2:1) into the sequence of four whole natural numbers (6, 8, 9, 12) in which, as we have seen, 8 is the harmonic mean and 9 the arithmetic mean of the interval between 6 and 12, the extremes belonging to a geometric series. Szabó, as noted, believed that this correlated with the canon's actual division into twelve segments, but Szabó also points to the range of meanings that the notions of ratio or *logos* and proportion or *analogia* had played in Pythagorean discussions up to the time of Plato and to which Plato had seemed to appeal in the *Timaeus* as responsible for bonding diverse parts into a whole.[20] Around that time, however, with the emergence of the type of geometry that would be codified by Euclid, the meanings of these terms were contracting in a way that resulted in the way these terms are generally used today, in which a "ratio" is understood in terms of how many times the smaller term divides the larger, with proportion or analogy understood as an equality of such ratios. Thus, Euclid writes: "Let magnitudes which have the same ratio be called proportional" (Euclid 1956, book 5, def. 6). Given Archytas's definition of the arithmetic mean as holding when the second of three terms "exceeds the third by the same amount as that by which the first exceeds the second" (Barker 1989, 42), it might be thought natural to write it as an equality between two pairs of terms, as in 12:9 = 9:6, for example, signifying the interval between 12 and 9 (3), being equivalent to that between 9 and 6. But of course, in the modern sense of ratio, "ratios" created by the arithmetic mean of an interval cannot be said to be equal: 12:9 ≠ 9:6 (or $\frac{4}{3} \neq \frac{3}{2}$).

The Euclidean sense of proportion is the sense in which *analogia* is discussed by Aristotle in relation to distributive justice in the *Nicomachean Ethics*. There, the just is described as a "species of the proportionate [*analogon*]. . . . For proportion is equality of ratios. Mathematicians call this kind of proportion geometrical" (Aristotle 1984, *Nicomachean Ethics*, 1131a 28–b14).[21] Thus in matters of distribution of honor, wealth, and other assets, Aristotle tells us that justice is not served if equal amounts are given to unequally deserving recipients or unequal amounts to equally deserving recipients. Rather, justice is an "equality of ratios" implying at least four terms—a proportion (*analogon*) "not of distinct numbers" (*arithmou idhion*), but of "number in general" (*alla alos arithmou*) (Aristotle 1984, *Nicomachean Ethics*, 1131a 31–32). In short, it involves a generalized Euclidean conception of proportion. Nevertheless, Aristotle goes on to distinguish this four-part $a : b :: c : d$ proportion from the "arithmetical proportion" relevant to cases of rectificatory or corrective justice in which "the equal is intermediate between the greater and the less" (1132a25–32b20). In this latter case the specific goodness or badness of the person judged is not relevant: "For it makes no difference whether a good man has defrauded a bad man or a bad man a good one, nor whether it is a good or a bad man that has committed adultery; the law looks only to the distinctive character of the injury and treats the parties as equal" (1132a1–5). Invoking the arithmetic mean is clearly a remnant of the earlier Pythagorean culture, but, as I suggested earlier (see the introduction) at a metalevel, Aristotle seems to think of the two different principles themselves as unified by the type of "equality of ratios" that reflects the strictly Euclidean geometric senses of ratio and proportion. This will contrast with Plato's more Pythagorean use of these notions, reflecting the broader musical sense with which he uses it—or so Hegel will claim.

Despite the contraction of the earlier Archytan sense of ratio of ratios to the more modern sense of a single "mean proportional," the general idea of three different means calling for unification would, despite not being prominent in Euclid's *Elements*, persist within Greek mathematics for centuries and would testify to the influence of the likes of Archytas and Eudoxus on later geometers such as Archimedes, Apollonius, and Pappus of Alexandria who had taken geometry beyond its Euclidean phase so as to have a focus on curves understood as conic sections (Knorr 1986, chs. 5–7). Thus, Pappus in the fourth century CE would note that Eratosthenes of Cyrene (276–194 BCE) had written a work "On Means," as well as a work on the mathematical basis of Plato's philosophy. Pappus would also give a diagrammatic representation attempting to relate geometric, arithmetic, and harmonic means between two points on a line (Thomas 1941, 2:569). These issues had especially been developed in the first centuries of the Common Era by neo-Pythagorean thinkers such as Nicomachus of Gerasa and Iamblichus, on whom Pappas would draw—both thinkers familiar to Hegel.

In line with such Pythagorean interpretations of Plato, a number of recent scholars have approached some of Plato's characteristic doctrines in ways that appeal to the different *analogia* of Archytas's musical theory. These interpretations appeal to a particular doubled ratio combining geometric and arithmetic means known as the "Golden Ratio," Maria Antonietta Salamone, for example, arguing that it was the Golden Ratio that Plato himself had in mind with the idea of the doubled ratio binding together the parts of the body of the cosmic animal in the *Timaeus* (e.g., Salamone 2019). Moreover, the Golden Ratio has commonly been postulated to be the double ratio invoked by Socrates in the construction of the celebrated "Divided Line" in the *Republic*—a figure heavy with epistemological significance for Plato. It will be later argued that it was not the Golden Ratio but the associated musical *tetraktys* that Hegel had taken to be what Plato had in mind, but exploration of the Golden Ratio will help clarify the nature of the issues involved.

2.3 Plato's Divided Line and the Golden Ratio

The Golden Ratio was another of those figures from ancient geometry afforded particular significance during the French Revolution. It itself had been reflected in the structure of the "pentagram," used as a friendship symbol by the original Pythagoreans, with whom the modern revolutionaries sometimes identified themselves (Billington 1980, 110).[22] While the subject of many inflated claims (Markowsky 1992), the Golden Ratio is a significant mathematical object in its own right, found in Euclid's *Elements* but linked more to developments in geometry that would postdate Euclid. In *Elements*, it is treated three times: in book 2, in relation to the Greek geometric algebra of rectangles; in book 5 in relation to the theory of proportional magnitudes as developed by Plato's colleague in the Academy and former student of Archytas, Eudoxus of Cnidus;[23] and in book 13, where it is indispensable for the construction of the five "Platonic Solids," usually attributed to Plato's junior colleague in the Academy, Theaetetus. It would seem to have been a "hot topic" in the early years of the Academy, and later Proclus would attribute the discovery of the "section" to Plato himself (Proclus 1970, 55), although Eudoxus would be described as first demonstrating its geometric nature. The Golden Ratio is perhaps the most significant topic in *Elements* that taps into the musical theories of the Pythagoreans, because it requires a division of a line that is subject to the requirements of both geometric and arithmetic means (fig. 2.1).

In the famous set piece in Plato's *Republic* book 6 concerning the "Divided Line," Socrates asks his interlocutor, Glaucon, to imagine a line that is divided into two unequal parts representing the visible and intelligible realms, respectively. While the text is not accompanied by an actual diagram, interpreters have generally represented it by a vertical line with the smaller lower segment representing the visible realm and the larger upper segment

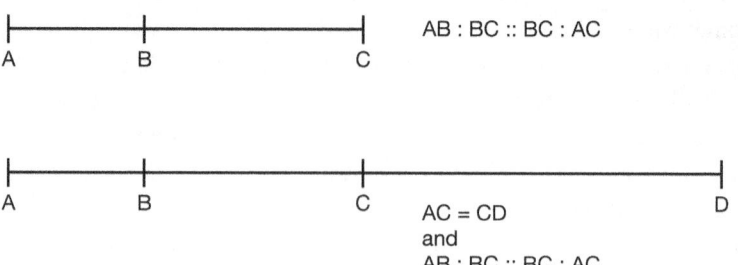

FIGURE 2.1 Two presentations of the Golden Ratio. In the upper figure: AB : BC :: BC : AC (AB+BC). In the lower figure: extending AC to D such that AC = CD makes BC the geometric mean of AC and CD and C the arithmetic mean of A and D.

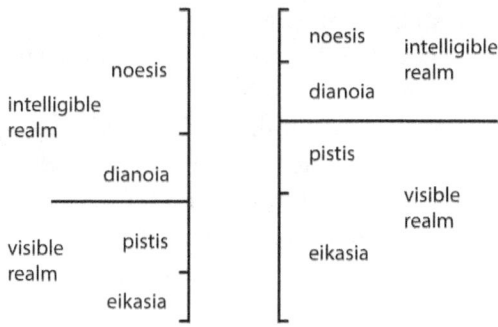

FIGURE 2.2 Two diagrammatic representations of Plato's Divided Line.

the intelligible realm, although some others have inverted this, with the larger segment below (fig. 2.2). Socrates then asks Glaucon to divide both segments "in the same ratio as the line." The four subsections of the line will now be taken to represent different cognitive attitudes onto the world—two to the visible world, two to the intelligible—together with the distinct types of intentional objects that are correlated with those attitudes. This sequence of descending intentional attitudes is the following, as translated by Jowett: reason (*noesis*), understanding (*dianoia*); conviction (*pistis*) and image-perception (*eikasia*).[24] It is important here that with *dianoia* Socrates explicitly appeals to examples of mathematical understanding.

Read according to its perhaps most obvious interpretation, the doubly divided line is meant to capture the similarity existing between the two relations. Image-perception stands to conviction in the way that understanding stands to reason, or image perception : conviction :: understanding : reason—schematically, $a : b :: c : d$. Here, Socrates starts with the lowest segment, the empirical *eikasia* or images such as shadows or reflections in water that are grasped as images of, and so explained by, the things that belong to the upper division of the lower segment, the visible realm. This ratio is now compared to that holding between the divisions of the upper segment, the intelligible realm. In the discussion of *dianoia*, the lower division of the intelligible realm, Socrates alludes to the "visible figures" that mathematicians use when reasoning but asserts that in such cases the reasoning is not *about* the various figures they draw but what they resemble: "They make their claims for the sake of the square itself and the diagonal itself, not the diagonal they draw" (Plato 1997, *Republic*, 510d). These are things to which the figures and diagrams stand as shadows or reflections so stand to the things they are shadows or reflections of.[25] We are now to think of the elements of *noesis* as the realities explaining them in the ways that concrete empirical objects explain their images.

Plato's basic idea seems clear enough. He intends the reader to acknowledge the existence of *idealiter*—the real, nonempirical squares, triangles, circles, and so on, of the mathematician's intentional activity—entities to which one must "lift the mind" beyond the drawn figures of the visible realm. Similarly, the reader is to lift the mind from the object of the mathematician's "hypothesis" that now stands as the proper object of the lower subsection of the upper, intelligible realm to the philosopher's idea.[26]

We might think of this interpretation as characterizing the conventional "Platonistic" reading of the Divided Line.[27] In relation to the objects of understanding, the abstract hypotheses of *dianoia*,[28] the philosopher, presumably unsatisfied with the extent of the mathematician's explanations, wants to reason from the existence of those explanations to "the unhypothetical first principle of everything" (Plato 1997, *Republic*, 511b). The upper division of the line thus represents a type of step upward from hypotheses to ideas that is analogous to the step upward from sensuous images to the also sensible entities that explain them. The very existence of those, as yet hypothetical, explanations had itself seemed to demand explanation, and it is that demand that takes the thinker from those already ideal objects to what we might call the *super*-ideal entities and principles of the realm of ideas.

There is, however, a spanner in the works awaiting this reading. Socrates's exposition concludes with the instruction to arrange the four separate line segments "in a ratio, and consider that each shares in clarity to the degree that the subsection it is set over shares in truth" (Plato 1997, *Republic*, 511c–d). And yet, as a number of readers have pointed out over the last half century, when the diagram is actually constructed in the way in which Socrates instructs Glaucon, the sections representing *pistis* and *dianoia* turn out to be of equal length. This, however, confounds the idea that these attitudes are meant to be contrasted in terms of a successively increasing clarity.[29] The proportion $a : b :: c : d$ has become a continuing one, $a : b :: b : c$. In terms of signaling differences within the degrees of clarity of these epistemic attitudes, the equal lengths of the middle sections are surely anomalous. However, it is underdetermined in Socrates's discussion exactly what the proportional ratios are meant to signify—other contrasting interpretations may be (and we will see, have in fact been) forthcoming.

Hegel's paraphrase of the account given by Socrates/Plato in his discussion in the *Lectures on the History of Philosophy* in fact portrays it as a tripartite division: "Plato embraced sensible consciousness and especially sensible representations, opinions and immediate knowing, under the term *doxa* (opinion). Midway between *doxa* (opinion) and science in and for itself there lies argumentative cognition, inferential reflection or reflective cognition, which develops for itself universal categories or classes. But the highest [knowing] is *noesis*, thinking in and for itself" (*LHP* 2:188; 3:13). While Hegel's translator here notes, "Hegel's account of the Divided Line here reduces Plato's four modes of apprehension to three" (*LHP* 2:188n35) it would appear that not only is this, in fact, mathematically warranted, but it is generally consistent with Hegel's pursuit of a Platonic structure with a "divided" or "broken" middle term.[30] In fact, this tripartite partitioning of the Divided Line is consistent with its interpretation according to the Golden Ratio, with its complex combination of arithmetic and geometric means, as proposed by numerous interpreters (see, for example, Brumbaugh 1954; Boyce Gibson 1955; Des Jardins 1976; Dreher 1990; Fossa and Erickson 2005).[31] In short, with the imagery of the Golden Ratio we are drawn back into the realm of Pythagorean harmony theory consistent with Plato's articulation of both the body and soul of the cosmic animal in the *Timaeus*.

I suggest that the type of consideration that may have attracted Hegel to the idea of a proportion subject to both geometric and arithmetic means is brought out by Gregory Des Jardins in his interpretation of the Divided Line understood as the Golden Ratio (Des Jardins 1976). We have seen that the intrinsic tripartite nature of the Divided Line (which itself makes it more compatible with the idea of a "divided" mean term) makes the "epistemological" reading problematic. However, Des Jardins attributes a quite different significance to the lengths than the traditional epistemological considerations. For him, the proportions are relevant in terms of the issue of the different and incommensurable *kinds* that are involved in the partition.

Des Jardins's argument requires the larger part of the Divided Line to represent visibles rather than intelligibles, which, while contrary to how the line is typically read, is not incompatible with Plato's actual description.[32] For Des Jardins, the equality of the two intermediary sections of the line is to be explained by the fact that the visible bodies of *pistis* (represented by the upper segment of the lower division) and the mathematical objects of *dianoia* (represented by the lower segment of the upper division) both belong to one kind, vis-à-vis the kind discrete countables. Moreover, it is the sameness of kind that is symbolized by another equality to be found in the line. When interpreted as the Golden Ratio, the length of the larger segment of the larger division (in Des Jardins's diagram, the lowermost segment, representing *eikasia*) is of equal length to the entire upper division. Des Jardins interprets this equality between *eikasia* and the combined dianoetic and noetic intelligibles (represented by the complete upper division) to signify that they too share in being of the same kind, the kind bodyless (Des Jardins 1976, 491).[33] Des Jardins's reading makes the most of the relations involved in terms that would surely have appealed to Hegel—the incommensurable nature of the products of the first division and the role of mathematical objects of *dianoia* as intermediaries between these two incommensurable realms of concrete countable things and purely intelligible forms.

The issues raised by such passages, I suggest, count as further evidence that, for Hegel, Plato's idea of a doubled or divided middle term was crucial for what it was that made his syllogism, in contrast to that of Aristotle, a rational one. As a final piece of evidence for the significance of Pythagorean harmony theory for Hegel's conception of the syllogism, however, in the following chapter we will turn to a consideration of his treatment of the category of magnitude through to its most mature form as *Verhältnis*, "ratio," in book 1 of *The Science of Logic*. Here we find considerable detail with respect to the influence and fate of the harmonically based Pythagorean mathematics on the categories of logic. It will also take us to how an idea from ancient Greek geometry as found in Carnot's projective geometry could have been significant for Hegel as providing a model for the way in which Aristotle's syllogism needed to be reconstructed.

3

The General Significance of Neoplatonic Harmonic Theory for Hegel's Account of Magnitude

> The means of 6 in relation to 12 are determined by the ratios 3:2 and 4:3. The sequence based on both of these means has been granted to the human race by the blessed choir of the Muses and has bestowed upon us the use of concord and symmetry to promote play in the form of rhythm and harmony.
>
> (PLATO), *Epinomis*

Many recent interpretations of Plato's central ideas of Socrates's Divided Line and Timaeus's "best" or "most beautiful" bond stress the role of Greek mathematics around the time of Plato as providing an important context for the comprehension of these puzzling notions. In particular, attention to the Euclidean "division in extreme and mean ratio," the Golden Ratio, has allowed some light to be cast on these doctrines. Nevertheless, as I have suggested, with respect to the best bond articulating the cosmic body in the *Timaeus*, Hegel seems to have had in mind some other—in fact, more general—"ratio" to which the Golden Ratio is related.[1] It would have been his familiarity with this more general ratio via books he possessed by late neo-Pythagorean mathematicians such as Nicomachus of Gerasa that could well have allowed him to recognize how elements of these ancient doctrines were being reintroduced into nineteenth-century mathematics by figures such as Lazare Carnot. We find evidence for this in one of the most puzzling sections of book 1 of Hegel's *Science of Logic*—his account of the category of magnitude that ends in his discussion of *Verhältnis* or "ratio."

3.1 Hegel's Exploration of the Category of Magnitude

Hegel's discussion of the concept of magnitude (*Grösse* or *Quantität*),[2] in section 2 of book 1 of the "Objective Logic," follows that of determinacy (*Bestimmtheit*) or quality (*Qualität*), and these two logical determinations of quality and quantity will continue to be woven together in complex ways throughout the *Logic* itself and, in a way crucial for us, into a distinction between judgment forms in Hegel's "Subjective Logic." As with the patterns typical of Hegel's *Logic*, a certain way of making a qualitative distinction will be superseded, *aufgehoben*, by a quantitative one that will itself eventually be replaced by a more complexly specified qualitative determination, which is now internally mediated by the specification of the quantity that had been *aufgehoben*.[3]

In the section "Quality" it had been learned that something, a field, say, will be made determinate by its distinctions from something similar but qualitatively different, a meadow or a forest, for example (*SL*, 153; 21:175). Here, there is a limit (*Grenze*) in semantic space distinguishing one type of thing from another—a "*middle point between* the two [*die Mitte zwischen beiden*] at which they leave off" (*SL*, 99; 21:114), and the syllogistic language of "middles" between limits suggests that we are on a path toward the goal of properly specifying the nature of such a logical relation. In contrast to qualitative difference, quantitatively a field is further made determinate by being distinguished from other fields of smaller or larger size. Such quantitative determinations presuppose the qualitative determinacies that they further divide—the size of a field is typically to be compared to that of another field, not that of a forest. (As the phrase goes, one must compare "apples to apples.") However, Hegel adds, there is a sense in which the determinate quantity has "for foundation a permanent being *which is indifferent to its determinateness*" (153; 21:174). This will prove to be an important idea and we have already glimpsed a rendering earlier (in the introduction) in the notion of "absolute quantity."

The quantitative determinateness that emerges from the incorporative supersession (*Aufhebung*) of the initial permanent being will itself come to be *aufgehoben* within a new qualitative determination that eventually succeeds it. This dynamic of qualitative and quantitative contrasts will develop in complex ways throughout the *Logic* and will become incorporated in subsequent overtly logical determinacies found in syllogistically related judgments, but it is the Timaean/Platonic "syllogism" that will be suggested by the particular "quantum" with which the section on magnitude will conclude, a particular type of ratio that Hegel labels the "ratio of powers." This, I suggest, will take us into the often-thought murky world of the neo-Pythagorean revival that affected middle and late forms of Platonism that had been resurrected around the time of the French Revolution.

In accord with the tripartite way the categories unfold throughout the "Objective Logic," the section "Magnitude" (*die Grösse*) is divided into three chapters, treating quantity (*die Quantität*), quantum, and quantitative ratio (*das quantitative Verhältnis*). As mentioned above, this last category is generally translated as either "quantitative ratio" or "quantitative proportion," the latter focusing on that type of ratios between ratios we see in structures such as $a : b :: c : d$. But Hegel, following the more Pythagorean approach of Plato rather than Aristotle, will interpret this structure as having a wider range of meanings than what is standardly understood as "proportion" qua equality of ratios. The section "Magnitude" will be followed by "Measure" (*Maass*), the contradictions of which, sending measure into measurelessness, will see the "being-logic" of book 1 transition into the "essence-logic" of book 2. As the metaphysical stance with its "essence-appearance" dichotomy throughout book 2 is broadly "Aristotelian," we might think of the transition from "being" to "essence" as to some degree coinciding with the idea that Greek speculative philosophy emerged out of the contradictions of the mathematical worldview of the Pythagoreans. Indeed, this is in keeping with the topics discussed in the chapter "Ratio," which starts with early Pythagorean conceptions of ratio but ends in ones that make explicit the more complex conceptions of ratio, albeit still Pythagorean ones, found in Plato's *Timaeus*.

The path through quantity to ratio will progressively show how a holistic or "structural" approach to mathematics will work to undermine the more "atomistic" approach characterizing the early Pythagorean conception of the *monas*. In his account of number in the discussion of quantum qua determinate quantity, Hegel alludes to the origins of arithmetic in simple counting or numbering procedures, in which since "the ones are external to each other, they are pictured in a sense image, and the operation by which number is generated is a reckoning on the finger tips, dots, etc." (*SL*, 172; 21:197–198).[4] What numbers *are* when determined in this way—"what four *is*, or five"—he adds, "can only be *indicated or shown* [*gewiesen*]" (172; 21:197–198). Presumably, here Hegel implies "indicated or shown" rather than "defined," and so as conceptually indeterminate. Such mechanical counting could go on indefinitely, and number is only made definite when this activity breaks off—when it finds a "limit" analogous to the qualitative limits distinguishing fields from meadows. I take Hegel's point to be that in counting the apples in a basket, say, one stops counting simply from the contingency of running out of apples to count! This is the sense in which the limit is accidental or "external" to the actual process of counting: "The limit is external, the breaking off point, how much is to be taken, is something accidental, arbitrary" (172; 21:197–198). One always counts finite numbers of things, but the activity of counting itself carries in it an infinite potential because it could be continued indefinitely.

It was this type of simple enumeration that was obviously at the origin of the Pythagoreans' initial conception of number. One counts things in terms of some unit. One might count off the size of a herd of goats by pairing each goat with a notch made on a piece of wood, say, but one measures the size of the herd by counting only goats, excluding other objects. When estimating the size of a herd one counts goats; when estimating the size of a fleet one counts ships. What is counted is, in each case, different, but in each case one employed some conception of a unit indifferent to what one was counting, a unit underlying the equivalent pairing of a certain number of goats with a similar number of notches on a stick or ships in a harbor. This indifferent unit is the *monas*. Hegel calls this approach to quantity that of "unit and amount," which is grounded in the Pythagoreans' initial conception of number and which proceeds "from the one of the *immediate* quantum in which unit and amount are only moments" (*SL*, 177; 21:202). It is difficult to see from this type of grounding of quantity in simple enumeration how what would in much later times be considered as numbers—negative numbers, say, or the "imaginary" number "i"—could possibly count as a number. Simple enumerating activity of this type will eventually become integrated within the properly scientific practice of "mathematics" in which determinate identities are somehow rationally or conceptually determined by "limits" that are not simply externally imposed by the nature of what one happens to be counting. But how? Hegel has in mind an evolution of the concept <number> that took place within the Pythagorean tradition itself—an evolution in which Eudoxus of Cnidus had played a pivotal early role.

While in the context of the *Lectures on the History of Philosophy* it is obvious whose ideas are being discussed, this is often not the case in these sections of *The Science of Logic*. Hegel's focus is principally on the abstract thought determinations themselves rather than on who had actually thought them, and while for Hegel there are often broad parallels between the logical development of categories in the *Logic* and the historical development of those ideas, in this section one often finds a confusing mix of historical periods. Nevertheless, there are a number of long digressions on topics of particular interest to Hegel, including Pythagorean mathematics and Newton's differential calculus, often in the context of "remarks" spread throughout the chapters. At various places in the discussion of magnitude, Hegel will also attempt to distance his approach from Kant's. We cannot here attempt to examine Hegel's views on mathematics in any depth, and later (chapter 5) we will engage with those parts of these sections that bear on the topic of Newton's mechanics and the role of the calculus in it. Here we will restrict ourselves to those parts of the text relevant to establishing some of his conception of the mathematical background to Plato's syllogism and its more general mathematical relevance. However, quickly sketching his position via its contrast to that of Kant can help orient us in relation to some of the basic features of Hegel's approach.

Hegel will start from a view of the origins of numbering something like that of Kant's description of number as "a representation that summarizes the successive addition of one (homogeneous [*Gleichartigen*]) unit to another"

(Kant 1998, B182), but he aims to counter Kant's derivation of mathematical objects from a process of construction in "pure intuition." "Numbers" as belonging to this primitive enumerating activity are indeed, for Hegel, "external" to the concept, but there is no synthesis involved in a simple counting that simply breaks off. That is, while agreeing with Kant that there is no conceptual synthesis involved, he also rejects the alternative of some specifically nonconceptual medium (Kant's pure intuition) allowing an alternative form of synthesis. However, despite the absence of conceptual synthesis at this basic level, there *is* something important that signals a role for conceptual activity presupposed by this purely mechanical and externally limited counting. Qua purely enumerable entities, the objects counted have been, like Kant's "homogeneous" units or the Pythagoreans' monads, entirely abstracted from all the actual empirical qualities manifested by the things being counted. That is, it is the same number 5 that is instantiated in five goats, on the one hand, and five ships, on the other, and in this sense things as countable can be no longer considered sensuous objects at all:

> Number is not an object of the senses, and to be occupied with number and numerical combinations is not the business of the senses. (*SL*, 181; 21:207)

> The intuition of figures or numbers is of no help to the science of figures and numbers; only the *thought* of them produces this science. (*SL*, 539; 12:42)

Qua pure countables,[5] the things counted are being treated something like supersensuous objects, and it is in this sense that number, as Hegel points out (*SL*, 178; 21:204), might be considered as standing "midway between the senses and thought" like the mathematical intermediaries attributed to Plato by Aristotle (Aristotle 1984, *Metaphysics*, 987b1). Moreover, being abstracted away from the empirically governed activity of counting will allow numbers, under certain conditions, to come to be conceived differently. An "irrational number" would not be conceived as a number if numbers were simply thought of as means by which one can count discrete goats or ships; but it will turn out that irrational numbers come onto the mathematician's radar as a consequence of a related type of measurement, the application of numbers to continuous magnitudes such as lengths, areas, and volumes.

At the beginning of the chapter "Quantum," Hegel notes that as *quantum*, quantity "has a limit, both as continuous and discrete magnitude [*sowohl als continuirliche wie als discrete Grösse*]" (*SL*, 168; 21:193), and while this distinction "in the first instance" has no significance, the interplay between these "two species" of magnitude will be crucial.

In spatial magnitude [*in der Raumgrösse*] geometry has, in general, continuous magnitude for its subject matter while the subject matter of arithmetic is discrete magnitude. However, with this disparity [*Ungleichheit*] of subject matters they also have an inequality in the manner and the completeness of delimitation or determinateness. Spatial magnitude has only delimitation in general; when considered as an absolutely determined quantum, it requires number. Geometry as such does not *measure* spatial figures—is not an art of measuring—but only *compares* them. (*SL*, 170; 21:196)

The disparity here between the two magnitudes expresses the view found in Aristotle that numbers, on the one hand, and lines, areas, and volumes, on the other, constitute different kinds of magnitude (Aristotle 1984, *Metaphysics*, 992a16; *Posterior Analytics*, 74a2–22). But Hegel suggests that if geometry is to be actually applied, then some sort of transgeneric equivalence between numbers and lines, areas, or volumes must be achieved. This shows his departure from Kant in relation to the distinction between the discrete and the continuous.

Kant is commonly taken as grounding geometry and arithmetic separately, in the pure intuitions of space and time, respectively,[6] although this may oversimplify his position.[7] As noted earlier and as will be explored further in the context of a contrast with Schelling (in chapter 4), Hegel does not subscribe to Kant's underlying concept of spatially and temporally opposed forms of "pure intuition," and so does not conceive of arithmetic and geometry as related in this way. Moreover, without pure intuition Hegel seems to give up the idea of any "pure" as opposed to "applied" mathematics. As the above passage makes explicit, geometry has primarily the continuous magnitude of space for its subject matter, although this notion for Hegel will be able to be extended beyond the immediacy of empirical space. Historically, however, it had been the attempted application of number to space, as in the assignment of units of measure to continuous spatial quantities, that had allowed these otherwise opposed determinacies to come into contact. This is reflected in the way that Hegel's progression from quality through magnitude to measure (*das Maass*) has the determinations of quality and quantity dividing and reuniting: "Abstractly expressed, quality and quantity are in measure united" (*SL*, 282; 21:323).

Considered in abstraction from continuous magnitudes, countable numbers can be subject to manipulations of increasing complexity, which introduces hierarchical relations between the "units" collected into "amounts" and the amounts themselves—Hegel here broaching topics that would later become central for set theory. For example, repeated counting on fingers can lead to a result such as "7 plus 5 make 12" being memorized, and from this, the idea of multiplication can follow by the reiteration of addition now applied

GENERAL SIGNIFICANCE OF NEOPLATONIC HARMONIC THEORY 63

to the resulting amounts: "by adding to one seven another seven and by repeating the operation five times" with the result being "equally memorized" (*SL*, 172; 21:198).[8] Hegel seems to suggest that the equalities resulting from these operations hide an underlying inequality. Equality exists between differently described amounts (as when the sum of amounts 2 and 3 equals 5), but because these "amounts" can, in the context of multiplication, be treated as units to be counted, that is, "as numbers, immediate to each other," they are thereby also "*unequal* in general" (*SL*, 175; 21:201).[9] But he now talks of a further "equality" that can be established between unit and amount when numbers are raised to their exponential powers, and this is an equality that brings the "equality of the determinations inherent in the determination of number" to completion (*SL*, 175–176; 21:201). This idea has connections to the relations established among the musical "means" in Pythagorean harmonic theory and will have ramifications for the way Hegel conceives of the determinations of concepts in general. It therefore warrants careful consideration.

The reiteration of addition to the amounts resulting from addition that we have observed in multiplication can in turn be applied to the operation of multiplication itself, such that the multiplication of 2 by itself can be thought of as 2^2 (two raised to the "power" 2), or multiplied by itself twice ($2 \times 2 \times 2$) as 2^3 (2 raised to the power 3).[10] Here, the powers themselves can be added in ways that correspond to multiplication among the base numbers raised to those powers:

$$2^2 \times 2^3 = (2 \times 2) \times (2 \times 2 \times 2) = 2 \times 2 \times 2 \times 2 \times 2 = 2^5 = 2^{2+3}$$

That is, via exponentiation, a type of equivalence can be established between multiplication at one level and addition at another, despite these being different operations. Hegel describes this situation as one in which "counting is the raising to a power." This, of course, could be continued indefinitely, counting powers from 1 to some "n" such that the underlying number, say 2, will be described as raised to the nth power, 2^n. The counting of powers in this manner could, of course, be further subject to the same developments of addition that we have seen in multiplication and exponentiation, but this would simply repeat the cycle of addition, multiplication, and exponentiation that is already in place. While counting was originally subject to determination from without by the number of the things (goats, ships, etc.) counted, the counting of powers seems to have entirely escaped this external determination: the "amounts" being counted, having been formed by prior operations, have been determined by factors internal to the system. It is for these reasons that Hegel can describe the development of exponentiation as completing the conceptual determination of number.

In the course of describing this passage from addition to multiplication to the taking of powers, Hegel makes the further, modern, rather than Greek,[11] point that each of these operations has a "negative counterpart"—what would now be called an "inverse function": for addition there is subtraction, for multiplication there is division, and for exponentiation there is "extraction of a root" (*SL*, 176; 21:201). There is, however, another "inverse" to exponentiation that, while not mentioned here, Hegel elsewhere pairs with exponentiation (237; 21:275 and 259; 21:298). This is the operation of determining the logarithm of a number.[12] Because this allusion to logarithms will link his idea of the complete conceptual determination of number back to the Pythagorean theory of the three musical means, we must pursue this somewhat confusing idea.

Logarithmic tables are aids to computation invented in the early seventeenth century that were still in use until the last quarter of the twentieth century, when they were made redundant by the development of pocket calculators, but the "logarithmic function" on which such tables were based is deeply embedded within modern algebra. This logarithmic function is an inverse of the exponential function (Hegel's "raising to powers") in that for any number x, its logarithm y is just the power to which some specified constant b (called the "base") must be raised so as to equal x. In short: $y = \log_b x$ if and only if $x = b^y$. This inverse relation utilizes the "counting of powers" discussed by Hegel in that correlations are established between addition and multiplication as seen in the equation above, $2^2 \times 2^3 = 2^{2+3}$—an equation that can be generalized as $b^m \times b^n = b^{m+n}$. Converted to logarithms, this can now be expressed as $\log_b n.m = \log_b m + \log_b n$, which in turn provides a way for converting between multiplications and additions. Thus, to multiply two numbers m and n, one finds their respective logarithms, adds those logarithms, and then finds the number whose log is that sum. Equipped with a table pairing numbers and their respective logs, calculations involving multiplication are thus greatly simplified. These pairings had been first described as ratios, "logarithms" being ratios (*logoi*) of numbers (*arithmoi*).

While the official date for the invention of logarithms is 1614, when the Scottish nobleman John Napier published the first "log tables," the idea behind this computational aid goes back to Archimedes (Pierce 1977, 22). Before Napier, Kepler had discussed their use in 1606 (Porubský 2010, 63–64) based on ones compiled (but not published until later) by a Swiss instrument-maker, Joost Bürgi. In fact, a similar method (called *prosthaphaeresis*) had been used by astronomers for about a century based on the trigonometric "cosine" function with which a similar conversion of multiplication to addition had been achieved.[13] Hegel seems to make this link to trigonometrical functions when he links logarithms not only to exponentiation (a link that had only been discovered a century after the discovery of logarithms) but also to certain "circular functions and series" (*SL*, 259; 21:298), by which he seems to be alluding to sine and cosine functions. Indeed, Hegel possessed a treatise on the mathematics of logarithms by the mathematics teacher at the Nuremberg high school during his own stay there, Johann Wolfgang Müller (Mense 1993, 680). It was clearly a topic about which he was well informed.

After their introduction, logarithmic tables would develop with respect to the choice of "base number" used,[14] but in the first instance they consisted of pairings of numbers between arithmetic and geometric continuous series that we have seen linked in Pythagorean music theory. For example, Bürgi's tables, using base 2, started by pairing the integers 0 and 1 (or 2^0), 1 and 2 (2^1), 2 and 4 (2^2), 3 and 8 (2^3), 4 and 16 (2^4), and so on (Cajori 1903, 6). In short, Bürgi's logarithms displayed the same "homomorphism" that we saw earlier in Pythagorean harmonic theory, where, in a more restricted sense, relations of multiplication—that is, the combination of perfect fourth and perfect fifth in the octave grasped from a harmonic point of view, a product—were correlated with relations of summation of steps of a scale.[15] Given that Hegel treats the three arithmetical operations (addition, multiplication, and exponentiation ("raising to the power") along with their inverses (subtraction, division, and [assuming] the logarithmic function) as constituting the complete determination of number, we can see the relevance that the ancient attempt to unify the three Pythagorean means could have for him. In short, the unity of the Pythagorean means provides an instance of the determinations of the more general conception of number itself. However, it must be kept in mind that numbers, qua discrete magnitudes, require being brought into contact with their incommensurable other, continuous magnitudes. By building up "modes of connection" among determinate numbers via "species of calculation" (*SL*, 171; 21:197),[16] the six interrelated arithmetical operations might give the complete determination of the concept of number, but they must somehow be integrated with relations among continuous magnitudes to give a determinate concept of magnitude itself. How are we to think of this interaction between determinations of these "incommensurable" magnitudes, however?

Hegel alludes to an answer to this question when he notes that in relation to "the *species of calculation*" that are "performed in arithmetic one after the other ... the thread guiding the progression is not brought out in arithmetic" (*SL*, 171; 21:197).[17] The suggestion here seems to be that the order or "one-after-the-otherness" of a progression is somehow the province of geometry rather than arithmetic, and this was a view that would come to be held by projective geometers in the nineteenth century. The French geometer Michel

Chasles, for example, would identify geometry as equally the science of order as of measure (Chasles 1837, 290).

By the beginning of the following century, Bertrand Russell would note that, although rarely discussed in the philosophies of his contemporaries, "the importance of order, from a purely mathematical standpoint, has been immeasurably increased by many modern developments" (Russell 1903, 199). Order had been shown to be at the heart of geometry by projective geometers such as Michel Chasles, but Russell would also point to the central role it played in arithmetic, declaring the cardinal numbers to be dependent on the ordinals (Russell 1903, 247–248). Indeed, as Stephen Houlgate points out (Houlgate 2014, 24), Hegel seems to anticipate this idea in his discussion of the distinction between extensive quantum and intensive quantum or degree (*SL*, 182–186; 21:208–213): "Intensive magnitude is at first a simple *one of many* '*more or less*' ... Just as twenty contains as extensive magnitude twenty ones as discrete, the specific degree contains them as continuity, a continuity which simply is this determinate plurality; it is *the twentieth* degree" (*SL*, 185; 21:212).

Considerations like these concerning the dependence of arithmetic on a feature predominantly found in geometry—that of order—would lead Hegel to treat the problem of the relation between discrete and continuous magnitudes in mathematics in a way that differed from Descartes's analytic resolution—the Cartesian "arithmetization of geometry" in which continuous magnitudes were understood as resolved into discrete ones, enabled by an expansion of the concept of number to include rational and irrational numbers as subsets of the more inclusive set of "real numbers" (Gouvêa 2008, §§5–7).[18] From Hegel's point of view, it would seem that the very idea of conceiving numbers as points on a number line stretching to infinity in both positive and negative directions already presupposed as a "guiding thread" the fundamentally geometric idea of a line as a continuous magnitude. Hegel thus posed an alternative to the opposing attitudes of either an unbridgeable opposition of continuous and discrete magnitudes or a reduction of one to the other: "What is overlooked in the ordinary representations of continuous and discrete magnitude is that *each* of these magnitudes has both moments in it, continuity as well as discreteness, and that the distinction between them depends solely on which of the two is the *posited* determinateness and which is only implicit. Space, time, matter, and so on, are continuous magnitudes ... [but] possess the absolute possibility that the one may be posited in them anywhere.... They contain in themselves, rather, the principle of the one; it is one of the determinations constituting them" (*SL*, 166–167; 21:190). Hegel's attitude gives expression to the "Philolaic" principles of the monad and the indeterminate dyad, the dual principles that, according to the unwritten-doctrines interpretation, Plato had adopted in his late dialogues, resolving the distinction in a way that nevertheless preserves both elements as somehow superseded (*aufgehoben*). We will see this solution being made more explicit as Hegel works through further determinations of the concept of magnitude.

3.2 Hegel's Mediated Mathematical Dualities: From Direct Ratio to Inverse Ratio

This developmentally holistic tendency in which "modes of connection" among determinate numbers are established via "species of calculation" (*SL*, 171; 21:197) continues through Hegel's treatment of the category "ratio" (*SL*, 271–281; 21:310–322). Without the provision of any historical context, Hegel's presentation is far from clear, but an initial contextualization within the treatment of ratio in Euclid's *Elements* books 5 and 7 will aid us. In book 7, Euclid treats ratios in a primarily arithmetical context, as they had been first treated by the arithmetically oriented Pythagorean mathematicians. Book 5, however, standardly attributed to Eudoxus of Cnidus, transfers the idea of ratio from discrete to continuous magnitudes, and the extension of the notion of "ratio" will become increasingly apparent as Hegel works through three different conceptualizations of ratio: direct ratio; inverse or indirect ratio; and the ratio of powers. The overall direction of the presentation will be to show that these arithmetic and geometric determinations of the notion of "ratio" are not independent of each other but are mutually determining within an overall system that unifies the divided notion of magnitude while preserving the incommensurability between the dual forms found within it.

The simplest form of ratio, direct ratio, in fact exemplifies the Euclidean geometric conception of ratio, and so its conventional modern conception, in which the "exponent" is the stable number of times that one quantity divides the other, as when both 1:2 and 2:4 share the exponent 2.[19] This will be a conception of ratio that is congruent with the idea of proportion (the Greek *analogia*) being understood as the equivalence of two ratios.

As we have seen, early Pythagoreans had assumed that the terms of all such ratios could be measured by the *monas*, the measuring "unit," such that the two terms can be considered as related as "unit and amount":[20] "One side was the unit, and this was to be taken as a numerical one with respect to which the other side would be a fixed amount and at the same time the exponent" (*SL*, 274; 21:314). Once the concept of number had been elaborated beyond the simple counting numbers, and certainly once the idea of incommensurable magnitudes was in play, it might be asked what difference with respect to the ratio 2:3 would it make to think of 2 as measuring 3 with an exponent of $1\frac{1}{2}$ or 3 measuring 2 with an exponent of $\frac{2}{3}$. But this disrupts the assumed asymmetry of unit to amount:[21] "Unit and amount were at first the moments of quantum; now, in the ratio, in quantum as realized so far, each of its moments appears as a quantum *on its own*" (*SL*, 272; 21:312). This starts the process within which the Pythagorean grounding of number in the unit or *monas*, which, as the basis of all number, cannot itself be a number, is gradually undermined to be replaced by a more systematic and holistic mode of determination. But it also disrupts the assumed asymmetry of a continuous series of ratios, introducing the idea of a series of numbers such as the natural numbers being read in the reverse direction. This will be made explicit in the transition from the direct to the "indirect" or "inverse" ratio.

We must keep in mind that the goal is to find a conception of ratio that resolves the oppositions between qualitative and quantitative determinations of magnitude encountered so far, and various problems can be seen to affect direct ratio from this point of view. For example, the continuing geometric series 1, 2, 4, 8 . . . can be continued indefinitely, denying it a proper limit, and so denying it ultimate determinacy. As we have seen, such a geometric series considered alone results in the problem of the cosmic "out of tuneness" identified by Plato as needing correction (see chapter 2.2). The problems facing direct ratio then lead to the postulation of the "inverse ratio," understood as the "*sublated* direct ratio" (*SL*, 274; 21:314), and which capitalizes on the possibility of reading any ratio in the inverse direction. This idea of an inverse ratio is to be found in Euclid, who defines it as one that "taking the consequent as antecedent in relation to the antecedent as consequent" (Euclid 1956, book 5, def. 13). Thus, if $a : b = c : d$, then $b : a = d : c$ (for example, if 2:4 = 8:16, then 4:2 = 16:8).

We clearly see in play here the geometrical equivalent of positive and negative numbers noted by Kant (Kant 1992a)—namely, the reversal of direction of a continuous magnitude. Read as a magnitude extending to the right, the ratio 2:4 has the exponent of 2; read as extending from right to left, it has the exponent of $\frac{1}{2}$. Hegel describes the "moments" of this exponent, 2 and $\frac{1}{2}$, as each being "the negative of the other," but "negation" here clearly has the sense of inversion. These moments are reciprocally determining inasmuch as their product is a constant (1). If we think of the invertible ratio in relation to a continuing geometric ratio it is clear that "the one moment [of the exponent] becomes as many times smaller as the other becomes greater" (*SL*, 275; 21:315).

The broader significance of the invertibility of the ratio is to be found, I suggest, in a book from Hegel's library (Mense 1993, 673), a volume edited by the classicist Friedrich Ast,[22] containing the "arithmological" works *The Theology of Arithmetic*, attributed to Iamblichus of Chalcis (Iamblichus 1988), a fourth-century CE neo-Pythagorean, and the two surviving books of *Introduction to Arithmetic* by Nicomachus of Gerasa from about a century before (Nicomachus of Gerasa 1926).[23] In this work Nicomachus addresses the three musical means in a way that continues Plato's earlier generalization of the significance of the numerical ratios involved, away from their application to harmonic and even cosmological theories.[24] Starting from the numerical distinction between odd and even natural numbers, Nicomachus builds a series of finer distinctions such as "even-times even" from "even-times odd" numbers that are opposed. Even-times even numbers are the numbers that are produced in a limited geometric series consisting of an even number of terms, as in the series 1, 2, 4, 8, 16, 32, 64, 128. Because such a series contains an even number of members, it will not contain a single middle term, but, rather, two (here, 8 and 16). In contrast, an odd-times even series thus provides a middle point from which the series can be seen as extending equally on either side and hence in "inverse" directions. An invertible series extending in either direction from a middle term seems to promise to unify its extreme terms by the fact that each of these terms limits the other by the requirement that their product is the middle term. The problem here according to Hegel, however, is that despite this mutual limitation the series can still be expanded into a "bad," that is, indefinite, infinite series (*SL*, 276; 21:316). For example, one could continue expanding the series above with terms that become, on one side, increasingly small, and on the other, increasingly large.

Recently, Luigi Borzacchini has pointed to the significance of a certain figurative *lamboid* number discussed by Iamblichus with this inverse feature—"a lambda with 1 as root and two infinite branches, the left one given by the sequence of the integer numbers, the right one given by the corresponding unitary fractions.... The two branches are in a radical opposition, and there is evidence that even their respective numerical bases were different: 10 for the integers, 12 for the parts" (Borzacchini 2007, 290–291).[25] The two branches are radically opposed in the sense that while the infinite growth of the left-hand series can be best understood as an accumulation of discrete magnitudes according to the function of multiplication, the growth of the right-hand series is to be understood as resulting from an infinite number of divisions of a presupposed finite continuous magnitude.[26] For Borzacchini this inverse series typifies the gulf separating the Greek recognition of the opposition between discrete and continuous magnitudes from the way the distinction is resolved with the modern idea of the real numbers (Borzacchini 2007, 291). For Hegel, the invertible ratio, while expanding the types of relation that can hold among numbers (adding division to multiplication, and, by implication, subtraction to addition), still cannot provide the idea of a self-contained quantum it initially promised to be. But addition and multiplication and their inverses do not exhaust the determinacies of number: exponentiation and its inverses, the taking of roots and logarithms remain. There is a link, however, between the invertible ratio and powers, inasmuch as the product of the two moments of the invertible ratio is a constant. For any three successive elements of a continuous geometric series, c, d, e, it is clear that the product of the extreme terms is equal to the square of the middle term, giving a determinate role to "powers" within the series. The focus can now shift to such "powers" or, perhaps, more strictly "potencies" (*Potenzenverhältnis*).

3.3 From Inverse Ratio to Ratio of Powers

The German *Potenz* contains the sense of both the exponential "power" to which a number is raised and the ability or potency of something, its *Macht* or *Mächtigkeit*. In fact, the two notions were similarly linked in the Greek of Plato's time, in that the word *dynamis*, used for "power," "might," "strength," or "capacity" (Liddell and Scott 1882), had the literal meaning "square," which was the geometric equivalent of the idea of a number raised to the second power (Szabó 1978, ch. 1.2).[27] The German *Potenz*, seemingly derived from the word *possest*, coined by the Renaissance Neoplatonist Nicholas of Cusa for the idea of a self-actualizing possibility, had been central to the language of Baader and Schelling, but the link to mathematics had been particularly stressed by the physician and Fichte-influenced nature philosopher, Adolf Karl August Eschenmayer. For Eschenmayer (Eschenmayer 2020), the dynamic and exponential connotations of *Potenzen* allowed the idea of natural forces that came in opposing pairs of plus and minus to be understood as expressions of an underlying unifying substance, as proposed by Baader in his *pythagoräische Quadrat* (Förster 2012, 241).[28] In an exchange with Schelling, Eschenmayer had criticized Schelling's treatment of these issues for errors due to his "complete misunderstanding of mathematics" (Eschenmayer 2020, 29). Hegel will be similarly critical of Schelling's mathematics (see below, chapter 4.1), but his way of interpreting the relevance of *Potenzenverhältnissen* will be mathematically more plausible than anything found in either Schelling or Eschenmayer.

Hegel wants to draw a major conclusion about the nature of quantum from the ratio of potencies. Not surprisingly, this final ratio will be shown to be a mathematical object at the heart of the crisis facing Pythagorean number theory—the crisis given expression as much by the incommensurability of the three means as by Pythagoras's theorem. Understanding the ratio of powers in the way discussed by Nicomachus allows us to make sense of the lesson that Hegel derives from it: it is a quantum that "is self-identical in its otherness"—that is, its otherness qua the type of number that it is. In the inverse ratio, an exponent was seen to be quantitatively similar but qualitatively different from its inverse. In the ratio of powers, a ratio between discrete magnitudes will be recognized as the same as that expressed between continuous magnitudes. Thus, here, quantum, positing itself "as self-identical in its otherness and in determining its own movement of self-surpassing, has come to be a being-for-itself." It is "posited in the potency of having returned into itself; it is immediately itself and also its otherness" (*SL*, 278; 21:318). Again, we return to the issue of the complete determination of magnitude, the three linked functions of addition, multiplication and exponentiation and their inverses. And, what's more, we will be taken back to Plato's syllogism from the *Timaeus*. But what is this peculiar ratio of ratios?

To answer this question, we need to find a form of double ratio that instantiates, as it were, the very concept of what it is to be a ratio. It is as if one is searching for a Platonic prototype—a particular meadow that is not only a meadow but also an exemplary individual instantiation of "meadowness."[29] While Hegel's presentation here is, once more, difficult to follow, illumination is again provided by what we know of what was happening to the Pythagorean theory of proportions during the first years of the Academy, courtesy of such later retrospective accounts like those of Nicomachus and Proclus to be found on Hegel's bookshelf.

In his summary account of the development of Greek geometry, Proclus would claim that to the "three proportionals already known," that is, the geometric, arithmetic, and harmonic means, Eudoxus of Cnidus, the originator of the theory of ratio and proportion for continuous magnitudes in *Elements* book 5, had "added three more and multiplied the number of propositions concerning the 'section' which had their origin in Plato" (Proclus 1970, 55).[30] However, these "three more" surely cannot be understood as the inverses of the arithmetical functions of addition, multiplication, and exponentiation; the "algebra" of this period was typically "geometric," and the "inverses" to which Eudoxus could have appealed must have been given a geometric meaning as concerning the opposed directions of continuous magnitudes.

The "section" referred to here is standardly understood as referring to the Golden Ratio that various interpreters have seen as at the heart of Timaeus's "best" or "most beautiful" bond as well as Socrates's Divided Line. As we have seen, the Golden Ratio is a ratio that is defined in terms of both geometric and arithmetic means that, as has been suggested, Hegel identifies as structuring the *gedoppelt Mitte* of the most beautiful bond. However, Hegel's analysis, I suggest, is more general than the accounts of those who are simply fascinated by the odd properties of the Golden Ratio. That ratio has an actual (albeit approximate, because of the irrationality involved) numerical value (1.61803399 . . .). Hegel is aiming at a mathematical object that is internally self-determining, and so free from being externally fixed as a number.

In direct ratio (which can be understood as a "ratio" in the conventional "geometrical" sense) Hegel had described the exponent of the ratio as an "immediate quantum," a certain amount of the unit monad—simply some number. The inverse relation had promised some more coherent conception of the unity within diversity, and, being able to be read in either direction, its exponent had two opposing aspects, but it too suffered from indefiniteness. However, Hegel says that in the case of the ratio of potencies "the unit," that is, that which had been the measure of the amount, "is at the same time the amount as against itself as unit" (*SL*, 278; 21:318). "If we compare the progressive realization of quantum in the preceding ratios, we find that quantum's quality of being the difference of itself from itself is simply this: that it is a ratio" (*SL*, 278–279; 21:319). Rather than determined in some external way so as to be fixed as an independent number, the exponent in the ratio of potencies is not a simple quantity but itself a ratio ("it is a ratio") that both is (because it is equal to it) and is not (because it is not the simple duplication of) the ratio being determined.

We might now recognize in the double ratio structure that Hegel is pursuing something similar to that found in Aristotle's use of a ratio of ratios in his treatment of justice in *Nicomachean Ethics* book 3. There, Aristotle's higher-level ratio had seemed to be one of the two ratios being compared: it seemed to have been the geometric ratio that, at the lower level, stood opposed to the arithmetic ratio. In contrast, Hegel seems to be searching for a higher-level ratio that both is and is not each of the lower-level ones. This is how Nicomachus seems to set out the achievements of Pythagorean ratio theory when incorporating the doctrines of Eudoxus that go well beyond his contributions to book 5 of Euclid's *Elements*.

In the discussion of the triad in *The Theology of Arithmetic*, Iamblichus sketches Nicomachus's doctrines in which the triad is said to have been called "mean and proportion" because of the "symmetrical" nature of the relation between the three terms, with the mean "midway between more and less" (Iamblichus 1988, 49). The two moments of the exponent of the inverse ratio, as we have seen, are unified in the sense that their product is the unit, 1. The extremes, however, were elements of an indefinite series extending in the opposed directions of greater and lesser. Some way is needed to prevent that indefinitely continuing series: the extremes must be tied back into the triad formed with the middle term. Effectively, it must be some internal configuration among the magnitudes themselves that ties them together. This is described as achieved by Eudoxus's extension of the three Archytan means by adding their three "subcontraries." The text then continues with reference to "three terms in the case of each mean, and three intervals (that is, in the case of each term, the differences between the small term and the mean, the mean and the large term, and the small and the large terms); and an equal number of ratios" (Iamblichus 1988, 50).

In *Introduction to Arithmetic* book 2, Nicomachus discusses this topic in much greater detail. Starting with a discussion of the properties of an arithmetical series of terms, he moves through the geometric and harmonic series and then the three new means introduced by Eudoxus. In the context of each discussion he is focused on finding some series of natural numbers that instantiate the mean in question, and then showing how proportions holding among the continuous "intervals" between the numbers can be reduced to ratios among the discrete numbers themselves. Thankfully, the translator (Nicomachus of Gerasa 1926, 281n3) provides a summary in a footnote.[31] Using a modern algebraic interpretation, the pieces start to fall into place.

We must focus upon the fact that the ratios to be established are, for the Greeks, primarily understood as holding between intervals on a continuous line—that is, between the extremes of a line segment. But to capture the role played by arithmetic we must understand the points and line itself as able to be situated within some type of coordinate system such as the later Cartesian coordinates that will be assumed here.[32] We can now consider an interval AB on the x axis stretching between two points with values a and b, respectively. This interval is divided by a varying point P whose value, x, is to be determined. Point P can thus be considered to divide the interval AB in the ratio $x - a : b - x$. We might call this the dividing ratio (fig. 3.1).[33]

From a Platonic perspective, the problem being addressed is that of finding some "rational," that is, mathematical, way of dividing the segment AB that is not simply dictated by some empirically given results, such as that of the divisions producing musical concords. A total of six dividing ratios need fixing, the three Archytan means and the added three Eudoxean "subcontraries."

We might call the six different ratios to be determined the "target" ratios and the ratios among the values, a, x, and b, of the individual points themselves the "determining ratios." The solution involves a simple type of algebra. Assuming that any term can be put into a ratio with itself, this means that there will be 9 (3 × 3) ways of determining the value of the target ratio, $x - a : b - x$, as below (fig. 3.2).

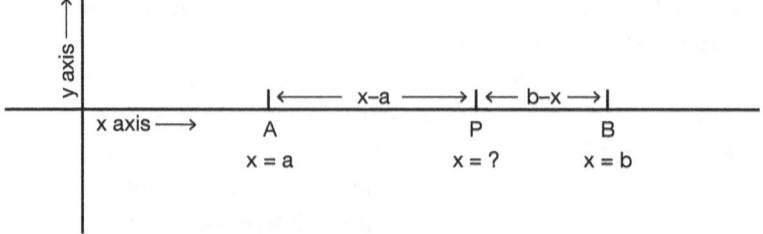

FIGURE 3.1 The dividing ratio, $x - a : b - x$.

1. $a : a,$
2. $x : x,$
3. $b : b,$
4. $a : x,$
5. $a : b,$
6. $x : a,$
7. $x : b,$
8. $b : a,$
9. $b : x.$

FIGURE 3.2 The nine determining ratios.

It is important to remember that pairing a target ratio with a determining ratio, as in the "equation" $x - a : b - x :: a : a$, for example, involves equating a ratio between originally continuous magnitudes with one between discrete magnitudes.[34] Algebraically, it now becomes simple to show that, when equated with the ratio $a : a$, $x : x$, or $b : b$, the difference ratio $x - a : b - x$ is determined such that x is the arithmetic mean of a and b. This is simply because the ratio between any term and itself has the value of 1, and is just to say that the "distance" from a to x is the same as that from x to b, which is the definition of the arithmetic mean. This now leaves only six further ways of determining the target ratio.

Today we find values for these doubled ratios by treating them as simple equations between fractions, and it can be easily shown that determining the value $x - a : b - x$ by either ratio $a : x$ or ratio $x : b$ determines p as the geometric mean of a and b.[35] Similarly, fixing the target ratio by the determining ratio $a : b$ produces the harmonic mean.[36] We have therefore now accounted for the three means of Archytas, leaving Eudoxus's three further "subcontrary" means to be determined by the remaining sixth, eighth, and ninth determining ratios, $x : a$, $b : a$, and $b : x$. Algebraically, these can be seen to be the inversions of the fourth $(a : x)$, fifth $(a : b)$, and seventh $(x : b)$, leading them to be called "subcontraries" to these corresponding ratios. Thus $b : a$ is described as the "subcontrary to the harmonic" (that is, to $a : b$) and $x : a$ and $b : x$

GENERAL SIGNIFICANCE OF NEOPLATONIC HARMONIC THEORY 75

are described as the first and second "subcontraries to the geometric" ($a : x$ and $x : b$).[37]

This terminology is significant. In Greek geometry, a "subcontrary" section of a triangle ABC produces a smaller triangle ADE within the first that is similar to it with $\angle ABC = \angle ADE$ and $\angle ACB = \angle AED$ (fig. 3.3). But the new triangle is a reflected version of the first, as if rotated on an axis through A. The subcontrary of a geometric figure is simply the inverse relation we have seen in the case of the inverse ratio, but applied to a planar figure. Inversion in this sense is thus the geometric version of the "negation" relation seen in arithmetic as holding between a number and its negation, n and $-n$.

In fact, the harmonic mean had initially been called the "subcontrary" mean, presumably because a subcontrary section of a triangle had been involved in the geometric representation of the harmonic mean.[38] Archytas is alleged to have changed the name to the harmonic mean. It would seem then that some type of reversal of order is responsible for the expansion of the three musical means to six in Eudoxus's 3 × 2 structure that corresponds to Hegel's "complete determination" of the concept of number.

With Eudoxus's 3 × 2 structure given to the Pythagorean musical means we start to get a sense of how the idea of reversible orders will be significant for the type of projective geometry that will grow out of these issues in early Greek geometry. Already we have caught a glimpse of this in relation to the significance of the reversal of direction in movements in space introduced by Kant in the context of his consideration of the meaning of "negative numbers" (see the introduction). We will see a further expression of this phenomenon that will affect what has been discussed above in relation to the

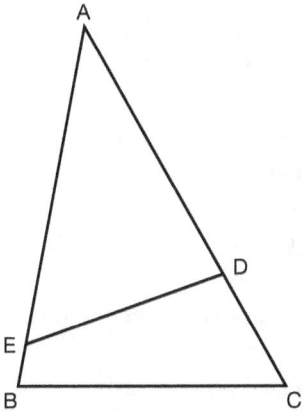

FIGURE 3.3 The "subcontrary" section of a triangle. Triangle ABC is sectioned by ED in such a way that ADE is an inversion of ABC ($\angle ABC = \angle ADE$ and $\angle ACB = \angle AED$).

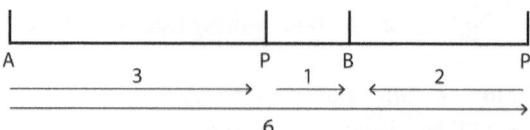

FIGURE 3.4 Internal and external divisions of an interval. Here, while the point P divides the directed interval $\overrightarrow{AB}$ "internally," the point P′ is said to divide it "externally." Because the direction of the $\overrightarrow{P'B}$ is opposite to that of $\overrightarrow{AP}$, it will be understood as having a negative value.

determination of "dividing ratios" created within a line segment by a movable dividing point. Once the idea of a segment being divided into parts that stand in a specifiable ratio, the consideration of the directionality of those parts introduces a new possibility—that of internal and external divisions of a line segment that stand in the same ratio.[39]

Consider a line segment AB that is divided at some point P such that the two new segments stand in a particular ratio, let's say 3:1 (fig. 3.4). There will now be some point beyond the original segment, P′, such that the ratio of the lengths of AP′ and P′B stand in the *same* ratio as AP stands to PB. For example, in the diagram below, where AP : PB is equal to 3:1, AP′ will have to be three times the length of P′B—here, 6:2. In such a case, P′ is said to externally divide the segment AB in the same ratio as P divides it internally. Expressed as a ratio of directed segments rather than simple lengths, however, the ratio resulting from external division will be understood as having a negative value in contrast to that resulting from the internal division. That is, $\overrightarrow{AP}/\overrightarrow{PB} = -\overrightarrow{AP'}/\overrightarrow{P'B}$ because the direction of $\overrightarrow{P'B}$ is opposite to that of the other segments, and so having a negative value in contrast to the other positives.[40]

What we have seen happening in this algebraic determination of these ratios is really a generalization of a fact noted earlier that each of the three Archytean means are able to be defined in terms of the other two. For any two extreme numbers, *a* and *b*, arithmetic and harmonic means can be calculated by the equations alluded to above. However, when *a* and *b* are members of a geometric series, such as the extremes of the musical *tetraktys*, 6 and 12, the harmonic and arithmetic means become unified with the extremes in a striking way, such that the product of the two means (8 × 9 = 72) equals the product of the extremes (6 × 12 = 72)—a result that only happens when the extremes stand in the geometric ratio. That is, a type of unity has been reestablished among the three means despite the internal "incommensurability" holding among them.

It was this entirely internal systematic or structural determination of these abstract mathematical objects in terms of their constitutive relations that underlies a point upon which Plato had insisted in contrast to even Archytas:

it was the relations among the magnitudes themselves that he thought fundamental and of significance beyond that which was found among empirical phenomena such as string-lengths involved in the production of concordant and discordant sounds. From this perspective, were it to turn out to be the case that there were no empirical harmonies involved, there would still be ideal "harmonies" existing among these Platonic objects. Plato was not speculating about the music of planetary motion but rather the type of logic ("philosophers' arithmetic") manifest in phenomena as widely divergent as music and cosmology.

This internal, purely mathematical determination of the now-expanded set of Pythagorean ratios provides an insight into just how complicated the crisis concerning incommensurability had been during the early years of Plato's Academy, with the consequences of Eudoxus's discoveries being worked out by mathematicians over the subsequent centuries. The phenomenon of incommensurability had at first undermined the Pythagorean dogma that all quantities were to be grounded in the *monas* as initially understood. This had led to a crisis for the geometric dimensions of Pythagorean thought, but Eudoxus had found a way to give the more or less—the continua of geometry—its own non-numerical form of determination. This was then linked to a reconceptualized Pythagorean doctrine of ratios by providing a type of internal algebraic redetermination of the three means. The historian of mathematics, François Lasserre, has described Eudoxus's breakthrough: "Instead of concentrating his attention, as Archytas, Plato and the philosophers of the Academy had done, on the presence of these means in Nature, for example in the field of harmony, Eudoxus concerns himself with mathematical properties of this concept of means, and soon discovers three new series possessing analogous properties" (Lasserre 1964, 59).[41] Such a process of generalization and axiomatization is usually thought typical of the progress of algebraic thought, and, as we have noted, was a fundamental feature of the "new" geometry of the nineteenth century (Nagel 1939). Here we can appreciate it as happening within the overall framework of Greek geometry.

Hegel could grasp that the lessons that Nicomachus and Iamblichus had drawn from these transformations were not the abandonment of the Pythagorean *monas* as much as its explicit reconceptualization. Now the *monas* could be understood as configured by this unified triad of triads, and so as internally articulated, somewhat along the lines that he had tried to express in his "triangle of triangles." As Iamblichus had put it, "The monad is even and odd and even-odd; linear and plane and solid" (Iamblichus 1988, 35). The monad's being even and odd testified to the fact that the seemingly incommensurable measures of odd and even or discrete and continuous had to be understood as internal to this fundamental measure. Iamblichus had driven home the point with continuing the series of the monad's being "perfect and over-perfect and defective; proportionate and harmonic; prime and incomposite, and secondary; diagonal and side; and it is the source of every relation, whether one of equality or inequality, as has been proved in the [that is, Nicomachus's] *Introduction*" (35). The indeterminacy of the "more or less" has now been explicitly worked *into* the very conception of the monad that had originally been conceived as antithetical to the more or less. In this way, the neo-Pythagoreans had drawn the consequences of the twist that, according to the "unwritten-doctrine" interpretation, Plato had given to the realm of ideas and, in particular, to the idea of "the Good" in his late works, moving away from the traditionally conceived "Platonistic" transcendent realm of middle-period works such as the *Republic*.

There is still, I suggest, another feature of Hegel's reception of this material that puts him on the side of the later Plato and his neo-Pythagorean followers and that contrasts with the attitudes of Schelling and the other *Naturphilosophen*. They had all drawn upon this tradition in their conceiving of those opposing forces in nature, *Potenzen* that divide into opposing positive and negative forces to be found in the various hierarchically arranged domains of the world. They, I suggest, were closer to the early Pythagoreans, such as Archytas, who had linked these mathematical structures directly to the empirical world and to be found in observations of harmonic relations among sounds and the movements of the planets. Plato had been critical of this and had conceived of these structures as somehow meaningful in their own right. Similarly, I suggest, Hegel took these structures more to manifest the movements of self-redetermining thought rather than thought that immediately mirrored the nature of the world itself. While the world could be considered as externalized thought, in the sense that its logic was a logic of the world itself, this process could not be conceived in the quasi-Spinozistic mode of Schelling as two identical but opposed manifestations of the same underlying absolute.

Without this Pythagorean-Platonic background, Hegel's discussion of the "ratio of potencies" as a quantum that has "returned into itself" and is "self-identical in its otherness" (*SL*, 278; 21:318) remains entirely obscure. The ratio of powers is a ratio that explicitly represents itself *as* a ratio, just as a ratio of intervals is represented by a ratio of numbers used in describing the intervals. As a prototypical ratio—we might call it Hegel's *Urverhältnis*—it gives expression not only to the "genus" or "concept" ratio; it gives expression to what it is to be a concept as such, because for Hegel a concept is something that instantiates itself in something other than itself. "By being thus *posited* as

GENERAL SIGNIFICANCE OF NEOPLATONIC HARMONIC THEORY   79

it is in conformity to its concept, quantum has passed over into another determination; or, as we can also say, its *determination* is now also as the *determinateness*, the *in-itself* also as *existence* [*als Dasein ist*]" (SL, 279; 21:320). We might now understand the sense in which mathematics, in Brady Bowman's phrase, represents for Hegel the "highest form of finite theoretical cognition," showing an "inner identity" with the method of philosophy itself (Bowman 2013, 170).

The presence in Hegel's library of those extant fragments of the writings of Nicomachus and Iamblichus, together with his familiarity with Pythagorean and neo-Pythagorean harmony theory and its relevance for Kepler's cosmological explanations, I contend, gives us the interpretative license to treat his "ratio of potencies" in this way. But there is another line of evidence to be found in Hegel's library that points in this direction as well—this time in the volumes by the contemporary French mathematician Lazare Carnot. On the basis of his understanding of the history of Greek geometry, transmitted through late neo-Pythagorean accounts that are still broadly accepted as accurate today, Hegel seems to have been well attuned to the possibilities contained within Carnot's new geometry that was, really, a revival of a very old geometry.

3.4 The "Ratio of Powers": From the Ancient Harmonia to the Modern Harmonic Cross-Ratio

I have suggested that a constellation of factors, including the presence of a translation of Carnot's *De la corrélation des figures de géométrie* in Hegel's library, signals a motive for thinking of Hegel's interest in ancient Pythagoreanism as quite different from the mystically inclined "nature-philosophical" interest of Schelling and Baader. As further evidence for this let us consider the particular "even-times even" sequence of four numbers that Nicomachus turns to in *Introduction to Arithmetic* after the deduction of the six means, a sequence he describes as containing "the most perfect proportion, that which is three-dimensional and embraces them all." This clearly is the structure that Hegel refers to as Plato's "most beautiful bond." It alone, Nicomachus notes, "would properly and truly be called harmony rather than the others, since it is not a plane, nor bound together by one mean term, but with two, so as thus to be extended in three dimensions" (Nicomachus of Gerasa 1926, 284–285).

It is not difficult to show that the number sequence given by Nicomachus to instantiate this "most perfect proportion"—the sequence 6, 8, 9, 12 referred to in Plato's *Epinomis* (991b)[42]—is an instance of the more generally expressed doubled proportion that would be reintroduced by Carnot in *De la corrélation* and subsequent works, and that would become a central feature of the projective geometry that developed during the nineteenth century. The name later given to this particular ratio of ratios, echoing *harmonia*, another name given to the musical *tetraktys*, would be the "harmonic cross-ratio," and it would be shown to be a particular instance of a cross-ratio or double ratio (in German, *Doppelverhältnis* [Struik 1953, 9]), which had important properties known in antiquity to Pappus and possibly also to Euclid (Coolidge 1934, 218). This cross-ratio between a pair of dividing ratios is discussed above, and takes the general form $AX : XB$, in which a variable point X is able to divide the interval between A and B both internally and externally in an equivalent but "inverted" way.[43] The two mean terms between the extremes are their harmonic and arithmetic means, and the extremes themselves stand in the ratio of the geometric mean. We have observed something like this structure in Aristotle's account of the ratio of ratios structuring the logic of justice, but this new double ratio avoids the suggestion of a structure reducible to one mean, the geometric. In the cross-ratio all the means are given equal weight.

In *De la corrélation*, Carnot does not place any great emphasis on the significance of the harmonic cross-ratio, although he does so more in its successor publication, *Géométrie de position* of 1803. In *De la corrélation*, published in 1801, it is generated via a figure called the "complete quadrilateral," the context in which the harmonic cross-ratio was found originally in the works of Apollonius of Perga, which had been revived by Girard Desargues in the seventeenth century. Much of the development of projective geometry in the nineteenth century would postdate Hegel, and it is not clear the degree to which Hegel, not being a mathematician, would have been in a position to anticipate the significance that would come to be assumed by the cross-ratio in mathematics later in the century. It is, of course, much easier to see such connections from this side of the history of the full realization of projective geometry—connections that might have been grasped only in the fuzziest outline at the time.[44] Nevertheless, we do know of Hegel's attraction to Plato's "syllogism" with its duplicated middle terms required by the tridimensionality of the body of the cosmic animal, his deep interest in Greek as well as contemporary geometry, his possession of and familiarity with Nicomachus's *Principles of Arithmetic*, and, of course, his deep commitment to the cosmology of Kepler.[45] But Hegel's appreciation of the possibility of this doubled ratio might also have been enabled by an innovation in the diagrammatic representation of magnitudes introduced by Kant in the 1860s—the innovation of assigning to line segments a direction, so as to allow them to be understood as "pointing" specifically in one direction as opposed to the other, and thereby representing magnitudes as qualitatively either positive or negative in a way that nevertheless presupposed an underlying absolute quantitative magnitude. This aspect of Kant's work would also influence Baader, Schelling, and other *Naturphilosophen*.

This idea had been introduced by Kant in an essay from his transitional period in the 1760s, "Attempt to Introduce the Concept of Negative Magnitudes into Philosophy" (Kant 1992a), the importance of which for Hegel has been stressed by Michael Wolff (Wolff 1999). There, Kant had employed the idea of directed line segments, later to be called "vectors" (Friedman 2013, ch. 5), in an attempt to explain the ontology of negative numbers. In the course of a sea voyage countervailing winds may cause a ship to travel in a distance away from its destination, leading the captain to record the ship's progress in its log in negative numbers, but of course the actual miles traveled—the actual quantities—are the same regardless of direction. When this idea reappeared in the new approaches to geometry found in both Carnot and Grassmann, the "absolute" value of a vector would be differentiated from its signed magnitude reflecting its direction. In fact, Carnot's turn to projective geometry around 1800 had taken place in a context in which the philosophical problem of negative magnitudes was being widely discussed (Martinez 2006, 25 and 46), and it is possible that his work was influenced by Kant's essay just as Hermann Grassmann's seems to have been (Petsche 2009, 222).

In relation to Hegel, a further factor accounting for the influence of Kant's essays on space in the 1760s is the appearance of a version of this idea of directed magnitudes in Nicomachus's *Introduction to Arithmetic* where Nicomachus emphasizes that for each of the three dimensions of space there exist two directions: "By these [three dimensions of space: breadth, depth, and length] are defined the six directions which are said to exist in connection with every body and by which motions in space are distinguished, forward, backward, up, down, right and left; for of necessity two directions opposite to each other follow upon each dimension, up and down upon one, forward and backward upon the second, and right and left upon the third" (Nicomachus of Gerasa 1926, 238).[46] This very point had been made by Kant in another essay from the 1760s linked to "Negative Magnitudes," the 1768 essay, "Concerning the Ultimate Ground of the Differentiation of Directions in Space" (Kant 1992b). Like Nicomachus, Kant stresses how the bidirectionality of each of the dimensions of space is centered on the body:

> Because of its three dimensions, physical space can be thought of as having three planes, which all intersect each other at right angles. . . . It is . . . not surprising that the ultimate ground, on the basis of which we form our concept of directions in space, derives from the relation of these intersecting planes to

> our bodies. The plane upon which the length of our body stands vertically is called, with respect to ourselves, horizontal. This horizontal plane gives rise to the difference between the directions [*Gegenden*] which we designate by the terms *above* and *below*. On this plane it is possible for two other planes to stand vertically and also to intersect each other at right angles, so that the length of the human body is thought of as lying along the axis of the intersection. One of these two vertical planes divides the body into two externally similar halves, and furnishes the ground of the difference between the *right* and the *left* side. The other vertical plane, which also stands perpendicularly on the horizontal plane, makes possible the concept of the side *in front* and the side *behind*. (Kant 1992b, 366–367; see also the editor's comments, lxxx–lxxxi)

We will see that this idea, together with the associated phenomenon of the handedness, or chirality, of certain three-dimensional objects discussed in this essay as "incongruent counterparts" would be significant in the development of the new nonmetrical forms of geometry in the nineteenth century.

Both Carnot and Grassmann were perhaps influenced by Kant's proto-vectorial approach to space, but both underlined the continuity of their projects with Leibniz's proposed project of a "situational analysis" (*analysis situs*). Leibniz had suggested this as an alternative to Descartes's analytic geometry, but it had been specifically criticized by Kant in "Differentiation of Directions in Space" (Kant 1992b, 365). We will later explore Leibniz's project and its relation to the failed seventeenth-century attempts to develop projective geometry, but here it is important to emphasize the ways in which Leibniz's *analysis situs* had reestablished a connection to ancient geometric algebra.

In the late 1670s Leibniz had first started to think of an alternative to the analytic geometry of Descartes and Fermat, aiming to introduce a type of algebraic approach to geometry but one that countered the reduction of continuous to discrete magnitudes found in analytic geometry. In a letter to Huygens in 1679 Leibniz speculated on the need for "another analysis which is distinctly geometrical or linear and which will express *situation* [*situs*] directly as algebra expresses *magnitude* directly. And I believe that I have found the way and that we can represent figures and even machines and movements by characters, as algebra expresses numbers or magnitudes" (Leibniz 1989b, 249).

In the analytic geometry of Descartes and Fermat, a geometric figure was able to be reduced to an equation with the help of coordinates that assigned to each point on the figure an ordered pair of numbers. That is, all the relations among continuous magnitudes were ultimately to be reduced to equalities holding between discrete "real" numbers. This was a version of what Hegel described as the atomistic system of "unit and amount" of the early Pythagoreans, but now carried out with the more developed system of real numbers,

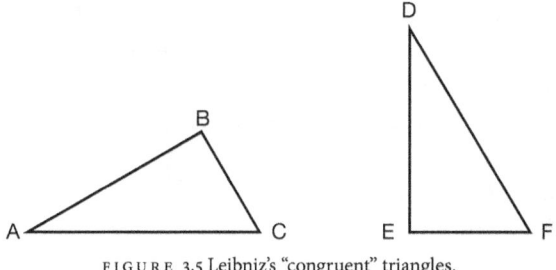

FIGURE 3.5 Leibniz's "congruent" triangles.

purportedly neutralizing the problem of incommensurability. But Leibniz would assert that "instead of using equalities or equations as in algebra, I shall here use relations of congruences, which I shall express with the character of ∝" (251). Leibniz then gives the example of two triangles, ABC and DEF as in figure 3.5, which he claims are congruent because the points on each "can occupy exactly the same place, and that one can be applied or placed on the other without changing anything of the two figures except place. So if one places D upon A, E upon B and F upon C, the two triangles, which are assumed to be equal and similar, obviously coincide" (Leibniz 1989b, 251).

On inspection, however, it is evident that ABC and EDF are what Kant described in "Differentiation of Directions in Space" as incongruent counterparts (*incongruentes Gegenstück*) of which right and left hands provided the prototypical instance: "The reflection of an object in a mirror rests upon exactly the same principles.... The image of a right hand in a mirror is always a left hand" (Kant 1992b, 370). In trying to superimpose a right hand on a left hand, one would have to reflect it through an imaginary fourth dimension. In the case of two-dimensional triangles, however, the required extra dimension is only the third. As we will see (below, chapter 4.3), projective geometry would render this type of reflection intelligible.

Kant's criticism was aimed at the relativistic conception of space presupposed by Leibniz's *analysis situs*, and Kant would carry the same argument forward when transitioning into his later transcendental idealism with its constitutive dichotomy of intuitions and concepts.[47] Thus he would argue that without the distinction between concepts and intuitions and especially the idea of the "pure intuition" of space, Leibniz was unable to account for the difference between incongruent counterparts.[48] Grassmann would similarly consider this to be an inadequacy of Leibniz's *analysis situs* (Grassmann 1995, 320), but he would respond to the inadequacy of Leibniz's account in a way that would effectively undermine Kant's own alternative. However, we have already seen something like Leibniz's (in)congruent triangles in the ancient idea of subcontrary triangles, which had become linked to possible inverse orderings of number sequences in portrayals of the ultimate unity of the three Pythagorean means.

Summing up, the revived form of geometric algebra that would develop in the nineteenth century would reproduce various features that had been implicit in Greek geometry and that had influenced Hegel. Just as Eudoxus had broken with the number-atomism of the early Pythagoreans and had conceived of ratios as holding directly between continuous magnitudes that were not specifiable in terms of numbers, Leibniz would introduce the idea of congruence between figures as fundamental, as opposed to Descartes's reduction of figures to equations that presupposed a system of discrete numbers. Leibniz's characteristic, however, did not accommodate the idea, to be found explicitly in Nicomachus and implicitly in Eudoxus, of the fundamental directedness or orientation of extended magnitudes, an idea that would with Grassmann be generalized to the orientation of two- and three-dimensional objects. Kant had signaled problems with Leibniz's conception of space in this regard, and this would be taken up and extended by Grassmann, but in a quite different way.

Toward the end of the nineteenth century, both Carnot's projective geometry and Grassmann's linear algebra would be developed and linked, absorbing other developments such as William Rowan Hamilton's theory of "quaternions."[49] Important developments would be made by the American mathematician Benjamin Peirce and the English mathematician-philosopher William Kingdon Clifford, the work of both influencing the experiments in logic of Peirce's son, Charles Sanders Peirce. In these developments, the sorts of foci adopted by the Greeks as well as Hegel, concerning the relations between lines, planes, and solids, would come to the fore, now with various "algebraic" ways of "adding" and "multiplying" two-dimensional oriented line segments (vectors) conceived as existing in three-dimensional space.[50]

Hegel's encounter with such directions taken in geometry had, of course, been limited to its very earliest phases. Nevertheless, it does not need stressing how significant the parallels between Nicomachus's summation of the ancient theory of means together with Carnot's rediscovery of it as well as Kant's introduction of the idea of signed geometric magnitudes would have been for Hegel, given the background we have sketched here. In the following chapter we will pursue the question of what Hegel may have recognized in those aspects of Carnot's work that would be later developed by Grassmann. In later chapters we will explore how this would be reflected in his approach to logic and the later logics of Peirce and other algebraists.

MIDDLE

Classical Meets Modern

4

Geometry and Philosophy in Hegel, Schelling, Carnot, and Grassmann

> But now, since the delineation of these [geometric] figures commences from different aspects and principles, and the various figures fall into place of themselves, in the comparison of these figures their *qualitative* unlikeness and *incommensurability* come into view. Geometry is thus driven, beyond the *finitude* within which it advanced step by step orderly and securely, to infinity—to the positing as equal of such as are qualitatively diverse. Here it loses the evidence that it derived from being otherwise based on fixed finitude without having to deal with the concept and the transition to the opposite which is its manifestation.
>
> HEGEL, *The Science of Logic*

In 1801, and so around the time of Hegel's own intense interest in geometry as well as the genesis of Carnot's geometric works, Hegel would give an account of the comparative virtues of the approaches of Fichte and Schelling, entitled *The Difference between Fichte's and Schelling's System of Philosophy*. Here Hegel had attempted to show how Schelling was countering the "formal" and "subjectivist" characteristics of Fichte's version of transcendental idealism with the addition of a more objective dimension. While addressing problems in Kant, Fichte's position was regarded as still hampered by features inherited from Kant's subjectivist approach. Thus, Fichte is described as conceiving of what Hegel terms a "subjective Subject-Object"—an individual subject that, while conceived as necessarily embodied (a "Subject-Object"), is still understood in a way such that its subjectivity necessarily transcends the limits of that embodiment (*Diff*, 81). To this, Schelling had opposed a more naturalistically conceived "objective Subject-Object" (82)—that is, the conception of an organic being located in the world, whose subjectivity is constrained by the given objective conditions of embodiment and location, conditions that extend beyond the limits of the subject's own conceptual grasp. Both forms taken on their own would simply reproduce the problematic dualism, but these opposed subjective and objective Subject-Objects were now to be understood as "united in something higher than the subject" (82). This "higher than the subject" meant for Schelling some type of Spinozistic "absolute," qua "indifferent"—that is, neither subjective nor objective—unification of the two Subject-Objects. Schelling would employ a quasi-geometric diagram to try to give a determinate expression to this view. Revealing differences would emerge between Hegel and Schelling concerning both how to understand this diagram and the relations among arithmetic, geometry, and philosophy more generally.

4.1 Hegel's Early Understanding of Geometry in Relation to Schelling's

In developing his nature philosophy around the turn of the century, and in the context of a dispute with Eschenmayer, who had accused him of misunderstanding the mathematical content of any such philosophy (Eschenmayer 2020, 28–29), Schelling would appeal to the geometric method of Spinoza and employ a quasi-geometric diagram to render his own position explicit. This was his "Constructed Line" (fig. 4.1), as put forward in his 1801 work, *Presentation of My System of Philosophy* (Schelling 2001a, §§46–50),[1] seemingly influenced by a diagram earlier used by Eschenmayer in an attempt to explain the nature of magnetic polarity (Eschenmayer 2020, 92–93; Châtelet 2000, 88–90). Eschenmayer's diagram had been based on the idea of a balance with a fulcrum at its midpoint and seems to have been inspired by the idea of oppositely directed "vectors" as introduced in Kant's 1763 essay.[2]

With his diagram, Schelling had meant to suggest that neither subjectivity (mind) nor objectivity (body) could be posited separately as in dualism—that is, as entities that are somehow understandable in themselves, and so as abstracted from the relation to the other. Rather, they must be presented only as aspects of a single absolute, much as Kant's idea that some actual distance traveled, some "absolute magnitude," underlies both the positive and negative miles logged in relation to reaching one's destination.

In Schelling's account, the single line seems meant to represent the self-identical absolute, A=A, but Spinoza's substance has two seemingly opposed aspects, the aspects of extension and thought, and within substance there are two opposed points of view from which substance itself is grasped as either thought or extension. Thus, the diagram seems meant to be understood in such a way that the application of the signs '+' and '–' to either of the terms, A or B, signals the absolute as grasped from these two opposed perspectives. Combined with this, however, the single line is also to be understood as containing a point, the fulcrum-like "point of indifference," midway between the ideal and real poles and indifferent to both.

The diagram by Eschenmayer upon which Schelling seems to have drawn was considerably more complex. In it, a series of exponentially related numbers extend indefinitely to the left and right of a midpoint marked by an "I" raised to the power of zero, "I^0," and seemingly representing Fichte's absolute

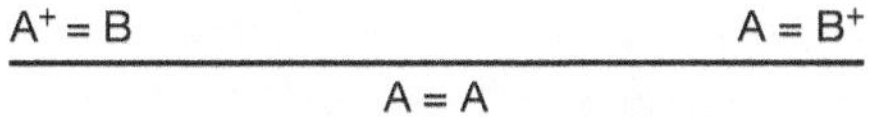

$$\frac{A^+ = B \qquad\qquad A = B^+}{A = A}$$

FIGURE 4.1 Schelling's Constructed Line.

ego (*Ich*). Extending to the left on the side of the finite ego, the terms pass from I^1, I^2, I^3 to an indefinite I^{+n}, and to right on the side of its opposing nonego, as I^{-1}, I^{-2}, I^{-3}, . . . I^{-n}. In this respect, Eschenmayer's diagram resembles the series of inverse ratios that Hegel traces in his discussion of ratio in book 1 of *The Science of Logic*, but while Hegel's inverse series concerns the arithmetic operation of multiplication with its inverse, division, Eschenmayer's works at the level of exponentiation with its inverse (or one of its two inverse operations) the extraction of roots. Eschenmayer's series of powers and roots may suggest Hegel's "ratio of powers," but it cannot be what Hegel has in mind, as it suffers from the indefiniteness afflicting Hegel's series of inverse ratios. In Eschenmayer there seems no equivalent to Plato's most beautiful bond at the heart of Hegel's solution to the problem of indeterminacy.

For Schelling, as for Eschenmayer, the idea is that as one goes in either direction, one moves toward a greater proportion of either mind or matter (ego or nonego) interacting within some worldly situation.[3] Schelling's midpoint or "indifference point" is not the Fichtean absolute ego presupposed by Eschenmayer, however, but a Spinozistic absolute, and the midpoint of indifference appears to represent something like the idea that Baader had expressed in his *pythagoräische Quadrat* a few years earlier, concerning a single unifying force underlying opposed signed forces of attraction and repulsion (Förster 2012, 241). As with Baader (Baader 1798, 15; Leuer 1976, 8), the imagery employed by Eschenmayer and Schelling seems to appeal to the fulcrum of a lever or balance, and there is no sense of a "divided" middle term.[4]

Despite his own presentations being meant to have something of the "axiomatic" form as found in Euclidean geometry and Spinoza's *Ethics*, Schelling's presentations were not particularly lucid or logically compelling, and he had attempted to make this more explicit by drawing on geometry in a follow-up essay, "Further Presentations from the System of Philosophy," published the following year (Schelling 2001b), which commences with a reflection on the relation of the philosopher's to the geometer's method. Schelling's appeal to geometry had clearly been meant to counter Eschenmayer's generally more arithmetic imagery, just as his more geometric divided line was meant as a contrast to Eschenmayer's sequence of numerical "powers."

Schelling's starting point is Kant's pure intuition of space as presupposed by the geometer's postulates:

> A geometer immediately sets about his constructions without any further instruction about pure intuition; even his postulates are not requirements for this intuition (of space) as such, about which it is assumed there can be no doubt or ambiguity, but necessary conditions of determinate intuitions (such as lines and figures).
>
> In the same way, intellectual or rational intuition is something fixed and decided for the philosopher in rigorously scientific construction, something about which no doubt is allowed nor explanation found necessary. It is that which simply and without restriction is presupposed, and can in this respect not even be called the postulate of philosophy. (Schelling 2001b, 376)

Schelling's imagery of the ever-present but opposed aspects of subjectivity and objectivity in cognition thus modified the idealist framework established by Kant and Fichte and was meant to resolve the contradiction with which we all live in our self-conceptions as subjects in the world. From one point of view, we grasp the world and ourselves in it naturalistically, and thus subject to lawlike regularities. This is at the basis of the dogmatic naturalism to which Fichte had fiercely opposed his Kant-derived idealism (Fichte 1994, §§4–5). From Fichte's opposing perspective, however, we consider ourselves as free agents, able to affect the world by exercising our wills. But while this "universal opposition of the ideal and the real, the infinite and the finite" remains a fixed opposition for "every pretended philosophy," "geometry ... and mathematics as a whole are entirely beyond this opposition. Here thought is always adequate to being, concept to object, and vice versa ... In a word, there is no difference here between subjective and objective truth; subjectivity and objectivity are absolutely one, and there is in this science no construction in which they are not one" (Schelling 2001b, 378). Mathematics thus provides a model for genuine as opposed to pretended philosophy, but, within mathematics, "in geometrical construction this coincidence of idea and reality shows up directly, since it is granted to geometry to display the archetypes, as it were, in outer intuition" (382). But while geometry is "subordinated to being," arithmetic is subordinated "to thought" (378)[5]—this asymmetry presumably representing Schelling's counterattack on Eschenmayer.

Differences between Schelling and Hegel would evolve over the next few years, although it is apparent that from this early period Hegel had not shared the conception of the nature of mathematics underpinning Schelling's quasi-Spinozist understanding of the diagram. Schelling's conception of mathematics as a whole is clearly of what is normally discussed as "pure" rather than applied ("there is no difference here between subjective and objective truth; subjectivity and objectivity are absolutely one")—that is, the classically "Platonistic" conception of mathematics. This mathematics, however, is cast in a distinctly geometric guise, Platonic "archetypes" being numberless geometric constructions.

In contrast, in the 1801 *Dissertation*, Hegel holds that "the whole of mathematics must not be regarded as purely ideal or formal, but also as real and physical" (*Misc*, 175). This, in fact, coheres with the more traditional view at that time that geometry was constrained in ways that contrasted it to algebra in that it was considered to be the science of space, and so limited by what could be empirically intuited (Nagel 1979, §§1–2). For example, geometry was assumed to be maximally three-dimensional because actual space as experienced is three-dimensional. Hegel thus represented a more traditional view of geometry than that of Kant, just as Carnot, as we will see, resisted the separation of geometry from the empirical sciences that was coming to be favored by "pure" mathematicians. Moreover, as we have seen neither did Hegel make a rigid distinction between geometry as the science of continuous magnitudes and arithmetic as the science of discrete magnitudes: both sciences, he believed, presupposed the concepts of continuity and discreteness, and this allowed interaction between them: "What is overlooked in the ordinary representations of continuous and discrete magnitude is that *each* of these magnitudes has both moments in it, continuity as well as discreteness, and that the distinction between them depends solely on which of the two is the *posited* determinateness and which is only implicit" (*SL*, 166; 21:190).

Such an outlook concerning the unity of a duality can also be recognized in Hegel's earliest "system fragments" from around this time. Thus, in the document *System der Sittlichkeit* (*System of Ethical Life* [*SEL*]), written in 1802–3, Hegel would employ a broadly similar way of describing the reciprocity between what Kant had distinguished as intuition and concept. While Kant had described judgments as involving the "subsumption" of intuitions by concepts, Hegel would add a necessary alternative form of cognition in which concepts are subsumed *by* intuitions. "Absolute ethical life . . . must be so treated that (a) concept is subsumed under intuition and (b) intuition is subsumed under concept" (*SEL*, 102). As Georg Sans has pointed out, this distinction between the reversed directions of "subsumption" between intuition and concept would evolve into a distinction found in *The Science of Logic* between opposed types of judgments: judgments of inherence and judgments of subsumption (Sans 2004, 94–97), about which we will have more to say in later chapters.[6] Here we might note that Hegel's way of addressing these issues in these years was, despite his use of Schellingian vocabulary, systematically different from Schelling's in a way exemplified by their different attitudes to the relations of geometry to arithmetic. As opposed to Schelling's Spinozist assumptions, as seen in his interpretation of the Constructed Line, Hegel's,

I suggest, can be seen as more Carnotian and, in a sense, Leibnizian, given Carnot's renewal of the project of an *analysis situs*.

For Hegel, as we have seen, both numerical and geometrical objects are defined by their positions within an evolving dynamic structure in which geometry offers ways of reinterpreting algebraic magnitudes, and algebra ways of reinterpreting the nature of geometry's objects. Neither side offers an ultimate means by which to take the measure of the other's claims. Hegel's position was therefore neither that of classical Euclidean geometric algebra nor Descartes's analytic geometry. Rather, the idea of the necessary unity of otherwise different genera of magnitudes, discrete or limited and continuous or unlimited, is more in line with the Philolaic duality principle of the later Plato. Nevertheless, despite the incommensurability involved, geometry would provide representations that, considered in abstraction from any exact arithmetical interpretations, were capable of being applied to the actual world or "executed." A new appropriate form of geometry was becoming available to Hegel in the form of Carnot's projective geometry, but Carnot would appear on Hegel's radar for other reasons as well.

4.2 From Infinitesimals as Ratios to the Ratios of Directed Line Segments

Hegel had been drawn to Carnot's approach to the philosophical problem of the infinitesimal magnitudes appealed to in the calculus of Newton and Leibniz, of which a succinct expression had been provided in 1734 by Bishop Berkeley in his description of infinitesimals as the "ghosts of departed quantities" (Berkeley 1996, 81). Moreover, according to the historian of calculus Carl Boyer, such "general doubt as to the nature of the foundations of the methods of fluxions and the differential calculus" had continued throughout the eighteenth century (Boyer 1959, 224). In his first mention of the dilemma of infinitesimals in *The Science of Logic* Hegel points to the way beyond this problem: "These magnitudes are so determined that they *are in their vanishing*—not *before* this vanishing, for they would then be finite magnitudes; not *after* it, for then they would be nothing" (*SL*, 79; 21:91–92). Later in the text it becomes apparent that he owes this solution to Carnot.

Hegel's interest in this problem is clear. Recently, John Bell has described two French works appearing in the same year, 1797, as "the last efforts of the eighteenth century mathematicians to demystify infinitesimals and banish the persistent doubts concerning the soundness of the calculus" (Bell 2019, 84). These were Joseph-Louis Lagrange's *Théorie des fonctions analytiques* and Lazare Carnot's *Réflexions sur la métaphysique du calcul infinitésimal*. Consistent with Mense's remark concerning the representation of leading contemporary works in mathematics and mechanics in Hegel's library, both these works are found there.[7] In *The Science of Logic*, mostly within three long "remarks" within the chapter "Quantum" concerning "quantitative infinity," Hegel discusses the different approaches of each (*SL*, 217–234; 21:253–273), and what he reports about Carnot's approach is telling.

Hegel summarizes Carnot's approach utilizing the "law of continuity"—a principle that had been introduced by Kepler as the "principle of analogy" in virtue of which "one can pass 'continuously' from any conic of his system into any other conic of that system" (Del Centina 2016, 568).[8] The law of continuity had been taken up by Leibniz and was generally thought to provide the basis of the application of geometry to nature (Bell 2019, 66–71), but it also clearly presages the shift from classical Euclidean geometry with its focus on the properties of individual geometric figures to projective geometry with its focus on correlations among geometric figures (Carnot 1801).[9] Reprising the earlier account of the preservation of the ratio of two magnitudes "*in their vanishing*" (*SL*, 79; 21:91–92), here Hegel describes how "*because of the law of continuity*, the vanishing magnitudes still retain the ratio from which they derive, before they disappear" (*SL*, 218; 21:254). With this, Hegel effectively paraphrases not Carnot himself, but a passage from the introduction by Hauff to his translation of Carnot's *Réflexions*—a passage that in fact translates an earlier quote from the French mathematician Sylvestre François Lacroix in support of Carnot's approach: "By virtue of the *law of continuity*, the disappearing magnitudes remain in the same ratio to that which they gradually approached before their disappearance" (Hauff 1800, ii).[10] That is, what has to be understood as continuous here is not magnitude per se but a continuous series of ratios between magnitudes. Hegel adds to his own paraphrase: "And this ratio or relation [*Verhältnis*] is so *continuous* and persistent that the transition consists rather in just bringing it out in its purity, thus causing any non-relational determination [*Verhältnislose Bestimmung*] . . . to vanish" (*SL*, 218–219; 21:254–255). In short, following Carnot, the correct understanding of Newton's method of infinitesimals involves a consequence of the principle of the "ratio of powers"—the idea that ratios as noncomposite are fundamental mathematical objects that can reciprocally determine each other. Carnot's "ratio" will not only be irreducible to the numbers from which ratios typically seem to be constructed; it itself will not have any fixed numerical value, being considered more like a variable than a constant. Once more, such "ratios" cannot be understood in the way that the word *ratio* is typically understood, preserving its odd "Archytean," pre-Euclidean usage.

Hegel's summary is faithful to Carnot's approach. In *Réflexions*, Carnot had started with the "imperfect idea" at the heart of modern infinitesimal analysis—that of a "singular species of being, which sometimes plays the role of true quantities, and at others must be treated as absolutely nothing, and which seem by their equivocal properties to hold a middle rank between substantial magnitudes and zero, between existence and not-existence" (Carnot 1797, 5–6). But he then appeals to a conceptual distinction between geometric magnitudes that are "given or determined by the conditions of the problem" and those that are "dependent on the arbitrary position of some point" (20). To the former, which he calls *quantités désignées*, he ascribes an objectivity independent of the calculator, while the latter, *non-désignées* or *auxiliaires* quantities, among which he clearly intends infinitesimals, he suggests, are introduced by the calculator simply to facilitate the calculation (22–23).[11] In the case of infinitesimals, the mathematician forms the idea of a quantity continually decreasing but is not interested in the value of this quantity per se. Rather the relevant object is the *ratio* established between this and another similarly decreasing quantity. Carnot sums up: "These infinitesimal quantities are only auxiliary quantities, introduced in the calculus solely to facilitate the expression of the conditions proposed. It is clear that it is absolutely necessary to eliminate them from the calculation to obtain the desired result, that is, the ratios or relations (*rapports*) sought" (30).

To this extent, to Carnot the idea of infinitely small quantities is a misconception, akin to the way negative quantities were to Kant. To conceive of these as determinate numbers that are exceptionally small is to fall prey to a conceptual confusion. It is to treat an indeterminate magnitude that corresponds to the use of a variable such as "x" as akin to the reality corresponding to a determinate "executable" expression, the three sheep, say, to which one refers with the expression "*these* three sheep."[12] Carnot's critique of the confused concept of an infinitesimal has also something of Kant's critique of the confusion between intuitions and concepts. However, Hegel's logical analogue of Carnot's algebraic distinction between constants and variables, as I have suggested, will be more that between the conceptual determinacies of "singularity" and "particularity."

Over the last decades, the development of Carnot's mathematics around 1800 has been closely examined by various historians of science (Gillispie and Pisano 2013, ch. 5; Schubring 2005, 315–317). *Réflexions sur la métaphysique du calcul infinitésimal* had apparently been a hastily rewritten version of earlier essays submitted to academies in the 1780s prior to Carnot's intense political and military preoccupations. Later in 1797, exile allowed him to resume his interests in "foundational" issues in mathematics, and it was during this time that his work took the distinctive geometric turn that started with *De la corrélation des figures de géométrie*. In particular, this refocusing on geometry seems to have been bound up with his engagement with the problem of negative magnitudes—the topic broached by Kant in the 1760s in an early expression of the type of vectorial analysis that would become influential with the nature philosophers and expressed in Schelling's Constructed Line.

Like the number zero, negative numbers had not been considered in Greek mathematics, but according to Alberto Martinez (Martinez 2006), they had been employed in Europe since the sixteenth century, especially for the recording of debts, but had always faced the objection of the impossibility of a number meant to be "less than nothing." In the seventeenth century, the English mathematician John Wallis had given a directional interpretation of negative numbers and in the eighteenth the Scottish mathematician Colin MacLaurin, taking up this form of analysis, had treated directionality as a qualitative as opposed to a quantitative determination, associating it with the logical notion of contrariety (Martinez 2006, 22). In Germany, the issue had engaged a number of major mathematicians, such as Abraham Gotthelf Kästner, upon whose work Kant had drawn in the 1763 essay (Kant 1992a, 210). This debate seems to have become particularly intense, however, especially among British mathematicians, around the turn of the nineteenth century (Martinez 2006, 25 and 46).

In 1779, the Scottish geometer John Playfair had contrasted geometry and algebra in a quasi-semiotic way by the idea that in the former, "every magnitude is represented by a line, and angles by an angle. The genus is always signified by the individual, and a general idea by one of the particulars which fall under it. By this means . . . the geometer is never permitted to reason about the relation of things which do not exist" (quoted in Martinez 2006, 77). In contrast, in algebra, where the connection of symbol to object is conventional, "the symbol may become the sole object of attention" and the analyst may "reason about characters after nothing is left which they can possibly express" (78).[13] It would be along much the same lines that Schelling would contrast the diagrams of geometry, which present the "universal in the particular" with the formulae of arithmetic that present "the particular in the universal" (Schelling 1967, 35; cf. 2001b, 381, 388), affording an objectivity to geometry contrasting with the subjectivity of arithmetic. Playfair had provided geometric solutions to the problem of "impossible numbers" such as the imaginary number i (Nagel 1979, 173–174), but this had been attacked by Robert Woodhouse in the *Transactions of the Royal Society of London* in which he employed ideas found in Berkeley to suggest a type of purely internal or structural understanding of the number system, such that they required no "external" interpretations such as offered by geometry (Nagel 1979, 178; Martinez 2006, 46–48).[14] Such disputes were clearly analogous to those about infinitesimals, and it is understandable that Carnot would have become engaged with them.

Carnot's earlier work on calculus had already appealed to the idea of ratio as a type of irreducible, nonmetrical mathematical object, and in his geometrical works he would go on to posit a geometric conception of ratio, which, like Hegel's "ratio of powers," was conceived as determined not by its component parts but by its relation to another ratio. This would be the harmonic cross-ratio, the roots of which go back, via Nicomachus's "most perfect proportion," to the state of geometry at the time of Plato's early Academy and, at least according to Nicomachus, to Plato's conception of the bond articulating the cosmic animal in the *Timaeus* as a type of syllogism. To appreciate the way Carnot's geometry could possibly play the role of a mediating context for Hegel's attempted revival of this ancient approach to logic, a closer look at the tradition of the projective alternative to Euclidean geometry in either of its ancient synthetic and modern analytic forms is necessary. It is clear why projective geometry might appeal to those who, despite its shortcomings, may have been inspired by the direction taken by Kant in his "Copernican revolution."

4.3 Ancient and Early Modern Roots of the Doubled Ratios of Carnot's Complete Quadrilateral

Around the turn of the nineteenth century, Carnot helped reintroduce an approach to geometry that had been proposed over a century and a half earlier by the French mathematician and engineer Girard Desargues and a small group of followers including Blaise Pascal. In 1639, Desargues had published fifty copies of a treatise, *Rough Draft of an Essay on the results of taking plane sections of a cone* (Field and Gray 1987). Appearing only two years after Descartes's *Géométrie*, which introduced his analytic approach, which would be adopted by Newton and others, Desargues's small work would languish until its later rescue. Desargues had developed ideas from the post-Euclidean geometer Apollonius of Perga (ca. 240–190 BCE), who had taken geometry beyond what was found in Euclid's *Elements* to the important examination of "conic sections"—the related group of curved two-dimensional figures, the circle, the ellipse, the parabola, and the hyperbola, produced when a three-dimensional cone is sliced by a plane at differing angles.

Surviving parts of Apollonius's *Conics* had been published in Europe at the turn of the seventeenth century around the same time as another important geometrical work, *Collection*, by Pappus of Alexandria (ca. 290–340 CE). Pappus's work attempted to present a summary of geometry from the earlier

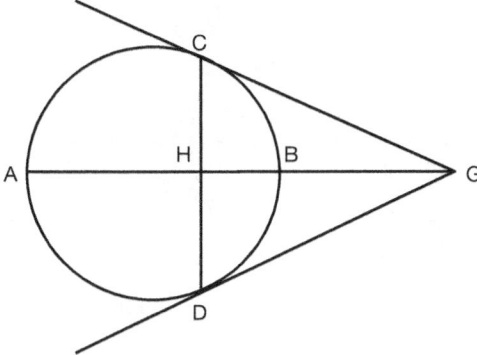

FIGURE 4.2 Harmonic section I—Apollonius. In absolute terms, ratio AG : GB is the same as AH : HB. (For the relevant proofs, see Heath 1896, propositions 62–65.)

"golden age" of Greek geometry and contained commentaries on Apollonius's theorems as well as on a since-lost work of Euclid, *Porisms*. Apollonius and Pappus together formed the basis for Desargues's distinctly nonmetric approach to geometry, which he opposed to Descartes's analytic geometry, which itself presupposed Euclidean geometry. These post-Euclidean developments in geometry built on the approach of the so-called problems tradition (Knorr 1986) with its use of the "regressive" rather than axiomatic method as known through later commentaries, such as those of Nicomachus of Gerasa, Iamblichus, and Proclus.[15]

In *Conics*, the harmonic mean of earlier music theory appears in constructions involving the curves of elliptical, parabolic, and hyperbolic conic sections being crossed by a straight line. As this is most simply illustrated by a circle, a circle will be used here, but it must be remembered that the proportions involved in the division apply to all other conic sections as well. That is, the genesis of this "harmonic" division will be independent of the angle of the plane cutting across the three-dimensional cone responsible for the figure being discussed—a circumstance that will be crucial for the later idea of "projective" geometry.

Consider a circle with a diameter AB that is continued beyond the circumference to some point G. Tangents are constructed from G to touch the circle at points C and D, and these points are joined by a straight line that intersects the diameter at point H (fig. 4.2). Drawing on a number of theorems from Euclid, Apollonius shows that the points H and G equally divide the interval AB in internal and external fashion, in that the ratio between the lengths of AH and HB is the same as that between AG and GB.[16] As noted earlier, the idea of conjugate internal and external divisions of a directed line

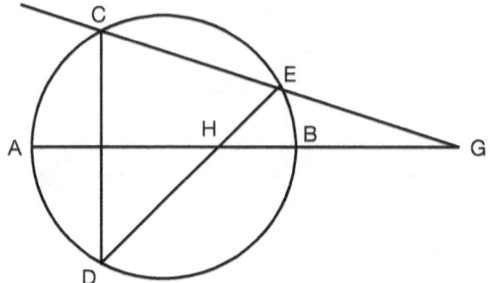

FIGURE 4.3 Harmonic section II—Pappus (after Heath 1921, 2:419–424).

segment would be revived in the wake of Kant's speculations in the 1760s on the origins of negative magnitudes, making this development an ideal context for the revival of Desargues's forgotten geometry.

Pappus constructs a similar figure, again involving a circle with a diameter AB extended to a point G beyond B (fig. 4.3). In Pappus's figure, a line from G is drawn that intersects the circle at two points, forming a chord EC. A perpendicular is now dropped from C to cross AB and meet the circumference of the circle again at point D. D is then joined to E such that DE crosses AB at point H.

The points H and G again divide the diameter of the circle in equivalent ways internally and externally as in Apollonius's figure, such that the ratio of lengths AH to HB is the same as that between the lengths AG and GB.[17] With the modification of a negative sign deriving from a consideration of directionality, this ratio would come to be known as the "harmonic cross-ratio," AH : HB = −AG : GB. The harmonic cross-ratio between the two ratios holds regardless of where G falls along the extension of AB. When G moves further away from B, H also moves away from B in the opposite direction, keeping the proportion between the ratios AH : HB and AG : HB equal. However, when AB = BG, making B the arithmetic mean of AG, H is found to divide AG in the ratio of 3:2. This is the musical *tetraktys* with the distances in proportions as given in the sequence 6, 8, 9, 12. This same double ratio appears in another proposition in Pappus's *Collection*, this time involving constructions on a quadrilateral figure with no *apparent* involvement of a circle (Heath 1921, 2:264, props. 130–131). (In fact, the "circle" is implicitly present.)

In the seventeenth century, Desargues had developed a geometry that related notions such as those of "projection" and "perspective," viewpoints and "points at infinity"—notions that had arisen from the treatment of perspectival representation by Renaissance artists (Andersen 2007; Field and Gray 1987, ch. 2). Desargues had rediscovered the theorem of homologous triangles or triangles in perspective (or "Desargues's Theorem"), based on further propositions in Pappus's *Collection* (Field and Gray 1987, ch. 8). This involved a construction (fig. 4.4) showing three "rays" radiating from a point, O, such that two "homologous" triangles (ABC and DEF) were constructed, each triangle having one vertex on each of the three lines. The sides of the two triangles are extended such that the pairs of corresponding sides (BC and EF, AC and DF, and DE and AB) each meet at three further points (G, H, and I). Desargues's theorem stated that these three further points, G, H, and I, were collinear, that is, they fall on one straight line. The two triangles are described as "perspective" from the point O, which is itself called the "centre of perspectivity" or "pole." For any such diagram, the line through the three collinear points, called the "axis of perspectivity" or "polar" (here, GHI), stands in a special relation to the pole (O). That relationship is in fact that which exists in Apollonius's construction above (fig. 4.2) between the point G and the line joining the points where the tangents from T touch the circle. In Apollonius's diagram, point G is the pole, and the line CD, the polar. In the nineteenth century it would be argued that this relation between "pole" and "polar" was an instance of a more general "duality" between points and lines in projective geometry.

Although figure 4.4 is formally a plane figure, the language of "perspective," "projections," "point of view," and so on, in conformity with its connection to the artist's concern with perspectival representation, suggests a reading of the figure as involving relationships in three dimensions. Thus,

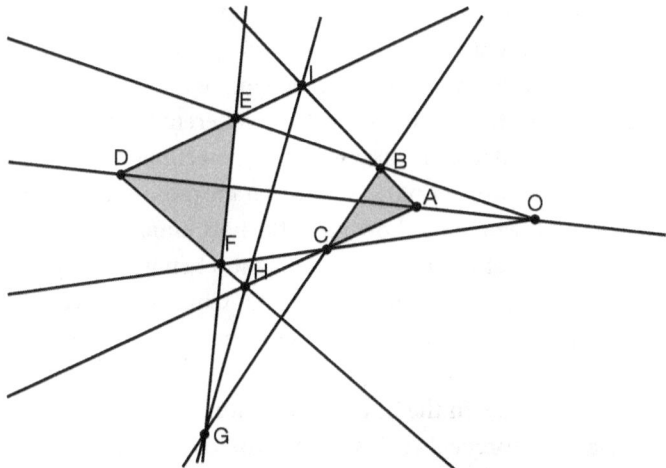

FIGURE 4.4 Desargues's homologous triangles. Triangles ABC and DEF are perspective from point O, the "centre of perspectivity." When extended, the corresponding sides of the triangles meet at points G, H, and I, which fall on the one straight line, the "axis of perspectivity."

in Desargues's diagram, two triangles are said to be perspective from a point, O, suggesting a sense in which a viewer located at O and observing such triangles arrayed within three dimensions on differently aligned planes would see them as superimposed. That is, these apparently different triangles are seen as the same when viewed from that "point of view." Moreover, when considered in three dimensions the basis of the relations manifest in these diagrams becomes clear. If Desargues's homologous triangles lie on two different planes, the extended sides of these triangles will necessarily meet on a single line because all points belonging to both of the two intersecting planes will fall on the line at which the planes intersect. In Hegel's logic, similar "two-dimensional" homologies will be explained by regarding them as "appearances" of an arrangement understood within a higher dimension.

All this means that figures that are invariant in Euclidean geometry are *not* so in projective geometry, in which what is circular from one perspective might be elliptical or even parabolic from some other, or what is a square from one perspective might be trapezoidal from another.[18] This is, of course, what we have seen studied in Apollonius's *Conics*, where various ways of sectioning a cone produce projective equivalences or correlations among the plane figures of circle, ellipse, parabola, and hyperbola. From a typically Euclidean perspective, these would all count simply as different objects. Indeed, as can be seen from Desargues's diagram, within the context of a projective geometry, the two triangles that Leibniz had used to illustrate congruence and that were criticized by Kant as incongruent (see earlier, chapter 3.3) are, in fact, congruent.[19] Regarded as a three-dimensional diagram, it can be appreciated how the two triangular shapes inscribed on differently oriented two-dimensional planes might come to be regarded as either congruent or incongruent depending on the location of the viewing point.

In order for projective geometry to be a coherent field of investigation, something must be held to be invariant across projections if all the traditional geometric objects lose this status. It is here that the cross-ratio relation would become so central. It would be shown that the harmonic cross-ratio could be generalized such that rather than the double ratio being fixed by the value of −1 it could also be fixed by any other constant.[20] Considered as a prototypical "object" in this new geometric environment, the cross-ratio would be thus more basic than the circles and squares that we typically think of as geometrical objects of study. In the nineteenth century the cross-ratio would be much more than a theoretical curiosity and would become important within practical disciplines such as military engineering. With its aid the distance between objects in the three-dimensional world could be calculated on the basis of information stored on two-dimensional maps.

A further consequence of projective geometry, separating it from Descartes's analytic geometry, was its reconceptualization of the notion of "infinity." From the time of the Renaissance, painters, attempting to get three-dimensional objects "in perspective," had come to represent straight lines that in reality are parallel as converging at the horizon. Interpreted within projective geometry, the line of the horizon could be understood as representing a line "at infinity"—a line made up of points at which different sets of "parallel lines" meet. That is, the horizon represents the "polar" that is coordinated from the "pole" of the artist's point of view. Via an associated theorem, from the "point of view" of any point on the line at infinity, the first "pole" would itself fall on the complementary polar.

That parallel lines meet was contrary to Euclid's famous "parallel postulate" according to which parallel lines do not meet (Euclid 1956, book 1, postulate 5), and in this way, projective geometry anticipated the various non-Euclidean geometries proposed later in the nineteenth century. But for a seventeenth-century audience it had also provided an image for the theological problem of how to conceive of the relation of finite human and infinite divine "points of view," a dimension to the fore in the work of Desargues's follower Blaise Pascal (Cortese 2015). From his comments on the role of the law of continuity in explaining the vanishing magnitudes of the infinitesimal calculus, Hegel surely would have been alert to these facts, as he would have been to the fact that Kepler had introduced this law in explaining how one of the foci of an ellipse came to be located at such a "point at infinity" when the ellipse was distorted into a parabola (Field and Gray 1987, appendix 4).[21] All this points to an attitude to geometry very different from that of Schelling.

Moreover, Hegel possessed Carnot's book containing the modern incarnation of Plato's most beautiful bond. Given the background circumstances that would have directed his attention to this aspect of Carnot's geometry, it is difficult to imagine that it would have had *no* impact on his thinking. In contrast, in relation to Hermann Grassmann, who was a student at the University of Berlin during Hegel's last four years there, 1827–31, there is no question of Hegel having been similarly influenced. However, some have been led to think of Grassmann having been influenced by Hegel because of a convergence between their views (Wolff 1999). While this is unclear, what is clear is that Grassmann had been deeply influenced by ideas from idealist and romantic thought sharing some features with Hegel's. These were ideas that he expressed in the heavily philosophical introduction to the revolutionary work he published in 1844, *Linear Extension Theory: A New Branch of Mathematics* (Grassmann 1995, 23–43). Combined with Carnot's ideas, Grassmann's provide compelling evidence for parallels between these directions in mathematics and the stance adopted by Hegel.

4.4 Grassmann, Idealism, and the Algebra of Geometric Vectors

Hermann Grassmann is now recognized as a major figure in nineteenth-century mathematics but during his life he would never obtain a university position in that discipline. Hermann was the son of a high school teacher, Justus Grassmann, who had "published a series of small books between 1827 and 1835 in which he wanted to expound a new philosophical and educational conception of mathematics while at the same time developing mathematics itself" (Otte 2011, 67). Justus Grassmann's mathematics, it is said, was deeply influenced by the type of nature philosophy introduced by Schelling. Along with this, he had been influenced by the work on crystals by Christian Samuel Weiss, a figure associated with Baader.

Weiss had been appointed as professor of minerology at the University of Berlin when it opened in 1810, and Hegel would take over his lectures on the philosophy of nature when he arrived in 1821 (Heuser 2011, 50). Weiss had adopted a geometric approach to crystal structure and had adopted Kant's theory of space from the "Negative Magnitudes" essay of 1763 for his purposes (Heuser 2011, 54). Hegel appears to rely on Weiss's work in his discussion of crystals in *Philosophy of Nature* (*E:PN*, §315, addition, plus editor's note, 2:330), and Hegel also possessed a PhD on crystal structure by a student at the University of Berlin, Franz Neumann, who favored the "synthetic" approach to geometry and, influenced by Weiss, applied it in his thesis (Mense 1993, 701–702).[22]

Justus's son Hermann is regarded as having continued and developed the novel approach to mathematics of his father. During his stay at the University of Berlin from 1827 to 1831 he apparently took no courses in mathematics but was most attracted to courses of the romantic hermeneutic theorist/theologian/philosopher Friedrich Schleiermacher, who would have a decided influence upon his approach to mathematics (Lewis 1977; Petsche 2009, ch. 2.3). Indeed, he had apparently closely studied Schleiermacher's published lectures on dialectics before composing *Linear Extension Theory* (Petsche 2009, xvii).

Partly because of the dialectical introduction to the *Linear Extension Theory* of 1844 that mathematicians found puzzling, Grassmann's work would not be taken up within mathematics for decades. However, as initiating the approaches of "vector analysis" or "linear algebra," it would eventually be regarded as one of the most important scientific developments in the nineteenth century and is now, along with calculus, a staple of higher education within mathematics. While its ideas are often unfamiliar to those who have not pursued mathematics beyond high school, some of its basic features that are relevant to our purposes are relatively easy to grasp. Crucial for our purposes is the fact that in vector analysis, the opposed signs of '+' and '−' that Kant had applied to line segments are generalized to figures of two, three, and even higher dimensions.

In his *Linear Extension Theory* Grassmann distinguishes between continuous vectors and discrete numbers understood as the "scalars" by which vectors can be multiplied or "scaled." Scalars themselves can be both positive and negative, and so directionality of directed continuous magnitudes from Grassmann's perspective does not solve the problem of negative magnitudes as envisaged by Kant.[23] Two basic "arithmetical" operations are allowed in Grassmann's vector calculus—the addition of vectors and the multiplication of vectors by scalars. The former operation would recall Newton's use of the "parallelogram of forces," in which the sum of two component directed force vectors can be thought of as the diagonal of the parallelogram of which the forces formed adjacent sides. The multiplication of a vector by a scalar allows a vector to be lengthened or shortened along the direction in which it points, while multiplying a vector by a negative scalar has the effect of reversing the direction of that vector. Thus, for the vector $\overrightarrow{AB}$:

$$\overrightarrow{AB} \times -1 = -\overrightarrow{AB} = \overrightarrow{BA}.[24]$$

Kant's original idea of opposed vectors, such as a ship's movement from east to west or west to east, pictured them as aligned on a single line, but Newton's parallelogram of forces pictured vectors interacting at different angles, such that combined they defined a two-dimensional plane. "Linear combinations" of vectors as in vector addition now pictured the resulting vector as belonging to the plane or "vector space" defined by the two vectors being added. Hegel had pointed to the internal relations among different arithmetical operations, as when one is able to conceive of multiplication as a type of iterated addition, and here too, a type of multiplication of vectors could be generated out of the iteration of vector addition.

Grassmann introduced the idea of multiplying vectors *by* vectors in such a way that there existed two such forms. In one, multiplying vector $\overrightarrow{AB}$ by vector $\overrightarrow{CD}$ results in a directionless number, or "scalar," rather than another vector. This, called by Grassmann "internal multiplication," is commonly called the "dot product" and is represented as "$\overrightarrow{AB} \cdot \overrightarrow{CD}$." The other form, Grassmann's "external multiplication," now called the "cross product" ($\overrightarrow{AB} \times \overrightarrow{CD}$), was conceived as a type of iterated "addition" and resulted in a vector oriented in three-dimensional space. Later, the forms of vector multiplication would be modified by William Clifford to produce a more perspicuous account that will be followed here.[25]

Clifford would replace Grassmann's external multiplication with two further forms resulting in a total of three types of vector multiplication.[26] Beside the dot product there was a "wedge product" ($\overrightarrow{AB} \wedge \overrightarrow{CD}$) and a "geometric product" (represented by juxtaposition, $\overrightarrow{AB}\,\overrightarrow{CD}$). Here, multiplying $\overrightarrow{AB}$ by $\overrightarrow{CD}$ to produce the wedge product could be conceived as involving the continuous displacement of vector $\overrightarrow{AB}$ in the direction of $\overrightarrow{CD}$ resulting in a two-dimensional parallelogram, a "bi-vector," with the two vectors as its sides. However, the order in which this operation is performed is significant. Displacing $\overrightarrow{CD}$ in the direction of $\overrightarrow{AB}$ will result in a parallelogram of a differently signed magnitude when compared to the result of displacing $\overrightarrow{AB}$ in the direction of $\overrightarrow{CD}$. That is, unlike the multiplication of numbers, the order in which the vectors multiplied is relevant to the value of the result. While, like arithmetical multiplication, the dot product is symmetric or "commutative,"[27] the wedge product is said to be anticommutative such that $\overrightarrow{AB} \wedge \overrightarrow{CD} = -\overrightarrow{CD} \wedge \overrightarrow{AB}$. Diagrammatically, an area with anticlockwise orientation is taken as positively signed, while an area with clockwise orientation is taken as negatively signed. This is the relation of Leibniz's questionably "congruent" triangles (fig. 3.5) discussed earlier. Moreover, the signed character of the spaces produced by this operation continues to higher dimensions. In three dimensions, volumes will have opposed orientations, as conceived by Kant with his incongruent counterparts (see above, chapter 3.4).

Clifford's geometric product was now defined in terms of the other two, with the geometric product simply being the sum of the dot product and the wedge product ($\overrightarrow{AB}\,\overrightarrow{CD} = \overrightarrow{AB} \times \overrightarrow{CD} + \overrightarrow{AB} \wedge \overrightarrow{CD}$). This strange idea of generating a product by the addition of two component products should by now be familiar. It is what we have seen harmonically in the "addition" of perfect fourth and perfect fifth intervals to form a complete octave, and in the addition of the logarithms of two numbers to form the logarithm of the product of those numbers. Moreover, Grassmann had earlier shown his vector analysis to be relevant to projective geometry.[28]

In short, the development of vector analysis in the nineteenth century would testify to the fact that the operations of addition and subtraction that Kant had identified for *phora* could be expanded to addition and multiplication among vectors interrelated within higher dimensions, giving a new form to the "geometric algebra" of the ancient Greeks. Introducing the geometric features of directionality or orientation would have specific consequences for the arithmetic operations of addition and multiplication in these systems, creating new forms of algebra. Kant had anticipated something

GEOMETRY AND PHILOSOPHY

of the significance of these developments for our conception of space with his observations concerning the significance of handedness for Leibniz's "congruent" triangles and his idea of three-dimensional "incommensurate counterparts." However, these developments in geometric algebra would disrupt the Euclidean presuppositions about geometry upon which Kant had relied. Viewed from where geometry was heading, Hegel's approach seems extremely percipient.

4.5 Schelling's Spinozistic and Hegel's Platonic-Carnotian Readings of the Constructed Line

I have suggested that in his Constructed Line, Schelling can be understood as drawing upon a distinction between the absolute value of a magnitude such as that of a line segment and the quasi-algebraic "signed" values that lengths may possess within some calculative system, a distinction suggested in Kant's 1763 essay and that would be exploited by new forms of geometry in the nineteenth century. While Hegel seems to concur with Schelling's claim that the absolute line represents something presupposed rather than postulated (Schelling 2001b, 376), a Platonic-Carnotian reading, I suggest, will have the line divided not by a single mean (in Schelling's case, as well as in Baader and Eschenmayer, the indifference point conceived as the fulcrum of a balance), but by a split or doubled mean. The frameworks provided by projective geometry and the algebra of geometric vectors allow us to understand Hegel's alternative here, with the original musical context of the three "means" being a helpful place to start.

As is clear in the case of a modern fretted instrument such as a guitar, the relationship between how far one's fingers have to move up and down the fretboard to produce the appropriate notes up and down the scale is a complicated matter. The frets on a guitar are not evenly spaced but get closer together the further one moves "up" the fretboard because they are spaced in a way that conforms to a logarithmic rather than a linear scale.[29] This allows the addition of, say, the five semitones constituting the perfect fourth with the seven semitones of the perfect fifth on the scale to produce a sound that is equal to the product of frequencies of the two individual tones produced—the full octave. The modern "equal-tempered" scale is not the same as that used by the Pythagoreans, but the same logarithmic principle holds for their restricted intervals of the octave, the perfect fourth and the perfect fifth. But such patterns of relations are far from being restricted to music and are spread widely in nature. Moreover, we see the same patterns when looking at "projective" phenomena in three-dimensional space.

Invariably, in introductory texts on the subject of projective geometry will be found allusions to viewing the rails on train tracks that, while actually parallel, seem to converge onto the horizon, the evenly spaced sleepers on which the rails rest appearing to become closer to each other as the tracks go into the distance. However, we might think of the reversed situation that holds when one looks along the fretboard of a guitar from some location at the body end of the instrument. With a little maneuvering, one can locate oneself at the appropriate viewpoint, O, from which all the frets, which in reality are progressively more widely spaced as one moves along the fretboard, appear evenly spaced. From O, the midpoint of that part of the fretboard corresponding to one octave (twelve frets) appears to be the sixth fret, while objectively as measured with a rule, the midpoint of this length is actually at the fifth fret. Because we are looking at a two-dimensional series of spaces from a point involving the third dimension, from Hegel's Platonic analysis the midpoint should be "split," and in a sense it is. We must understand our subjective point of view when located at some "O" as a view onto a world that can be equally grasped from no point of view—that is, from the shifting point of view of the rule-wielding measurer.

I have suggested elsewhere (Redding 1996, ch. 3) that Schelling's Constructed Line had formed the starting point of Hegel's reworking of Fichte's account of intersubjective "recognition" as presented in his practical philosophy and that would come to be at the center of Hegel's theory of "spirit" (*Geist*), and this view, I believe, coheres with the more developed reading of Hegel's interpretation of the Constructed Line being suggested here. How exactly to understand Hegel's account of intersubjective recognition in the famous vignette from *The Phenomenology of Spirit* concerning the "master-slave dialectic" is difficult and controversial, but there is certainly a moment in it that, as John McDowell has argued, the opposition between master and slave is meant to represent the Kantian split between "empirical" and "transcendental" dimensions of self-consciousness (McDowell 2003). Read in the Platonic way, Schelling's diagram could be understood as giving a schematic representation to the relation between two interrelated intentional attitudes onto the world. One might be thought of as a perspective onto the world to be had from some point within it, and the other a related "view" from a point at infinity—some problematic "view from nowhere." The latter, however, can now be given an interpretation from a practical point of view: it will be the intentional attitude that coincides with the application of some objective measuring device to the world.

In the context of an examination of Hegel's theory of judgment, it will be argued that this geometrical analogue of Kant's empirical and transcendental dimensions of self-consciousness reflects a duality found between the opposed conceptions of predication in Hegel's "judgments of inherence" and "judgments of subsumption." In contrast to the univocal account of judgment form found in both Aristotle and Kant, Hegel's dual judgments will reflect his commitment to the Platonic idea of the split middle term. This in turn will be related to his novel interpretation of the relation of logical form and content in judgments. In this homologously equivalent model of judgment, these inverse judgments can be understood as having different logical functions while representing the same "absolute" content: one type of judgment serves the function of the acquisition of empirical content in contexts governed by perspectival features, while the other, that of entering into inference relations with other judgments. After all, "measuring devices" such as rulers and tape measures are really devices for comparing properties of objects—inches, centimeters, and so on being lengths we chose for such purposes. In turn the syllogism makes explicit this type of "identity in difference" between the two premises as united in the conclusion.

In the following chapters it will be argued that those features we witness in Hegel's departure from Schelling on geometry will be reproduced in his modifications of Aristotle's syllogistic. This latter issue, however, can only be understood in terms of Leibniz's earlier rethinking of Aristotle's syllogism. It is widely recognized that Leibniz had anticipated many of the developments within mathematical logic found in the nineteenth century. But this itself must be understood in relation to Leibniz's own attempts to resist the "analytic" dimensions of modern thought by reinvoking the nonmetrical geometrical thought of the ancients in ways that anticipated nineteenth-century mathematical developments such as projective geometry and vector analysis.

5

The Role of *Analysis Situs* in Leibniz's Modernization of Logic

> In philosophy, I have found a means of accomplishing in all sciences what Descartes and others have done in Arithmetic and Geometry by Algebra and Analysis, by the *Ars Combinatoria*. . . . By this all composite notions in the whole world are reduced to a few simple ones as their alphabet; and by the combination of such an alphabet a way is made of finding, in time by an ordered method, all things with their theorems and whatever is possible to investigate concerning them.
> LEIBNIZ, "Letter to Duke Johann Friedrich of Hannover, October 1671"

Descartes and other early moderns had typically interpreted human cognitive engagement with the world in a very different way from that of the ancient Greeks. In the new approach cognition was grasped subjectively, expressing what Hegel characterized as the typical *Innerlichkeit*, innerness, of the modern subject. From this perspective, the relation of being and thought—"extension" and "intension"—would be seen as a type of global problem, and perhaps the simplest response had been that of effectively collapsing the distinction by the device of thinking of thought's "extension" as limited to the mind itself. This was at the heart of the new "way of ideas" approach that would come to be known as "subjective idealism." What one "really" experiences, on this model, is not what it seems to be. I think I see a tree beside a lake, but what I'm really perceiving is my idea of a tree located beside my idea of a lake! The objects directly perceived are Platonic "icons" located in the individual's mind rather than in the world, observed by an inner "homunculus"—a "little man" trapped, as it were, inside the skull. Philosophy had thus become obsessed about how one can be assured that the arrangements we *really* see—that is, those arrayed on some type of inner screen viewed by the homunculus—are good representations of what one *thinks* one sees—various arrangements of independent objects in the "outside world."

Hegel, as an early critic of the way of ideas, is now sometimes discussed in relation to the critique offered by Wilfrid Sellars of what he called "the myth of the given," but here I want to focus on aspects of Hegel's way around the Cartesian framework that drew on an alternative offered by Leibniz in a logico-epistemological approach that may be seen as a generalization of the "revolution" that Copernicus had established in cosmology. This would be reflected in Leibniz's logic, inasmuch as he would conceive of a way of translating between extensional and intensional interpretations of judgments based on the idea of a type of reversal of direction from which the contents of a judgment could be considered, a conception linked to his use of the metaphor of "perspective." On this approach, the "subjectivity" that Descartes and other way-of-ideas thinkers had made thematic was not to be captured by conceiving of one's experience as unfolding on the stage of some "inner theater," but more in terms of the consequences for a subject's experience of the particularity of their placement and orientation within the world. That is, a subject perceives the things of the world around them and the arrangements and interactions of those things from a particular perspective or *point de vue*, as famously sketched in Leibniz's *Discourse on Metaphysics*. While Kant is standardly associated with a philosophical extension of this "Copernican revolution,"[1] the recognition for having taken Copernicus's method seriously must, as Friedrich Kaulbach once argued, equally go to Leibniz (Kaulbach 1973, 333).

Leibniz is now known, among other things, for his invention of the modern mathematical approach to logic, which involved the application of algebra to Aristotle's syllogistic in a way similar to that made famous by Descartes's invention of analytic geometry. However, Leibniz also reacted adversely to Descartes's reduction of geometry to arithmetic and suggested a nonmetrical form of analysis that he called situational analysis, *analysis situs*. This, it seems, had been based on what he knew of the work of Desargues and especially his follower Pascal.

5.1 Leibniz's Ambivalent Revival of Plato's Philosophical Arithmetic

Interest in Leibniz's logic was limited until the end of the nineteenth century when it was "rediscovered" in a context within which the innovatory nature of his thought could be appreciated. Since the 1950s especially, Leibniz has increasingly come to be seen as having anticipated significant ideas found not only in Boole and the algebraists but in Frege and Russell as well (e.g., Rescher 1954). By the 1990s, careful reconstructions of the logic contained in the 1686 essay, "General Inquiries about the Analysis of Concepts and of Truths" (Leibniz 1966, ch. 7), were being carried out by Wolfgang Lenzen (Lenzen 1990, 2004), Chris Swoyer (Swoyer 1994), and others, and this type of analysis has continued to be developed (e.g., Malink and Vasudevan 2016).

Leibniz's logic is now seen as amounting to more than a vague anticipation of the later approach of George Boole in which Aristotle's syllogistic was interpreted into an algebraically tractable form in the context of an emerging set theory. For Lenzen, while the systematic concept calculus developed in

General Inquiries was mathematically equivalent to Boole's later algebra of sets (Lenzen 2004, 13–14, section 4), this work was further extended to a calculus of propositions, on the one hand, and a modal logic, on the other, with the latter anticipating the basic ideas found in modern possible-world semantics (section 6). In relation to the same work, Swoyer claimed that Leibniz had anticipated the modern distinction between syntax and semantics, a distinction not clarified until Tarski's development of the idea of "models" (Tarski 1954). As well as this, Leibniz had anticipated the use of particular algebraic models, the algebra for which, involving "partially ordered sets" (posets) and diagrammatic "semilattice" structures, have only been explicitly developed from the early twentieth century (Swoyer 1994, 25; Malink and Vasudevan 2016, section 3.1).[2] Below I give a quick sketch of some of the basic ideas suggested by these authors, relating them to what we have seen at work in ancient logic and as anticipating logical developments in the twentieth century. For our purposes, however, it will be the implications of Leibniz's unrealized project of *analysis situs* and its connections to the nineteenth-century revival of geometric algebra that will be emphasized.

Lenzen has reconstructed the series of axiomatic logical systems from Leibniz's texts written throughout his career. The series commences with the simplest system developed between 1676 and 1679, which was a class-based logic utilizing as a principle for inference the type of transitivity of containment relations that we have seen in Aristotle's ambiguous use of this notion. In a way that had been at best implicit in Aristotle, Leibniz treated these containment relations as fundamentally intensional. As one interpreter of Leibniz's logical achievements has put it, "Leibniz was fully aware of the difference of these two methods of interpretation of Aristotle's logic, and he was the first to construct an intensional interpretation, if only in terms of his characteristic numbers. It was his idea to use pairs of numbers which has led us to the general construction of a set theoretical intensional model of Aristotelian logic" (Glashoff 2010, 263).[3]

This would be one major difference between Leibniz's approach and that of Boole, who would interpret his calculus extensionally. That is, from Leibniz's intensional viewpoint, the concept <human> is conceived as containing the concept <animal> just as the concept <animal> contains the more general concept <organism>. This was the inferential principle traceable back to Plato's diairetic pyramid and operative in Aristotle's "perfect" syllogisms, although Aristotle seemed to blur this with suggestions of an extensional interpretation. However, the reverse container-contained relation holds when these structures are interpreted extensionally from "bottom up," as when the class of animals is now understood as containing the subclass of humans. As noted above, in some of these works Leibniz had also suggested that *numbers* be assigned to terms such that the concept <human> could be conceived as containing the concept of <animal> just as the number 6 contains as a divisor or "factor" the number 3 (e.g., Leibniz 1966, 17), reproducing Aristotle's transitive containment relations: if the last term C is contained in the middle, B as in a whole, and B is so contained in the first, A, then C is contained in A. It is important to remember, however, that a type of algebra was available to Leibniz that had not been available to Aristotle, such that the assignment of numbers to parts of sentences allowed the idea of basic arithmetical operations being applied to them. This would allow the judgment/equations to be linked systematically to each other in terms of a numerical value, 1 or 0, that would later be understood as one of two "truth-values," "true" and "false."

According to Lenzen, the strongest logic in Leibniz's series is to be found in *General Inquiries*, which is "deductively equivalent or isomorphic to the ordinary [that is, extensionally interpreted] algebra of sets." Thus, Leibniz "'discovered' the Boolean algebra 160 years before Boole" (Lenzen 2004, 7). Swoyer calls this calculus the "calculus of real addition" because of the way that Leibniz conceives of a process of adding concepts together in a way analogous to the arithmetical operation of adding numbers. It was this that constituted the algebraic approach that Leibniz brought to the implicitly geometrically conceived Aristotelian syllogism:

> Although Leibniz stresses that his calculus is amenable to alternative interpretations, he very frequently interprets its characters as signifying concepts and real addition as an operation for conjoining them; for example, the real addition of the concepts rational and animal is the complex concept rational animal. In order to accommodate real addition in the object language, Leibniz employs what we would now regard as a character-forming operator that allows us to join characters like 'A' and 'B' to produce the composite character 'A $\oplus$ B.' In interpretations in which the characters of his calculus denote concepts, 'A $\oplus$ B' signifies the compound concept that is the real sum of the concepts A and B. (Swoyer 1994, 7)

Leibniz had put the '+' sign inside a circle to put the reader on notice that conceptual addition did not always behave like simple numerical addition. In fact, confusingly, the concepts that seem to be "added" are those that have been established by a process akin to "division." Later, Boole would clarify the respective roles of logical "addition" and "multiplication."

Conceptual addition shows many of the features found in the actual addition of numbers,[4] but one of the axioms of the system diverges from the numerical analogue. This is the axiom "A $\oplus$ A = A," which will appear also in Boole and be a distinctive feature of algebras of logic as distinct from numerical algebras. Later, in the nineteenth century, algebra would become sufficiently abstract so as to allow the clear distinction of its operations from numerical calculation. For example, "group theory" would display the structures and processes underlying the fundamental arithmetical operations of numerical addition and multiplication as representing particular instances of more general binary operations on sets (Anonymous 2008, 2.1).[5] In England, this process of abstraction of algebraic operations away from domains of numbers would include the independent development of algebraic logic by mathematicians such as George Boole and Augustus De Morgan.[6]

For his part, Leibniz had attempted to develop a system of logical calculus after the axiomatic style characteristic of Euclid's geometry, in which theorems are deduced from a set of fundamental axioms. Thus, in Leibniz's universal characteristic, primitive symbols are to be joined in basic equations from which more complex syntactically well-formed "sentences" could be built. This allowed propositions to be thought of as akin to equations and, like Boole roughly two centuries later, Leibniz would employ a version of arithmetic reduced to two numerals, 1 and 0, rather than the usual ten.[7] Here it is worth pausing to reflect upon the peculiar relation in which this approach would stand to Greek mathematics.

Leibniz's allusion to Pythagorean mathematics is obvious from the choice of "Monadology" for the name of his metaphysical system. However, the development of the modern digital number system had required the Indian-originated "Arabic" system of numbers that ranges from 0 to 9, not the Greek-originated "Roman" system with its still largely Pythagorean 1 to 10. In short, the number zero, problematic for the Pythagorean conception of number, was required for the development of modern algebra.[8] However, there is something of the Pythagorean approach in Leibniz's choice of the binary number system. As has been remarked, the Greeks had conceived of magnitudes as organized into different kinds: linear numbers could not be treated in the same way as rectangular numbers, nor rectangular numbers in the same way as cubic numbers. But in relation to their number theory, the fundamentally opposed kinds of number in the Pythagorean view were even and odd numbers. In the type of binary "arithmetic" introduced by Leibniz and Boole for the purposes of propositional logic the following equalities held:

$$1 + 1 = 0,$$
$$1 + 0 = 1,$$
$$0 + 1 = 1, \text{ and}$$
$$0 + 0 = 0.$$

This is the same pattern that exists in the Pythagorean system for adding odd and even numbers, for which the pattern holds:

> odd + odd = even,
> even + odd = odd,
> odd + even = odd, and
> even + even = even.

Summing up, when facing the type of calculus of which Leibniz conceived, these sentence-equations could be grasped as equations having one of two numerical values, and as able to be manipulated in ways that allow various combinations of numbers to be computed. Regarded logically, however, they could be regarded as assertions that had the value of being either true or false (or as Leibniz usually expressed it, as equal to *oui* or *non*). From the latter perspective the outputs of the computational process would thus result in sentences whose "truth-values" were logically understood on the basis of the outputs of algebraic computations performed on sets of elements. Hegel's effective logic teacher, Ploucquet,[9] had followed Leibniz down this computational path (Marciszewski and Murawski 1995).

A particularly crucial issue for Leibniz had been how to derive the needed propositional logic from his more basic concept calculus. The relation of Aristotle's term logic to a properly propositional logic would become a major issue among the logicians in the second half of the nineteenth century, with the general recognition of the presence of problems compromising Boole's efforts. As for Leibniz, Lenzen describes his extension of his 1686 system to his system of propositional logic in a process that involves "mapping the concepts and conceptual operators into the set of propositions and propositional operators" making it a "seemingly circular procedure" (Lenzen 2004, 7):

> Now a characteristic feature of Leibniz's algebra L_1 (and of its subsystems) is that it is in the first instance *based upon* the propositional calculus, but that it afterwards serves as a *basis for* propositional logic. When Leibniz states and proves the laws of concept logic, he takes the requisite rules and laws of propositional logic for granted. Once the former have been established, however, the latter can be obtained from the former by observing that there exists a strict analogy between *concepts* and *propositions* which allows one to re-interpret the conceptual connectives as propositional connectives. (Lenzen 2004, 8)

Something like this "strict analogy between *concepts* and *propositions*" would be the subject of critiques of Leibniz's logic by both Kant and Hegel,[10] and in the later nineteenth century Boole and his followers would be plagued by similar problems of how to relate concept and propositional calculi. Frege would say of Boole's system that its two parts, its class and propositional calculi, "run alongside one another, so that one is like the mirror image of the other, but for that very reason stands in no organic relation to it" (Frege 1979, 14).

The purported "circularity" in Leibniz's procedure is significant for Hegel's criticism of Leibniz's conception of judgment in the "mathematical syllogism" (*SL*, 602–604; 12:104–106) as well as for Kant's more general critique of Leibniz's logic. Leibniz was able to move with apparent ease between his class calculus and his propositional calculus because of the phenomenon we have noted in which he assumed the equivalence of intensional and extensional readings of the relation of class inclusion found in the idea of the reversal of the containment metaphor. Perhaps the best-known expression of this is found in *New Essays on Human Understanding* where Leibniz has Theophilus comment on Aristotle's securing of inferences in a syllogism via the transitivity of conceptual containment:

> The common manner of statement concerns individuals, whereas Aristotle's refers rather to ideas or universals. For when I say *Every man is an animal* I mean that all the men are included amongst all the animals; but at the same time I mean that the idea of animal is included in the idea of man. 'Animal' comprises more individuals than 'man' does, but 'man' comprises more ideas or more attributes; one has more instances, the other more degrees of reality; one has the greater extension, the other the greater intension. (Leibniz 1996, 486)[11]

Leibniz thus disambiguates Aristotle's "containment" metaphor at the heart of his syllogism with its apparent confusion of extensional and intensional readings: "So it can truthfully be said that the whole theory of syllogism could be demonstrated from the theory *de continente et contento*, of container and contained" (486). But then Leibniz goes on to qualify the idea of containment: "The latter [the relation of container and contained] is different from that of whole and part, for the whole is always greater than the part, but the container and the contained are sometimes equal, as happens with reciprocal propositions" (486).

This seemingly arbitrary distinction between "part-whole" and "container-contained" is crucial here and differentiates Leibniz's approach to what is only implicit in Aristotle but explicit in later algebraic interpretations of Aristotle's logic. The relation of "inclusion" is meant as reflexive in the way found in the arithmetical relation of "less than or equal to" (symbolized by '$\leq$') holding between two numbers, while "is part of" is treated like "less than," which is not reflexive: 3 is less than or equal to itself but not less than itself. In Leibniz's distinction, while a whole cannot be a part of itself, a "container" can contain itself.

It is in relation to this that Leibniz is sometimes thought to anticipate a more "geometric" alternative to that of class inclusion, the algebra of "partially ordered sets" underlying modern "lattice" or "semilattice" structures (e.g., Swoyer 1994, 25), modeled on sets of numbers that are ordered according to the relation of "less than or equal to" ('≤'), a relation characteristic of geometrical continua. In later algebraic logic, it would be Peirce who would explicitly introduce the binary relation that is generally denoted by the symbol '≤.' While applying paradigmatically to numbers, this "less than or equal to" relation can be generalized beyond numbers to capture binary relations between entities that are transitive, anti-symmetric, and reflexive. This idea of an entity having this type of "reflexive" self-relation is the type of idea that Hegel would identify as distinctly modern—a feature of modern mathematics that seems to correspond to the special role of "singularity" found in algebra and in modern thought more generally.

Leibniz's logical writings were never presented in a unified or systematic form; what is found there is really only an array of suggestive hints, the power of which has only been recently recognized. Moreover, they are not often discussed in relation to the "geometric" alternative that he also presented to Descartes's analytic approach, his *analysis situs*. To help see the type of possibilities unleashed by his overall approach it might be useful to look to the example provided by one of Leibniz's eighteenth-century followers, the Swiss mathematician Johann Heinrich Lambert, referred to at the time as the "Alsatian Leibniz" (Basso 2010). Lambert himself would anticipate some of the developments of nineteenth-century projective geometry and would be involved in disputes with Hegel's effective logic teacher, Gottfried Ploucquet, over the development of Leibniz's ideas.

5.2 The Cosmology of an Alsatian Leibniz—J. H. Lambert

Lambert is now often known for his role as a correspondent of Kant during the years of the gestation of Kant's critical philosophy, but Lambert's views were widely known and discussed in the eighteenth century. There are certainly many reasons to assume that Hegel would have been familiar with Lambert's views—most prominently, perhaps, was that Lambert had coined the term *Phänomenologie*, appropriated by Hegel for his own *Phänomenologie des Geistes* (*Phenomenology of Spirit*). But Lambert had also been involved in a very public dispute with the Tübingen logician and philosopher Gottfried Ploucquet over the development of Leibniz's logic (Lemanski 2017, 58–63),[12] and connected to this dispute had been Lambert's own project of pursuing a type of alternative to Euclidean geometry with many of the features of projective geometry (Andersen 2007, ch. 12).

If Leibniz's approach to the redetermination of experience can be described as Copernican, Lambert's views as expressed in his *Cosmological Letters on the*

Arrangement of the World-Edifice of 1760 (Lambert 1976) might be described as bringing out the *hyper*-Copernican consequences implicit in Leibniz himself. To the astronomer Tobias Mayer he would write: "I do not believe that one can become more Copernican than I have become in these letters" (Jaki 1976, 20). In the *Letters* Lambert writes that "insofar as Copernicus made the first step, there remains for us and for our descendants still a thousand other steps to take and even then we shall not be perfectly Copernican by a long shot" (Lambert 1976, 175).

Lambert speaks of the adoption of the Copernican "idiom" or "language," which is able to be translated into "the ordinary tongue" (176), and speculates on the language that might be spoken by astronomers who lived on the moon: "Their ordinary language sounds as if the moon had no motion at all. But since they constantly see the earth at the same spot of their sky, the earth has to appear to them as completely or almost completely motionless, or having no other motion that the one which it seems to have around its axis." Just as astronomers on earth have learned to translate their natural language into a language in which the earth is described as moving around the sun, the astronomers on the moon would learn to speak in a new way in which the moon is described as rotating around the earth. However, "the moon would have to let both the moon and the earth move around the sun, and on the basis of this twofold analogy they could doubt for good reasons the resting of the sun and would in the end stir everything from rest" (176). In fact, this was the analogy that Lambert himself drew concerning the structure of the universe. Just as the planets revolve around the sun, the sun itself forms part of a cluster with other suns that all rotate around some central body, and that body in turn, along with other similar bodies, rotates around a further massive central body, the result being the galaxy to which we belong, the Milky Way. And the process is reiterated, the Milky Way along with other galaxies rotating around a further massive central body, this being repeated for perhaps a thousand steps.[13]

Lambert's cosmology gives us a good example of the possibilities opened up by the hyper-Copernican idea of a continual reiteration of the initial Copernican reversal, forming a type of indefinite continuous geometrical progression: moon : earth :: earth : sun :: sun : some further central body, and so on. In climbing Lambert's ladder of languages, one moves from some determinate cognition to the higher step positing the condition of that cognition, and then to the further condition of the condition of the original cognition, and so on, just as Leibniz had talked of reiterating the process of reason giving, giving a series of "reasons for reasons" (Leibniz 1989a, 28).

Ascent via such a series of languages or conditions invites the picture of ascent up a conceptual ladder—a scaling of Plato's diairetic pyramid so as to achieve some more comprehensive point of view. But why stop at a "thousand steps"? As to the telos of such an ascent, Leibniz could invoke the medieval concept of knowledge expressed in the language of God, as found in Ockham, for example (Ockham 1980), and as reconceived later by Galileo as the language of mathematics. In the Bible, the image of a ladder leading all the way to heaven had come to Jacob in a dream, but in the *Critique of Pure Reason* (Kant 1998, A321–332/B377–389), Kant would envisage a logically articulated ladder for the mind's "analytic" ascent of "prosyllogistic chains" as leading only to a comprehensive view of appearances rather than to any God's-eye view of things in themselves. From Kant's point of view, Leibniz had failed to grasp the depth of the limitations of our cognitive lives, but Hegel's critique was of a different nature. Images such as these all suffered the same indeterminacy as that found in an unconstrained geometric series. Leibniz himself, however, had already shown concerns about such epistemic structures in relation to the type of "analytic" origins of his own logic.

5.3 Leibniz's Own Geometric Alternative to Philosophical Arithmetic: The Idea of an *Analysis Situs*

At times, Leibniz expressed concerns about Descartes's analytic geometry and opposed to it an envisaged alternative nonquantitative form of "analysis" for geometry that he called an *analysis situs*, an analysis of situation (De Risi 2007), an approach to the analysis of space that was clearly in conformity with his distinctive holistic and relational approach (Redding 2009, ch. 1.3). As noted earlier, both Carnot and Grassmann would describe their respective forms of geometric analysis as a Leibniz-inspired "geometry of position" (Carnot 1803a, i–ii; Grassmann 1995, 317–318). Leibniz would return to the idea of an *analysis situs* intermittently up until his death but never really developed it; however, the idea would have consequences for the development of both geometry and logic in the nineteenth century.

Toward the end of his stay in Paris in the 1670s Leibniz had started to discuss this form of analysis, by which he seems to have had in mind an attempt, in a type of "holistic" or "structural" way, to render each element determinate in terms of its relatedness to other elements in the structure. This can be understood as a move in the conception of mathematics away from that of science of quantity to include notions of order. It seems to have been meant to counter the shortcomings that Leibniz had come to attribute to Descartes's effective arithmetization of geometry, and so it marked a limited move back to the Greek "geometric algebra," with geometry being given at least parity status to arithmetic with the nonreducibility of continuous to discrete magnitudes. At the same time, it promised a way beyond the hard dichotomy of a stark choice between geometric algebra and the analytic geometry of Descartes and Fermat as providing some ultimate framework for investigation of the world. Others besides Carnot and Grassmann would draw inspiration from this project. In the eighteenth century, Leonhard Euler would give the title *geometria situs* to what would later be called "topology,"[14] the geometry of continuous multidimensional surfaces. Toward the end of the nineteenth century, the French mathematician Henri Poincaré would create the discipline of algebraic topology, the application of algebra to topology, referring to his project as an *analysis situs*.

Descartes's analytic geometry had initially been met with resistance on the part of those who believed Euclidean geometry, with its axiomatic proof structure, to be more rigorously grounded than the newer algebra. Newton himself had harbored such concerns, these being related to his retention of the broadly geometric framework for his celestial mechanics and his reluctance to apply within his *Philosophiæ Naturalis Principia Mathematica* the calculus that he had earlier invented. Here, Leibniz was generally on the side of the algebraists, but this was tempered by a degree of resistance that also suggested the ineliminability of geometry. Thus, like Descartes's analytical geometry, the idea of an *analysis situs* represented a fundamentally modern transformation of the traditional Euclidean approach, while at the same time resisting a Cartesian-style reduction of continuous to discrete magnitudes. As one historian of this process has put it, Leibniz's version signaled a "new relation between algebra and geometry" such that "the evolution of the two fields was henceforth intrinsically linked in a dialectical process" (Dorier 1995, 237). This idea would, in fact, drive much progress in mathematics through the nineteenth century, with the reemergence of projective geometry after Carnot and Grassmann's linked theory of linear extension, and, as we have seen, it is clearly expressed in Hegel's explicit comments on the relations of geometry to arithmetic.

The modernity of Leibniz's approach can be discerned in his conception of geometry as the science of space. Euclidean geometry, it is usually said, had been conceived as the science of spatial figures—figures able to be constructed with ruler and compass, lines, triangles, hexagons, circles, and so on. As we know, the conception of space itself—space considered as a void—was largely foreign to the thought of Aristotle, for whom such a conception of empty space was literally "nothing," and thus had no properties, such as extension.[15] From an Aristotelian perspective, then, there could therefore be no "science of space" itself. In contrast, the Stoics had argued in favor of the idea of "void space," and similar notions had appeared in late Neoplatonists such as Proclus, but the problematic nature of this notion persisted into the early modern period. As the historian of science Edward Grant noted (Grant 1981), during this period there was indeed "much ado about nothing," that is, about void space. Newton, for example, who needed the conception of void space, argued that space was a nonmaterial substance, in fact the extension of an immaterial but nevertheless infinitely extended God (Grant 1981, 244). It was this absolute conception of space that Leibniz had contested in his correspondence with the Newtonian Samuel Clarke (Redding 2009, ch. 1). Connected to a relational account of space, Leibniz's idea of a situational geometry seems to have offered to provide him with a way of making spatial relations determinate in a way that did not raise the problems raised by Newton's theologically derived idea of absolute space.

In the context of projective geometry this relational theory of space would be expressed in terms of the idea of "projective" correlations among differently aligned planar figures. In turn, this would introduce an alternate way of understanding the significance of Cartesian coordinates in analytic geometry. From Newton's absolutist perspective as represented by Clarke, point-like locations in space could themselves be thought of as absolutely determined, with space thought of as constituted by an infinite totality of such points. Thus, with the new concept of number that had been introduced by Stevin and Descartes, space could be conceived as a type of infinite and continuous three-dimensional version of the coordinated plane of Cartesian geometry, in which each point was isomorphic with an ordered sequence of, now, three "real" numbers. As with Newton's earlier identification of infinite space with God, this complete arithmetization of space could allow its conception as both infinite and having determinate locations. Leibniz's opposed holistic or relational conception of space, however, would deny that any *point* could have any such absolute location, each point gaining its identity in relation to other points. Cartesian coordinates could be still employed, but in a way analogous to the way in which coordinates had been employed in Greek geometry, by being generated in relation to determinate geometric figures. Later, with the development of Grassmann's vector analysis, coordinates could be introduced as "base vectors" in terms of which the magnitude of other vectors could be measured. But these base vectors would themselves be subject to the types of transformations applicable to the vectors measured by such base vectors. Such coordinates could not measure absolutely.

Part of Leibniz's resistance to the Cartesian reduction of geometric figures to algebraic equations seems to have been that, like the Greeks, he thought that geometry could not be eliminated because of its role in the determination of arithmetical entities (De Risi 2018, 249). However, exactly what Leibniz had in mind with the term *analysis situs* has remained unclear. Without sciences such as topology or vector analysis existing in Leibniz's time, it is difficult to simply identify what he meant by *analysis situs* by invoking them. The projective geometry of Desargues and Pascal, however, the form of geometry that would be reinvented by Carnot, did exist, and Leibniz himself knew of it and seems to have been particularly influenced by it. Indeed, Leibniz had possessed the letter in which the precocious sixteen-year-old Pascal had set out a major theorem of projective geometry ("Pascal's theorem") that he had discovered (Mesnard 1978). Given Leibniz's "Copernican" attention to the idea of reflection upon the conditions of perspectivally constrained perceptual knowledge, projective geometry surely would have recommended itself to him, as it had to his Alsatian follower Lambert (Andersen 2007, ch. 12).

Leibniz's idea of an *analysis situs* was discussed during the eighteenth century. As we have noted, Kant, for example, invoked it in his essay of 1768, "Concerning the Ultimate Ground of the Differentiation of Directions in Space." Hegel may have known of it through this, but he probably would have been familiar with the associated mathematical idea of "points at infinity" introduced by Kepler in 1604 (Field and Gray 1984, appendix 4), in whose views he seems to have taken a particular interest since his time at Tübingen (Paterson 2005, 73).[16]

With the idea of parallel lines *meeting* at infinity, projective geometry had removed a restriction found in Euclidean geometry to the idea that any two lines can be conceived as intersecting.[17] It is not coincidental, then, that Lambert is now recognized as having challenged Euclid's "parallel postulate" in a way that anticipated the non-Euclidean geometries of the nineteenth century (Ewald 1996, vol. 1, ch. 5). These issues had thus been in the air at the end of the eighteenth century when Hegel was in the process of shaping those ideas that would go on to define him as a philosopher in the nineteenth. It is significant in this regard that J. K. F. Hauff, with whom Hegel could possibly have been associated around the end of the 1790s, had gone on to become a professor of mathematics at the University of Marburg and was known for his work on the "theory of parallels" (Halsted 1896, 105).

5.4 Lambert's Geometry of Thought and Hegel's Critique

From the 1750s Lambert had developed ideas in relation to the geometry of perspective that bore similarities to the projective geometry to be revived in the nineteenth century. According to Kirsti Andersen (Andersen 2007, ch. 12), although his anticipation of various projective theorems would be later acknowledged by Poncelet in the 1820s, Lambert's work seems to have had little effect on the later revival of projective geometry. Some of these works would remain unpublished, and the published ones would remain largely unnoticed. Where his works were appreciated it was in the context of their practical application, as in perspectival painting, rather than in strictly scientific circles.

In these works, Lambert had been concerned with the way that spatial arrangements in a horizontal plane were projected onto a vertical plane, as in a landscape projected onto the plane of an artist's canvas. He apparently did not know of the work of Desargues (Field and Gray 1987, 42), and called his geometry *Linealgeometrie*, literally "ruler geometry," since, as in projective geometry, all constructions could be carried out with a ruler alone, without the compass typical of Euclidean geometry. Also as in projective geometry, Lambert used the ideas of an "eye point" or viewpoint, and points at infinity called "vanishing points" that could be conceived as lying on a *Grenzlinie*, a limit-line. He also made use of the idea of converging straight lines being "perspectively parallel" as well as that of any triangle being able to be understood as a perspective transformation of an equilateral triangle. However, he did not pursue the search for invariances across projections that would be central to nineteenth-century projective geometry, the context within which the harmonic cross-ratio would be so significant.

While Lambert's work on the geometry of perspective may not have been widely appreciated in scientific circles, there are reasons why this may not have been the case with respect to students at the Tübingen Seminary in the last decades of the eighteenth century. Lambert had been involved in a very public precedence dispute with Gottfried Ploucquet, the logic and metaphysics master there, over the use of "Euler diagrams" in logic (Lemanski 2017, 58–63). The dispute, however, was not restricted to the issue of precedence, as both disagreed over how to interpret the logical calculus of Leibniz, which they both adopted and developed. For his part, Ploucquet had denied the possibility that any universal calculus or characteristic could be appropriate for finite beings such as ourselves, as it presupposed a type of knowledge inaccessible to such beings (Lu Adler 2017, 43).[18] In contrast, Lambert in his *Neues Organon* used both geometric and algebraic signs to represent thoughts and conceived of a universal algebraic language akin to Leibniz's universal characteristic to supply, as it were, semantic content for the formulae of that calculus (43).

Hegel was certainly familiar with Lambert's work and in *The Science of Logic* is explicitly critical of his project of giving a mathematical notation to logic "based on lines, figures and the like, the general intention being to elevate—or in fact rather to debase—the logical modes of relation to the status of a *calculus*" (SL, 544; 12:47). His savage critique seems to add to the arguments of those who deny that mathematical logic could be significant for Hegel's project of logic. As Hegel points out, "Since the human being has in language a means of designation that is appropriate to reason, it is otiose to look for a less perfect means of representation to bother oneself with.... It is futile to want to fix it by means of spatial figures and algebraic signs for the sake of the *outer eye* and a *non-conceptual, mechanical manipulation,* such as a *calculus*" (545–546; 12:48). But exactly what is the target of Hegel's critique here? One thing seems certain: Hegel is clearly against the aspiration of Lambert's geometric calculus to the status of a *characteristica universalis.* To a certain extent, Hegel's critique more or less repeats Ploucquet's criticisms of the project of the construction of a universal language as found in both Lambert and Leibniz, but I suggest it is nevertheless not the same.[19]

Since Ockham there had been a common theological view that God thinks in a logically perspicuous language that might be considered as the ideal to which we finite beings aspire. Lambert's moon-dwelling astronomers needing to learn the language of earthlings, who in turn would need to learn the language of inhabitants of the sun and so on, might be thought of as one way of conceiving of the relation of finite perspectival languages to some infinite aperspectival one. Lambert's series of new languages to be learned really just presents us with a linguistic analogue of Leibniz's imagery of ascent up the Platonic ladder, at each step of which one postulates, in a Copernican way, the conditions that might hold for the experience of the world to be had from the rung below. Kant, however, put an end to such optimistic imagery, putting an infinite distance, not Lambert's very great cosmological distance (his "thousand steps"), between ourselves and our ideal destination. For Kant, our inability to ascend the Platonic/Jacobian ladder to some ultimate god's-eye view or divine language is based in our absolute finitude separated by an infinite gap from God's absolutely infinite nature. Ploucquet's criticism of Lambert thus seems akin to Kant's criticism of Leibniz, but Hegel, I suggest, refused this dichotomy, and so too the image of the relation of human to divine nature on which it was based. The universal characteristic is a flawed model for logic read either optimistically, as the, at least in principle, achievable divine perspective, as with Leibniz or Lambert, or pessimistically, as forever out of our grasp, as with Kant or Ploucquet. But this criticism need not flow over entirely into the idea of a logical calculus per se. Indeed, as rector of the high school at Nuremberg, prior to using his own logic text, Hegel appears to have used the logical calculi of Lambert and Ploucquet for upper high school instruction in introduction to philosophy courses.[20]

The idea of "base vectors" in vector analysis would free this form of analysis from any presupposed absolute metric, and, as we will see below (chapter 8), certain proponents of the use of logical calculi in the nineteenth century would similarly object to any idea of a universal logical language, of the sort that, in the spirit of Leibniz, was being proposed by Gottlob Frege. For example, W. E. Johnson (presumably unknowingly) would essentially repeat Hegel's criticisms of Lambert in arguing that, as the use of any formal logical calculus depended on the use of human reasoning and human language for its interpretation, human language itself could not in turn be reduced to such a calculus (Johnson 1892, 3). Moreover, in the spirit of Johnson and his colleague John Venn, Hegel, in an address as rector at the Nuremberg Gymnasium, would point to the benefits for spiritual developments of engaging with "alienated" concepts that have been "divorced" from their immediate spiritual content, as when the learner of a foreign language has to start with memorizing mechanically combined meaningless sounds (*Misc*, 296–297).[21] In order to determine Hegel's actual attitude to the relevance of mathematics to logical thinking, this is perhaps an appropriate place to examine exactly what Hegel *does* say about the status of mathematics, and especially geometry, in those passages in *The Science of Logic*'s penultimate chapter, "The Idea of Cognition," alluded to by Brady Bowman, in which geometry is treated as "the highest form of finite theoretical cognition" (Bowman 2013, 170).

Consistently, the attitude that Hegel expresses toward the relevance of mathematics for philosophy mirrors the view that Aristotle had attributed to Plato: numbers and geometrical figures are not themselves objects of philosophical cognition, as had been thought by the Pythagoreans, but have more the status of "intermediaries," which help when raising the mind to higher things. It is thus no coincidence that the discussion of mathematical "theorems" in "The Idea of Cognition" leads into "The Idea of the Good," the idea to which mathematical intermediaries lead for Plato. As Aristotle was apparently fond of recounting, Athenians who had gone to a lecture Plato was to deliver, "On the Good," had come away frustrated because Plato had spent most of the lecture discussing mathematics.[22]

As we have seen, for Hegel, numbers are born from practices concerned with countable worldly things, but number itself "is not an object of the senses, and to be occupied with number and numerical combinations is not the business of the senses; such an occupation, therefore, encourages spirit to engage in reflection and the inner work of abstraction" (*SL*, 181; 21:207). However, calculating with numbers relies on the manipulation of empirical objects—dots, fingers, written symbols, and so on. This affords arithmetic an ambivalent status: it is "of great, though one-sided, importance. For, on the other hand, since the basis of number is only an external, thoughtless difference, the occupation proceeds without a concept, mechanically" (181;

21:207). The very same applies to geometry. Like numbers, geometric objects are not objects of the senses, for "the determinations of space that are its subject matter are already abstract objects" (724; 12:226). And yet, like numbers, geometric objects rely on physical phenomena such as diagrams that are able to be applied to the empirical world, such that "the intuitive character that geometry possesses because of its still sensuous material only gives to it that level of evidence that the senses generally provide to thoughtless spirit" (724–725; 12:226).[23] In short, space is not itself empirical, but "it is only because the space of geometry is the abstract emptiness of externality that it is possible for figures to be drawn in its indeterminateness in such a way that their determinations remain perfectly at rest outside one another with no immanent transition to the opposite" (725; 12:226).

For the Greeks, the activity of reflecting on the nature of number, *arithmos*, had separated from the simple use of numbers in practical life, *logistikos* (Klein 1968, pt. 1), and had created a theoretical practice that provided a place for the conceptual process in which these theoretical objects transitioned into their opposites. The very concept of what a number was, for example, had been transformed under the pressure of the original discovery of the incommensurability of discrete and continuous magnitudes. Here, we may surely ask, would such a process have been possible without numbers having been written down or geometric diagrams drawn, allowing early geometers to come up with their axioms and theorems? Figures can be drawn in that "abstract emptiness of externality," and once drawn, they are there as empirical objects "perfectly at rest outside one another with no immanent transition to the opposite" (*SL*, 725; 12:226), allowing the reflection upon them that generates contradictions. Thus, immediately after, Hegel goes on to suggest that it is just that externalization that allows the discovery of phenomena such as incommensurability that will drive the conceptual process of redetermination. "Now, since the delineation of these [geometric] figures commences from different aspects and principles, and the various figures fall into place of themselves, in the comparison of these figures their qualitative unlikeness and incommensurability come into view. Geometry is thus driven, beyond the finitude within which it advanced step by step orderly and securely, to infinity—to the positing as equal of such as are qualitatively diverse. Here it loses the evidence that it derived from being otherwise based on fixed finitude without having to deal with the concept and the transition to the opposite which is its manifestation" (725; 12:226).

The incommensurability encountered within mathematical practice, I have been suggesting, was for Hegel grounded in the fundamental identity within difference between discrete and continuous magnitudes. If this then drives geometry beyond finitude to "infinity," might we not think of a comparable incommensurability within the logical realm to similarly drive "formal logic" to infinity, as long as that formal logic is properly conceived? To follow up this thought it is necessary to take up Hegel's attitude toward the most developed form of logic of his age—Leibniz's algebraized version of Aristotle's geometric logic.

6

Hegel's Supersession of Leibniz and Newton: The Limitations of Calculus and Logical Calculus

> Hegel is often regarded as a philosopher who did not take mathematics very seriously. The fact that he devoted a substantial portion of *The Science of Logic* to the infinitesimal calculus speaks to the contrary.
> JOHN L. BELL, *The Continuous, the Discrete, and the Infinitesimal in Philosophy and Mathematics*

When Leibniz relies upon the type of equivalence or interchangeability between "intensional" and "extensional" readings of judgment/equations (Leibniz 1996, 486), we might think of him as consciously accepting what Aristotle had simply assumed—that the categories were simultaneously categories applying to things themselves, on the one hand, and to *thought* about things, on the other. In the *Jäsche Logic*, Kant would repeat the idea of an inverse relation between intension (*Inhalt*) and extension (*Umfang*):

> Every concept, *as partial concept*, is contained in the representation of things; as *ground of cognition*, i.e., *as mark*, these things are contained *under* it. In the former respect every concept has a *content*, in the other an *extension*.
> The content and extension of a concept stand in inverse relation [*in umgekehrten Verhältnis*] to one another. The more a concept contains *under* itself, namely, the less it contains *in* itself, and conversely. (Kant 1992c, §7)

But Kant's account of this inverse relation would be complicated by the fact that his critical philosophy was based upon a break with Leibniz's way of thinking of how objects were contained, or, in Hegel's language, "subsumed," under concepts. For this task, Kant would introduce a distinct type of nonconceptual cognition, the intuition, the singularity of which would demarcate it from the necessary generality of concepts. This nexus of the three-way relation between Leibniz, Ploucquet, and Kant provides the context within which Hegel's subjective logic might be best approached.

6.1 Reactions to Leibnizian Hyper-Copernicanism: Kant and Ploucquet

It was the reciprocity of intensional and extensional readings of judgments that underlay Leibniz's use of two interchangeable conceptions of reference to specific individuals. In order to give judgments about individuals a proper place within Aristotle's syllogistic, Leibniz had followed earlier nominalist logicians by conceiving of singular judgments on the model of universal judgments. As universal judgments from an Aristotelian perspective could be regarded as referring to kinds, a judgment about Socrates from this perspective could, given the new individualization of essences, be thought of as referring to Socrates as a type of singular universal or individual essence—the medievalists' *haecceity*.[1] But Leibniz also adapted the particular judgment form for this purpose as well, and this would allow a contrasting intensional reference to Socrates.[2] From this perspective, just as the concept <philosopher> could be thought of as referring to philosophers in general, the range of its reference could be reduced by "adding" further specifying concepts, as in producing the concept <Athenian philosopher>, say. Add enough specifying concepts and one can eventually limit the class of philosophers one has in mind down to one. For example, one might form the concept <Athenian philosopher, executed by his fellow citizens for allegedly corrupting the youth of Athens>, and so uniquely pick out Socrates. This could stand as an early template for Russell's famous "description theory of proper names" (Russell 1905). But what if concepts that are added together in acceptable ways produce a "definite description" for which there are *no* instantiations? We might, after all, have just as easily combined concepts in a rule-governed way to produce a description "Athenian philosopher who was crowned king for his role in the Peloponnesian Wars."

As Lenzen has pointed out, the Leibnizian answer to this is that what is picked out is the metaphysically problematic entity of a possible person: "For Leibniz, the *extension* of a predicate A is not just the set of all *existing* individuals that (happen to) fall under concept A, but rather the set of all *possible* individuals that have that property" (Lenzen 2004, 16). In short, for Leibniz the "extension" of a term could not be limited to the entities of the actual world but must extend to the realm of other merely possible worlds, and with this had arisen a modal status not found in Aristotle—that of mere logical possibility. Merely possible non-beings would come to find an indispensable role in modern thought akin to the indispensable "impossible numbers" found there as well (Nagel 1979). Forming a hypothesis about, say, the possible viral origins of a new illness is now generally thought to represent a stage within scientific inquiry, and the hypothesis has to be regarded as meaningful even if such a virus turns out not to exist.

For Aristotle possibilities had been potentialities in the sense that, as from the point of view of Aristotle's biology, human semen contains potential human individuals. In contrast, Leibniz's use of possibility seems to be more connected to the propositional logics of the Stoics within which the conditional sat more easily than it did within Aristotle's syllogistic (Bobzien 2020). Consequently, Leibniz's algebraization of logic seems to have reversed the relation between actuality and possibility as found in Aristotle. Actual individuals belong to a world that, for various reasons having to do with various features of it in relation to necessary features of the God that created it (his infinite goodness and so on), is a world that, from an infinite set of possible worlds, has been chosen because it is the best of those possible worlds.

We might then say that Leibniz's two devices for picking out individuals—one that adapts the traditional universal quantifier and one that adapts the particular quantifier—are analogous to the use of constants and variables in algebra, respectively. The former picks out directly a concrete specific individual, Socrates, for example. However, when one picks out Socrates by the combination of concepts, <Athenian philosopher, executed by his fellow citizens for allegedly corrupting the youth of Athens>, one is first identifying an abstract possibility, and then "subsuming" an actual individual (if that individual exists) under that abstract conceptualization. Following Leibniz, Ploucquet would employ a similar type of distinction between ways of picking out an object with his distinction between "exclusive" and "comprehensive" forms of particularity (Ploucquet 2006, §§14–15).[3] Following Ploucquet, Hegel would adopt it, but for Hegel, the interchangeability of these terms found in Leibniz would be constrained in important ways that had to be reflected in logic itself. We will examine this in more detail in later chapters (chapters 9 and 10), but the basic principles involved are relatively straightforward.

It is clear that one may infer a particular judgment from a singular judgment—what is now known as the rule of "existential generalization." If one knows that Socrates was killed for supposedly corrupting the youth of Athens, then one knows that someone was killed for supposedly corrupting the youth of Athens. Working within an epistemic environment as idealist logics standardly do, this inference is one way, however. One may know that somebody was killed in this way, but not know who. There are occasions, however, when something like the reverse of this inference is appropriate. If from the forensic evidence it becomes clear that Jennifer's apparent suicide was in fact a case of murder, the detectives come to know that some actual person killed her; they just do not know which one. Putting a proper name to this "somebody" ("existential instantiation") now becomes the task of their inquiry. They start narrowing down the class of individuals who fit a list of very particular characteristics (had a motive, was in the vicinity at the time, and so on).

For Kant, using logic to reason about the actual world would send him in the direction of differentiating "general logic" as a logic of concepts of possible objects from "transcendental logic" as a logic for the cognition of actual objects, actual objects being accounted for by the role played by a new type of cognition that Kant had introduced, singular empirical intuitions. Without making such a distinction, Kant believed, Leibniz had been led into the types of contradictions that he pointed to as the "Antinomies of Pure Reason." Hegel had learned these Kantian lessons of the contradiction-generating problems of Leibniz's logic but attempted to resolve them in ways that resembled but differed from the solution that Kant offered in terms of his fixed distinction between intuitions and concepts as opposing species of cognitions.

Effectively, Hegel would employ a solution with which Kant had flirted in the 1760s prior to his transition to the critical philosophy and in the context in which he discussed negative magnitudes in terms of opposed directed line segments. It is the distinction between two types of predications we have alluded to above, and that can be found in Aristotle between the strict logic applicable indifferently to members of kinds and the less precise practical logic that could be applied to judgments about actual individuals. This was the distinction Hegel attempted to capture in terms of that between predication understood as "subsumption," on the one hand, and as "inherence," on the other. These were issues that were apparent within Ploucquet's way of addressing Leibniz's attempts to incorporate singularity into the Aristotelian syllogistic.

When Lenzen writes that Leibniz first establishes his class-based system as "based upon" the propositional calculus, I take it that he means that the whole business of coming up with intensional and extensional classes starts with a consideration of propositions in the sense that both classes would seem to develop from initial acts of classifying entities into groups—that is, of making basic judgments. The idea of a class of animals grouped in virtue of having a heart is presumably meant to have come about by a process involving judgments of the sort *This animal has a heart, so does this animal, this one too,* and so on. Thus, in *New Essays*, Theophilus (representing Leibniz) explains to Philalethes the essential role of general terms in language. If speaking of individual things, were we to have only proper names to apply to them "we would not be able to say anything. . . . But if by 'particular things' you mean the lowest species (*species infimae*), then, apart from the fact that it is often difficult to determine them, it is obvious that they are themselves universals, *founded on similarity*" (Leibniz 1996, 275, emphasis added).

Lenzen's criticism of the circularity involved in Leibniz's idea of an initial classification founded on similarity effectively repeats Aristotle's criticism of Plato's diairetic method considered as a method of discovery in the *Prior Analytics* (Aristotle 1989, *Prior Analytics*, 46a32–46b38). Plato had spoken somewhat loosely of a procedure of "collection" (*synagoge*) in which things "scattered about everywhere" are collected into "one kind" allowing a type of definition (Plato 1997, *Phaedrus*, 265d). But this presupposes that we already know which things to add to the collection and which things to omit, and does this not presuppose the diairetic division of genera into species as already in place?[4] But Hegel would be concerned with the threat to empirical content attendant on such a response to the problem of circularity facing the idea of perceptually based judgments. Propositional logic holds not for simple classes of actual things but for classes of possible things, with actual things becoming located in presupposed spaces of possibilities.

In transitional essays of the 1760s prior to his "critical turn" and its impermeable distinction between concepts and intuitions (Kant 1992a, 1992b), Kant would put his criticism of Leibniz in a different way that would be closer to that developed later by Hegel with his distinction between the two forms of predication within judgments (Wolff 1999). There Kant had differentiated between dual judgment types in terms of the different ways that negation is handled in each. With the *Critique of Pure Reason*, however, Kant would replace this with the generalized concept-intuition distinction, and the distinction between these two judgment types would become problematic, although remnants of it would continue to play a role.[5] Hegel in contrast would consistently refuse to go down the path of a homogeneous judgment form, the modern version of which would annihilate the type of kind distinctions that allowed judgments to be applied to the world—a mathematical model for such an annihilation of kind distinctions we have seen in Leibniz's great mathematical invention, the calculus. For Hegel, judgments must show and retain dual forms, and, as in Kant in the 1760s, these dual forms would be differentiated by the types of negation (internal and external) characteristic of each, a duality that would disrupt the classical laws of logic.

According to Lenzen, while Leibniz was aware of the fundamental distinction between term and propositional negation, he had trouble not confusing them (Lenzen 2004, 17–18), a feature that is not surprising given his general thesis of the simple interchangeability of intensional and extensional interpretations of judgments. Here we might follow Lenzen's account of Leibniz transitions between simple categorical judgments and properly propositional ones.

First, Leibniz subjects the traditional square of opposition to the following transformations: the E-judgment "No As are B" is converted into the judgment "All As are *non-B*," such that the A- and E-judgments are now opposed by their term-negated predicates. This was a type of conversion appropriated from medieval logic. Next, the I-judgment "Some As are B" would be regarded as the external or propositional negation of the newly described E-judgment, resulting in external "not" being applied to "Every A is non-B" to produce "It is not the case that every A is non-B." Lenzen now describes Leibniz's mature concept calculus as growing out of three transformations of this syllogistic starting point. The first drops the quantified aspects of the subject terms—"Every A is B" becomes simple "A is B" or "A contains B" (Lenzen 2004, 14–15). This results from treating extensional and intensional readings of a judgment as equivalent. Next, he introduces the idea of conceptual addition described above, combining concepts such as A and B into A $\oplus$ B. Finally, he disregards the syllogistic limitation of premises to two, introducing the idea of a longer set of premises.[6]

The details here are complex, but a fundamental outcome of these changes was to allow Leibniz to transfer the idea of containment that operates at the level of the relations between subject and predicate within a judgment, as when "A is B" is understood intensionally as "A contains B," to the relation of implication that relates a judgment or set of judgments, on the one hand, the premises, to a further judgment, the conclusion, on the other. That is, the syllogism is understood as the conclusion being somehow contained in the list of premises. Using Greek letters for propositions, we might write that A is B = $\alpha \supset \beta$. That is, a categorical assertion like "Humans are animals" is given the form of an implication along the lines "Being a human implies being an animal" or "If something is a human, then it is an animal."

Leibniz's various attempts to translate a class calculus into a propositional one would place great pressures on the presupposed "arithmetic," however. Although he described the determination of individuals as involving a process of conceptual addition, as we have seen, the inferential relations between propositions were best captured by the idea that a concept was determined as the product of its component concepts (Leibniz 1966, 17). This was one problem accompanying the conflation of the categories that Hegel, following Ploucquet, would distinguish as singular and particular. To think of a specific individual, Socrates, as both brave and wise, might be to think of bravery and wisdom as both "inhering" in him in an "additive" way. However, if Socrates is grasped as just "some or other" possible individual "subsumed" under the concepts <brave> and <wise>, then he might best be thought of as an instance of the product of these concepts. Both forms of determination would come together in Leibniz's idea that every individual had a "complete concept." On this view, that I am sitting at my desk, typing on this keyboard at this very moment, must be as much part of my concept as my being a human being, for example, and in this sense, any property predicated of me will ultimately be, in Kant's terminology, "analytic" rather than "synthetic," and any proposition will be a matter of extracting the predicate from the subject considered as a complex concept. When this type of "philosophical arithmetic" would be rediscovered in the nineteenth century with the work of George Boole, such issues would come to be addressed in a more self-conscious and explicit way.

Boole would repeat Leibniz's attempt to derive a calculus of propositions from the starting point of a calculus of classes, although Boole would start from an explicitly extensional interpretation, and the problems inherent in this approach would be worked on by algebraists like Jevons, Peirce, Venn, Johnson, and Schröder. Of the algebraists, it would be MacColl who would conceive of the propositional calculus as nonderivative in a way that resulted in a distinct form of modal logic that, I will suggest, resembles Hegel's. Here, however, let us remind ourselves of the two eighteenth-century critical responses sketched above, those of Kant and Ploucquet. Kant's official response, as we have seen, was his critical philosophy as it developed from 1770 onward, with its dichotomy between two structurally different forms of cognition—intuition and concept—although he had earlier played with a distinction based on different judgment structures differentiated by their different treatments of negation. Ploucquet's would remain closer to the framework of Leibniz and attempt to work with the distinction of two types of referential mechanisms, exclusive and comprehensive particularity, resulting in different judgment types akin to those found in Kant's transitional work of the 1760s. However, Ploucquet would argue that the cost of this was the need to abandon the Leibnizian dream of a univocal "universal characteristic," thus aligning himself with those later algebraic logicians who would develop Leibniz's calculus ratiocinator at the expense of his *characteristica universalis*.[7]

Within this general framework we might sharpen Hegel's location by focusing on similarities between his critique of Leibniz's logical calculus, on the one hand, and his differential and integral calculus, on the other.

6.2 Hegel on Newton's Celestial Mechanics and the Role of the Calculus

Differential and integral calculus, or simply "the calculus," is usually described as having been invented by Newton and Leibniz during the second half of the seventeenth century, leading to a fierce priority dispute. In retrospect, while each seemed to have worked largely independently, both drew on a considerable body of mathematical techniques that had been developed by others from earlier in that century, including, crucially, Descartes's analytic geometry, as well as on techniques that dated back to the Greeks, including Euclidean geometry, of course, but especially ideas developed by Eudoxus and Archimedes (Heath 1897). The recent developments in algebra in particular had arisen in relation to the needs of the incipient scientific revolution in areas such as astronomy, optics, and the behavior of projectiles, for example, for which the static determinations of Euclidean geometry had been found wanting.

Two linked problems expressed geometrically in relation to which the calculus would emerge concerned curves, in particular finding ways of calculating tangents for and areas under curves. The former, "differential calculus," would allow the calculation of ratios of change, the latter, "integral calculus," would allow the calculation of continuously accumulating magnitudes. Besides being known for his role in the coinvention of the calculus,[8] Newton is, of course, famous as the author of *Philosophiæ Naturalis Principia Mathematica* of 1687 (Newton 2016), generally thought of as the decisive text for the founding of modern physics, in which these new mathematical techniques could be applied. However, the method applied in *Principia* was no straightforward expression of the calculus that would develop throughout the eighteenth century in algebraic form. Instead, it was heavily dependent upon ancient geometry. In contrast, the form it had taken in Leibniz is usually said to have been more algebraic, and this aspect would develop, especially in continental Europe, over the next century. This was the form found in Lagrange, who, in his *Mécanique analytique* of 1788, would proudly declare that there were no diagrams to be found between its covers. This heavily algebraized approach to mechanics is what Carnot had reacted against, reviving a geometric approach that had come to be regarded as old-fashioned.

We earlier observed aspects of Hegel's exploration of Carnot's geometrical alternative to Lagrange's algebraic interpretation of the calculus (see above, chapter 3.3). For Hegel, Newton's concessions to geometry did not go far enough, and in the 1801 *Dissertation*, he would argue that Newton's laws were just "mathematical" correlations of quantities that did not give expression to genuine "forces" in the world (*Misc*, 174–176). In particular, he there contests the conventionally accepted interpretation that, with his "inverse square law,"[9] Newton had supplied an appropriate explanation of the three empirical laws of planetary motion earlier given a geometric explanation by Kepler.[10] Effectively appealing to the ancient link between power (*dynamis*) and square, Hegel refers to "the true reason why what a certain force brings about must be displayed by a square, and why all quantities referring to that force must be displayed by relations that follow from the construction of a square" (*Misc*, 177). That which is "displayed by a square" is Newton's inverse square law that declares the gravitational attraction between bodies to be inversely proportional to the square of the distance between them, and this

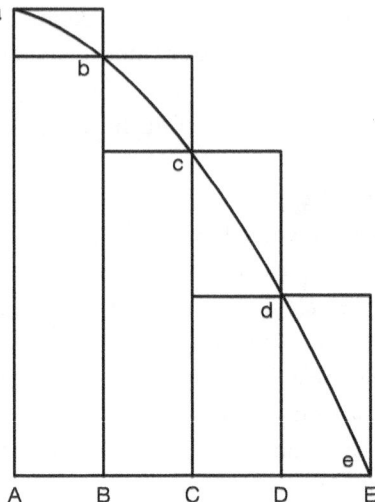

FIGURE 6.1 Newton's use of the method of exhaustion in *Principia*. For calculating the area under a parabolic curve, Newton applied the "method of exhaustion" utilized by Archimedes for calculating the length of the circumference or the area of the circle. Or, otherwise put, it was a method for calculating the value of the irrational number π (pi), the ratio of the circumference of the circle to its radius being 2π : 1. Carnot, in *Reflections on the Metaphysical Principles of the Infinitesimal Analysis*, refers to this method (Carnot 1797, 7–12).

must be subject to a proper explanation. Newton's law is not the *explanans* of Kepler's geometrically presented laws it is purported to be. In the Preface to *The Phenomenology of Spirit*, Hegel would write of mathematics, by which he seems to mean pure mathematics,[11] that it "does not consider ... the relation of line to surface, and when it compares the diameter of a circle with its circumference, it runs up against their incommensurability [*Inkommensurabilität*], which is to say, a ratio lying in the concept, or an infinite, which itself eludes mathematical determination" (*Phen*, §45). Differential calculus would ignore the incommensurability of such magnitudes when in differentiation it reduced a square quantity (x^2) to a linear one ($2x$). Such criticisms are filled out in Hegel's account of magnitude or "quantum" in *The Science of Logic*.

It is part of the standard account of the development of modern integral calculus that in *Principia* Newton had built on an ancient technique for measuring the circumference and area of a circle. Utilizing the pairing of quadratic equations and conic sections allowed by Descartes's analytic geometry, Newton's approximated the area under a curve by conceiving it as made up of a series of rectangles. If the rectangles are thought to become thinner and thinner, the approximation will be understood as becoming more and more accurate (fig. 6.1).

In Archimedes's original application to the circle, a first polygon is constructed inside the circle (as in fig. 6.2). If P denotes the combined lengths of the sides of the polygon, then the circumference of the circle will be greater than P. Consider now a second polygon constructed outside the circle, the sums of the sides of the polygon being P'. It is also clear that the circumference of the circle is less than P'.

Now consider repeatedly doubling the number of sides of both polygons, such that the difference between P and P' steadily decreases. The size of the circumference of the circle can now be estimated with greater and greater accuracy. (Archimedes himself went from a six-sided to a ninety-six-sided polygon and achieved a value for the ratio of the circumference to the diameter of the circle [the number π] as lying between $3\frac{1}{7}$ and $3\frac{10}{71}$.)

It is important to keep in mind that the actual value of π, as the Greeks were very aware, is irrational—that is, the magnitudes of the circumference and the radius of the square were for them incommensurable. Rational numbers such as $3\frac{1}{7}$ and $3\frac{10}{71}$ were understood as only approximations of π, but in the modern number system, π was understood as fully determinate, despite the fact that when expressed in decimal form (as, say, 3.14159 . . .), this expression could never be actually written down. Its expansion would continue infinitely. In Newton's conception of the method of exhaustion as continued to infinity, the width of the bases of the rectangles (AB, BC, CD . . .) and of the corresponding arc-segments (ab, bc, cd . . .) would be conceived as approaching zero. From the Greek point of view, this transformation of a polygon into

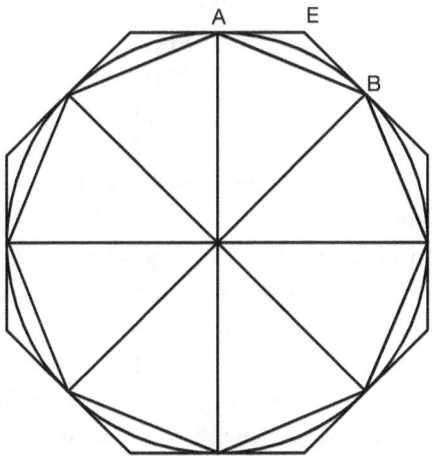

FIGURE 6.2 Archimedes's method of finding the length of the circumference of a circle between lower and upper limits.

a circle would entail equating incommensurable magnitudes. From the modern point of view, it would give rise to the problem of infinitesimally small magnitudes, Berkeley's "ghosts of departed quantities."

In the *Dissertation*, when Hegel distinguishes from "pure geometry" that "geometry that endeavours to subject the circle to calculation to express numerically the relation of the circumference to the radius" and that "seeks refuge in the hypothesis of an infinitely-sided regular polygon" (*Misc*, 177–178), it is clear that he has in mind this Archimedean background and its modern extension in the calculus. The implicit reference to Archimedes becomes explicit in the longer discussion in the chapter "Quantum" in *The Science of Logic* where Hegel refers to the "cyclometry" of Archimedes, that is, his celebrated work, *Measurement of a Circle* (*SL*, 261; 21:300; Heath 1897, 91–98), another classic work of geometry in Hegel's library (Mense 1993, 670).

In relation to the metaphysical problems of Berkeley's ghostly magnitudes, as we have seen, Carnot treated infinitesimals neither as real but infinitely small magnitudes nor as "nothings." They were "auxiliary quantities, introduced in the calculus solely to facilitate the expression of the conditions proposed" (Carnot 1797, 30). Thus, he would consider them in terms of continuously varying ratios that could not be thought as reducible to determinate relations between discrete numbers. This is what Carnot had appealed to with the methodological "principle of continuity" that had been put forward by Kepler.[12] Thus, in his treatment of the relationship of Newton and Kepler in the *Encyclopedia*'s *Philosophy of Nature*, Hegel concurs with "the accomplished exposition in a work '*Traité de mécanique élémentaire*' " by Louis-Benjamin Francoeur demonstrating that Newton's laws could be deduced from Kepler's laws of planetary motion (*E:PN*, §270, remark, p. 264). Significantly, Francoeur, who had been among the first to matriculate from the École Polytechnique set up by Carnot, where he had been taught by Monge, claims in relation to the approach to mechanics adopted there that "we cannot go beyond that which has been expressed by M. Carnot in his *Principes fondamentaux de l'équilibre et du mouvement*," Carnot's work on mechanics published in 1803 (Francoeur 1807, 8).[13]

In his discussion of the rival, purely algebraic interpretation of the calculus by Lagrange, Hegel treats the issue in relation to the ancient problem of incommensurability. In the extended method of exhaustion that had been discussed by Carnot (as the "method of approximation" [Carnot 1797, 7–12]), an arc is treated like a tangent, but the arc, adds Hegel, "is surely *incommensurable* with the *straight line*: its element is, from the start, of another *quality* than the element of the straight line." And yet, calculus requires "that straight lines when infinitely small, have passed over into curved lines"

(*SL*, 232; 21:270).¹⁴ This attempt to connect "*elements* within the mathematical object *which are qualitatively different*—curves with straight lines, linear dimensions and their functions with plane or plane dimensions and their functions, etc. . . . can only be taken . . . as the mean between a *greater* and a *lesser*" (*SL*, 257; 21:296). Hegel continues:

> Lagrange's exposition of the rectification of curves, since it proceeds from the principle of Archimedes, involves the *translation* of the Archimedean method into the principle of modern analysis, and this affords us an insight into the inner, the true meaning, of an endeavour which in the other method is carried out mechanically. . . . But Archimedes' principle, that the arc of a curve is greater than its chord and smaller than the sum of the tangents drawn at the endpoints of the arc and contained between these two points and the point of their intersection, does not yield any direct equation. (257; 21:296)

What Hegel has in mind is clear. If we take a segment of Archimedes's figure above (fig. 6.2), it can be appreciated that the length of a chord between two points on a circle A and B is always smaller than the arc of the circle between A and B, which in turn will be smaller than the combined lengths of the two intersecting tangents, AE + EB, drawn from those points. That is, straight and curved lines, like square and linear numbers, cannot be summed from the perspective of Greek geometric algebra because they are qualitatively different or, to express it otherwise, they belong to generically different types of mathematical quantity. They can, however, be treated as continuously transforming ratios.

It is not so much the "ghosts of departed quantities" that is the problem for the calculus but the ghost of a departed qualitative difference between continuous and discrete magnitudes involved when Archimedes's technique is so "translated" into modern analysis. Like Plato, Hegel finds the structure of the "more or less" as an irreducible feature of the empirical world but draws from this a different conclusion. Plato, despite his acknowledgment of the necessity of indeterminacy, and hence the necessity of the empirical world as an aspect of being, had still retained the Pythagorean evaluation of such indeterminacy as "bad," unilaterally privileging the ideal over the empirical in ways that had been resisted and, indeed, reversed by Aristotle. Like Aristotle, Hegel wants to bring Plato's forms into the world, but this must be done in a way that does not compromise the place of the nondiscrete determination of "greater or lesser" within the world. Moreover, the discrete forms of the ideal world can only be brought to the empirical world because those forms contained the "bad" dimension of more or less implicitly within them. The calculus, however, obliterates a role for the greater or lesser by reducing the "mean between a greater and a lesser" to a unit.

This is not the place to try to assess Hegel's critique of the calculus; it is generally recognized that the problems concerning the rational foundations of the calculus were not resolved (if "resolved" at all) until well after Hegel's time. The year of Hegel's death, 1831, roughly coincides with the birth of abstract algebra in the nineteenth century with Galois's postulation of the notion of a "group."[15] However, it is important to be clear about the general lines along which Hegel's critique proceeds. As Thomas Posch has underlined in his study of Hegel's *Philosophy of Nature*, Hegel was critical of the combination of the annihilation of qualitative differences in the modern positive sciences and the promotion of their results to the status of a "world-view"—in Newton's case, a natural philosophy (Posch 2011, 198). By its elimination of "the more and less" that applies in the realm of geometry in favor of complete numerical determinacy, the calculus represents a type of modern version of conventional, that is, middle-period, Platonism, and it is this that is behind Hegel's odd-sounding claim that Newton's celestial mechanics is not an empirical science.

The genuinely empirically based modern scientists were, for Hegel, Galileo and Kepler, who had "*proven* the laws they have discovered by showing that the full compass of the singular things of perception [*Einzelheiten der Wahrnehmung*] conform to them" (*SL*, 297; 21:340).[16] This is because they had not attempted to eliminate the element of indeterminacy to be found in the empirical world from their representations by eliminating its properly geometric content—a content whose magnitudes were limited to the "more or less." As he says of Kepler in the *Dissertation*, "He posited nothing but the relation of those factors that can truly increase and decrease, and did not spoil the pure and truly celestial expression of these relations by determining the quantities of gravity, which has no quantity" (*Misc*, 184).[17] But as we have seen, Carnot too fitted this description, Hegel describing his treatment of quantitative ratio as being "not unlike the grasping of an empirical *existence conceptually*" (*SL*, 219; 21:255). In contrast, "the analysts show by the comparison of a result obtained with strict geometrical procedure and with the method of infinite differences that the result is one and the same in both cases; that there is *absolutely no place for* a more or less in exactitude" (*SL*, 220; 21:256, emphasis added).

This does not mean that Newton's analytic approach did not represent a type of progress. "One must deem that the science of astronomy, insofar as it concerns mathematics, owes much to Newton" (*Misc*, 185). Hegel recognizes that the introduction of the calculus allowed an expansion of the finite sciences that would not have happened were modern science limited to the resources of Euclidean geometry. His criticism is directed rather to the pretension of Newtonian analytical mechanics to be an empirically based natural philosophy. In a self-negating move, Newtonian mechanics had helped eliminate the geometric mode of thought that had allowed Kepler's earlier empirical discoveries about the world and upon which it itself depended.[18]

With his role in the development of the calculus, and despite the reservations expressed with his idea of an *analysis situs*, Leibniz had been at the forefront of the movement building on Descartes's "analytic" reduction of geometry to arithmetic. Moreover, he had also been at the forefront of the similarly modern movement in logic in which the "geometric" dimension of Aristotle's syllogism was reduced to a type of logical arithmetic. This, rather than that of his undeveloped *analysis situs*, would be the analytic style of thought for which he would be remembered. Hegel, in his critique of Leibniz's paradigmatically modern "quantitative" conception of judgment, would treat it as involving the elimination of qualitative differences between kinds in ways analogous to the elimination of qualitative differences among magnitudes involved in the calculus. Nevertheless, Hegel was not opposed to this type of "translation" of the qualitative to the quantitative per se: in fact, rationality, he thought, depended on it. He was rather opposed to the conception of "thinking as understanding," a conception of thinking that fixes the determinacies of what is being thought in ways preventing their further redetermination. Schelling's Constructed Line, reinterpreted in Hegel's somewhat Carnotian way, would provide Hegel with a picture of how we should think of the relation between otherwise incommensurable qualitative and quantitative thoughts.

6.3 Parallels between Hegel's Attitudes toward Leibniz's Calculus and Logical Calculus

In the "Subjective Logic" of *The Science of Logic*, the first instance of Hegel's qualitative judgments of inherence is the "judgment of existence [*Dasein*]," meant to give expression to some immediate taking in of the objective world such that the judgment is measured by what is found in the world via perception. As immediate, the contents of such judgments are not "true," however, and the "positive" judgment of existence has its truth in its negation—that is, has its truth in the contesting judgment of another judge who may, from their different point of view, judge things differently. It is this interaction of judgments that, later in the context of the more complex "judgment of the concept," will be characterized as a syllogism. This syllogism will be the proper medium for the formation of truth, not the separate individual judgments tied to the direct experience of the individual subjects.

This context of dialectical interaction with another reasoning observer invites being understood in terms of Hegel's now well-known "recognitive" theory of self-consciousness in which a subject's self-consciousness is dependent on existence within a reciprocal relation to another in which each recognizes and is recognized by their other (Redding 1996, ch. 5). This makes the issue of the logical form of any judgment more complex. My judgments will have a dimension that gives expression to how the world for me simply is, but they must also have a dimension that is less immediately reflective of my contingent location in the world, from which the limitations of my viewpoint can be appreciated. This is a dimension typically understood by some other differently located and oriented "Subject-Object" who can thereby take the measure of the conditioning of my claims by features of the world not apparent to me.

That a subject perceives the things of the world and their arrangements and interactions from a particular perspective or *point de vue* had been famously sketched by Leibniz in his *Discourse on Metaphysics*. Committing the same type of reduction of spatial volumes to points of which Hegel complains in the context of calculus, Leibniz had claimed that while a finite monad neither exists "in" space nor has extension, it nevertheless represents the universe as if from a point of view, "rather as the same town is differently represented according to the different situations of the person who looks at it" (Leibniz 1998, §9). The difference between the apparent spatial "locations" involved here is cashed out in terms of the specific relations among representations and appetitions making up the states of each monad. Leibniz would try to bring his logic and epistemology together in a conception of the Copernican-styled correctable perspectival dimension of perceptual knowledge. Epistemologically, this was described as the capacity to translate knowledge involving clear but confused ideas into that involving clear and distinct ones. In this way he would conceive of a type of translation of the contents of traditional categorical judgments, representing how the world is experienced immediately from a particular point of view, into algebraically tractable judgments now understood as akin to equations, the value of which could be designated in terms of the opposition true and false conceived as the values 1 and 0 of a binary arithmetic. Thus, he would conceive of a "universal characteristic" within which ideas could be expressed in a way that ultimately freed them from their initially perspectival enframing, an idea that, it has been claimed, guided him through the studies that led to the calculus (Bos 1980, 60).

Epistemologically, the corrective translation for Leibniz was properly from clear and confused cognitions to some comparatively more distinct ones. Located at any one moment as if on a step of a ladder, one can grasp some truth informed by confused ideas by seeking an explanation or reason for it—a move legitimated by the principle of sufficient reason and taking one to the next higher rung. Moreover, for Leibniz, each step is able to be repeated, the inquirer thus seeking a reason for that reason, making movement up the ladder, as described in the essay "On Contingency," a matter of giving "reasons for reasons" (Leibniz 1989a, 28). For Lambert, this would be thought of in terms of the idea of reinscribing experience within an ascending series of new languages—moon-dwellers needing to express their experiences in the language natural to earth-dwellers, who in turn need to speak the language of those located on the sun, and so on (above, chapter 5.2). Logically considered, such translations from clear and confused to clear and distinct concepts (or more perspectival to less perspectival expressions) would be understood via the capacity of the terms of the "judgment-equation" to be linked internally to the terms of other such judgment-equations. All this could now be understood as allowing a type of cognitive "ascent," thus providing a model for the type of ascent conceived within Platonism as conventionally understood. But as both Playfair and Carnot had complained in their own ways, this could be understood as a path leading from real executable quantities to the empty abstractions that can be found in algebra. While these latter "auxiliary" or "non-designated" quantities (Carnot 1797, 22–23) played important roles in computational processes, lines of translation back to the applicable magnitudes that were the equivalent of Leibniz's "clear and confused ideas" had to be maintained.[19]

Schelling's Constructed Line, able to be understood as expressing Nicomachus's "most perfect proportion" or the modern cross-ratio of projective geometry, had presented the possibility of a more circular conception that unifies opposing judgment types and nevertheless preserves their mutual opposition. Hegel's idea of the translation of qualitative judgments of existence into quantitative judgments of reflection would involve the same type of annihilation of differences in genus or kind as that found in the calculus, and as in the case of the calculus, this would undermine the experiential content of the judgment by ablating it of the dimension of the "more or less." Consonant with this, Hegel's idea of the translation of judgments could not be pictured as providing a Leibnizian ladder to some God's-eye point of view. Rather, it would provide the means for the transformation of those objects of which the judgments were judgments (see above, chapter 3.2).

Hegel had opposed an understanding of the type of *de-re* judgments made on the basis of perceptual experience as structured according to the "top-down" Platonic conception of *diairesis* in which two actual colors such as green and blue could be regarded as instances of the more general concept, *color*. As qualitative, blue is differentiated from green in much the same way that a meadow is differentiated from a field. There will be colors in which this differentiation is difficult to make, as the color blue is experienced as stretching along a continuum that will gradually shade into green. Clearly, judgment here is structured more by the "indeterminate dyad" of the more or less: a certain shade will be judged to be more green than blue rather than definitively either green or blue, such a continuum of qualities being entirely appropriate for the empirical domain. But this is not to describe determinate shades of colors like green or blue as providing fixed singular *infima* for this structure. The concept <blue>, say, can also be treated as a Hegelian particular, a more abstract concept with which it can be asked of some object, "Is it or is it not blue?" in the mode of Kant's judge "who compels witnesses to answer the questions he puts to them" (Kant 1998, Bxiii). Demanding a yes-or-no answer in this manner would force experience to "answer" in a way that abstracts from the "more or less" quality of the experience. Later we will see the logician W. E. Johnson capture this distinction as one between "determinables" and "determinates" rather than genus and species (below, chapter 8.4), but here it can be noted how this capacity to redetermine the content of a judgment provides a type of translatability between particular and singular ("existential generalization" and "existential instantiation") not enabled by Kant's fixed distinction between intuition and concept. The same retranslatability will apply at the top of the abstractive phase of this cyclical process as well, at the point of a redeterminable *supremum*.

Hegel's treatment of the abstraction from concrete givenness in judgment driven by negation takes the initial positive judgment of experience to the maximally indeterminate judgment found at the apex of the cycle he calls the "infinite judgment" (*SL*, 567–568; 12:69–71). In relation to the task of telling someone something about the world, an infinite judgment is *widersinnig*—contrary to sense—and its contrariness to sense is a function of its having been entirely stripped of the "more or less" structure of sensory experience. In Carnot's terms, one may think of an infinite judgment as an auxiliary judgment. The infinite judgment serves a purpose, as stripping the original judgment of sense so as to leave "pure form," as it were, brings out that aspect of a judgment that allows it to link up in distinctly logical patterns with other judgments similarly conceived—patterns that can be exploited by a type of algebraic calculus, the "calculus ratiocinator" that accompanies Leibniz's *characteristica universalis*. However, its usefulness depends on any such "pure" form being repopulated with sensory content but now in ways that are dictated predominantly by the logical form of the judgment itself. Hegel addresses the nature and functioning of the Leibnizian scaffolding of the universal characteristic in the section of the "Subjective Logic" of *The Science of Logic* devoted to the so-called mathematical syllogism, the fourth syllogistic figure (602–604; 12:104–106).

Aristotle had limited the number of syllogistic figures to three, the fourth being a later addition. Hegel reinterprets the four figures, courtesy of his own singular-particular-universal distinction, in ways that, I have suggested, may draw upon the idea of opposed—internal and external—ways of "dividing" an interval found in the cross-ratio model as revived by Carnot. For Hegel, the fourth syllogistic figure effectively represents a syllogism in which the arrangement of the three terms constitutes the greatest departure from Aristotle's "perfect" syllogistic paradigm based on the iteration of predicates understood as "containing" the subject. It is the syllogistic equivalent of the earlier "infinite judgment." Hegel describes the conception of predication at work in this syllogism in the following way:

> If two things or two determinations are equal to a third, then they are equal to each other.—The relation of inherence or subsumption of terms is done away with.
> A "third" is in general the mediating term; but this third has absolutely no determination as against the extremes. (SL, 602; 12:104)

In this context he goes on to discuss the "logical calculus" of Leibniz and Ploucquet, focusing on a feature of Leibniz's logic that is highly significant in relation to the later Fregean turn in logic (Angelelli 1990). In his *characteristica universalis* Leibniz had effectively abandoned the traditional subject-predicate conception of judgment and, adopting an approach from Johannes Raue, treated subject terms as themselves predicates. What were formally understood as subject and predicate terms are now grasped as linked in virtue of being predicates that are both true of the same objects or range of objects—some common third (a *tertium commune*) not represented in the original judgment.[20] This is effectively how predication comes to be understood in the specifically propositional logic. Just like the "infinite judgment" treated earlier, this conception of syllogism is maximally indeterminate, the *tertium commune*, says Hegel, has "absolutely no determination as against the extremes" (SL, 602; 12:104). It is this conversion of subject terms to predicates that Hegel conveys with the idea that in the mathematical syllogism all terms have been reduced to universals, leading the original S-P-U structure, after transiting through the reorderings of the second and third figures, to assume the ultimately degenerate form of U-U-U (602; 12:104).[21] From the perspective of Plato's three-dimensional syllogism, the three constitutive dimensions of the world have been collapsed into one.

Hegel's familiarity with aspects of Leibniz's logic that were not recognized until much later make this short section of the "Subjective Logic" a rich source for understanding Hegel's thoughts about where formal logic was heading. The mathematical syllogism effectively marks the collapse of the Aristotelian tradition in logic, and what Hegel himself sees as the future of logic has to be constructed from out of these ruins. Effectively, the mathematical syllogism is a syllogism whose component judgments are those "infinite judgments" that resulted from abstraction from the content of judgments of existence—they are auxiliary judgments with maximally indeterminate content. Leibniz had tried to revolutionize Aristotle's syllogistic by treating the terms of judgments as the names of classes, such that to say P of some S is to say that there is at least one thing that belongs to both classes P and S. However, such classes had to be understood both extensionally as classes of actual things, and intensionally as classes of concepts, and he had attempted to map such a class-based logic onto a propositional logic. Lenzen points to the circularity of the latter and to the way in which the logical properties of the propositional contents of such judgments would require that they be extended from classes of actual things to logically possible things (Lenzen 2004, 16).[22] This is why, as Hegel says, such "thirds" have "absolutely no determination." Existing, actual things are maximally determinate: that red tomato in my garden manifests some specific shade of red—it has a way of being red. But merely possible things are maximally indeterminate: there is no specific shade of red possessed by those possible tomatoes that I might have planted over there in that different garden bed but did not. In terms of the diagrammatic representations discussed earlier, the indefinitely red possible tomato is that entity represented by the intersection between two concept classes—that of red things and that of tomatoes. Such a thing is a "posit," akin to the imperceptible point at which two lines intersect.

Just as how in the calculus a magnitude had been stripped of its "genus" so as to be subject to a type of universal computation, here objects are represented as stripped of their generic determinations for a parallel purpose, computation now being carried out on *abstracta*—propositions—which are related in ways reducible to patterns among binary "truth-values." The language of Hegel's criticism repeats that of his criticism of the loss of qualitative distinction in Leibniz's calculus: "The quantitative determination, which alone comes into consideration in it, is only *by virtue of the abstraction* from qualitative differentiation and from the concept determinations.—Lines, figures, posited as equal to each other, are understood only according to their magnitude. A triangle is posited as equal to a square, not however as triangle to square but only according to magnitude, etc." (*SL*, 603; 12:105). It is appropriate to look at the rediscovery of Leibniz's logical innovations within both sides of the revolutionary changes taking place in logic in the second half of the nineteenth century.

END

The Modern as Redetermined Classical

7

Exploiting Resources within Aristotle for the Rehabilitation of the Syllogism

> The Aristotelian logic ... involves the universal thought-forms or the foundation for what has been known as logic right down to most recent times. It is Aristotle's undying merit to have recognized and drawn attention to these forms and to have brought them to light. ... But these forms, which are set forth in the Aristotelian books as logical forms, are still only the forms of thinking at the level of the understanding; they are not the forms of speculative thinking or of rationality as distinct from the sphere of the understanding.
>
> HEGEL, *Lectures on the History of Philosophy*

When discussing Aristotle in the *Lectures on the History of Philosophy* (*LHP* 2:225–262; 3:59–99), Hegel is generally intent on portraying him as a misunderstood Platonist whose views were distorted by the Scholastics, whose "wide-raging metaphysics of the understanding and formal logic have nothing Aristotelian about them at all" (231–232). Aristotle's own thought, he claims, did not proceed according to the demonstrations of formal logic; had it done so "he would not have arrived at any speculative thesis" (261). Nevertheless, he clearly identifies Aristotle as responsible for the "syllogism of the understanding" that forms "the foundation for what has been known as logic right down to most recent times" (260). However, he hints at why Plato's more philosophical logic based on the dialectical syllogism cannot bypass the more prosaic Aristotelian logic of the understanding. In relation to Aristotle's formal logic, "what occupies our conscious interest is, as a rule, concrete thinking or thinking immersed in outer intuition; the forms of thinking are, so to speak, immersed in it. It is an endlessly mobile network, and to have pinpointed these forms, this fine thread permeating all, to have brought this to consciousness, is a masterpiece of empiricism" (260). How does this sit with those claims made earlier in the context of his discussion of Plato?

During the discussion in the *Lectures on the History of Philosophy* of the ontological "syllogism" structuring both the body and soul of Timaeus's cosmic animal, Hegel had devoted a packed paragraph to a comparison of Plato's rational syllogism and Aristotle's formal syllogism of the understanding derived from it. When he notes that "in the syllogism of the understanding there are two extremes and one middle term [*zwei Extreme ... und eine*

Mitte]" the contrast with Plato's is apparent. Moreover, he continues, "the extremes have a value of independent characteristics, and so a particular form belongs to each of these terminal points. The first is the singular, the second particular, and the third is the universal" (*LHP* 2:210; 3:40). This latter point, as we have seen (chapter 1.2 above), is not entirely the case. Officially Aristotle excluded singular terms from his syllogisms because every term must be capable of playing the role of both subject and predicate in a judgment and singular terms cannot be predicates. But there is nevertheless a degree of ambiguity here: Aristotle had occasionally used examples of syllogisms containing singular judgments, seemingly admitting a singular term in subject position of a minor premise that would not need to appear as the predicate term of another premise.[1] But such singular reference would not have been appropriate in the context of the type of demonstrative syllogisms of science described in the *Posterior Analytics*, as science, as he makes explicit, specifically deals with universals and not with individuals per se.[2] From the perspective of science, individuals are only significant inasmuch as they instantiate some kind. Socrates will be an appropriate object of scientific investigation only inasmuch as he instantiates some genus, a human being qua "rational animal," for example. But as we will see, Hegel would exploit scattered suggestions in Aristotle that concerned a type of reasoning about individuals as individuals—singulars—rather than "particular" instances of kinds, thereby linking Aristotle's logic to more modern developments.

As we have seen from Einarson and Smith, Aristotle had taken over the language of Plato's harmonic model to give structure to the syllogism, but while Plato had bound the parts of the cosmic animal together by using both geometric and arithmetic means, the suggestion seems to be that Aristotle, in the formal syllogism, conceived of its structure as employing only one of them. This, I suggest, was the geometric mean, the type of mean found in the narrowed Euclidean conceptions of ratio and proportion in the move away from Pythagorean arithmeticism. It was this move that produced Aristotle's ambivalent advances in logic. On the one hand, it allowed for the characteristic generality to be found in logic; on the other, it would be responsible for the shortcomings of the "logic of the understanding" that would continue in its modern transformation in the hands of Leibniz and Kant. Hegel's goal would be to reconstitute Plato's original conception of the syllogism by bringing out the implicit doubled mean to be found in the syllogisms of Aristotle's *Prior Analytics*. This means incorporating the concrete singulars into the framework of Aristotle's syllogism, which only officially works with those indeterminate abstract subjects that correspond to Hegel's category of particulars.

7.1 The Formal Aristotelian Syllogism and Its Iterable Geometric Mean

In the discussion of the syllogism in *The Science of Logic* Hegel notes the following about the limits of Aristotle's approach: "Aristotle confined himself rather to the mere relation of *inherence* by defining the nature of the syllogism as follows: *When three terms are so related to each other that the one extreme is in the entire middle term, and this middle term is in the entire other extreme, then these two extremes are necessarily united in the conclusion.* What is here expressed is the repetition of the *same ratio [gleichen Verhältnisses]* of inherence of the one extreme to the middle term, and then again of this last to the other extreme, rather than the determinateness of the three terms to each other" (*SL*, 591; 12, 93). The first sentence here effectively repeats Aristotle's own description of the perfect syllogism in terms of the iterable "is in" relation in the passage from the *Prior Analytics* we have quoted above (Aristotle 1989, *Prior Analytics*, 25b32–26a3)—the relation that Hegel describes here as the "inherence" of the predicate in the subject, to which Aristotle had "confined himself." In contrast, Hegel's phrase concerning the "determinateness of the three terms to each other" recalls his specification of Plato's syllogism in the *Timaeus* and Nicomachus's most perfect proportion.

Aristotle's uniformly applied "is in" or "belongs to" relation effectively is the same as the iterable "measures" relation as set in the *Sectio Canonis*. The reiteration of the "is in" or "measures" relation between terms models the syllogism on an indefinitely extendable geometric series of terms presupposing that initial and ultimately inadequate conception of ratio that Hegel treats as "direct ratio." By being confined to an iterated inherence relation, such that the first term being in the second and the second's being in the third implies that the first is in the third, Aristotle's "perfect" syllogism clearly could be continued indefinitely, and so lacks the type of unification found in the Platonic model, the bond that "makes a unity of itself together with the things bonded by it" (Plato 1997, *Timaeus*, 31c). The concept <animal> being contained in the concept <human>, which is in the concept <Greek>, allows us to grasp that the concept <animal> is thereby contained in the concept <Greek>. But why then restrict the number of premises to two? Equally, the concept <Greek> might be conceived as contained in that of <Greek philosopher>, which is contained in <Greek philosopher from Athens>, and so on. Later, Leibniz would free this restriction of premises to two—a move away from the traditional syllogism that would be repeated in the nineteenth century.

There is a further problem in simply drawing on the iterated measures relation as a model for the syllogism, however, given Aristotle's own needs.

Aristotle was clearly motivated by the need to apply logic to the world in such a way that worldly things could be conceived as constraining or "measuring" the concepts being applied to them. In Aristotle's iterable-measure model, the measure-measured relation proceeds unidirectionally from universal to particular instance, as from <animal> to the concept of a particular type of animal, the concept <human>. This problem, we will see, is a generalization of the problem alluded to earlier (see chapter 1.2) concerning the idea that perception of Callias is somehow simultaneously that of an indefinite man and the specific man, Callias—the problem that, described in more modern terms, is conceived of as conflating "intention" and "extension." Such a distinction was not self-consciously made by Aristotle, but it *would* be made by Leibniz, and this would allow him to exploit the potential implicit in Aristotle's syllogism to both increase the number of premises in an inference and conceive of how the problem of singularity might be overcome.

First, Leibniz would allow premises within syllogistic structures to be piled on top of one another as indicated above, so as to conceive of logic as a type of ladder that allows the mind to scale a series of ever increasingly abstract concepts, an ascent that leads from some fact to its condition and that then asks for the condition of that condition, and so on. Kant, in the "Transcendental Dialectic" of the *Critique of Pure Reason*, would refer to such a series of inferences as a "chain or series of prosyllogisms" (Kant 1998, A331/B388), a series that can be continued because it has a fixed "exponent" (A331/B387).[3] This, it will be recalled, was the characteristic that Hegel ascribed to the relation of "direct ratio." Plato's own dialogues had, of course, provided plenty of images of such an ascent: one such is Diotima's speech in the *Symposium* that shows the way in which the mind can be taken from a mistaken and childish concern with sensuous appearances to a vision in which one gazes out over "the great sea of beauty," the complete cosmos grasped in a way that understands the truth, beauty, and goodness of the whole (Plato 1997, *Symposium*, 210d–e). But Leibniz also believed he had a solution to the directional problem implicit in Aristotle's desire to bring empirical findings to bear on science. The intensional-extensional distinction would allow Leibniz's favored metaphor of one concept's containment in another to be read in two opposed ways, such that it could accommodate movement either up or down Porphyry's tree: "When I say *Every man is an animal* I mean that all the men are included amongst all the animals; but at the same time I mean that the idea of animal is included in the idea of man" (Leibniz 1996, 486). This involves the type of reversal of directions seen in Kant's "Negative Magnitudes" essay and the approach to space developed in the new nineteenth-century geometries. Moreover, such a reversal of direction reflects the transition from direct ratio to the inverse (or invertible) ratio as Hegel treats it in his exposition of ratio in book 1 of *The Science of Logic* (see above, chapter 3.3) As we will see, for both Peirce and Hegel, directionality would provide a rich resource to be exploited for logical ends.

There are at least hints of this reversal of directionality already implicit in Aristotle, however. For example, immediately following the description in the *Prior Analytics* of the syllogism utilizing the "is in" conception of predication, and so describing various terms as "so related to each other that the last is in the middle as a whole and the middle is either in or not in the first as a whole" (Aristotle 1989, *Prior Analytics*, 25b32–26a3), Aristotle had switched to the language of predication as a "said of" relation, "if A is predicated [*katigoristhai*] of every B and B of every C, it is necessary for A to be predicated of every C" (26a1–3).[4] Moreover, with this he reverses the standard Greek word order: A is *predicated* of B only if B "contains" A in the sense of "inherence." As with other instances of a certain indeterminacy in Aristotle, here there seems to be a blurring between two conceptions of judgment structure, a *de-re* conception, in which concrete properties are said to inhere in things, and a *de-dicto* conception, in which abstract properties are said of a thing. In the former, properties are characterized by the "more or less" relation among points on a continuum, while in the latter a concept is understood as "true of" a thing in a binary, "yes-or-no" sense. It has been suggested (above, chapter 4.1) that this idea of the reversal of directionality found in Schelling's "Constructed Line" would give Hegel a novel way of conceiving of the relation between different judgment forms. As with Hegel's "invertible" ratio, the change of directionality has allowed the series to be read in one direction as a continuum and in the other as a series of *discreta*. Aristotle's conflation of intensional and extensional judgment types that run in contrary directions must be made explicit, and these two judgment types must then be shown to be equivalent in a way that preserves this opposition. In Hegel's discussion of ratio this was achieved by the final "ratio of powers," which we have related to the cross-ratio structure that reemerged in nineteenth-century geometry. In the context of *The Science of Logic*'s "Subjective Logic," this will be achieved in a model that shows homologous equivalence between judgments, whose opposed function-serving logical forms are indicated by a distinction between two senses of predication that he calls predication as "inherence" and predication as "subsumption."

This, I suggest, is at the heart of Hegel's attempt to transform the Aristotelian formal syllogism back into a Platonic ontological one that employs the "doubled" middle term. But historically, Hegel's solution would also be forward looking, because the conception of logic as containing, and so needing to unify, two different systems—broadly an Aristotelian "term" logic and a Stoic "propositional" one—is present in Leibniz and would become central to the logic revival of the second half of the nineteenth century started by George Boole. To understand the possibility for this happening, however, it is important to understand the way the indefiniteness of logical form in Aristotle had allowed the type of generality needed for notions of logical inference to be systematically developed.

7.2 The Achievements and Limits of Generality in Aristotle's Logic

As we have seen, the algebra that is usually accredited with the introduction of generality into arithmetical procedures had been achieved geometrically in Greek mathematics, in which the use of diagrams had allowed the type of abstraction and indeterminacy otherwise achieved with algebraic symbols. The idea of Aristotle's having achieved the required generality for logic by similarly geometric means might now be linked to his idea of inference as an iteration of the spatially imagined "is in" relation. Such an interpretation raises the issue of the role of diagrams in logic.

When one thinks of "logic diagrams" one invariably thinks of the types of quasi-geometric containment diagrams—for example, Euler diagrams or Venn diagrams—found in Leibniz and those coming after him. That Aristotle himself used diagrams, as urged by some, is largely conjectural, but even if it turned out that Aristotle had not, the containment idea of conceptual relations founded on his use of figures is so strong that it makes the use of such diagrams seem very natural for Aristotelian logic.[5]

Containment diagrams such as those using overlapping circles, rectangles, or squares to represent logical relations do not per se differentiate between intensional and extensional readings. Think, for example, of a partitioned rectangle in which the rectangle itself is meant to represent Greeks living in the golden age of classical philosophy, with the left-hand partition representing Athenians and the right-hand partition representing non-Athenian Greeks, as in figure 7.1. The diagram could easily suggest different "extensional" and "intensional" interpretations.

One intuitive way of thinking of the spatial representations involved in figure 7.1 would be to think of distinct points in each partition (able to be indicated by a dot, say) as representing each specific Athenian Greek—Plato and Socrates, say, being found in the left partition, with individual non-Athenian Greeks, such as Archytas or Philolaus (both from southern Italy), being found in the right. This idea of specific individuals as countable instances of the collection "Athenians" would be a natural interpretation for

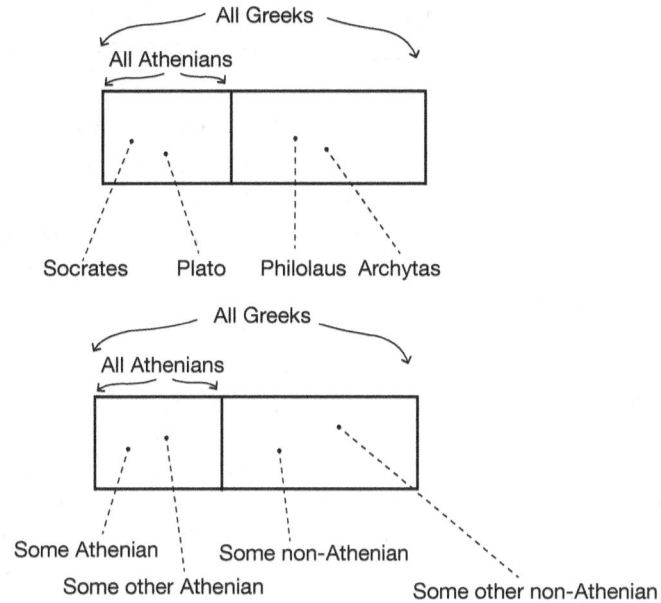

FIGURE 7.1 Containment diagrams able to be interpreted extensionally and intensionally.

an early Pythagorean (or, later, a medieval nominalist) because this was how the early Pythagoreans thought of the extensive magnitudes such as areas as made up. They are composed of monads "in position." But Eudoxus's conception of proportions between irreducibly continuous magnitudes of areas might suggest another interpretation. Now, as in the lower diagram, the left partition might be thought of as representing Athenians in the more indeterminate sense of whoever is Greek and comes from Athens, with a similarly generic understanding of the right partition. In short, in the first interpretation, the areas would be thought as akin to sums of proper names, while in the second they would function more like determining descriptions. The left partition is, in one account, populated by concrete singulars, in the other, by abstract particulars. The former is arithmetical, the latter geometric.

In the nineteenth century, the French geometer and historian of geometry Michel Chasles would appeal to the existence of two different types of geometry—one in which the monadic point plays the role of the fundamental element from which extensive magnitudes are generated, and another in which the line or plane plays the equivalent fundamental role of that from which all other entities are derived (Chasles 1837, 408–409). Clearly, early Pythagorean geometry and its modern "analytic" equivalent instantiate the former, and, while Chasles is not particularly clear on the opposing form, I suggest that it was with Eudoxus that continuous magnitudes had come to be grasped as basic, resulting in Greek "geometric algebra." Projective geometry had made this duality into its own fundamental principle. A line can be defined in terms of the two points it joins, or a point can be defined as where two lines meet, giving points and lines a type of equivalence, such that for every theorem in projective geometry concerning relations among points an equivalent one can be found concerning relations among lines (Nagel 1939, §§45–60). We have seen that Hegel posits a similar type of equivalence between discrete and continuous magnitudes that is reflected in his account of space in the *Philosophy of Nature*. There Hegel writes that space is the following:

> (1) In the first instance the point, i.e., the *negation* of the immediate and *undifferentiated* self-externality of space itself. (2) The negation is however the negation of *space*, and is therefore itself spatial. In that this relation is essential to the point, the point is self-sublating and constitutes the *line*, which is the primary otherness or spatial *being* of the point. (3) The truth of otherness is however the negation of negation, and the line therefore passes over into the *plane*. (*E: PN*, §256)[6]

This mutual implication of indefinite spatial continuum ("the immediate and *undifferentiated* self-externality") and the initially dimensionless (and so non-spatial) point simply reflects Hegel's underlying idea of the way both continua and discreta contain the principle of the other within them. We might then think of the ambiguity of these containment diagrams when seen from this point of view as expressive of a principle that is shared by both projective geometers and Hegel, and as enabling them to understand logical diagrams in two different ways.

For example, diagrams using the partitioning of areas might be used to illustrate certain truths such as "All Athenians are Greeks" but "Only some Greeks are Athenians." Interpreted extensionally along atomistic lines, grasping this truth would correspond to seeing that all the identifiable individual points falling in the Athenian partition also belong to the overarching area representing all Greeks, while the existence of identifiable points in the non-Athenian partition demonstrate that not all Greeks are Athenians. From the perspective of geometric algebra, however, things would be slightly different. The same truths might now be understood as diagrammatically encoded without the need to specify those actual individuals being referred to. Now the truth that "All Athenians are Greeks" would correspond in a natural way to claims expressed intentionally with the idea that the concept <Athenian> contains the concept <Greek>, or that all possible Athenians are Greek.

However, containment diagrams are not the only type of diagrams used by logicians, and while the diagrams that work on the basis of the part-whole

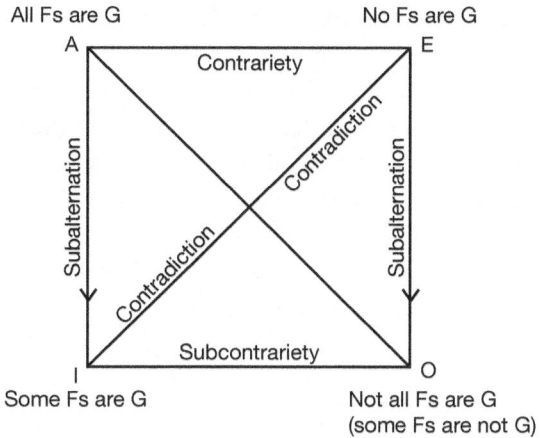

FIGURE 7.2 The square of opposition.

relation among areas might most naturally suggest the extensional interpretation, I suggest another type of diagram is more naturally suited to the intensional. Rather than exploit relations of containment, these exploit notions of order and contrast, and one might consider as a basic example the traditional "square of opposition" invoked by later logicians, such as Apuleius in the second century CE and Boethius in the sixth, to capture the logical relations holding among judgment types as set out by Aristotle in *De Interpretatione* (fig. 7.2).[7]

Located at the top corners of the square of opposition (the A and E corners) are found contrasting positive and negative versions of "universal judgments" (as in "All Athenians are mortal" and "No Athenians are mortal"), and at the two bottom (I and O) corners, similarly contrasting positive and negative versions of the opposing "particular" judgments (as in "Some Athenians are philosophers" and "Some Athenians are not philosophers" or "Not all Athenians are philosophers").[8] The downward direction of the verticals is meant to suggest the idea of a type of inferential passage from the more general to the less general, with A- and E-propositions being related to I- and O-propositions, respectively, by the relation of "subalternation."[9] Aristotle's logic, it is generally accepted, had been a logic of terms rather than propositions—that is, predication understood as a predicate's being "contained in" a subject rather than "said of" the subject—and such class-based term relations are suggested by the verticals. In contrast, it had been the Stoics who had developed the type of logic that is now considered propositional logic with an opposed "said of" conception of predication. In the square, it is the diagonals read as contradiction that suggest such a Stoic propositional logic. While supposedly giving expression to Aristotle's syllogistic, the square would in this way come to be understood equally as expressing a propositional logic. Thus, while Boethius himself seemed to have conflated the Aristotelian and Stoic traditions (Martin 1991), his logic would be important for the later development of propositional logic by figures such as Abelard in the twelfth century.

Boethius had focused on the way that Aristotle had clarified the status of negation in logic by going beyond the way Plato had used negation to divide categories in his method of *diairesis*, repeated in Porphyry's tree. For example, dividing the category of living things on this model would result in a distinction between rational living things and nonrational ones. But the square of opposition distinguishes three types of "negation." Contrariety holds "horizontally" across the top of the square between judgments of the form "All As are B" and those of the form "No As are B"—contrariety being a weaker form of negation, asserting that while two such propositions cannot both be true, they can both be false. The stronger relation of contradiction, however, holds across the diagonals of the square. For example, "Some As are B" contradicts "No As are B," the truth of one of the pair implying the falsity of the other. Here, truth and falsity are completely divided in the style of Porphyry's tree (Correia 2017, 5). Along with these, the relation between I-judgments and O-judgments is that of subcontrariety: together, both cannot be false but can be true.[10]

As we have seen, Aristotle had not seemed to have been fully aware of the sorts of problems surrounding mixing extensional and intensional interpretations that would become an issue in modern logic. Strongly inclined to a type of empiricism, he seems to have thought of the particular judgments that would come to be located at the "I" and "O" corners as providing the type of judgments appropriate for application to the empirically available world. But this results in an oddity concerning the types of judgments that may feed into our reasoning processes, as seen in the problems of the relation between the indefinite "man" and "Callias, the man." In the twentieth century, issues of this type would come to be discussed as involving confusions between the conceptions of what it is to be a member of a class (Socrates as a member of the class "philosophers"), and what it is to be a subclass of a class (empiricists as a subclass of the class "philosophers"), but earlier Kant had insisted that purely conceptual judgments such as Aristotle's particular judgments would need the participation of singular "empirical intuitions" in order to be applied to the actual world. For Hegel, however, the strict separation of singular intuitions from particular concepts was exactly the problem that he complained about in Aristotle's formal logic as opposed to Plato's. He would therefore insist on some way of translating or converting judgments involving singular conceptual determinations into particular ones, and here he took his lead more from Leibniz.

Leibniz, like later algebraic logicians of the nineteenth century, would appeal to both class relations and propositional relations—ideas of containment and ideas of order—and would translate between sentences with predicational forms that Hegel would distinguish as inherence and subsumption. Kant would criticize this type of free translation of forms as resulting in contradictions or "paralogisms" and would strictly distinguish between two types of logic that he called "general" and "transcendental." This would be the terrain on which Hegel would fashion his own logic but modeled on the structure of Timaeus's most beautiful bond or Nicomachus's "most perfect proportion." However, resources for the inclusion of singular judgments could already be found in Aristotle's own logic.

7.3 Resources for Reasoning about Singulars in Aristotle

As we have noted, there is no proper place for singular judgments as such in Aristotle's demonstrative syllogistic, but more generally he clearly recognizes the existence of such judgments. Laurence Horn (Horn 2017) has pointed to a passage in Aristotle's *Prior Analytics* suggesting what Horn calls a "singular square"—a square like the square of opposition, but dealing with singular judgments—where Aristotle addresses the issue of the relations between contraries and contradictories (fig. 7.3):

> It makes a certain difference in establishing and refuting whether one believes 'not to be this' and 'to be not this' signify the same thing or different things (for example, 'not to be white' and 'to be not white'). For these do not signify the same thing, nor is 'to be not white' the denial of 'to be white': instead 'not to be white' is.... 'It is a not white log' and 'it is not a white log' do not belong to something at the same time. For if it is a not white log it will be a log, whereas it is not necessary for what is not a white log to be a log. (Aristotle 1989, *Prior Analytics*, 51b5–31)

Importantly, Aristotle lists a variety of examples with similar grammatical structures: the negations between "he can walk" to "he can not-walk" (presumably meant as something like "he can stay still" or perhaps, "he can run"), "it is good" and "it is not-good" ("it is bad"), and so on. Hegel would link the relation of contrariety among predicates to his judgments of inherence, but the most significant resource from Aristotle for thinking of the role of singularity in logic would again come from the treatment of justice in *Nicomachean Ethics* book 5 to which we have earlier alluded and in which different means, geometric and arithmetic, are to be applied in cases of distributive and rectificatory justice, respectively. To fully grasp this, however, we need

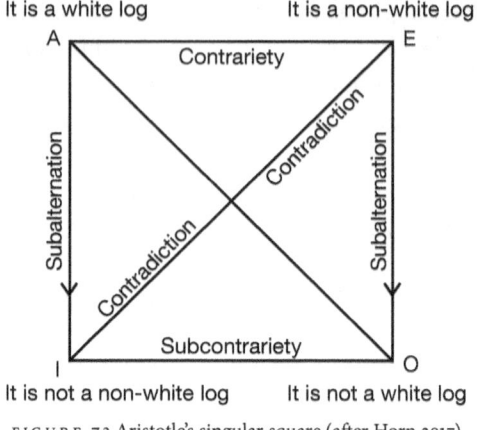

FIGURE 7.3 Aristotle's singular square (after Horn 2017).

to understand Aristotle's way of distinguishing the metaphorical from nonmetaphorical use of analogy.

Aristotle clearly distinguishes between two different types of analogy, one among similarities found within a genus, and the other among similarities found across boundaries separating entities belonging to different genera. The latter were cases he designated specifically as metaphor. For example, when one says, "Here stands my ship," one uses the word "stands," which would otherwise be said of something that is not a seagoing vessel—typically, a person or some other legged animal—and one does so to capture the second-order similarity (the "ana-logy") between the relation (the *ratio*, *logos*) of the ship's property to the ship (its lying at anchor) to that holding between the person's posture and the person (Aristotle 1984, *Poetics*, 1457b6–12). That is, a ship is to that ship's attitude as a person is to their attitude of standing. Prior to Aristotle, such a distinction seems missing in both the Pythagoreans and Plato. For example, Myles Burnyeat (Burnyeat 2000, 55–58) points out that Plato did not think of the application of words like "measure," "harmony," and "concord" beyond the musical sphere as only a metaphor. But for Aristotle, only in nonmetaphorical similarities, that is, where there is no genus crossing, was scientific demonstration possible (Aristotle 1984, *Posterior Analytics*, 75a29–75b6; Cantù 2010). Thus, while he seemed to accept the Pythagorean account of ratios in relation to music as well as in a variety of other areas, he did not extend this, as did Philolaus and Plato, to cosmology (Gibson 2005, 27–28). He presumably thought of the "harmony of the spheres" idea as no more than a metaphor. In short, Aristotle's account of metaphor was part of a broader theory of "analogy" or proportion theory, and while distinguished from the approach to similarities found in demonstrative science, it was nevertheless still afforded a type of normative use within practical reason, as we have noted in the account of justice in the *Nicomachean Ethics* where something about the qualitative singularity of the person or action being judged is grasped as relevant for one form of justice but not the other.

A further place in which Aristotle's practical philosophy impacts on the formalities of his demonstrative logic is the well-known discussion of future contingent propositions in *De Interpretatione*, chapter 9. While in modern thought we think of the propositional content of a judgment, if true, as eternally true, this was not Aristotle's view for certain contexts: "Suppose, for example, that the statement that somebody is sitting is true; after he has got up this same statement will be false" (Aristotle 1984, *Categories*, 4a24–25; see also *Metaphysics* 1051b8–18). In modern classical quantified predicate calculus, following Frege and Russell, the bare assertion "This man is sitting" would be strictly understood as incomplete and as short for "This man is sitting at time t_1"—that proposition remaining true when the man later stands at time t_2. But for Aristotle, the belief is complete as it is, and changes its truth-value with time.[11] The consequences this has are expressed in the example given in *De Interpretatione* concerning tomorrow's sea battle.[12]

Aristotle suggests that a statement such as "There will be a sea battle tomorrow" is, when considered today, neither true nor false, and that it will only become true or false tomorrow depending upon whether the sea battle occurs (Aristotle 1984, *De Interpretatione*, 18b10–25). Thus, to preserve the indeterminacy of the future, Aristotle seemed willing to deny a logical principle that would be dear to the Stoics and to later forms of propositional logic, the principle of bivalence that states that every judgment must be either true or false.[13] (Moreover, with this he also seemed to deny his own law of the excluded middle—a characteristic, as we shall see, of modern intuitionistic logic.) In short, while Aristotle denied the principle of bivalence so as to avoid what he took to be its fatalistic consequences, the Stoic logician Chrysippus would affirm bivalence in the course of arguing for a causally deterministic universe and a very different conception of human freedom (see, e.g., Bobzien 1997).

In book 3 of the *Nicomachean Ethics*, Aristotle had linked this possibility of agency to the cognitive action of "deliberation." Things that are *eph' hemin*— that is, "things that are in our power and can be done"—are things about which we can deliberate, but in "the case of the exact and self-contained sciences there is no deliberation" (Aristotle 1984, *Nicomachean Ethics*, 1112a31–b1). Moreover, Aristotle claims that if an action is possible, then so is its contrary. If virtue is in our power, then so too is vice (1113b6–8).[14] This coincides with what he says about substances and their individual instances in the *Categories*. While substance itself "does not admit of a more or less . . . it seems most distinctive of substance that what is numerically one and the same is able to receive contraries. . . . For example, an individual man—one and the same—becomes pale at one time and dark at another, and hot and cold, and bad and good" (Aristotle 1984, *Categories*, 3b31–4a20). As is obvious from the example, while substances are discrete, their inherent properties lie on continua along which properties transition into their opposites. Once more, deliberation as a type of reasoning about specific individuals invokes different logical principles from those found in demonstrative thought about nonspecific and so generalizable instances of kinds. As Hegel stressed, the views of Aristotle should not be simply equated with the type of formal syllogistic found in the *Prior* and *Posterior Analytics*.

This logical dichotomy in Aristotle between the type of reasoning appropriate to specific individuals, on the one hand, and the scientific reasoning that treats individuals as indeterminate instances of their kinds, on the other, provides resources for Hegel's expansion of the Platonic syllogistic with its doubled or divided mean. These distinctions would be now applied systematically within the otherwise "formal" logic that runs through his treatment of judgments and syllogisms in the "Subjective Logic" of *The Science of Logic*.

7.4 Disambiguating Aristotle's Singular-Particular Conflation in the Syllogism

In the "Subjective Logic" of *The Science of Logic* Hegel famously describes the syllogism as the "truth" of the judgment (*SL*, 593; 12:95), and the most developed form of judgment, which transitions into the syllogism in Hegel's subjective logic, is called the "judgment of the concept" (*SL*, 581–587; 12:84–89). This is a directly evaluative judgment about some specific and existing human action or action product: Hegel's examples are "This act is good" and "This house is bad" (*SL*, 583; 12:85), the demonstrative "this" in each case indicating the actual existence and, at the time of the judgment, presentness to the judging subject of the house or act in question. There is an absolute value, some real involved that is good or bad, something that is presupposed by each of the positive and negative opposed judgments, and the opposition of the predicates "good" and "bad" is of course what Wolff describes as the mathematically (rather than linguistically) based opposition described by Kant (Wolff 1999). Moreover, "good" and "bad" are typically at the extremes of a graded continuum with a midpoint that is neither particularly good nor bad and at which the good becomes bad and the bad good. The opposed predicates represent opposed ways in which that concrete content can be taken. This combination of an accessible singular existing subject and contrarily opposed predicates of "more or less" will retrieve features of earlier "qualitative" aspects of judgments belonging to earlier cycles of developing judgment forms to be found in Hegel's account of judgment. Color judgments show a version of this, for example, where judgments of green transition into judgments of blue, but here the contraries are not, as in the judgment of the concept, limited to two. Importantly, as the "truth" of these earlier judgment forms, the judgment of the concept brings to the fore earlier negated but ultimately ineliminable features of such judgments.

The form of judgment exemplified by opposed judgments such as "This house is good" and "This house is bad" will be seen to expand into an apodictic judgment in which the subject-predicate relation becomes mediated by a middle term that effectively contains the justification of that initial judgment—for example, "This house, as so and so constituted, is good." Here the middle term is a particular that gives a general reason for the judgment, mediating the relation between the singular subject "this house" and the evaluative universal "good." It allows us to understand why *a* house or *any* house so characterized would be considered good. Even if this house were the only existing house to be "so and so constituted," there will always be other possible houses of which this evaluation could be made. Thus, judgments of this type open up otherwise questionable ontological domains, such as that of abstract logically possible alternatives to the actual, just as algebraically introduced numbers had opened up similarly questionable ontological domains, like those of negative, imaginary, and other "impossible" numbers (Nagel 1979). In his logic Hegel both recognizes and responds to this situation in a way analogous to that in which Carnot had recognized and responded to the situation within contemporary algebra.

This tripartite singular-particular-universal structure (S-P-U) can now be easily expanded into a traditional formal syllogism, the "syllogism of existence." In its first figure, this S-P-U structure is shorthand for a modified Aristotelian syllogism (*SL*, 590; 12:93):

S-P (this house is so and so constituted)
P-U (a house so and so constituted is good)
∴ S-U (this house is good).

In the premises S-P and P-U, with two extremes linked by a doubled middle term (one referring to the concrete way *this house* is constituted, the other to *any house* displaying such features), Hegel surely recognized the doubled ratios or proportions found in Plato's *Timaeus* and *Republic* and Nicomachus's *Introduction to Arithmetic*. Within the Aristotelian framework, however, with its blurred singular-particular relation, this appears as a simple geometric proportion, $a : b :: b : c$.[15]

Looking for a more Aristotelian alternative to Hegel's modification we might write:

1. All houses so and so constituted are good.
2. This house is so and so constituted.
∴ 3. This house is good.

However, in relation to the formally identical syllogism, "All humans are mortal, *Now Gaius is a human*, Therefore Gaius is mortal," Hegel points out that "the major premise is correct only because and to the extent that the *conclusion is correct*" (*SL*, 611; 12:112).[16] Here Hegel is following Kant's analysis of evaluative aesthetic judgments in the *Critique of the Power of Judgment* (Kant 2000, pt. 1, section 1, book 1): there are no rules for this type of goodness, and so one could not deduce from some kind of definition of a good house that this one, possessing the relevant features, must therefore be good.[17] Saying what is good about houses depends upon making first-order judgments about specific houses. And yet our judging practices necessarily involve using justifications of this sort. There must be some type of inferential commerce between judgments about singular houses (this house or that one) and about indeterminate particular houses (a house with such and such features). This, I take it, is the syllogism interpreted in a Platonic way with "divided" middle term. It must be able to have characteristics of both singular (a Fregean object) and universal (a Fregean concept).

The form of Hegel's syllogism will develop through two further figures into a final degenerative fourth, with the second and third figures being represented by successive reorderings of the original S-P-U structure. Thus, the second figure is given as P-S-U (*SL*, 597; 12:99) and the third S-U-P (*SL*, 600; 12:102). A reader with some familiarity with Aristotle's logic will recognize the Aristotelian equivalent of this. In Aristotle, the two syllogistic premises share a "middle term" (*meson*) that is eliminated in the conclusion. Paradigmatically, as in the first figure (Aristotle 1989, *Prior Analytics*, 26b33), this middle term will be subject of one premise and predicate in another to conform with the transitivity of the containment relation. In the second figure, however, it plays the role of predicate in both premises (26b34–36), and in the third, that of subject of both premises (28a10–12).[18]

As has been suggested, for Aristotle it is because only the first pattern shows the transitivity of the containment relation underlying the proof of the inference that the second and third figures must be converted back to those "perfect" syllogistic inferences found in the first figure. Because Hegel distinguishes the (syntactic) subject-predicate distinction from the (semantic) distinction between the singular, particular, and universal determinations of the concept, his account of the figures will be more complex. This is where the principle of homomorphic equivalence promises to illuminate the *movement* of the middle term. As modeled by a pair of incommensurable ratios, on the Hegelian reading, the movement of the middle term can be understood as a transition from a judgment displaying an internal mean to its inverse, a judgment with a corresponding external dividing mean. For the moment, this will supply us with sufficient interpretative tools to return to the type of judgments from which Hegel's account starts—judgments that will develop into the implicitly syllogistic judgment of the concept sketched above. One further point needs to be made about syllogisms, however.

From Hegel's choice of examples of judgments of the concept it is clear that he has in mind what has been described as involving the application of "essentially contested" concepts (Gallie 1964). What Hegel's examples bring into view, I suggest, is that it is the contestability of such judgments that will lead to efforts on the parts of the judges to say why the other should accept them—that they will, in Wilfrid Sellars's terminology, be given a place in the "space of reasons" (Redding 2007, ch. 2.4). This is the idea that has been developed by Robert Brandom in his "inferentialist" interpretation of Hegel's logic—at least the logic he sees implicit in Hegel's *Phenomenology of Spirit* (Brandom 2019). However, from within the classical Fregean perspective he adopts and adapts, the essential duality of judgment form in Hegel becomes invisible. As we see below, Hegel's analysis of judgment structure will be more in line with the approach of sophisticated algebraic syllogistic logicians following in the wake of Boole's revival of Leibnizian logic—later nineteenth-century algebraic logicians like C. S. Peirce, Hugh MacColl, W. E. Johnson, and, a little later, Arend Heyting.[19]

7.5 Disambiguating Aristotle's Singular-Particular Conflation in the Judgment

In his account of judgment, Hegel starts from an initial form of judgment something like what would be called "primary judgments" in the form of logic introduced by George Boole—they are the immediately perceptual *de-re* judgments in which the adjectival predicate term is understood to "inhere" in the subject term in a way that captures how a perceivable quality is experienced as inhering in the concrete substance it qualifies. Hegel calls these "judgments of existence [*Dasein*]," and his favorite example is "The rose is red" (*SL*, 558–559; 12:61–62; *E:L*, §172). Clearly, we need to be careful as to how we understand the subject phrase "the rose"—it could, as in the subject of the judgment of the concept, be meant in the sense of "this rose" (indicating some actual and hence directly perceivable rose), it could be meant in the sense of an indifferent "some rose" (existing somewhere and somewhen), or it could be meant in the sense of "the rose as such"—the genus rose, as it were. In the latter two cases the sentence could be uttered without any actual rose in view.[20] It is clear that Hegel intends the former. In the *Encyclopedia Logic*, for example, he uses the demonstrative phrase explicitly (*E:L*, §172, addition; §174, addition). But the most appropriately Hegelian "proof" of the essential demonstrability of the subject of the judgment of existence will come from the judgment of the concept, understood as the "truth" of the earlier form. The house or act that was good or bad, it will be recalled, was this house and this act.

In making an empirical judgment concerning the color of some specific rose, it is natural to think of the predicate offered as being "measured" externally by the perceived quality of the thing appearing as subject of the predication. But like later critics of "primary judgments," Hegel will focus on the logical shortcomings of such judgment forms. His "positive judgments of existence" are barely judgments at all, and, rather than aspiring to truth, are capable only of "correctness" (*Richtigkeit*) (*SL*, 562; 12:65; *E:L*, §172, remark and addition). Moreover, they have their "truth" in the "negative" judgments that succeed them, which in turn will lead to more complex judgments in which the predicate "is said of" or "subsumes" the subject term.

This latter form will characterize a type of quantitative judgment that he calls a "judgment of reflection" and that in contrast to being *de-re* in the sense of about some *res* or substance might better be described as *de-facto*—judgments not primarily about specific things such as roses but rather purported circumstances or states of affairs involving those things. To describe a judgment as one in which the predicate "subsumes" the subject is, Hegel puts it, to say that that predicate "measures" the subject term.[21] Just as negation in the initial judgment form occupies a point "internal" to the subject-predicate relation, I have suggested that so does its equivalent "position," that is, affirmation. When this rose is said to be red, what is affirmed is the predicate, being red, of the subject, this rose. This is shown by the appropriate contrast class into which the claimed redness of the rose is being put. The rose is red rather than yellow, blue, pink, and so on. "When it is said that, for instance, the rose is not red, only the *determinateness* of the predicate is thereby denied and thus separated from the universality which equally attaches to it; the universal sphere, *color*, is retained; if the rose is not red, it is nonetheless assumed that it has a color, though another color" (*SL*, 565; 12:68).

The negation that we have seen in the passage from the positive to the negative judgment of existence drives a type of abstractive process in which an element with the initial determinacy of concrete singularity is driven first to a less determinate particularity and then to a maximally indeterminate universality. Importantly, these more complex and abstract judgment types encountered on the way might be judged to be true even when immediate appearance says otherwise, as in looking at a red rose by moonlight, for example, when it may perhaps appear to be dark purple or even black, one may, taking in the total circumstances involved, still judge it to be red. This might be regarded as a consequence of the type of "Copernican" reversal at the heart of modern science. The sun's seeming to move is countered by a consideration of the broader circumstances or conditions under which such a perception has occurred. And yet, like Carnot's criticism of the metaphysical reality of infinitesimals and other impossible numbers, Hegel will be critical of the idea that such *abstracta* correspond to some metaphysical reality. He will thus resist the type of "ladder" analogy in which thought can climb to more and more abstract levels—a ladder leading to something like the "God's-eye view" found in Leibniz or a series of increasingly abstract languages as those found in Lambert's analogy of the languages spoken on the moon, on the earth, on the sun, and so on. From these accounts, what prevents us humans reaching our goal is the infinite number of steps involved.[22] What will correspond to the God's-eye "view from nowhere" in Hegel—the locus of the "infinite judgment"—will be closer to the "points at infinity" introduced by Kepler via the use of the principle of continuity and taken up by Desargues and Pascal and, later, Carnot. As Carnot would stress, mathematical devices such as infinitesimal magnitudes should be stripped of their metaphysical associations: they exist within systematically linked practices and are ultimately tied to executable concepts. "Points" at infinity as vanishing points on a horizon will be linked to viewing points in the world as corresponding "pole" of the "polar." Translated into judgments, the contextual or indexical judgment of inherence is linked to an equivalent but inverted judgment of reflection, just as the latter will be linked to the former. Each judgment form takes the measure of the world in its own way, and, importantly, each will be able to take the measure of the other. Their unity will be in accord with the principle of homomorphic equivalence, and its ultimate expression will be the syllogism. Hence the infinite judgment will represent the zenith of the ascending abstractive phase of a loop that will then descend though a transformation of the judgment form in which it returns to another type of concrete judgment. As with the "triangle of triangles" the imagery is that of being drawn deeper and deeper into empirical reality so as to grasp its true structure.

What needs stressing here is the fact that while qualitative judgments will be able to be translated into quantitative ones and vice versa, a translation enabled by the fact that they share the same absolute content, neither will be able to represent the definitive logical form of judgment itself. Any judgment for Hegel must be understood as effectively able to be given either form, but equally these opposed forms are forms of a single, absolute, content. Judgments must have an irreducibly "dual" form that, as will be seen, is found in the algebraic syllogistic logicians of the nineteenth century but not among Fregean classicists. These are the opposed judgment types that are united in the syllogism.

The first phase of each of these cycles of judgment form that Hegel will trace will commence with some version of the concrete *de-re* judgment, although these will include quasi-substantial ones in which the names of kinds rather than individuals are the initial subjects of Hegel's second cycle. This first phase will involve abstraction to something closer to the equivalent propositional or *de-facto* form with its typical external locus of affirmation or negation. While the first one or two steps in each cycle might be thought of as ascending successive rungs up the Platonic "ladder" it is important that this process cannot be simply iterated in the way that seems to be available within Aristotle's framework and that is found in the logics of Leibniz and Kant suggesting the "ladder" image. The indeterminacy of a continuing geometric series needs to be overcome in a way that, involving a reversal of direction, allows the extreme terms to be bound together.

The circularity characterizing the development of the judgment- and syllogism-forms in Hegel's subjective logic will in fact be an instance of a more general circular pattern of development marking not only Hegel's objective and subjective logics but the whole *Encyclopedia of the Philosophical Sciences*, within which Hegel had set out his mature thought. Thus, he would come to describe each part of his system as "a philosophical whole, a circle coming to closure within itself, but in each of its parts the philosophical idea exists in a particular determinacy or element [*einer besonderen Bestimmtheit oder Elemente*]. The individual circle [*einzelne Kreis*], simply because it is itself a totality, also breaks through the boundary of its element and founds a further sphere. The whole thus presents itself as a circle of circles" (*E:L*, §15)[23]—a structure surely recalling the earlier "triangle of triangles." In the context of *The Science of Logic*, Hegel refers to these logical cycles as "cycles of determination":

> In the different cycles of determination and especially in the progress of the exposition, or, more precisely, in the progress of the concept in the exposition

of itself, it is of capital concern always to clearly distinguish what still *is in itself or implicitly* and what *is posited*, how determinations are in the concept and how they are as posited or as existing-for-other. (*SL*, 95; 21:110)

Hegel's cyclical account of judgment- and syllogism-forms in the "Subjective Logic" will here be treated as such cycles of determination or, as I shall put it, *redetermination*.

Determination (*Bestimmung*) had been a term of art within Kant's philosophy. As George di Giovanni has put it, "To single out an object, whether by trait, direction, or production, for the sake of recognizing it as possibly or actually in existence (*Dasein*) is the overarching meaning that in Kant holds together the derivatives of *bestimmten* and the variety of contexts in which these are used" (di Giovanni 2021, 145). Di Giovanni points out that, for Kant, "everything existing is thoroughly determined" (Kant 1998, A573/B601), but, of course, knowledge of something in its complete determination is, for Kant, beyond human cognition. Human theoretical cognition does not extend to "things in themselves." Effectively, *for us* objects are known determinately along two different axes, the conceptual and the intuitive. An object is conceptually determinate—that is, logically possible—if "of *every two* contradictorily opposed predicates, only one can apply to it" (Kant 1998, A571/B599). On the other hand, an object is known as actual rather than simply logically possible via the sensuous content of empirical intuition. Here, the discrete, all-or-none character of conceptual determinateness contrasts with the fact that the empirical determination of the actual via intuition comes in terms of the "more or less." Just as the extensive magnitudes of space and time are continuous or "flowing," so too is the "intensive magnitude" of objects of empirical consciousness, varying between the values of 1 and 0 (A165–176/B207–218).

As suggested above, Hegel does not accept the Kantian dichotomy of concepts and intuitions, but neither does he simply reject it, as found in modern predicate calculus, for example, with its ontological reduction to objects and concepts. Rather, the features distinguishing the intuitions and concepts at work in empirical consciousness will for Hegel be found internal to the conceptual. Essentially, empirical judgments of objects will vary in "intensive magnitude" between maximum (Kant's 1) and minimum (Kant's 0) just as had Kant's empirical intuitions. Thus, the cycles of redetermination through which the proper concept of judgment unfolds can be thought of such that the abstractive phase moves from maximum to minimum values of intensive magnitude and the reverse phase from minimally determinate *abstracta* back down to some new concrete maximum. The details of these processes will be explored when some of the resources provided by the post-Boolean algebraic logicians have been introduced. Hegel did not have the advantage of being able to utilize the products of the work of these later figures, but he *was* able to utilize some of the basic logical ideas to be found in Leibniz and Ploucquet, who had anticipated, at least in broad outline, aspects of these developments.

8

The Return of Leibnizian Logic in the Nineteenth Century: From Boole to Heyting

> The design of the following treatise is to investigate the fundamental laws of those operations of the mind by which reasoning is performed; to give expression to them in the symbolical language of a Calculus, and upon this foundation to establish the science of Logic and construct its method; to make that method itself the basis of a general method for the application of the mathematical doctrine of Probabilities; and, finally, to collect from the various elements of truth brought to view in the course of these inquiries some probable intimations concerning the nature and constitution of the human mind.
> GEORGE BOOLE, *An Investigation of the Laws of Thought*

Toward the end of the nineteenth century, a then relatively unknown German mathematician, Gottlob Frege, reviewed a work that systematized and presented to the German scientific community a new form of logic (Frege 1960). The work reviewed was the first volume of what would eventually become the three-volume *Vorlesungen über der Algebra der Logik* (*Lectures on the Algebra of Logic*) by Ernst Schröder (Schröder 1890–1905), a work that was regarded as having brought to maturity a form of logic commenced about half a century before in England with George Boole.[1] Boole had attempted to modernize the ancient tradition of logic by the application of algebra to the Aristotelian syllogism, not knowing that much of what he proposed had been advanced by Leibniz a century and a half before him. Frege himself had been working on a different type of logic, now generally known as classical predicate calculus with quantification, that, especially being promoted by Bertrand Russell in the new century, would become the official logic of the movement of analytic philosophy.[2] Outside academic philosophy, however, Boole's logic would continue to be influential. This broadly Boolean framework of logic that we might characterize as "Leibniz Mark II," I will argue, provides a more appropriate context than Frege's within which to further examine Hegel's own logic.

As had been pointed out by the British logician Philip Jourdain (Jourdain 1914, iii), both algebraic Aristotelians and Fregean anti-Aristotelians could, in retrospect, be said to have developed ideas that had been earlier sketched by Leibniz,[3] but in each case the focus was on different parts of Leibniz's dual project. If one thinks of Leibniz's anticipated revolution in logic as combining a *characteristica universalis* and a calculus with which to perform combinations of characters of the former, then in general the Booleans would uncouple the calculus from the idea of a universal concept language, which they generally discarded. For them, formal logic was not an autonomous meaningful language but a "disinterpreted" mathematical calculus, in need of reinterpretation. In contrast, Frege held to both parts of Leibniz's project with the primary focus on the idea of logic as a universal concept-script (*Begriffsschrift*) (Frege 1997). The conception of the truths of arithmetic as resting upon the truths of logic in this sense would be known as "logicism."

Among the post-Booleans, the rejection of the logicist idea of logic as a universal language is exemplified in the algebraic approach of the Cambridge logician W. E. Johnson, who tended to treat logic as what Peirce had described as a *logica utens*, a type of formal device useful in specific contexts to aid human reasoning, but which itself depended upon human reasoning and human language for its interpretation.[4] As Johnson put it in the early 1890s, a logical calculus "aims at exhibiting, in a non-intelligent form, those same intelligent principles that are actually required for working it" (Johnson 1892, 3).[5] That is, in order for these "disinterpreted" strings of symbols to be grasped as logical, they must once more be reinterpreted, which suggests two things: they must rely upon the resources of everyday language and thought for their reinterpretation, and reinterpretation will in turn result in new meanings being given to those elements—meanings different from those they intuitively had possessed before this procedure.

Here Johnson's point aligns with Hegel's criticism of the reduction of logic to the algebraic formalizations of Euler or the geometric ones of Lambert. While determinations of the concept may be "like lines or the letters of algebra, *diverse*; and . . . also *opposed* and allow, therefore, the signs of *plus* and *minus* . . . they themselves and especially their connections . . . are in their essential nature entirely different. . . . Since the human being has in language a means of designation that is appropriate to reason, it is otiose to look for a less perfect means of representation to bother oneself with" (*SL*, 544–545; 12:47–48). As Elena Ficara points out in relation to this passage and a similar one pertaining to Leibniz from the *Encyclopedia*, "Hegel emphasizes the difficulties of fixing a *complete* hieroglyphic language, and the fact that the conceptual and logical relations require signs that are susceptible of a continuous revision" (Ficara 2021, 55). That is, from this point of view common to both Johnson and Hegel, human reason could not be definitively formalized in an axiomatic way because it is forever possible for humans to reflect on and revise those axioms.[6] Ironically, this seems to suggest that the most

RETURN OF LEIBNIZIAN LOGIC IN THE NINETEENTH CENTURY 171

mathematical among the modern logicians—the algebraic Aristotelians for whom formal logic *was* mathematics rather than an ideal language within which the foundation for mathematics was to be laid bare—could entertain a philosophical conception of logic that is closer to Hegel than is the Fregean paradigm. This chapter will explore those features of the logic of a number of the algebraists that help shed light on aspects of Hegel's "Subjective Logic." In the final two chapters, specific examples of these convergences will be explored.

8.1 George Boole's Logic and Its Immediate Aftermath

Leibniz's logic had remained relatively unknown until revived at the turn of the twentieth century by the French logician Louis Couturat (Couturat 1901, 1903), and by this time mathematical or "symbolic" logic had been well established by its "second founder" (Lewis and Langford 1932, 9), the English mathematician George Boole. Boole, without any foreknowledge of Leibniz, had retraced Leibniz's path with the application of an algebra linked to a binary number system to the Aristotelian syllogism. We will be familiar with the basic general features of Boole's logic from what we have learned of Leibniz, but some important differences need to be noted. Boole starts off with a calculus of classes, but this time understood explicitly from an extensionalist perspective. Nevertheless, problems of the sort facing Leibniz surrounding the relation between the logic of classes to one of propositions would remain. Thus, Frege would criticize Boole's system for the fact that its two parts, its term and propositional logics, "run alongside one another, so that one is like the mirror image of the other, but for that very reason stands in no organic relation to it" (Frege 1979, 14). From the perspective of nineteenth-century geometry, however, these two parts could be understood as instantiating a particular type of "duality" that had come to the attention of mathematicians (Nagel 1939, §§45–60; Demey and Smessaert 2022). Frege had thought he had solved this problem, and it would be central to his and Russell's case against the algebraists. Frege and Russell, however, would count as distant targets of criticisms that Hegel had aimed at Leibniz.

Boole's approach to algebra was in line with the "disinterpretational theory of algebra" that had been developed by a group of Cambridge mathematicians, George Peacock, Duncan Gregory, Augustus De Morgan, and the computing pioneer Charles Babbage earlier in the century. Members of this "analytical society" were intent on bringing to England the European algebraic approaches to differential calculus found in Lagrange and others—the very interpretation that Carnot had a few decades earlier opposed.[7] They brought to mathematics, however, an approach that would resemble one aspect of Hegel's method in logic, in that they regarded the operations of algebra as able to be abstracted from application to the specific domain to which they were directed, paradigmatically, the arithmetical manipulation of numbers. Boole's logic would emerge as an early expression of this "symbolic" approach.

In 1847 Boole published a short work, *Mathematical Analysis of Logic*, which applied algebra to syllogistic logic, but he would later, in 1854, add the more substantial work for which he would come to be known, *An Investigation of the Laws of Thought, on Which Are Founded the Mathematical Theories of Logic and Probabilities*. In the first book Boole makes it clear that the algebraic calculus he is applying to logic "does not depend upon the interpretation of the symbols which are employed, but solely upon the laws of their combinations" (Boole 1847, 3). Like Leibniz, Boole chose to work with an algebra applied to a binary rather than decimal number system, and early in his presentation uses "the symbol 1 to represent the Universe" (14), or sometimes, "the logical universe" (68). In *The Laws of Thought* this would become "the universe of discourse" (Boole 1854, 30). Although not explicitly defining '0,' Boole used it to designate the nonexistence of a class. The parallels with the general framework within which Hegel's logic would commence, the distinction "being" and "nothing" (*SL*, 59–60; 21:68–70), are striking. This distinction would be immediately *aufgehoben* in Hegel, however, signaling its highly questionable status as a fundamental distinction—from a logical point of view, the concept nothing (like the set containing nothing) is not nothing. Boole, however, would get trapped in this dichotomy that was meant to distinguish being from nothing, on the one hand, and true from false, on the other.

Within this class-based logic, inferential processes would be understood in much the same way that Aristotle had understood "perfect syllogisms," that is, the "part-whole" model in which one class is included in another as part of a whole. But for Boole the model was now understood explicitly extensionally not intensionally as it had been by Leibniz.[8] If x is an element of class X, and class X is included in class Y, then x is an element of Y. If, for example, Socrates is a human, and the class of humans is contained in that of mortals, then Socrates is mortal.

The ancient distinction between arithmetic and geometric relations that Hegel comments upon in relation to Plato would also find a place in Boole's logic in his employment of operations on classes traditionally found in arithmetic, those of "product" (multiplication) and "sum" (addition), operations seemingly confused by Leibniz in his idea of conceptual addition (above, chapter 5.1).[9] For example, that "the product xy will represent, in succession, the selection from the class Y, and the selection from the class Y of such individuals of the class X as are contained in it, the result being the class whose members are both Xs and Ys" (Boole 1847, 14).[10] Thus, the product of two sets, X and Y, would be understood as itself a set, consisting of all the "ordered pairs" that resulted from pairing each element of the first set with every element of the second. In contrast, the sum of two sets X and Y consisted of a set formed by merging the members of the two sets into one.[11] This allowed the component judgments within syllogisms to be now represented by class relations. For example, "All Xs are Ys" means that "to select out of the Universe all Ys, and from these to select all Xs, is the same as to select at once from the Universe all Xs. Hence, $xy = x$" (20). "Factoring" this equation produces $x(1-y) = 0$, which can be interpreted as declaring the nonexistence of things that are both X and not Y.

Leibniz had realized that the containment relations underlying relations of logical inference could also be thought to hold between collections of sentences about them just as it held among objects themselves. Similarly, Boole applied his algebra to propositions as well as to collections of objects. The underlying algebraic ideas of product and sum now allowed for two types of logical relations holding among propositions—conjunction as in "p and q" and disjunction as in "p or q," respectively. The relation between these two logical connectives, reminiscent of the similarly defined "arithmetic" and "geometric" means in Plato, would instantiate the type of "duality" that had been discovered within nineteenth century geometric algebra (Nagel 1939, §§45–60), as shown in "De Morgan's Laws," which state that the negation of a disjunction is equal to the conjunction of the negations, and, inversely, the negation of a conjunction is equal to the disjunction of the negations.[12]

The differentiation of term and propositional logics, however, necessitated making a distinction between two different types of propositions that Boole called "primary" and "secondary propositions," and some form of this distinction would be held by all the algebraists who followed Boole. Boole's distinction is essentially the same as that between Hegel's judgments of inherence and judgments of reflection, and both reflect the type of underlying duality expressed in De Morgan's Laws.

Boole gives as an example of a primary proposition the sentence "The sun shines," which includes an object, the sun, within a group of objects, things that shine (Boole 1854, 38).[13] In this sense, the judgment "classified" the object that was referred to in the subject term by identifying it as a member of the class referred to by the predicate, the class of shining things. As examples of secondary propositions Boole gives the compound propositions "If the sun shines the earth is warmed" and "It is true that the sun shines." Unlike "The sun shines," neither of these propositions is *about* the sun. The latter, for example, is about the primary proposition (that is in turn about the sun): it says of that proposition that it is true. It corresponds to what the medievals had called a *de-dicto* proposition, a proposition *about* something said, some *dictum*.[14] A similar situation holds for the hypothetical, as neither the antecedent nor the consequent asserts anything of the sun. In fact, what seems to be asserted by the entire utterance is a relation of dependence between the two primary propositions.[15]

Later, Russell would separate the question of the meaning of a conditional "If the sun shines the earth warms" from that of the inference from an assertion "The sun shines" to another, "The earth warms," but this distinction between an "inference" (something that a reasoner does in moving from one judgment to another) and an "implication" (a certain kind of compound proposition whose truth-value is dependent upon those of its component propositions) would only emerge clearly during the years between Boole and Russell (Prior 1949).[16] Russell's criticism was based on the claim that Boole's primary propositions were not propositions at all, and should have no place in logic. Unfortunately, this would rule out many everyday claims believed to be capable of being true or false, such as in an example that would be used in a dispute between Russell and MacColl, the assertion "Mrs Brown is not at home." It would also rule out Hegel's qualitative "judgments of inherence," such as "This rose is red." From Hegel's perspective, such "positive judgments of existence" needed to be *aufgehoben* within the logical system, but of course to be *aufgehoben* means to be preserved in being negated; it does not mean simple elimination or reduction to some other form as favored by Russell.

The logical behavior of Boole's logical connectives "and" and "or" is rather rudimentary. On the one hand, if one knows that the sentence "a and b" is true, one can infer that the sentence "a" is true, and one can infer that the sentence "b" is true. On the other hand, if one knows that "a" is true, one thereby knows that "a or b" is true (and similarly, one knows that "a or b" is true if one knows that "b" is true). Bertrand Russell would go on to define the material implicational connective "if . . . then . . ." in terms of the notion of logical product or logical sum together with negation. To know that "a implies b" is, he would claim, to know that either "a" is true and "b" is true or that "a" is false and "b" is true or that "a is false and b is false." The only combination to be ruled out is the conjunction "a" is true and "b" is false. Russell's definition of "implies" would later be criticized,[17] but it brings out the general feature of the interdefinability existing among the various logical connectives in such mathematical formalizations. Eventually different "logics" would come to be described as differentiated by what could be considered basic and the ways in which what was derived had been derived.

The first to recognize Boole's logic from a philosophical point of view, and to adopt a critically transformed version of it, had been William Stanley Jevons, but Jevons objected to what he perceived as Boole's having forced properly logical laws into the straitjacket of mathematical ones. Boole, he thought, did not pay sufficient heed to specific human intuitions about logical relations, and he criticized Boole's interpretation of the word "or," arguing for it having an "inclusive" rather than "exclusive" sense.[18] As a model of the practice of human inferring, Boole's logic from this perspective needed to be tested against the evidence.

After Jevons, Boole's work would be taken up by the Cambridge philosopher John Venn (1834–1923), and two claims contained in his influential book *Symbolic Logic* (Venn 1881) are worth noting. First, to counter the type of skepticism found in Jevons to the specifically algebraic aspects of Boole, Venn stressed how such a generalized algebra abstracted from the familiar interpretations of the symbols involved—a point that would be repeated later by his younger colleague Johnson (1892). This disinterpretation, Venn thought, allowed science to progress to new conceptions:

> A thorough generalization assumes sometimes an entirely unfamiliar aspect to those who were previously acquainted only with some very specialized form of the generalized process:—thus we all know what a step it is to most beginners to extend "weight" into "universal gravitation." In such cases the realization of the generalization may amount almost to the acquisition of a new conception, rather than to the mere extension of one with which we were already intimate. (Venn 1881, xxi)

In relation to this we might mention one justification for classical learning Hegel gave when delivering an address when headmaster of a school in Nuremburg in 1809. There he describes an alienation (*Entfremdung*) "that is the condition of theoretical erudition," a necessary "divorce" (*Scheidung*) of the soul from its "natural condition and essence" by means of which it is led into a "remote and foreign world" (*ferne, fremde Welt*)" (*Misc*, 296–297). The mechanical drudgery involved in learning a foreign language cannot be avoided as "the mechanical . . . awakens the mind's desire to digest the indigestible food forced upon it, to make intelligible what is at first without life and meaning, and to assimilate it." This mechanical element in language study, he notes, "constitutes the beginning of logical training. . . . In learning grammar therefore, the understanding itself first becomes learned" (297).[19]

The second feature concerns Venn's attempt to sketch the historical roots of algebraic logic in which he mentions, besides the earlier work of Leibniz, the later works of Ploucquet and Lambert (Venn 1881, xxxii). Lambert, he goes on, had recognized the logical analogue of the four algebraic operations, addition, subtraction, multiplication, and division, as well as the inverse relations that hold among them, subtraction being the inverse of addition, division of multiplication (Venn 1881, xxxiv and n2).[20] We have noted the roles that these basic arithmetical operations and their inverses had played, along with exponentiation and its inverse, in Hegel's elucidation of the "complete concept" of number in book 1 of *The Science of Logic*.[21] Moreover, in an observation that would surely have struck a chord for Hegel, Venn noted that while Lambert realized logical division is the inverse of multiplication, "he failed to observe the indefinite character commonly assumed by inverse operations.... He regarded the inverse as being merely the *putting back* a thing, so to say, where it was before" (xxxv). In Hegel's logical cycles, the role of inverse or negation is to bring about redetermination. Restoring meaning to disinterpreted concepts allows breaking with the understandings that shaped the past.

Like Jevons, all of the post-Booleans saw the need to go beyond the limitations of Boole's logic, and it is Peirce who is generally seen as having made the most progress there. To understand his advances, however, his work must be examined in the context of that of the rival approaches of Frege and Russell.

8.2 Peirce and Frege: Rival Approaches to the Logic of Relations

A feature of Frege's logic that has been celebrated concerns the way that it allowed for the logical representation of relations, thus overcoming a major shortcoming of the Aristotelian tradition in which the subject-predicate structure of sentences meant that only "monadic" (one-placed) predicates could be said of a subject. While Aristotle's approach was adequate for simple judgments of inherence as in "This rose is red," it was far from adequate for representing the logical structure of more complex judgments. For example, in relation to the two sentences "Jane is reading *War and Peace*" and "Arnold is reading *Madame Bovary*," the Aristotelian analysis would treat "is reading *War and Peace*" and "is reading *Madame Bovary*" as distinct, simple predicates—as unrelated as the predicates "blue" and "round," for example. Clearly, it would be preferable if both predicates could be understood as containing the same concept <to read> that could be applied to a variety of possibly readable things. This is what Frege had achieved by bringing the algebraic relation of function to argument to replace the traditional subject-predicate relation.

While the algebraic notion of function had been used by mathematicians for centuries, subtle changes in its meaning had occurred in the nineteenth century.²² Frege generalized the idea of functions applied to sets of numbers to functions understood as relating combinations of propositions to one of the two truth-values, true and false.²³ This required the proposition, now regarded as an abstract entity capable of having properties of being true or false, to be the most basic unit of meaning. That is, the proposition was no longer considered as somehow assembled from the independently meaningful subject and predicate terms of Aristotelian term logic. The components of propositions were rather abstractions arrived at by the device of removing the referring terms from the original sentences so as to create sentences with gaps—Russell would call these "propositional functions." Such incomplete entities would only become proper propositions when these gaps left by the removed referring terms were filled, and this could be done by the use of algebraic variables that were in turn "bound" by universal and existential "quantifiers."

In the 1870s and 1880s, the American philosopher and scientist Charles Sanders Peirce had sketched an alternative to the direction being taken by Frege and had found a way to extend Boole's algebra to capture relations. Moreover, he had independently introduced the idea of universal and existential "quantifiers" just a few years after the publication of Frege's *Begriffsschrift*. Peirce's solution would make explicit features that others have recognized as implicit in Leibniz's logic of 1682, and it would maintain more of the operational sense of "function" than that implicit within the entirely abstract set-theoretical approach of Frege and Russell.

Peirce would draw upon the advances in linear algebra made by his father, Benjamin Peirce, an eminent mathematician, whose work *Linear Associative Algebra* (Peirce 1881) the younger Peirce had edited and prepared for publication after his father's death.²⁴ In a series of papers, starting in 1870, and drawing on the work of both Boole and his contemporary Augustus De Morgan, Charles extended Boole's algebraic logic to encompass relations by treating a two-placed predicate as a name of an ordered pair of objects, thus making explicit the "geometric" idea of partial order that has been described as implicit in Leibniz (Swoyer 1994). Whereas Boole's basic logical relation had been the '=' of an equation, Peirce introduced a sign '$\prec$' to signify the relation of as small as or less than or equal to (standardly written as '$\leq$') (Peirce 1870, 367). Typical of the disinterpreting tendencies of modern algebra, this relation that had standardly held among numbers, could now be given a more general meaning, being defined in terms of the properties holding of a relation between nonspecified objects, those of reflexivity, anti-symmetry, and transitivity. With this, relations of class inclusion became just one way among others of establishing an order among elements. Moreover, while the familiar

Aristotelian relations of class inclusion used by Boole had been transitive, they were not reflexive.

For Leibniz, the idea of reflexivity expressed in the idea of a container containing itself had been a way of introducing a "modern" individualist dimension into an Aristotelian logic that had been incapable of giving explicit recognition to what Hegel referred to as singularity, *Einzelheit*. Similarly, for Peirce, it represented an important modernization of the Aristotelian syllogistic. With this geometric idea of order, something of Plato's "greater or lesser" was being reintroduced into the otherwise "all or nothing" quality of Aristotle's concept of class inclusion.[25]

In the early 1880s (Peirce 1885; Peirce et al. 1883), Peirce and his students would also introduce quantifiers into logic paralleling the innovation that had, unknown to Peirce, been made independently by Frege in 1879.[26] The details are technical, but the differences between the two approaches are relatively easy to understand. As for "universally quantified" judgments as in "All metals are heavy," for Frege, the "all" really refers to an "all" of propositions, not individual metals. The sentence asserts that for all things x, sentences of the form "If x is a metal then x is heavy" are true. The Aristotelian "some" quantifier would in turn be treated as what Frege called an "existential quantifier." From the perspective of the early Pythagoreans or the medieval nominalists, "Some ancient Greeks were philosophers" would be naturally understood as saying of a list of ancient Greeks—Socrates, Thucydides, Aristophanes, and so on—that one or more of them were philosophers. In contrast, for Frege, "Some ancient Greeks were philosophers" meant that there was at least one unspecified something (x) of which it was true that that thing was both an ancient Greek and a philosopher.

Peirce's approach to quantification, using algebraic notions of sum and product, was, in this regard, closer to the more natural (Pythagorean/nominalist) one in virtue of his employment of the notion of the idea of an "index," and this would allow an explicit comparison with the "object-involving" dimension of Hegel's judgments of existence. Thus, drawing on the idea of a pointing index finger, Peirce writes: "I call such a sign *index*" which "asserts nothing; it only says 'There!' . . . Demonstrative and relative pronouns are nearly pure indices, because they denote things without describing them; so are the letters of a geometrical diagram, and the subscript numbers which in algebra distinguish one value from another without saying what those values are" (Peirce 1885, 260).

In 1904 Russell had believed that a judgment or thought about an object—in his example, Mont Blanc—actually contained that object as a component, but this view outraged his correspondent, Gottlob Frege, for whom what a judgment asserted, its "content," had to be something abstract, a "proposition" understood as an entirely abstract object capable of truth or falsity (Frege 1980, 163). Russell himself would soon adopt Frege's view, establishing the modern paradigm of formal logic, but in 1904 he had not thought his proposal an outrage to common sense, regarding the content of the judgment as "a certain complex (an objective proposition, one might say) in which *Mont Blanc* is itself a component part" (169). From 1905, as put forward in Russell's famous "description theory" of proper names (Russell 1905), such names would no longer be thought of as directly referential—in Hegelian terms, such singular determinations would be replaced by particular ones, as when proper names in sentences are replaced by "definite descriptions" containing conceptual predicates subsuming all possible individuals of which the predicate was true.

In contrast, Peirce's account of quantification as developed in 1885 did not have this consequence, and he used the sign "Σ," suggesting a sum (and contrasting with "Π" suggesting a product) with a variable x to represent a concept that is true of individuals that are represented by the associated indices. Thus, "$\Sigma_i x_i$ means that x is true of some one of the individuals denoted by i or $\Sigma_i x_i = xi + xj + xk +$ etc." (Peirce 1885, 277–278).[27] The system developed by Russell had not retained this capacity to refer to a conjunction of specific individuals as found in Peirce.

Russell's description theory would later be criticized in modal terms by Saul Kripke and others (Kripke 1972), but the seeds of this resistance, both in regard to the nongenerality of names and the modal issues involved, are to be found in Peirce and, after him, MacColl and Johnson—and before them, Hegel.

8.3 MacColl's Modal Logic

Hugh MacColl, whose work would, at least until recently, be largely forgotten after his death in 1909, had published a series of papers from the late 1870s and, after a break, again in the 1890s, the latter being brought together in 1906, in a book, *Symbolic Logic and Its Applications*. Like Peirce, MacColl had worked in the algebraic tradition commenced by Boole. He had corresponded with Peirce and Schröder and had a decisive influence on both (Peckhaus 1999; Anellis 2011). Russell, while critical of MacColl's algebraic approach to logic, would nevertheless acknowledge him as having been the first to displace the focus of recent logic from class relations to relations of implication among propositions (Russell 1906, 255). MacColl's modal logic would show an array of striking parallels with Hegel's approach to "subjective logic."

MacColl's approach to the logic of modality would fail to catch on, and it would be C. I. Lewis (Lewis 1918; Lewis and Langford 1932) who would be regarded as rejuvenating modal logic, despite the fact that "twenty years before Lewis, [MacColl] defined the concept of strict implication, and earlier than Peano he accounted for inclusion by means of implication" (Astroh and Read 1998, ii). Nevertheless, "during the second half of the 20th century . . . MacColl's major domains of research, i.e., modal and non-classical logic, gradually turned into acclaimed fields of research" (ii), and interest in his work would be revived in the later decades of that century.

Significantly, at the very start of *Symbolic Logic and Its Applications* MacColl asserts the reinterpretative approach to logical symbolism in that "there is nothing sacred or eternal about symbols" and that "all symbolic conventions may be altered when convenience requires it, in order to adapt them to new conditions, or to new classes of problems" (MacColl 1906, 1). This clearly reveals a "contextualist" attitude opposed to any that aimed at some ultimate "universal language" that we might think an appropriate medium within which to express a knowledge of the world as grasped from a "God's-eye view"—an attitude more like that of Hegel's conception of the capacity for logical categories to be redetermined.

In this relatively short book, MacColl, as Russell acknowledged, took logic to be primarily about the implicational relations existing among propositions, and attempted to accommodate class relations on the basis of this. It was from this perspective that he would approach modal issues by distinguishing a plurality of modal semantic predicates, that would be applied to propositions as subject terms, thereby creating propositions of a "higher order."

In his more influential approach to modal logic, C. I. Lewis would understand propositions in the Russellian way, and would conceive of modal operators, "necessarily" and "possibly," as applying to those propositions, such that their truth or falsity would be now understood as modified "adverbially" as necessarily or possibly true or false.[28] MacColl however, presupposing Boole's duality of "primary" and "secondary" propositions, would treat modal notions in the way that Boole treated truth and falsity, as predicates of higher-order propositions whose subjects were themselves propositions. Thus, he would add to the familiar "true" and "false" a further three semantic predicates that he would label "certain," "impossible," and "variable," giving five second-order judgment types—judgments that were true, false, certain, impossible, or variable (MacColl 1906, 6–7).[29] The last of these judgment types were, like Hegel's judgments of existence or Boole's primary judgments, context-sensitive judgments (Stelzner 1999)—judgments that were "sometimes true and sometimes false" (MacColl 1906, 18).

In contrast to Lewis's modal contradictories, MacColl's "certain" and "impossible" were modal contraries, able to be understood as if located at the "A" and "E" corners of a modal version of the Aristotelian square of opposition.[30] To these, MacColl's "sometimes true and sometimes false" added a third modal category of contingency. Hegel too had given an important place to contingent predications, and MacColl's opposition between the contraries necessary and impossible reflected the contrary predicates of Hegel's "judgment of the concept" (*SL*, 581–587; 12:84–89), an evaluative judgment in which opposing pairs of contrary predicates such as "good" or "bad" measured some object or act "against the concept as an *ought* which is simply presupposed, and is, or is not, in *agreement* with it" (*SL*, 582; 12:84). It was the logical form of such a judgment, it will be remembered, that was revealed as a syllogism (587; 12:89), exemplifying Hegel's description of the syllogism as "the truth of the judgment" (593; 12:95).

The critique of MacColl's idea of judgments that are "sometimes true and sometimes false" would be central to Russell's critique of MacColl's book in his review of it (Russell 1906). Russell's review starts favorably, acknowledging that it deals with "whole statements or propositions, not, like most writers, with classes. 'The complete statement or proposition,' [MacColl] says, 'is the real unit of all reasoning'" (Russell 1906, 255; MacColl 1906, 2). This, however, is misleading, as clearly MacColl had not intended "proposition" to be taken in the sense used by Frege, defining a proposition as "a statement, which, *in regard to form*, may be divided into two parts respectively called *subject* and *predicate*" (MacColl 1906, 2). Ignoring this, Russell describes MacColl as primarily concerned with the relation of "*implication*; his formulae state that one statement implies another, not (directly) that one class is contained in another" (Russell 1906, 255).[31] Russell, however, soon turns to his main criticism: MacColl has overlooked "two relevant and connected distinctions . . . , namely (1) that between a verbal or symbolic expression and what it means, (2) that between a proposition and a propositional function" (256). Frege had effectively directed the first criticism against Schröder, and Russell's second criticism similarly has a Fregean provenance.

Russell says of MacColl's example of the first-order proposition "Mrs. Brown is not at home" that while uttering it one might seem to have said something true or false, and although in everyday life we use "true" and "false" in this way, such sentences should have no place in logic. MacColl's sentence, he goes on, represents a propositional function, and not a complete proposition, and only propositions are capable of being true or false. Russell represents the gap existing in the structure of the propositional function that needs to be filled by the variable "x" in his replacement of MacColl's sentence with

"Mrs. Brown is not at home at the time x." To get a proper proposition, it would be argued, one needs to "bind" this "x" by the existential quantifier, so as to assert that there exists a specific time (say, for example, 3:00 p.m. on June 21, 1905) of which the sentence is true. Filling the subject gap in this way now allows the resulting proposition to be true regardless of when it is said because it has been turned into an assertion about that specific time, and can be conceived as being itself made at no particular time.

MacColl, who had debated these issues with Russell, complained about this departure from everyday language, stating that "to say that the proposition A is a different proposition when it is *false* from when it is *true*, is like saying that Mrs. Brown is a *different person* when she is *in* from when she is *out*" (MacColl 1906, 19).[32] Were it a consequence of using Russell's definitions that assertions we standardly count as being true or false (such as "Mrs. Brown is not at home") could no longer be considered true or false, then so much the worst for Russell's definitions. We will then be free to try others. As we will see with Johnson, the dualities found in algebra allow for the choice of what to take as fundamental and what to take as derived, and that such a choice is one to be made for specific situations. In this way, MacColl could take the concepts <impossible> and <certain> as equally basic as <true> and <false> rather than as ways of being true or false. In this sense, modal logic was irreducible to nonmodal logic.

8.4 Johnson's Algebraic Logic

William Ernest Johnson had been a junior colleague of John Venn at Cambridge and continued to teach there through the period within which was conceived and developed the "classical" version of modern logic deriving from Frege and given early forms in the *Principia Mathematica* of Whitehead and Russell (1910–13) and the *Tractatus Logico-Philosophicus* of Ludwig Wittgenstein (1922). Like Venn, Johnson practiced logic in the general style of Boole's algebraic interpretation of the Aristotelian syllogism,[33] but had followed Peirce in attempting to liberate the traditional syllogism from its restriction to one-placed predicates as found in Aristotle. As with Peirce, this would be done in a mode different from that found in Frege and Russell, and in a way that avoided an absolute break with the syllogistic tradition.

Johnson would extend the range of predicates in judgments to accommodate complex relational predicates (Johnson 1921, xxxv and ch. 13), treating relations as expressed by "a specific kind of adjective" that, unlike ordinary adjectives, is transitive.[34] This extension of the idea of a predicate thus accommodates Frege's idea of multiplaced predicates and a similar extension of the concept of the subject would alter the traditional idea of the substantival nature of the latter. While "the substantive alone can function as subject, and the adjective as predicate," nevertheless, "an appropriate adjective can be predicated of a subject belonging to any category, including adjective, relation and proposition, the subject as thus functioning becomes a quasi-substantive" (Johnson 1921, xxxiv).[35] For example, while "red" might start as a simple nontransitive adjective characterizing a typical substantive, an apple, for example, this adjective itself can become the "quasi-substantive" subject of a different type of predication, involving a type of higher-order characterizing of the original property, as when one says something like "Red is not a relaxing color." Johnson, however, would stress that understanding the meanings of sentences like the latter is dependent on a grasp of the meanings of sentences in which words like "red" are used in the predicative form, as in "This apple is red."

Peirce's treatment of multiplaced predications had, as we have noted, departed from Frege by treating the relevant propositions involved as having an "indexical" dimension, something like that expressed in Hegel's initial "judgments of existence." In a similar spirit, Johnson would talk of certain judgments as involving what he called "instantial affirmation"—an affirmation, not properly asserted but seemingly more presupposed, concerning the existence of some substance about which the judgment *says* something determinate.[36] As he would point out (Johnson 1921, ch. 6, §4 and ch. 9, §3), in some uses of the phrase, "an A," a speaker will have in mind a specific instance of the class A—as he puts it, "a certain A" that the speaker knows to exist. In other contexts, however, the phrase "an A" will relate simply to an indefinite or nonspecific "some A or other" that may not be directly known. This distinction repeats Ploucquet's between "comprehensive" and "exclusive" particularity—Hegel's "split" middle term.

This type of instantial affirmation must in turn be distinguished from what in the Frege-Russell tradition would be treated as an existential judgment symbolized by the use of the "existential quantifier." As we have seen, in Frege's logic, when the existence of something with such and such properties is affirmed, this can be read as not involving the type of specification involved in Johnson's "instantial affirmation." Evidence may point to the existence of some person or other of whom some description may happen to be true without it being the case that some specific individual can be identified as that person.[37] Using the device appealed to earlier in relation to Aristotle's logic, we might think of this indefinite character as being picked out as that abstract point determined as that point at which a number of lines, representing different generally characterizing predicates, intersect. But while Johnson's distinction has no equivalent in Frege, it does have an equivalent in Hegel. In Hegel's system, a judgment with instantial affirmation is one, as in the judgment of existence, in which the subject referred to will be, for example, "a certain rose." In contrast, a reflective judgment will be typically one without instantial affirmation, one about "some rose or other."

Such distinctions among judgments would in turn have implications for Johnson's conception of inference. Like Peirce, Johnson would go beyond the traditional syllogism by clarifying the difference between an inference proper and the type of "... if ... then" judgment—the "conditional" or "implicative"—with which inference had been commonly confused (Abeles 2014). In traditional propositional logic, an inference would come to be explained along the lines of the Stoic idea of *modus ponens*, in which an asserted conditional, "if p then q," together with an assertion of the antecedent "p," is taken as warranting the assertion of the consequent, "q." Johnson, however, would insist that the use of the conditional judgment (which, like Boole, he would class as a secondary judgment) presupposed the more traditional conception of judgment (Boole's primary judgment) as well as that of the existence of inferences among such judgments. In relation to Hegel, Johnson's treatment of difference between types of judgment and the relation of inference to implication can help clarify the role of "reflection" more generally within Hegel's complex conception of the syllogistic process as involving relations among different types of judgments. Such distinctions are all bound up with one for which Johnson would be most remembered and which draws him close to Hegel—that between determinables and the determinates that instantiate them.[38]

Johnson first introduces the distinction between determinables and determinates—a duality typical of algebraic logics—as one between two types of classifying adjectives, which, moreover, is not hard and fast but one of degree (Johnson 1921, xxxv). A determinable is what would most often be thought of as an abstract concept equivalent to Hegel's "subsuming" abstract universals or typical Kantian concepts. In Johnson's basic example, color is a determinable, and it is resolved into an array of determinates: specific colors such as red, green, blue, and so on. The fundamental feature of this distinction that he stresses is its difference from the traditional "genus-species distinction"—effectively the distinction between a class and its subclasses as found in Porphyry's tree. Basically, determinables are not to be conceived as divided into their determinates by some *fundamentum divisionis* in the way that, say, the class of animals can be divided, by the concept <rational>, into the subclasses of human and nonhuman animals. That is, there is no specifiable dividing further concept, which, when added to the concept <color>, distinguishes blue things, which fall under that concept, from red, green, or yellow ones, which do not. Here the sharp logical determinacies of the ideal realm are compromised by the "more or less" character of the distinctions found among things in the actual world.

Clearly, there is something of Kant's concept-intuition distinction in Johnson's determinable-determinate division. A determinable is an abstract concept, like the concept <color>, while a determinate is more concrete and qualitative, like specifically colored intuitions—red, green, and blue ones, for example. But the determinable-determinate relation is not fixed; it is contextual and relative. While more concrete than a determinable, a determinate has a level of generality and logical structure that gives it the features associated with concepts. Thus, while the determinable-determinate distinction has something of the discrete-continuous difference that separates Kantian concepts from intuitions, in Johnson, as in Hegel, this is now made internal to the realm of conceptuality.

One's capacity to distinguish green from blue, for example, is more like one's ability to distinguish the opposed spatial directions of right and left. One distinguishes such directions immediately without reliance on some determinate concept of what makes this direction to be to the right in contrast to that opposing one that is to my left.[39] And just as with the right-left distinction in which a series of things arrayed to my left gradually pass over into a series of things arrayed to my right, a color that is judged to be determinately blue can be seen to gradually transition into one that is determinately green. In this sense, the "space" of color has a form something like that possessed by space and time in Kant's transcendental approach, the form of "pure intuition." But here, space and time are not absolute but conceived as "directed" in virtue of being centered upon the cognizing subject, more like that found in the precritical Kant, the neo-Pythagorean Nicomachus of Gerasa, and, I have argued, Hegel (chapter 3.4 above).

While their respective terminologies do not line up exactly, clearly Johnson, with his determinable-determinate distinction, is trying to capture the sorts of differences that Hegel had tried to capture with his particular-singular distinction, and both go in the general direction of what Hegel had in his discussion of Plato characterized as a divided or broken "mean."[40] The red said to inhere in this apple has a type of phenomenal determinacy that the more general "subsuming" concept of red lacks. There is something "that it is like" to experience this apple's specific shade of red, but any such specific "singularity" cannot be ascribed to the apple in judgment without it accruing features of "particularity" responsible for the logical features of that judgment. Describing the apple as red amounts to implying that it is not green, and so on. Importantly for Johnson, all these classifications can be redetermined, such as when in a different context the word "red" comes to function itself as a determinable, of which something further can be said. This clearly is useful in those contexts alluded to by Venn, in which in the course of scientific investigation, a property comes to be redetermined. For example, one may come to think of the property red as being the capacity to reflect electromagnetic waves of certain wavelengths, rather than as having a certain look.

The phenomena captured by Johnson's determinable-determinate distinction lead to his being at odds with the standard way of understanding negation in the twentieth century, which largely derives from the quantified predicate calculus of Frege and Russell. Moreover, along with this, it also puts him at odds with the standard way of thinking about assertion. All this results in a much more Hegelian approach to judgment.

In the standard classical predicate calculus that developed in the wake of the work of Frege and Russell, negation is treated "truth-functionally" as a one-placed logical operator (typically symbolized by the sign '~') that serves to reverse the truth-value of the proposition. Truth and falsity are thereby treated as complementary, meaning that if a particular proposition p is true, then its negation, $\sim p$, is false, and if p is false, then $\sim p$ is true. Just as in modern algebra, in which subtracting 5 from 3 is treated as a form of addition (i.e., adding –5 to 3), Frege would treat the denial of p as the assertion of $\sim p$.[41] Both Johnson and Hegel, however, reject the analysis of the denial of p as the assertion of its contradictory.[42] When Johnson notes that "the relation of *incompatibility* lies at the root of the notion of contradiction" (Johnson 1922, 15), he is alluding to the incompatibility of determinates considered as existents "in the same sense as the object presented to perception is an existent" (Johnson 1921, xiii). It is in this sense of being concrete that a determinate, which in Hegel's terms, is conceived as something "inhering" in a substance, can exclude other incompatible determinates, as when an apple's redness excludes its greenness, making the relation among determinates that of contrariety. It is in this sense, then, that for Johnson contrariety "lies at the root of the notion of contradiction."

8.5 Heyting's Intuitionistic Logic

As a student of the Dutch mathematician L. E. J. Brouwer, Arend Heyting attempted to formalize the logic implicit in the "intuitionistic" approach to mathematics that Brouwer had advocated against the Platonistic orientation of Frege and Russell.[43]

Brouwer's intuitionism (or "constructivism") had clear idealist origins in Kant's understanding of mathematics as based on the "pure intuitions" of space and time,[44] but responding to the need to accommodate non-Euclidean geometries, Brouwer had reduced these to the intuition of time alone.[45] He criticized logic as relevant to mathematical proofs. The proofs themselves he regarded as based on a subject's intuitions of mathematical structures, with concepts being relevant only to the communication of those proofs to others. In particular, he argued against any role for the classical laws of excluded middle and double negation elimination in mathematical proofs. This rigid distinction between the proof itself and its communication in language was softened by Heyting, however, who developed a logic relevant for such mathematical proofs in a decidedly nonclassical way and proposed a different interpretation of the algebraic structures underlying Boolean logic (Moschovakis 2009). This would give Heyting's logic features similar to ones found in Johnson and Hegel.

Heyting weakened Boole's logic by dropping the laws of excluded middle and double negation elimination as axioms. The reasoning here was the need to exclude the possibility that mathematical truths could be established indirectly, as found in the type of reductio ad absurdum or proof by contradiction that dated back to Aristotle in which one could establish the truth of p by demonstrating the falsity of not p—a type of proof rejected by Brouwer.[46]

In intuitionistic logic, the concept <true> is to be understood as equivalent to proven within the subject's experience by a specific "witness," and <false> as similarly indicating refuted by the experience of a disconfirming witness. A nonmathematical analogue might be that just as the proposition "The apple in the box is red" requires proof by the experience of it as being red, the proposition "The apple in the box is not red" requires proof by an equivalent experience of that apple as having some specific disconfirming non-red color, say, green. This approach has the consequence that "true" and "false" are no longer complementary notions: that is, "not p" is not defined as the contradictory of "p," such that "not p" is false when "p" is true and true when "p" is false.

In light of this, Heyting's alternative way of defining negation was to utilize the consequence that Russell had employed in his definition of material implication—the medieval principle of *ex falso sequitur quodlibet*, from a falsehood anything follows. Thus, in intuitionistic propositional logic, the negation operator is defined in terms of the claim that a false proposition implies any proposition ($\sim p \supset (p \supset q)$),[47] and so implies false ones. But if implication is to be used in the definition of negation, clearly the relation of implication cannot itself be defined in ways that employ the negation operator, as is done in classical logic. The relation of implication must be defined in a different way, and so a different pattern of dependence must be found among the logical connectives.

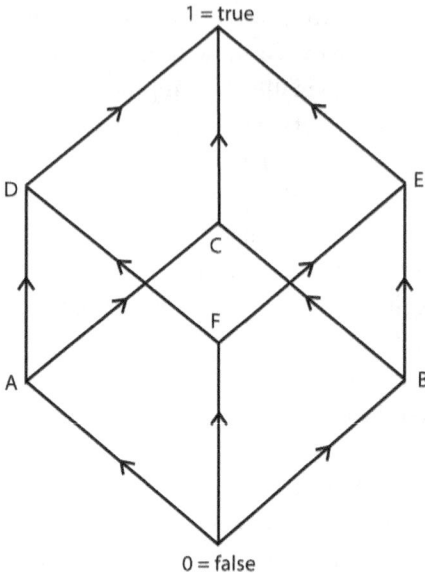

FIGURE 8.1 A "Hasse diagram" able to be interpreted differently by Boolean and Heyting algebras.

Any details of this alternative would take us too far beyond our concerns here, but the general way in which Heyting's logic departs from the conventional laws of logic as found in Boolean algebra can be illustrated in terms of his peculiar interpretation of a type of logical graph that had developed for the "order-theoretic" approach introduced by Peirce and that draws on the idea of composable directed line segments or "vectors" developed by Grassmann. Using these resources, the types of diagrams that had been traditionally used in logic could be associated with underlying algebraic systems that could specify the properties of those logical systems in more determinate ways. This allows the appreciation of how different logical systems like Heyting's, on the one hand, and conventional Boolean logic, on the other, can be contrasted.

We can think of this type of "Hasse diagram" as represented above (fig. 8.1) as something like the traditional "square of opposition" in that it locates judgments at nodes connected by arrows representing inferential relations. In figure 8.1, the nodes A, B, C, D, E, and F can be taken as representing different judgments, with inferences among those judgments represented by connecting arrows, such that A → C represents that the proposition A implies proposition C. However, as the diagram also represents A as implying D, then A can also be understood as representing the conjunction of C and D (standardly symbolized as "C ∧ D"), since a conjunction of judgments implies each conjunct.[48] By the same reasoning, if both F and A imply D, then D can be understood as representing the disjunction A or F (symbolized as "A ∨ F").[49] Such Hasse diagrams effectively give expression to those partially ordered sets discussed earlier in which elements within a set are related in ways that are transitive, reflexive, and anti-symmetric. It is usual to represent the orientation of the lines (or "edges") connecting nodes (or "vertices") as all having the same direction, typically upward, to allow the individual arrow "points" to be omitted.[50]

Such a diagram for a Boolean logic typically has the form of a "lattice"[51] with maximum and minimum vertices that correspond to the Boolean values, 1 and 0, understood as true and false, respectively.[52] As implication is a transitive relation among judgments, the judgment at the lowermost node represented as implying A, B, and F thereby implies judgments at all other nodes, and being lowermost, is implied by no other judgment. In line with Russell's conception of material implication, it can be regarded as a falsehood, as a falsehood implies any judgment and is implied by no other true judgment. Similarly, the topmost node can be regarded as a truth, for a truth is implied by any other judgment. But when interpreted according to Heyting's system, because of the peculiar way that negation is defined, 0 and 1 do not play quite the same roles as they play in the Boolean system. Formally, Heyting's algebra is not a lattice but a "semilattice."[53]

Typically, the relation of implication can be defined in terms of conjunction or disjunction—the logical equivalents of arithmetical multiplication and addition, respectively—together with negation. Here, however, because negation is no longer complementary, the implicative conditional (if p then q) must be introduced in another way.

Rather than setting out these definitions in terms of some set of basic axioms, intuitionists have largely followed the path introduced by the "proof-theorist" Gerhard Gentzen in the 1930s, where "introduction" and "elimination" rules are used to define logical connectives, and this has provided a way of introducing logical implication directly rather than from conjunction or disjunction together with negation.[54] These differences mean that the laws of double negation and excluded middle no longer hold for a Heyting algebra, as demanded by the intuitionist's philosophy of mathematics. Nevertheless, these principles can be added to the Heyting algebra as separate axioms, and when they are so added, a typical Boolean logic results. In this sense, considered as a logic, Heyting algebra might be thought to accommodate the broader sorts of inferences to which Aristotle had appealed (such as judgments with roles for properly singular subjects) but that had no place within the stricter logic of his *Prior Analytics*. This in turn has different metaphysical connotations in that intuitionistic logic can be regarded as appropriate for reasoning within a world in which certain states of affairs, such as the existence or not of tomorrow's sea battle in Aristotle's famous example, will be regarded as indeterminate, with judgments about them as lacking a truth-value. As with Johnson's logic, then, Heyting's seems to appeal to a wider sense of logic than that acknowledged by classical logic in its ancient and modern forms. That is, there is a logic of thought that in principle cannot be reduced to the grammar of some universal language as in Frege's concept-script.

This, I have been arguing, is how Hegel conceived a broader scope for logic. The logic of human reasoning cannot be reduced to a formal calculus, but, nevertheless, the possibility of such formal calculi being formed reflects the capacity for thought to reflect upon itself. This capacity in turn implies the capacity for thought to redetermine the categories within which it thinks. But there might here be even further specific parallels between such directions taken in modern logic and those shapes implicit in Hegel.

Since the 1980s, in the area of computer science, a type of logic has developed, called "linear logic," so called because it draws explicitly upon the linear algebra started by Grassmann and that had come to influence Peirce's logic. Linear logic has added a further "exponential" connective to the "additive" and "multiplicative" ones we have observed in Boolean logic.[55] Just as "multiplication" underlies logical conjunction, and "addition" logical disjunction, exponentiation provides an algebraic analogue for implication when no longer understood as derived from the other two along with negation.[56] With this third "arithmetical" operation, linear logic is meant to unify the otherwise opposed and independently conceived Boolean and intuitionistic logics.

Parallels to Hegel and Peirce here seem striking.[57] It will be remembered that Hegel had added the operation of exponentiation to addition and multiplication to give a complete determination of the notion of "number." In relation to linear algebra, Peirce had argued that there could be only three underlying forms of such algebras to which all other forms could be reduced, and that these corresponded to his three distinct logics: predicate logic, propositional logic, and modal logic (Houser 1997, 2–3). Clearly, these three logics broadly align with those applying to Hegel's fundamental judgment forms: judgments of inherence, judgments of subsumption, and judgments of the concept. Moreover, as we have seen, within linear algebra itself, Clifford had expanded the forms of "multiplication" found in Grassmann's approach from two to three, with these three being linked in peculiar combinations of addition and multiplication.

Such technical developments, of course, are light-years away from anything that Hegel could even have imagined, but the general parallels with his attempts to bring the ancient mathematics of the three interrelated "musical means" to illuminate a conception of logic he thought implicit in Plato are difficult to dismiss.

9

Hegel among the New Leibnizians: Judgments

> Judging is therefore *another* function than conceiving; or rather, it is *the other function* of the concept, for it is the *determining* of the concept through itself. The further progress of judgment into a diversity of judgments is this progressive determination of the concept. What kind of determinate concepts *there are*, and how they prove to be necessary determinations of it—this has to be exhibited in judgment.
>
> HEGEL, *The Science of Logic*

In chapter 7 we touched upon the cyclical pattern of development of Hegel's treatment of the forms of judgment in the "Subjective Logic" of *The Science of Logic*, where the cyclical alternations between two underlying "qualitative" and "quantitative" judgment forms—what I have called "cycles of redetermination"—results in the increasing complexification of subject and predicate terms of judgment expressions. What we have seen of Johnson's idea of the redetermination of subject and predicate terms of judgments away from the simple picture of the qualification of a substance might now provide a template for how we are to think of Hegel's cycles as progressing.[1]

In *The Science of Logic* Hegel describes such cyclical movement through its own triadically grouped categories as resulting in the "animation" or "ensoulment" of such categories, the suggestion being that each cycle ends with a transformed or "ensouled" version of the category with which it had commenced, with this transformed category in turn initiating the following cycle. Hegel's earlier triangle of triangles had become a circle of circles:

> By virtue of the nature of the method just indicated, the science presents itself as a *circle* that winds around itself, where the mediation winds the end back to the beginning which is the simple ground; the circle is thus a *circle of circles*, for each single member ensouled [*als Beseeltes*] by the method is reflected into itself so that, in returning to the beginning it is at the same time the beginning of a new member. (*SL*, 751; 12:252)

Once more, this structure of the first becoming last and the last first in a process that involves the first and last terms swapping places with a middle is none other than the unity of the three Pythagorean means found in Plato's syllogism.

In the judgment cycles the mediating second member of these categorical cycles will be abstract in relation to the more concrete first and third members, although in the sequence of syllogistic figures, the middle term will be occupied in turn by each of the determinations of the concept. Moreover, in the cycle of judgments the suggestion seems to be that the "ensoulment" of the final category has resulted from structures associated with the negated first and second categories being somehow "reflected" back into the first category, and so producing the third. Indeed, negation seems to be at the heart of this dynamic:

> The one thing needed to *achieve scientific progress* . . . is the recognition of the logical principle that negation is equally positive. . . . Because the result, the negation, is a *determinate* negation, it has *content*. It is a new concept but one higher and richer than the preceding. . . . It is above all in this way that the system of concepts is to be erected. (*SL*, 33; 21:38)

The cyclical movement through the forms of judgment is thus just one expression of this circular methodology, but it is an expression that, I believe, sheds light on the more general process. Importantly, like the triangle of triangles it also challenges the more conventional linear imagery of Jacob's ladder to heaven central to the logic of Leibniz and others. Earlier I have suggested that in relation to his theory of judgment this feature of Hegel's logic is connected to a dynamic of disinterpretation (or abstraction) and reinterpretation (or concretization) of concepts, an attitude to logic that Hegel has been shown to share with algebraists of the late nineteenth and early twentieth centuries such as Venn and Johnson (see chapter 8). In this and the following chapter, we will further explore parallels between aspects of Hegel's logic with its principle of local homomorphism expressed here as the homologous equivalence of opposed qualitative and quantitative judgment forms—a model ultimately deriving from the Platonic conception of the relation among the three musical means—and the various alternatives to classical logic offered by Peirce, MacColl, Johnson, and Heyting with their distinctive features of the logical equivalents of the "dualities" of projective geometry.

9.1 Hegel's First Logical Cycle: From Instance to Its Ensoulment as Genus

In the context of Hegel's "Subjective Logic," the same phenomenon of "ensoulment" of the subject terms of *de-re* judgments can be observed in the cycles through which judgment forms progress from the initial simple judgments of experience to the developed judgments of the concept, which, as we have seen, are in fact implicit syllogisms. For example, the first cycle leading from the *de-re* judgment of experience through the more *de-facto* form of the judgment of reflection and then to the new *de-re* judgment of necessity sees the objects of the original judgments, determinate singular objects such as some particular rose perceived in its here and now, transformed into the kinds that they instantiate—in this case, "the rose as such." The original singular rose has become "ensouled." "*This* rose . . ." has become equivalent, as it were, to "this *rose* . . ." The rose experienced this way in my here and now has become one of a kind, and so equivalent to other instances not being experienced in my here and now. Similar dynamics are then shown to operate in the subsequent cycles, those driving the judgment of necessity from its immediate form to its equivalent ensouled form, which then initiates the following cycle, taking the immediate form of the judgment of the concept to its syllogistic "truth."

In the initial cycle we thus see the subject term of an original judgment of experience, "the rose" of "The rose is red," undergo abstraction, first from the specific rose instantiating this red (determined in its singularity) to a less determinate rose that is colored some red, in the sense of having a color that is not-green, not-yellow, and so on. The original color first thought of as something simple and immediately given has now been shown to have the logical structure of particularity—in Johnsonian terms, the color possessed is now thought as a determinate of a determinable (Johnson 1921, ch. 11). Confronted with a further negation (now, "external" sentence rather than predicate negation, the denial of the complete *dictum*), the subject of the utterance is redetermined as an otherwise entirely abstract posit such as Leibniz had in mind with his "third" linking two predicates (*SL*, 602; 12:104), an entirely indeterminate entity about which two abstract predicates (now Johnsonian determinables) such as "rose" and "red" can be said to be true or false.

We can regard this process of negation-driven abstraction as one of desemanticization—an initial phase of a cycle of redetermination with "ascending" and "descending" phases. Here, desemanticization involves a process that in Kantian terms could be described as involving the loss of "intensive magnitude" from its maximum (value = 1) at the start of the ascent to its minimum (value = 0) at the apex (see above, chapter 7.5). Otherwise expressed, desemanticization has resulted in the loss of those concrete empirical "witnesses" that for intuitionists are necessary for any judgment to be proven or refuted, and so to have meaning. While at the apex we have reached a domain of abstract objects (propositions) that satisfy the laws of classical logic, this has been at the expense of the applicability of those objects to the world in acts of judgment. Hegel had argued that with this type of abstraction a completely senseless form of judgment, the infinite judgment, had resulted. It must be remembered, however, that such judgments can only be properly regarded as senseless when abstracted from their relation to other more determinate judgments. Rightly conceived, the infinite judgment is the sort of judgment correlated with a "viewpoint" understood as located at a point at infinity.

These apparently senseless judgments will be regarded in a different light, however, when understood from the perspective of the principle of homomorphic equivalences, which has it that two judgments can have the same absolute content or underlying substrate while grasped in opposed indexical and nonindexical ways that serve different functions related to content and form. That is, a judgment that, in intuitionistic terms, comes with a witness, such as "This rose is red," can be regarded as having the same absolute content as the entirely abstract judgment into which it has developed that comes with no witness, as in "There exists (in some indeterminate spatiotemporal location) a rose that is red." Within the type of truth-functional semantics of classical predicate calculus this latter assertion will, in isolation from others, be regarded as having a meaning simply because it has a truth-value, regardless of whether this is known or not. In contrast, for Hegel or Heyting, at least when conceived in isolation in this way, it does not have a determinate meaning, Hegel pronouncing the "infinite judgment" to be without sense.

This, however, does not condemn such a judgment form to have *no* role within the logical processes of reasoning. This situation might be compared to the use, for Carnot, of nonexecutable "auxiliary numbers," such as infinitesimals, within mechanics, or "points at infinity," within projective geometry. For Hegel, the attainment of this senseless status is precisely what allows the meaning of the judgment to be redetermined in the way that Venn would suggest was necessary for the development of scientific concepts from those employed in everyday life. And so, from this point of maximal abstraction, redetermination must involve a process of resemanticization. For Hegel, this will effectively involve a reversal of the process of abstraction, that of concretization. Before examining this, however, let's pause to consider the type of homomorphic equivalence that might be thought to hold between these inverse forms of judgment involving predication as inherence and predication as subsumption, respectively.

In an earlier chapter I appealed to the relation between logarithmic and linear readings of the musical intervals involving the three Archytan means: geometric, arithmetic, and harmonic. In modern algebra, the logarithmic relation in which an equivalence is established between products of elements in one system and sums of elements in another is an instance of a "homomorphism" between groups. As central to the abstract nature of modern algebra, group theory allows the extension of the idea of combinations of elements as sums and products from the literal meaning of these terms as operations on numbers. In the abstractive spirit in which Boole had taken "sum" and "product" to be given distinctive logical meanings, I suggest that the notion of "homomorphism" allows this as well. In short, Hegel's two types of judgment might be thought of as belonging to two distinct "axiomatic" systems of logic, one something like Heyting's and the other something like Boole's, such that inherence-predication within Heyting's intuitionistic logic plays the same functional role within *it* as subsumptive-predication plays within Boole's classical logic. Homomorphism, of course, does not mean that the meanings of these systems are identical, just as the addition of $\log x$ to $\log y$ is not the same operation as the multiplication of x and y found in $\log x.y$. Neither homomorphism nor homology implies identity. Nevertheless, a homomorphism is a type of equivalence. In Hegelian terms, it is a type of "identity in difference."[2] It was this type of identity among otherwise incommensurable ratios that had been the Pythagorean core to Plato's "beautiful bond." In the realm of modern nonclassical logic, the attempt to show the unity between otherwise distinct Boolean and intuitionistic logics by "linear logic" has invoked the third of the arithmetical operations, the exponential, in a way that once again seems to echo the dynamics of Plato's bond and Hegel's account of the complete determination of the concept of number.

In Hegel's logical cycles of redetermination it is this identity-in-difference that in turn allows the resemanticization of judgments in the "downward" parts of those cycles. From the top of the first cycle—an apex of abstraction—the downward path will then address the need to resemanticize the judgments found there, but this will not simply lead back to the original "immediate" judgment form, as the process of reconcretization must be such that it responds to the new logical form that has been achieved by the judgment in the process of abstraction—a logical form allowing the judgment to link to others in "reflective" truth-functional ways. Clearly these new judgments will need to be given *some type* of empirical content so as to be made determinate, but this must be done in such a way that such judgments will no longer be understood as being made determinate simply on the basis of any purportedly immediate experience of the object being judged, as had been the case of the simple experienced properties of specific concrete substances, such as the rose's color or smell. Copernican skepticism will reflect the felt naïveté of calling the world exactly as one finds it, and experience will be now thought of as unfolding within a context in which, as Kant had put it, reason "in order to be instructed by nature" must approach it "not like a pupil, who has recited to him whatever the teacher wants to say, but like an appointed judge who compels witnesses to answer the questions he puts to them" (Kant 1998, Bxiii).

In this new form of subsumptive empirical judgment involved in the downward phase of the cycle, the judgment of reflection, the object and properties involved will have different logical forms from those of the originating simple judgments of existence. In particular, the predicate of the new judgment will, as Hegel states in the *Encyclopedia Logic*, be "of the sort that, by means of it, the subject demonstrates itself to be related to another" (*E:L*, §174, addition)—that is, the property indicated by the predicate will be, as in Johnson's extension of the subject-predicate form, a relational one. In one of Hegel's examples, a plant is said to be curative,[3] and of course the property of being curative, attributed to a plant, requires reference to another object— let's say, a curable sick human or other animal to whom the plant can be administered. The property is thus manifested in quite a different way from the way a plant's color is manifested: one usually cannot "read off" the property of being curative from the simple experience of the isolated plant. The form of experience relevant for attributing this property to a plant will be complex and will involve, say, feeding the plant to various humans or animals with particular illnesses, observing and correlating the results obtained with another group who are not given the plant, and so on. Here we are in the realm of Johnsonian facts capable of conjunctive coexistence. We might call this the "experimental manifestation" of a relational property such as that of being curative.[4] Judgings in these contexts are, of course, still related to experience, but they are related in a different way. Hegel's shorthand is to say that here the relation of the substance to its property is "mediated."

Clearly, in relation to Hegel's judgments of reflection we are in the general territory of the type of logic pertinent to reasoning within the modern natural sciences—the type of reasoning that Hegel here calls *Räsonnement*. Being in the vicinity of what we might call "Newtonian reasoning," we should expect this logic to exhibit the sorts of limitations found in the context of Hegel's discussion of mathematics in the Logic of Being. There Hegel brought the mutual dependency of qualitative considerations found in geometry and quantitative ones found in arithmetic to a criticism of the reductively algebraic approach to mechanics of Lagrange. While it "may seem fitting to define the judgment of reflection as a judgment of *quantity*," nevertheless, the quantity of the judgment of reflection is "not just sublated quality [*nicht bloss die aufgehobene Qualität*], and therefore not merely *quantity*" (*SL*, 569; 12:72). The property of being curative, we have noted, is not manifested qualitatively in the immediate experience of the plant itself. But when we inquire into the relevant properties of the related object—say, a patient's state of health—presumably this is to be understood as capable of qualitative manifestation, such as the color and warmth of their skin, the strength of their pulse, and so on. Here the patient's color, for example, will not be understood as significant "in itself," but as indicative of something else—it will be taken as a sign of the patient's more systemically conceived "condition." Nevertheless, the qualitative phenomenon does not simply disappear into the intelligible significance it possesses as a sign. It must be somehow preserved, just as Kepler's ellipses did not disappear into the abstract linear vectors of Newton's mechanics. The doctor can only gain epistemic access to the patient's general condition via awareness of particular clinical manifestations. Such qualitative determinations are "sublated" but are not "just sublated" (*SL*, 569; 12:72).

Newtonian science achieves the level of logical organization typical of its Copernican-styled judgments of reflection, with its equations showing quantitative relations among measurable parameters—mass, velocity, distance traveled in a measurable time, and so on. But as we have seen, Hegel believes that limited to this level, Newtonianism does not grapple with the physical reality of what it is that is responsible for the correctness or otherwise of such equations—in Newton's case, the reality of force.[5] In his championing of Kepler over Newton, Hegel had, like Carnot in his mechanics,[6] criticized the idea of interacting independent forces: "The *concept* of *gravity* contains not only the moments of being-for-self, but also that of the continuity which sublates being-for-self. These moments of the concept suffer the fate of being grasped as distinct forces corresponding to the forces of attraction and repulsion" (*E:PN*, §269, remark). At the level of its judgments, we might say that Newtonian *Räsonnement* is restricted to the quantitative organization of judgments of reflection, in particular, universal judgments of "allness" (*Allheit*) in which "the 'all' is the all of all the *singulars* [*alle Einzelne*] in which the singular remains unchanged" (*SL*, 572; 12:74). Universality here is mere "*association* [*Gemeinschaftlichkeit*] of such singulars as comes about only by way of *comparison* [*Vergleichung*]" (572; 12:74). Nevertheless, Hegel in no way wants to eliminate this phase from the greater dynamic of reason—as in Johnson, such simple conjunctions of facts can be reinterpreted into more relevant logical relations—and his allusions to the "logic" of this process are far from being some naïve philosophy of science.

We see more of the relevance of the reflective judgment form when Hegel treats the logic of scientific induction as a type of syllogism, the syllogism of induction, in the later discussion of syllogisms (*SL*, 612; 12:113 and *E:L*, §190), and it is worth examining this here in order to display the functional relationships within which the judgments in question stand and from which they attain their logical form. Again, it will be helpful to compare Hegel's logic to that of Johnson, who also locates induction within a syllogistic form.

9.2 Hegel and Johnson on the Inductive Resemanticization of Judgments

In commenting on the "much cited" syllogism "All humans are mortal, *Now Gaius is a human*, Therefore Gaius is mortal," Hegel notes that "the major premise is correct only because and to the extent that the *conclusion is correct*" (*SL*, 611; 12:112). Hegel here follows the criticism of syllogistic reasoning common to the medieval nominalists for whom "all humans" was not a reflection of the natural kind "human" but merely a shorthand way of giving a complete list of humans. It is in this sense that the generalization is correct only because each of the possible conclusions are correct. Nevertheless, this "empty, *reflective semblance of syllogistic inference*" has a function as a reduced form of inference that operates within the context of scientific induction, a process in which the reasoning runs in the reverse direction from conclusion to major premise. Clearly this exploits the fact that the syllogism can be set out in a quasi-diagrammatic way akin to the *ekthesis* of a proof in relation to a diagram in Euclidean geometry—a parallel between Aristotle's syllogism and geometrical method noted by Einarson (Einarson 1936, 162). This introduces an element of directionality that would be exploited by Peirce in particular in expanding the capacity of Aristotle's formal syllogism.

In the *Encyclopedia Logic*, Hegel writes of this type of reduced syllogism (to which he adds "all metals are electric conductors, *therefore*, for example, copper is, too") that "in order to be able to assert those major premises that are supposed to express the *set of all* of the *immediate* individuals and to be essentially *empirical* sentences [*empirische Sätze*], it is required that already *previously* the sentences about the individual Gaius, the *individual* copper are confirmed for themselves as correct" (*E:L*, §190, remark). The syllogism involved must therefore be somehow understood as running in the reverse direction of that of the standard syllogistic model because the relevance of its otherwise empty form "All As are B, this C is A, therefore this C is B" comes from the way that the known conclusion can play an evidentiary role in affirming the major premise.

Some initial interpretation must be given to the judgments involved in induction of this sort, and Hegel treats the middle term of this syllogism as determined as singularity, giving the inductive syllogism the structure of U-S-P. Here the term "S" represents not *a* singular thing but the set of "all" relevant singulars (in the *Encyclopedia Logic*, Hegel says "*all singular concrete* subjects" [*E:L*, §190]), the syllogism being thus expanded into the configuration shown in figure 9.1.

```
    S
    S
U — — P
    S
    S
   ad
infinitum.
```

FIGURE 9.1 *SL*, 612; 12:113; cf. *E:L*, §190, addition.

The universal judgment (U-P) mediated by this set of singulars will be the expression of an empirical law such as "All metals conduct electricity," the mediating middle term here being the "complete set" of individual metals—gold, silver, copper, lead, and so forth. That is, it would seem then that the effective major premise of this syllogism will be a set of "empirical sentences" such as the set of sentences "Gold is metal," "Silver is metal," "Copper is metal," with the minor premise being a corresponding set of sentences stating the results of experiments, "Gold conducts electricity," "Silver conducts electricity," "Copper conducts electricity," and so on. Induction, then, is no simple "syllogism of mere *perception* or of contingent existence [*der blossen Wahrnehmung oder des zufälligen Daseins*], but the syllogism of *experience* [*Erfahrung*]—of the subjective gathering together of singulars in the genus, and the conjoining of the genus with a universal determinateness on the ground that the latter is found in all singulars" (*SL*, 612–613; 12:114).[7] Induction, then, does not proceed from the contingencies of experience but takes place in a constrained environment in which, as in Kant's metaphor, specific questions are posed to experience forcing it to answer from a fixed set of terms. It is important to keep distinct two different applications of "all" here. On the one hand, there is the "all" of the nominalistically interpreted class of "all metals," which is really just the sum of individual metal kinds (gold, silver, copper, etc.). On the other, there is the "all" of the sentences involved, the totality of "Gold is metal," "Silver is metal," "Copper is metal," etc.

Again, Johnson's modern transformation of the Aristotelian syllogism together with his porous determinable-determinate distinction will result in a schematization of the process of induction helpful in understanding Hegel's. Just as Johnson had extended the traditional subject-predicate model of the judgment to include quasi-substantive subjects and relational predicates he similarly employs a "functional extension" of the traditional Aristotelian deductive syllogism. In a way that parallels Hegel's homomorphic idea of the identity-in-difference of qualitative and quantitative syllogistic forms, Johnson talks of two different inferential principles at work in the syllogism—the "applicative" and "implicative": "The former may be said to formulate what is involved in the intelligent use of the word 'every'; the latter what is involved in the intelligent use of the word 'if' " (Johnson 1922, 10). Taken separately, these would clearly reflect the logical principles at work in qualitative class and quantitative propositional logics, respectively—what we have alluded to in the discussion of intuitionistic logic in terms of the relation of "inference" to "implication." Indeed, it would seem that considerable energy had been spent by algebraic logicians of the second half of the nineteenth century in trying to figure out how these two logical forms fitted together (see, for example, Abeles 2014), with Johnson having been later regarded by Arthur Prior as having given the most developed and satisfactory account (Prior 1949). For Johnson, the syllogism properly understood demanded that both principles play a role, and induction shows a complex combination of both. Later, Heyting's logic would too, as we have glimpsed, conceive of a way of translating between distinct inferential and implicational forms rather than simply taking the latter to be the basis of the former.

The form of inference governed by the applicative (Hegel's qualitative) principle is modeled on an extensionally interpreted inference of subalternation (A→I) in the square of opposition. It states that "from a predication about 'every' we may formally infer the same predication about 'any given'" (Johnson 1922, 11), and, similar to Hegel's P-S-U model of the syllogism, Johnson's syllogism has the general form "Every X is Y, this is an X, therefore this is a Y." But this inference is achieved only with the help of the *implicative* principle as formulated fundamentally as a relation among *propositions*, the general form of which will be *modus ponens*, "p" and "if p then q," therefore "q."

As in Hegel, directionality plays a crucial role here in Johnson's account. Like Hegel, for whom "the fundamental character of induction is that it is a syllogistic inference" (*SL*, 613; 12:115), Johnson takes induction as operating on the same principles as the deductive syllogism but as going in the reverse direction. Summarily stated, the inductive syllogism reverses the deductive inference from "every" to "any" so as to move from "any" to "every" although operating only "in certain narrowly limited cases" (Johnson 1922, 28).[8] Later, Johnson starts to fill in more of this account in relation to what he calls the "functional extension of the syllogism," which involves "a conjunction of disconnected syllogisms of this type:

> "Everything is p if m; This is m; Therefore This is p."
> "Everything is p' if m'; This is m'; Therefore This is p'."
> "Everything is p'' if m''; This is m''; Therefore This is p''." (103)

This expanded syllogism is clearly similar to Hegel's inductive syllogism, whose middle term consists of the "complete set of singulars."

Johnson describes induction in a way that recalls Hegel's account of the cognitive status of geometrical figures. It is a matter of "apprehending the universal in the particular," and this has a meaning at the subpropositional level in which the universality of the predicate is apprehended in the particularity [that is, Ploucquet's "exclusive particularity" or Hegel's "singularity"] of the subject: "The procedure by which these generalisations [i.e., among propositions] are established may be shown by psychological analysis to involve an intermediate step by which we pass from one instance to others of the same form" (Johnson 1922, 192). Elsewhere, Johnson expresses this with the idea that "the passing from 'any' to 'every' is justified only when the passing from 'any one' to 'any other' is justified" (28–29). Johnson's idea of this type of "intermediate" inferential step passing from "any one" to "any other"—an alternative form of ampliative inference to induction upon which induction seemingly relies—looks like what Hegel calls "inference by analogy" but also suggests the approach of Charles Sanders Peirce to a nondeductive alternative to induction that he called "abduction." As Peirce's idea of abduction is more fully developed and as it also seems to have clear parallels in Hegel, it is worth reviewing it briefly in this context.

Over many years Peirce experimented with a nondeductive or "ampliative" form of logical inference, which he had originally named "hypothesis" but later called "abduction," as distinct from the more commonly discussed induction. Like Johnson, he had approached both these forms from within an overall syllogistic framework. Again, Peirce relies heavily on the diagrammatically based idea of reversal of direction when moving along paths of some diagram. Induction can be readily thought of as a reversal of the deduction of I-judgments from A-judgments in the traditional square of opposition, but the addition of abduction involves more complex paths and requires the context of a syllogism for its setting out. Thus, while induction passes from result and the minor premise of a syllogism to its major premise, abduction passes from a combination of the result and the major premise to the minor premise.[9] I suggest that the "result," from which, together with the major premise, abduction makes its inference in Peirce, is significantly like the judgment that, in Hegel's account, expands into the syllogism—the judgment of the concept as exemplified by "This house is bad [as opposed to good]" (*SL*, 583; 12:85).

First, Peirce claims that "abductive inference shades into perceptual judgment without any sharp line of demarcation between them" or alternatively that perceptual judgments "are to be regarded as an extreme case of abductive inferences" (Peirce 1998, 227). The point at which Hegel's judgment of the concept expands into a syllogism might equally be described as one that the judgment "shades into" an inference, or vice versa. Next, just as Hegel's developed paradigm of judgment, the judgment of the concept, was a directly evaluative one, Peirce treats the judgments from which abduction occurs as paradigmatically aesthetic, while thinking of aesthetic experience as paradigmatic of the type of normativity found in both ethics and logic itself (Peirce 1992, 198–199). Clearly, these must be judgments that involve a maximum of Kantian intensive magnitude. Thirdly, as Michael Hoffmann has pointed out, Peirce linked abduction to a diagrammatic mode of reasoning—"meta-diagrammatic abduction"—that he thought introduced new ways of seeing things: "Our vantage point determines the set of available theoretical models. It is possible to generate new models simply by shifting the perspective on a problem" (Hoffmann 2010, 581). He identified this form of reasoning with the use of diagrams in projective geometry, and in particular regarding the construction involved in Desargues's theorem of the homologous triangles (as in fig. 4.4 above). When Desargues's triangles are seen as lying on two intersecting planes within three-dimensional space, the reasons for the collinearity of the points of intersection of their extended sides becomes readily apparent (Hoffmann 2010, 582–583).[10]

In short, for Peirce as well as for Hegel, there is a peculiar type of inference that starts from an overtly evaluative judgment grounded in a type of felt response to a thing with some distinctively perceivable quality and that is capable of achieving some type of redetermination of the content involved by virtue of its generalization. Thus, while Peirce stresses the role of emotion in abductive inference (Peirce 1992, 199), Hegel indicates that the judgment of the concept in its initial form is based on nothing more that "a subjective *assurance*" (*SL*, 583; 12:85). That this type of judgment is initially subjective in this way is in turn linked to the purpose of this type of inference. For Hegel, the point of the judgment of the concept is to make explicit something that was only implicit within the initial judgment given its subjective basis. What the inference aims to do is to bring out something of the essential structure of the kind to which the perceived object belongs and to grasp it as responsible for the initial subjective assurance felt by the judge.

In Hegel, this unfolds in the context of the dialectical engagement of the judge with another judge. Challenged with an opposing judgment and attempting to justify her own, one judge is led to formulate that it is because the house is so and so constituted that it is good. That is, what is reasoned to in this form of reasoning is a form of judgment closer to a minor premise that captures how this house (a singular), as a particular instance of a kind, is, because of this fact, good. This judgment has a split middle term inasmuch as the house is conceived as both immediate (it is this house) and mediated (it is whatever about it that is responsible for my judging it to be good). Here, the mere sentiment underlying the initial judgment is replaced with a conception of its cause.[11] Similarly, Peirce describes abduction as reasoning to the minor premise as involving a movement from "effect to cause," in which the cause "explains" the situation as experienced (Peirce 1992, 194).[12]

We will return to these parallels between Hegel and Peirce in the following chapter in examining Hegel's approach to Aristotle's syllogistic figures. Here, however, it is worth pointing to the parallel between Hegel's "syllogism of analogy" and Peirce's conception of abduction, both providing a model for Johnson's "intermediate" inferential step from "any one" to "any other" in his treatment of induction. In accord with this, Hegel's syllogism of analogy is to be found as a form of what he calls the reflective syllogism that supersedes the syllogism of induction and that, as superseding it, brings out its true nature. Of course, the idea of a "syllogism of analogy" should bring to mind Aristotle's version of this type of practical inference operating with the transgenus proportion (*analogia*) or double ratio, $a : b :: c : d$, a form that he could nevertheless not incorporate into his formal syllogistic. In relation to this, Hegel appeals to the idea of this syllogism as "containing *four terms*, the *quaternio terminorum*" and this raises the question of "how to bring analogy into the form of a formal syllogism" (*SL*, 615; 12:116), which contains three. We might expect that a three-termed analogy with a split middle term is what will explain such a *quaternio terminorum*.

While Aristotle's difficulty with integrating analogical inferences was premised on his conception of a univocal middle term,[13] Hegel seems to be suggesting that such an analogical dimension is unavoidable in any inferential process and that it is allowed by the ambivalence of the middle term. As succeeding the syllogism of induction, the syllogism of analogy brings out what it is that actually makes induction a genuine inference. Thus, as with Johnson, this type of analogy is involved at the level of inference from "any one" to "any other" that is required in order to group a lot of singulars into a collection that could be used as the basis for an inference from "any" to "all." The induction found in the syllogism of reflection must be one that, as Hegel writes, "rests upon *analogy*" (*E:L*, §190). In the corresponding section of *The Science of Logic*, Hegel goes about addressing Aristotle's problem by distinguishing three terms from a fourth: "There are *two* singulars; for a *third*, a property immediately assumed as common, and, for a *fourth*, the other properties that one singular possesses immediately but the other first comes to possess only by means of the syllogism" (*SL*, 615; 12:116–117).

In the two examples given in the *Encyclopedia Logic*, "Gaius, a human being, is a learned individual; Titus is also a human being; hence he is also likely to be learned" and "The Earth is a heavenly body and has inhabitants;

the Moon is also a heavenly body; hence, it is probably also inhabited" (*E:L*, §190, addition), there is a probabilistic inference from one singularly determined body to another on the basis of some immediately grasped property or properties inhering in each.[14] Because what is being compared are, in the first instance, singulars, as in "the Earth" and "the Moon," the inference in its initial form must involve a type of identification as in "The Moon is *an* Earth," thereby making the Earth itself one of a kind, one "earth" among others including the moon. But it also allows the type of geometric double ratio in which the sun is to the earth as the earth is to the moon (sun : earth :: earth : moon). This will therefore be a step toward the type of Copernican redetermination of the objects involved, with the development of general terms (star, planet, satellite, and so on), as in Venn's conception of the development of theoretical from everyday language.

These intervening analogical steps bring into focus the fact that the identities involved in induction cannot simply hold between the qualities themselves as immediately given, thus giving the lie to all empiricisms that rely on equating some initially given "sensory ideas" or "sense-data." The syllogism of analogy brings out the point that the relevant identities are between the relations (or "ratios") themselves: the identities being posited are between the ways that this quality inheres in this thing, that quality inheres in that thing, and so on. As in Carnot's projective geometry, the basic objects involved are "correlations" among conventionally different figures, not the figures themselves. But I suggest also that the association of the syllogism of analogy with the syllogism of induction demarcates Hegel's position from the typical theological realism founded on analogy, as in Thomas Aquinas, for example (Ashworth 2017). Abstracted from its correctable role within the syllogism of induction, the syllogism of analogy works at the level of the *Vorstellungen* of religion and not at the level of philosophy.[15] Finally, both Johnson and Hegel appeal to a type of intuitive dimension to these initial one-to-one inferences: Johnson simply calls this an "intuitive inference" that involves the "apprehension of the universal" in the particular/singular, while Hegel alludes to an "instinct of reason" (*E:L*, §190, addition).

Hegel's examples clearly portray the syllogism of analogy as fallible and as being "more superficial or more rigorous" (*E:L*, §190, addition), belonging to the comparative estimation of the "more or less." The source of this fallibility, it would seem, is the feature he underlines about the "reflective syllogism" of which the inductive and analogical syllogisms are subtypes—they are subjective. This is why this corrective or "reflective" type of inference is necessary. Analogously, despite his criticisms of Newtonianism, he clearly thinks that Newtonian mechanics provides a type of knowledge—it is just not the type of knowledge that it aspires to be. Hegel does not have a lot to say about how his notion of the inductive syllogism may be extended to this, but again Johnson, with his explicit differentiation between applicational and implicational principles and their "counter" forms, is able to suggest a path.

In his description of "a conjunction of disconnected syllogisms" alluded to earlier and of the form "Everything is p if m; This is m; Therefore This is p," "Everything is p' if m'; This is m'; Therefore This is p'," "Everything is p'' if m''; This is m''; Therefore This is p''," the terms "m," "m'," "m''," etc. stand for individual determinates of the determinable M, while "p," "p'," "p''," etc. stand for similarly individual determinates of the determinable P. "If then we can collect these major premisses into a general formula holding for every value of M and P in accordance with the mathematical equation $P = f(M)$, then we have an example of what may be called the functional extension of the syllogism . . . where the major or supreme premiss may be expressed in the simple form $P = f(M)$" (Johnson 1922, 104). That is, while the general empirical law is expressed in determinables, "the terms which occur in these different minors and conclusions are specific values of the determinables"—that is, determinates of those determinables (Johnson 1922, 103–104), the intuitionists' witnesses.

With this, and giving as examples Newton's inverse square law and Boyle's law, Johnson effectively supplies a logical form to fit the empiricists' conception of natural law as simple covariation among specific measurable parameters. In cases such as these, numerical values are the determinates of determinables such as "distance," "velocity," and so on. But, of course, the implications involved are only valid when the "everything" referred to in the law is shorthand for the sum of those individuals indicated by the demonstrative "this" in each of the disconnected "syllogisms"—what Hegel describes as the association (*Gemeinschaftlichkeit*) of singulars or the "complete set of singulars."

Were this all to work on the level of propositional logic with its implicative and counterimplicative principles there would be no genuine inference or no new knowledge, and this is surely behind Hegel's refusal to accept both Leibniz's mathematical syllogism as the formal core of logic and Newton's "explanations" of Kepler's laws. The measurable singulars of judgments of reflection, deprived of some universal determination, are now "measured and determined" (*zu messen und . . . zu bestimmten ist*) entirely by the abstractly universal predicate under which the singular subject is "*subsumed* as an accidental" (*SL*, 569–570; 12:72). But such abstractions are entities for which Kant's intensive magnitude equals zero. For the implicational structures involved to become proper inferences (syllogisms)—for them to become part of a properly explanatory process—requires something akin to the move insisted upon by contemporary scientific realists in their criticisms of positivistic "correlations," some principle such as "inference to the best explanation." But this, as both Johnson and Hegel insist, requires something beyond the implicational structures involved: Johnson requires the exercise of a properly "counter-applicational" principle; Hegel, a further application of the "inference by analogy" operating now at the level of kinds. Merely shared abstract, that is, subsuming, universals do not constitute the true measure of things—genuine explanation must progress beyond shared universal characteristics to some underlying determination that makes something what it is—its genus. "Instead of 'all humans,' we now have to say 'the human being'" (or "the man as such" [*der Mensch*]; *SL*, 574; 12:76).[16] For Hegel, the empirical correlations need to be explained by the essential properties of the objects involved. For Johnson, the formal "everythings" that are merely finite sums need to become genuinely categorical. Both have reached a more traditional Aristotelian conception of explanation, but neither rests there.

9.3 The Secondary Substances of the Second Judgment Cycle

At the end of the first judgment cycle we have a new *de-re* judgment with a type of "secondary substance" as its subject—some natural kind or concrete universal.[17] Thought has moved from being able to reflect on the experience of this rose or the Earth to reason about instances of the kinds rose or planet because judgments can be made about these kinds as such. Judgments about these secondary substances or natural kinds thus initiate a second cycle within which this judgment form will be transformed along the general lines observed in the first (*SL*, 575–581; 12:77–83). As in the first cycle, this cycle will ascend through a phase of abstraction to a maximally indeterminate judgment form (the hypothetical judgment) and then descend through a phase of concretization (the disjunctive judgment) so as to ultimately issue in the judgment of the overtly evaluative judgment of the concept. Nevertheless, there is a sense in which the cycle itself is "reflective" in relation to the preceding and succeeding cycles, indicating the problematic status of the kind as itself a substance.[18] In this cycle, the shortcomings of judgments limited to this phase of development reflect the point we have been making about the limitations of Aristotle's logic—its inability to give proper expression to the determination of singularity, the singularity distinguishing Callias from some indefinite particular instantiation of the human kind. It will be the determination of singularity that will be restored in the judgment of the concept, the judgment form that represents the supersession of those of the two earlier cycles. What is judged there is not a house considered as a mere instance of "the house as such" but rather this house considered as a better or worse instantiation of a how a house ought to be. The need to transition into the explicitly modal logic of the judgment of the concept will raise questions for those who find in Hegel some type of Aristotelian realism about kinds, that is, the kinds as determined within the second cycle.

What the judgment of necessity divides into are the universals, genus and species, but Hegel reminds us that "the species is a species only in so far as, on the one side, it exists in singulars [*in Einzelnen existiert*]" (*SL*, 575; 12:77–78), or, as he puts it more bluntly in the *Encyclopedia Philosophy of Nature*, "Things are singularities [*einzelne*] however, and the lion in general does not exist [*der Löwe überhaupt existiert nicht*]" (*E:PN*, §246, addition, p. 198). The closest the subject of judgments of this cycle can approach to singularity is as the indeterminate particular: "The subject is subject . . . only as a *particular* [*nur als Besonderes*]" (*SL*, 576; 12:78)—that is, it is an indifferent instantiation of some universal. Again, the subjects of such judgments are as found in Aristotle's conception of science: there is no science of Socrates qua Socrates, only the science of Socrates in the determination of being a human. Hegel notes that we must not confuse the subject of the sentence "The rose is a plant" with that of the sentence "The rose is red" (576; 12:78). The former names a species, and predicates of it a genus; the latter names an individual, and predicates of it a qualitative inherent property. The three categories of universal, particular, and singular are not fully intelligible considered in isolation. Like the three Pythagorean means, they are to be considered as a unity of determinations among which some degree of incommensurability exists. From the categorical judgment the judgment of necessity will pass through two more forms, the hypothetical judgment and the disjunctive judgment, the latter of which will bring out something that was only implicit in defining a species in terms of a higher genus. It was only a particular instance of that genus.

I suggest we see Hegel's cycles as a device to progressively unearth logical relations that exist implicitly within the rational practices of our shared logical life. As in Brandom's Sellarsian account, we might think of these as involving the pragmatic "language game" of the asking for and giving of reasons, but in contrast to Brandom's rather general way of conceiving of this activity, I suggest that Hegel's account is more specifically directed to those dialectical language games that Aristotle refers to in the *Topics* and which are linked to the ability to "puzzle on both sides of a subject" (Aristotle 1984, *Topics*, 1.2, 101a35–37)—a type of language game more specifically connected to philosophy in which is preserved a certain residual incommensurability between perspectives rather than those more "demonstrative" forms of scientific reasoning considered in the *Posterior Analytics*—for example, in which singulars are absorbed into the more general category of particular instances of kinds. Again, in contrast with Brandom's more Fregean approach, Hegel, pursuing the theme of the syllogistic "doubled mean," adopts an account of inference more like that of the algebraist Johnson with his opposed but complementary "applicative" and "implicative" principles at the heart of syllogistic inference. Moreover, with the move of making the explicitly evaluative "judgment of the concept" the truth of the type of judgments found in scientific reasoning, Hegel is denying that the logic of our reasoning about values can be reduced to or somehow explained by the types of judgments we make in the positive sciences. In fact, the types of explanations found in the positive sciences are only understandable against the background of such evaluative practices. While this rejection of "scientism" itself is not such an unusual philosophical attitude in the present, offering a type of systematic logic for the reasoning presupposed by the workings of empirical science, as Johnson attempted in his *Logic*, is not so common.

9.4 The Judgment of the Concept and Its Syllogistic Truth

In recent discussions of Hegel's metaphysics there has appeared a tendency to point to the notion of "normativity" as that which separates Hegel's philosophical attitude from that of traditional metaphysics. This move, it is claimed, provides an alternative to the traditional view interpreting Hegel as a premodern theocentric metaphysician—its error being that of confusing what he posits as norms with descriptions of independent features of the world. In this way, Hegel is often described as having effectively generalized the role that Kant had given to normativity in his practical philosophy. While Kant had emphasized normativity and rule following in practical life, Hegel had extended this approach to encompass theoretical reason as well, liberating it from the remnants of a representational conception of knowledge still present in Kant.[19] While there is something right about this account of Hegel, I want to argue that there is something incomplete as well, at least to the extent that it can reflect the way the concept of normativity in general has been shaped by Kant's specific approach to the normative nature of practical philosophy. When we look to Hegel, we find "values" as central, in relation to which "norms" are abstractions, and it is the logical structure of evaluative concepts that is at the core of Hegel's final conception of judgment, the "judgment of the concept."[20]

Hegel starts the section on the judgment of the concept with the observation that the capacity to say "The rose is red," "The snow is white," and so on will hardly be taken as "a sign of great power of judgment" (*SL*, 581; 12:84), and this immediately puts him at a critical distance from standard modern conceptions of judgment in logic in which judgments like those about the respective colors of roses and snow will be thought of as prototypical judgments because they are the sorts of judgments most likely to be met with agreement. From the perspective of modern classical logic, truth is taken primarily as a property of judgments, and the least problematic judgments will be deemed as prototypically true. In contrast to such simple judgments, the sorts of evaluative judgments that Hegel considers under this heading will be thought of as the most problematic, ones most likely to be met with disagreement, and so in need of evidence. These are the types of judgment that apply to objects the type of concepts that W. B. Gallie described as "essentially contested" (Gallie 1964).

We have seen how the notion of "measure" with which "The Doctrine of Being" concluded played a role that anticipated the notion of "essence" found in "The Doctrine of Essence," and Hegel appeals to the link of "measure" and "essence" here: the evaluative predicates "'good,' 'bad,' 'true,' 'right' etc., express that the fact is *measured* against the concept as an *ought* which is simply presupposed [*als dem schlechthin Sollen gemessen*], and is, or is not, in *agreement* with it" (*SL*, 582; 12:84). Traditional subject-predicate structure will thus be favored here as, from the results of the first cycle, we can understand a kind term as containing presuppositions about that which is referred to by that kind.[21] The cycle of redetermination that unfolds in the course of this judgment form will purportedly reveal what it is that makes this judgment the most developed form in terms of which all the earlier judgments are to be understood.

The cycle is relatively easy to follow in its basic development. It starts with an "assertoric" judgment that connects to a "concrete singular" a predicate that "expresses this same singular as the *connection* of its actuality, its determinateness or *constitution*, to its *concept*. ('This house is *bad*,' 'this action is *good*.')" (582; 12:85). The kind "house" will bring with it a list of features essential for houses—houses provide protection from the weather, from intruders, and so on—and the goodness or otherwise of some specific house can presumably be measured against the typical contents of such a list. But there is a difference between both houses and actions as kinds and what, in the spirit of Aristotle, are thought of as natural kinds. Aristotle tended to run these notions together into a concept of natural kind that contained a distinctly evaluative dimension, but the conception of natural kind that had emerged within the generally explanatory framework of Hegel's judgment of necessity seemed to swing free from this dimension, which is introduced only in the following cycle. The course of this third cycle of judgment, starting from the judgment of the concept, will link evaluation to what is distinctive about the non-natural kinds that we think of as human actions and their products.

In the case of the natural kinds of the second cycle, that empirical regularities had come to be packed into the kind terms would suggest that those kind terms themselves might provide an objective measure to which an individual instance had to conform to count as an instance of that kind. To be a rose, this thing has to be a genuine plant, has to have the characteristics definitive of one of the four subgenera of the genus *Rosa*, and so on, but in the case of houses and actions, the logic of judgment is very different. A plant that does not satisfy the defining characteristics of a rose is simply not a rose. In contrast, a house that does not live up to the normative characteristics of a house is a bad house, but a house, nonetheless. There is a dimension of the more-or-less in this structure's instantiation of the concept <house>. Hegel suggests that the credentials of such evaluative judgments express, in the first instance, "only a subjective *assurance*" (*SL*, 583; 12:85). Such essentially contestable judgments lead to reason giving, and this now locates the house within a logical space of evaluative concepts—human actions and products are, by their nature, possibly good and possibly bad—but it has also located the concrete judgment itself in that same logical space, such that it is a possibly good/possibly bad instance of judgment. Only explicitly evaluative judgments can adopt this type of reflective metaconceptual standpoint in which the activity of judging can itself be brought under the scope of the concepts being applied in the original judgments. It is in this sense that judgment has here reached its completed, self-sufficient form: it has realized the concept of what it is to be a judgment.

We are now back on "Copernican" territory, in which we are asked to consider the possibility that the immediately given object is not the proper "measure" of the concept applied in the judgment—perhaps the apparent object simply reflects the conditions from which the judgment issues rather than the object's true nature. Just as in the case of reflecting on the possibility that it is *me* who is actually moving when I report the sun to be moving, here negation leads to the consideration that perhaps it is something *about me* rather than the proper concept of a house, my ultimately naturally based predispositions to respond, that have been the ground of my judging. To offset this possibility, I have to bring the judgment back to the house itself, abstracted from presuppositions held about it. Thus, Hegel puts the focus squarely back on the singularity of a specific existing house: "Purified of such a singularity, the subject would be only a universal, whereas the predicate entails precisely this, that the concept of the subject ought to be posited with reference to its singularity" (*SL*, 584; 12:86).

This third cycle thus corrects the conception of logical structure that was found in the second. It reinjects the determination of the singularity of the object judged that had fallen out of the second cycle in which "the subject is subject... only as a *particular*" (*SL*, 576; 12:78). The content of the judgment must have as a component the actual thing itself in its full determinacy. It is only then that judgment can be provided with an adequate measure for its own measurings, and a measure that is equally available to another judge. The insight about the nature of reasoning that the insistence on singularity rather than mere particularity brings forth is that in the case of human actions and products a singular instance can come to measure the normativity of the concept being applied in a way that works in the opposite direction from that in which the abstract concept or definition measures its instances.[22]

I have suggested that Hegel's differentiation of the judgment of the concept from the judgment of necessity of the earlier cycle reveals his critical attitude to an ontology of Aristotelian kinds, and this might be expressed by drawing Hegel's account closer to Plato when understood as the late Plato of the "unwritten doctrines"—Plato as an advocate of the duality of the one and the indeterminate dyad of the more or less and of the sensible rather than the suprasensible status of *paradigmata*.[23] Hegel's position here might be most easily clarified by contrasting the notion of "the good" as it features as a predicate in the judgment of the concept against the way that it features in the logic of Kant's practical philosophy. Kant's considers the moral notion of the good as a self-sufficient concept able to give a determinate content to the will. Simply put, the categorical imperative can tell the will what it ought to do. When, early in the *Groundwork of the Metaphysics of Morals* Kant writes that "it is impossible to think of anything at all in the world, or indeed even beyond it, that could be considered good without limitation except a *good will*" (Kant 1998, 7), one might imagine Hegel's (decidedly Greek) critical response to the *very idea* of a good "without limitation." From the duality of the one and the indeterminate dyad, to describe anything as without limitations is to construe it as "bad." Indeed, this is the bad indeterminacy of Kant's purely intelligible moral law that Hegel sees as its problem. Here we might think of Kant as the moral equivalent of Newton. Like Newton, Kant must rely on the empirical to give his laws any content, but he cannot properly accommodate the moral status of anything empirical within the logical framework of those laws. That is, they only admit abstractions. Hegel's conception of evaluative judgments, on the contrary, presupposes the existence of paradigms that can be taken as instantiations of norms. These are the Platonic *paradigmata* that, according to Sayre (Sayre 2005), had, by the time of the post-Parmenidean dialogues, ceased to exist exclusively in the transcendent beyond and had found a place in the empirical realm of the "more and less."

Progress through the forms of judgment had shown how judgments had acquired contents that would become progressively transformed or redetermined.

The concept of the judgment of existence has shown it to start with some nameable concrete object as part of its content, but the first judgment cycle showed that object to be redetermined as a concrete universal, a kind. Kinds had started as the proper objects of the categorical judgments commencing the second cycle, but by the third cycle concrete singulars had reappeared—now singular actions or action products as claimants to the status of their concepts. But not only objects had appeared within judgment contents, judging subjects had been "located" in relation to those objects by the judgment form as well.[24] In the judgment of the concept, the existence of the judging subject had become explicit as the problematization of the judgment is simultaneously a problematization of the subject qua normative judge making that judgment. To make an evaluative judgment is to bring one's judging to the status of something to be judged. Here, different judges bring their different measures to evaluate or measure the measurings of their opponents. In turn, all these contents now become incorporated into the syllogism, with the difference that the syllogism contains places for different, opposed judging subjects. This is why Schelling's Constructed Line could offer a suggestive model for Hegel's understanding of both the syllogism and the intersubjective practice in which the measures brought to judgment by one judge are themselves the object of evaluation—measure—by others, the form of interaction that Hegel calls "recognition." By the end of the progress of syllogistic forms, which to a large degree mirrors the development of forms of judgment, it becomes apparent that "the concept in general has been realized; more precisely, it has gained the kind of reality which is *objectivity*" (SL, 624; 12:125). The truth of conceptuality has been revealed to be the type of dialectically mediated forms of practice structuring human life, guided by the idea of value—the good. With this, Aristotle's conception of the good life is made more Platonic by being interpreted as that of logical life.[25]

It is this underlying object-centered and subject-placing conception of judgment that is in turn connected to that aspect of Hegel's approach that links him to the algebraic tradition rather than the classical tradition of modern logic, and that finds an important place for conceptual polarities that get expressed most explicitly in evaluative judgments with their peculiar logic. We will focus on these issues in the following chapter.

10

Hegel beyond the New Leibnizians: Syllogisms

> It must be granted that a study that has for its subject matter the modes of operation and the laws of reason must be of the greatest interest in and of itself—an interest at least not inferior to the knowledge of the laws and the particular shapes of nature. If it is not reputed a small matter to have discovered some sixty species of parrots, one hundred and thirty-seven species of veronica, and so on, much less ought it to be reputed a small matter to have discovered the forms of reason. Is not the figure of a syllogism something infinitely higher than a species of parrot or veronica?
>
> <p style="text-align:center">HEGEL, <i>The Science of Logic</i></p>

In the previous chapter we touched on some broad parallels between the ways in which both Peirce and Hegel conceive of a form of nondemonstrative inference that works its way up a syllogism in the opposite direction from deduction but that is not merely inductive. Such moves, it was suggested, illustrate the way both Hegel and Peirce had augmented the inferential possibilities implicit in Aristotle's formal syllogism by making use of the notion of directionality that had been introduced within Kant's protovectorial treatment of directed line segments in his transitional work. With this Kant had anticipated the way directionality would play a central role within the revival of geometry in the nineteenth century that would challenge the assumptions about the relation of geometry to arithmetic of the "analytic" mainstream initiated by Descartes. It is now time to explore some of the ways in which this development had been implicit in Hegel's account of the syllogism. In this chapter we will explore this first in relation to Peirce's later linkage of nondeductive inference forms to the second and third syllogistic figures, then in relation to other more recent attempts to transform the 2 × 2 traditional square of opposition into the 3 × 2 structure of a hexagon, and finally into viewing the hexagon as a two-dimensional projection of a three-dimensional cube.

10.1 Hegel, Peirce, and Aristotle on the Three Syllogistic Figures

In an early paper from 1878 in which he refers to what he would later call "abduction" as "hypothesis" (Peirce 1992), Peirce sets out to establish the three linked inferential forms of probabilistic reasoning: deduction, induction, and hypothesis. While all inferential forms can be reduced to Aristotle's favored "perfect" syllogism of Barbara, a mood within the first figure reasoning from premises "All As are B" and "All Bs are C" to "All As are C," "it does not follow that this is the most appropriate form in which to represent every kind of inference" (Peirce 1992, 187). Barbara typifies deductive reasoning but is in fact "nothing but the application of a rule" that is laid down in the major premise, applied to a case stated in the minor premise to produce a result. Inductive or hypothetical reasoning, however, "being something more than the mere application of a general rule to a particular case, can never be reduced to this form" (187). But, as we have seen (in chapter 9), one can, as Peirce puts it, "row . . . up the current of deductive sequence" (188) as when in induction, one infers from a combination of the result (the conclusion) and the case (the minor premise) to the rule (the major premise).

Peirce's example involves the sampling of populations. Consider a situation in which I draw a handful of beans from a bag and, on finding them all to be white, infer that in fact all the beans in the bag are white. I can set out the inference thus:

> These beans were in this bag.
> These beans are white.
> ∴ All the beans in the bag were white. (188)

It is clear that this inductive inference is just an inversion of a deductive one:

> *Rule.*—All these beans in the bag were white.
> *Case.*—These beans were in the bag.
> *Result.*—These beans are white.

But Peirce now points out that there is a further way of arranging the parts of the deductive inference to get a nondeductive one, the resulting inference being neither from population to sample nor from sample to population:

> Suppose I enter a room and there find a number of bags, containing different kinds of beans. On the table there is a handful of white beans; and, after some searching, I find one of the bags contains white beans only. I at once infer as a probability, or as a fair guess, that this handful was taken out of that bag. This sort of inference is called *making an hypothesis*. It is the inference of a *case* from a *rule* and *result*. We have, then—
>
> > Deduction
> > *Rule.*—All the beans from this bag are white.
> > *Case.*—These beans are from this bag.
> > ∴ *Result.*—These beans are white.

Induction
Case.—These beans are from this bag.
Result.—These beans are white.
∴ Rule.—All the beans from this bag are white.

Hypothesis
Rule.—All the beans from this bag are white.
Result.—These beans are white.
∴ Case.—These beans are from this bag. (Peirce 1992, 188)

However, there is yet another way of generating these alternative nondeductive forms of inference that, in a way that recalls Hegel's use of negation in generating alternative conceptions of judgment, uses denial rather than affirmation. Again, starting with the "perfect," first syllogistic figure of Barbara, by using the law of *modus tollens* one can derive from the denial of the conclusion, the denial of either of the major or minor premises. Peirce gives the following example. First, the deductive form of Barbara:

Rule.—All men are mortal.
Case.—Enoch and Elijah were men.
∴ Result.—Enoch and Elijah were mortal.

From this, two further valid deductive inferences can be formed by denying the result. First, if the result is denied while the rule is affirmed, we must infer the denial of the case:

Denial of the Result.—Enoch and Elijah were not mortal.
Rule.—All men are mortal.
∴ Denial of Case.—Enoch and Elijah were not men.

On the other hand, if, having denied the result, we affirm the case, we must infer the denial of the rule:

Denial of the Result.—Enoch and Elijah were not mortal.
Case.—Enoch and Elijah were men.
∴ Denial of the Rule.—Some men are not mortal. (Peirce 1992, 190)

It will be remembered that in Aristotle's syllogistic, figures in the second and third figures need to be converted to figures in the first figure. What Peirce has done is simply to have reversed this conversion, in a type of counter-conversion of second and third figure forms from the first. Thus, the inference in which denial of the result infers to the denial of the case is in a mood of the second figure (the mood of Baroco), while that in which the denial of the result infers to the denial of the rule is in the third figure (in the mood of Bocardo). But also, the former is a form of hypothesis, while the latter is a form of induction. Peirce has thereby aligned his three forms of inference deduction, hypothesis (abduction), and induction with Aristotle's three syllogistic figures. I suggest that broad parallels can be found with Hegel's own similarly functional interpretation of the three syllogistic figures.

It is no simple matter working out how Hegel conceives of the relation of his three main forms of syllogism in *The Science of Logic*, the syllogisms of existence, reflection, and necessity, to Aristotle's own three syllogistic figures. Like Aristotle, Hegel represents syllogisms as sequences of three terms. For Aristotle, the basic sequence meant to represent "perfect" deductive syllogisms in the first figure, such as that of "Barbara," is given as that of a sequence of letters standing for major extreme, middle term, and minor extreme, as in "A B C." Let us recall Aristotle's description of the first figure: "Whenever, then, three terms are so related to each other that the last is in the middle as a whole and the middle is either in or not in the first as a whole, it is necessary for there to be a complete deduction of the extremes. (I call that the *middle* which both is itself in another and has another in it—this is also middle in position—and call both that which is itself in another and that which has another in it *extremes*." Here we see the reciprocity of the "is in" and "said of" conceptions of predication as Aristotle immediately continues: "For if A is predicated of every B and B of every C, it is necessary for A to be predicated of every C" (Aristotle 1989, *Prior Analytics*, 25b32–40). That is, the "is in" relation works its way from right to left (last to first), while the "said of" relation progresses from left to right (first to last). With this explanation, it could be said that Aristotle construes the relations involved semantically, as via the relations among the meanings of the terms. But when he describes the alternative second and third figures, in chapters 5 and 6, respectively, he mixes semantic with purely syntactic descriptions based simply on relations of order.

In introducing the second figure, he writes: "When the same thing belongs to all of one term and to none of the other, or to all of each or none of each, I call such a figure the *second*. In it, I call that term the *middle* which is predicated of both and call those of which this is predicated *extremes*; the *major* extreme is the one lying next to the middle, while the *minor* extreme is the one farther from the middle." This, as with his description of the first figure, explains the figure in terms of the semantic relations holding among the terms. However, he then adds a description in terms of the movement of the middle term as one might illustrate by rearranging the order of otherwise meaningless counters on a table: "The middle is placed outside the extremes and is first in position" (Aristotle 1989, *Prior Analytics*, 26b34–27a1). The account of the third figure follows the same pattern: two linked semantic characterizations followed by a syntactic one: "If one term belongs to all and another to none of the same thing, or if they both belong to all or none of it, I call such a figure the *third*. By the *middle* in it I mean that term of which they are both predicated and by *extremes* the things predicated. By *major* extreme I mean the one farther from the middle and by *minor* the one closer. The middle is placed outside the extremes and is last in position" (28a11–15).

When we come to Hegel's three-term sequences, the significant difference in relation to Aristotle's is that while Aristotle's "A," "B," and "C" are apparently meaningless placeholders, Hegel uses capitals "S," "P," and "U" signifying the three semantically related conceptual determinacies of singularity, particularity, and universality.[1] His order also reflects the more natural (to both German and Greek) word order of subject followed by predicate, meaning that his "S P U" for the first syllogism has the reverse word order from Aristotle's "A B C" when understood semantically. Hegel reflects the movement from subject to predicate, and so from the less general to the more general, while Aristotle's reflects the movement from the more general to the less general.

A further complication is that Hegel applies the schemata of the figures at different levels of analysis. Thus, he describes Aristotle's three figures within the description of the formal "syllogism of existence," a sequence that leads to the "fourth figure"—the Leibniz-Ploucquet "mathematical" syllogism. But the pattern is essentially repeated when the formal syllogism of existence, via the mathematical syllogism, transitions into the syllogism of reflection and then the syllogism of necessity. Not only is the same configuration repeated within each of these syllogisms; it is repeated in the pattern holding among them as well.

Given all this, it might be thought optimistic to recover much in common between Peirce's use of the three figures for the purposes of his functional differentiation between different types of inference—deduction, induction and abduction—and Hegel's utilization of them for similar ends. Nevertheless, enough commonality can be observed to suggest some sort of convergence between Peirce and Hegel here. Moreover, it is the directionality allowed by these primitive logical diagrams, I suggest, that enables this.

The movement of the middle term generating the second and third figures from the first effectively repeats the idea of "external" alternatives to the "internal" division of a line segment that we have seen opened up as consequence of Kant's idea of the significance of the directionality of such a segment. We have seen this "dividing ratio" involved in the genesis of Nicomachus's "most perfect proportion," the precursor of the modern harmonic cross-ratio. Hegel will use the idea of moving the "middle term" in either of the two directions of the line defined by the two "extremes" to attempt to capture something like what Peirce envisages as "rowing up" the deductive stream along two different routes, one that takes him from the result to the minor and then to the major premise (induction) and one that takes him from the result to major premise and then to the minor premise (hypothesis).

In Aristotle's second syllogistic figure, the middle term, "B," is moved outside the interval between extremes to the left so as to become "first in position," leaving the sequence "B A C," and leaving A, the most general term as the new middle term—that is, the one common to the premises and eliminated in the conclusion. The equivalent move in Hegel would have to move "P" within the initial sequence "S P U" in the direction that would leave "U" (the most general term) in the middle, as in "S U P." Here, of course, the middle term "P" has become last, not first, but this conforms to the fact that the directionality of Hegel's sequence in relation to Aristotle's is reversed. This is, in fact, the shape Hegel gives as the third figure of the syllogism of existence and, similarly, the third figure of the syllogism of reflection, which he calls the "syllogism of analogy." Despite the rearrangement of second and third figures, Hegel's pattern reproduces Aristotle's reasonably faithfully.

Correspondingly, Hegel's second figure, "P S U," in which the "P" counter has been moved to the left, will correspond to Aristotle's third. In Aristotle's third, the middle term "B" has been moved to the right to be last in position, producing the sequence "A C B," leaving the least general term, "C," the new middle term. This corresponds to the associated semantic interpretation because this is the only term of which both other terms can be predicated. Similarly, in Hegel's second figure, the term "S," qua singular term, as new middle term is the only term of which a particular and a more general universal can be predicated.

Hegel's second figure, "P S U," is the one we have seen at work in the treatment of induction that we compared to Johnson's in the previous chapter, the syllogism of induction being the second syllogistic form of the syllogism of reflection, which is itself the second syllogism in the major syllogistic triad. Peirce's sequence of the three syllogistic figures coincides with Aristotle's, and so, again compensating for the difference due to the directionality and associated reordering involved, Hegel's account of induction coincides with Peirce's account, as does his account of the "syllogism of analogy" with Peirce's account of "hypothesis."

There is clearly something of Peirce's hypothesis in Hegel's syllogism of analogy. As in Hegel's example arguing from "*The earth* has inhabitants" and "The moon is *an earth*" (that is, is a thing of basically the same kind as *the earth*) to the conclusion "Therefore the moon has inhabitants" (*SL*, 614; 12:115) is to hypothesize. Clearly this is a fairly crude type of hypothetical reasoning, although we might imagine something like this as a part of the "logic of discovery" phase of inquiry, as when the atom was conceived on the model of the solar system, and it might be thought as in need of the reciprocal "logic of verification," served by the process of induction as treated in Johnsonian fashion. But we have already seen a rather more substantive form alluded to in relation to the application of the "principle of continuity" in Kepler, who, in grasping the similarity of the four conic sections, had argued that just as there are two foci in an ellipse, so too should there be two foci in a parabola. From this he went on to conceive of the second focus as at some infinitely distant point, anticipating the types of "points at infinity" postulated by the projective geometers. Contrary to a view such as that found in Popper's epistemology, where "conjectures" have little logic to them in contrast to the falsifying "refutations" that they face (Popper 1962), Peirce and Hegel extend their conceptions of logical structure to that first phase of inquiry.

10.2 Hegelian Expansions of the Square of Opposition: From Logical Square to Logical Hexagon and Beyond

Aristotle's syntactic device generating the extrasyllogistic figures clearly echoes the pattern of the beautiful bond in Plato's *Timaeus* in which the "middle term has become the first and the last" and "the last and the first have become the middle terms," but not in Plato's way such that they thereby have "all become one" (*LHP* 2:210; 3:39). That the second and third figures of Aristotle's syllogism asymmetrically rely on the first reflects the lack of such closure. One can then appreciate how Hegel would want to exploit and develop it in ways that took it beyond Aristotle's own use of it. This type of mechanical manipulation in which elements are rearranged like counters on a table presupposes the type of desemanticization that, as has been argued, allows resemanticization in a way like that which Hegel sees working within the mathematical tradition to allow its progression.

Peirce's image of different paths being traversed among three locations suggests an increase in the dimensionality of the "space" of the syllogism beyond that of the linear ordering of three terms. Leaving the result one can pass though the rule on the way to the case or alternatively pass through the case on the way to the rule, for example. Here, alternative orders come into focus in a way that resembles the puzzle concerning the seven bridges of Königsberg that had sparked Euler's invention of his *geometria situs*. In Peirce's version of the puzzle, the possibility of two such pathways from each of the three starting points will suggest six possible trips involved. Similarly in Hegel's case, while there are only three ways of ordering "three counters" in a row, there are six if one includes the possibility of changing the direction of the order. This "3 × 2" picture also appears in the various permutations available when three conceptual determinacies (singularity, particularity, universality) are distributed over the two syntactic parts of the judgment, subject and predicate.[2] We have seen this "3 × 2" picture before: first in Eudoxus's expansion of the three Archytan musical means by the addition of their subcontraries (above, chapter 3.3) and then in the way that directionality gives a doubled structure to each of the three dimensions of space, into front-back, up-down, and right-left, in Kant as well as in Nicomachus of Gerasa (above, chapter 3.4). In light of these convergences, it seems significant that during the twentieth century a number of logicians, without any connection to Hegel, would independently argue for an expansion of the traditional square of opposition into a logical hexagon, converting its 2 × 2 structure into a 3 × 2 structure.

In the 1960s, the French logician Robert Blanché extended into a hexagon a *modal* interpretation of the traditional square of opposition that had been proposed by the Polish logician Jan Łukasiewicz (Blanché 1966; Łukasiewicz 1953).[3] Employing the pair of strong modal contraries we have observed in MacColl, necessity and impossibility, Łukasiewicz had located the propositions "necessarily p," "impossibly p," "possibly p," and "not necessarily p" at the corners, A, E, I, and O, respectively, of the traditional square (fig. 10.1).[4]

Blanché then exploited the subcontrariety relation between I- and O-judgments across the bottom of the square to add a third modal category, contingency. Thus, the compound "contingently p" could be understood as equivalent to the conjunction of both "possibly p," and "not necessarily p."

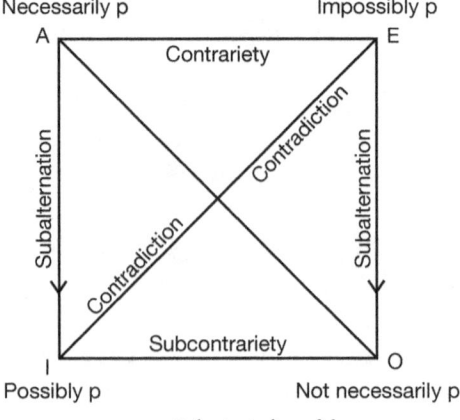

FIGURE 10.1 Łukasiewicz's modal square.

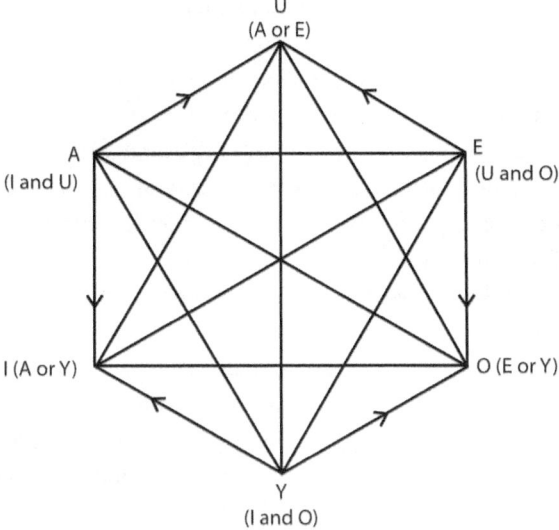

FIGURE 10.2 Blanché's hexagon (after Blanché 1966).

Because a conjunction implies both individual conjuncts, a lower vertex, Y, can be connected to the modal square such that the Y-judgment can be understood as implying each of the I- and O-judgments, adding to their subalternation implication from the A- and E-judgments, respectively.[5] Similarly, an upper vertex, U, can be added, representing the judgment "not contingently p" (and so the contradictory of Y), because "not contingently p" can in turn be understood as the disjunction of the A-judgment, "necessarily p," and the E-judgment, "impossibly p," because implied by both (fig. 10.2).

Blanché's experiments with this hexagonal diagram were linked to the French structuralist movement of the mid-twentieth century, Blanché mentioning the work of the anthropologist Claude Lévi-Strauss in noting that "the organization of concepts by contrasting couples appears to be an original and lasting form of thought" (Blanché 1966, 15). This idea had earlier become prominent within French ethnography around the turn of the twentieth century with the work of Émile Durkheim and Marcel Mauss (Durkheim and Mauss 1903), who would identify a type of rough-and-ready form of practical and evaluative reasoning rooted in the distinctions right and left and male and female as effectively universal among preliterate cultures. These, of course, exemplify the type of Pythagorean table of linked contraries given by Aristotle (Lloyd 1966). Blanché notes, however, that these oppositions had effectively been eliminated from modern classical logic, in which negation had become exclusively "external," and in which the relation of contradiction holding between propositions had come to predominate over the contrariety between terms. Moreover, among the logical relations that Blanché sought to represent was a distinction between two different senses of contrariety found in Aristotle: a weaker sense, as incompatibility among multiple terms within a particular field, and a stronger sense of polarity or opposition between two terms (Blanché 1966, 42). Clearly, the former coincides with the incompatibility among color concepts in Hegel's judgments of existence, while the latter the opposition between the opposed concepts of good and bad in the judgment of the concept.[6]

With a little manipulation, Blanché's hexagon can be transformed into the type of lattice diagram found in Boolean algebra. Let us first only retain the directed, that is, inference-indicating segments from figure 10.2 (A → U, A → I, E → U, E → O, Y → I, and Y → O) to get a stripped-down version. Next, because a Hasse diagram relies on all inferential "arrows" pointing in the one direction, we will need to reverse the positions of I and A and O and E nodes of the stripped-down hexagon, while retaining the directions of their connections to the top U and bottom Y vertices, so to get the diagram in figure 10.3.

We know that for a Hasse diagram a proposition represented at the highest node is implied by all propositions located at connected lower nodes, and that a proposition represented at the lowest node implies any proposition located above it. We can therefore add a maximum node above I, U, and O and a minimum one below A, Y, and E. What results is the type of lattice diagram as found in Boolean logic or the semilattice diagrams as found in Heyting logic, corresponding to their respective logical interpretations of partially ordered sets (fig. 10.4).

In the 1950s and 1960s, Blanché had not been alone in thinking of hexagonal extensions of the traditional square of opposition, and a similar hexagonal extension had been proposed in 1955 by the Polish logician Tadeusz

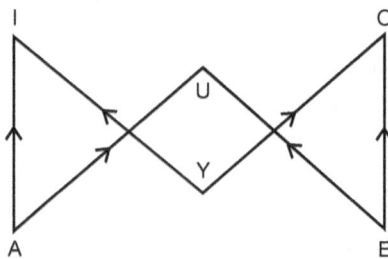

FIGURE 10.3 A rearranged Blanché hexagon.

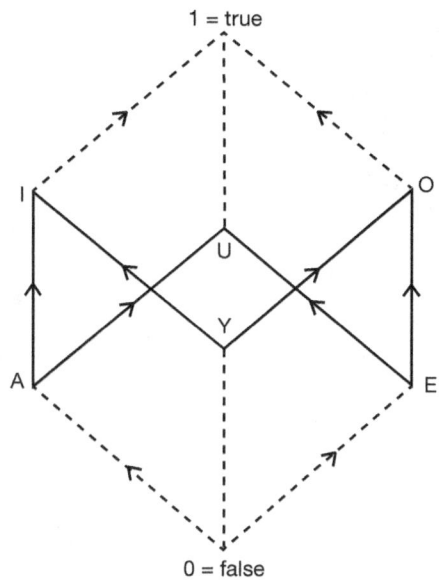

FIGURE 10.4 Adding maximum and minimum vertices to the rearranged hexagon.

Czezowski (Czezowski 1955; see also Englebretsen 1986). In this case, the relevant "square" to be expanded was not Łukasiewicz's modal version of the traditional square but the type of singular square that Horn had noted in Aristotle (Horn 2017) such that Czezowski employs (like Hegel) a distinction between singular and particular propositions: "The name, 'This S' in the subject of a singular proposition I regard to be a proper name denoting a given individual from the extension of the S term, just as 'Francis Bacon' denotes one of the members of the Bacon family" (Czezowski 1955, 392). And so, while for Blanché the U node represented the disjunction of A and E nodes, for Czezowski it represented an affirmative singular proposition of the type "This S is P" (Hegel's positive judgment of existence), while its diagonally opposite Y node represented the contradictory of that singular proposition (392).

The nodes of Czezowski's hexagon thus gave representation to the following six judgment types: A: universal positive, E: universal negative, U: singular positive, Y: singular negative, I: particular positive, O: particular negative. There are significant similarities and, not surprisingly, differences between Czezowski's and Blanché's diagrams (fig. 10.5). Comparing them, it can be seen that while both have A → U, A → I, E → O, and Y → O, Blanché's E → U and Y → I are missing from Czezowski's, and Czezowski's U → I and E → Y are missing from Blanché's.[7]

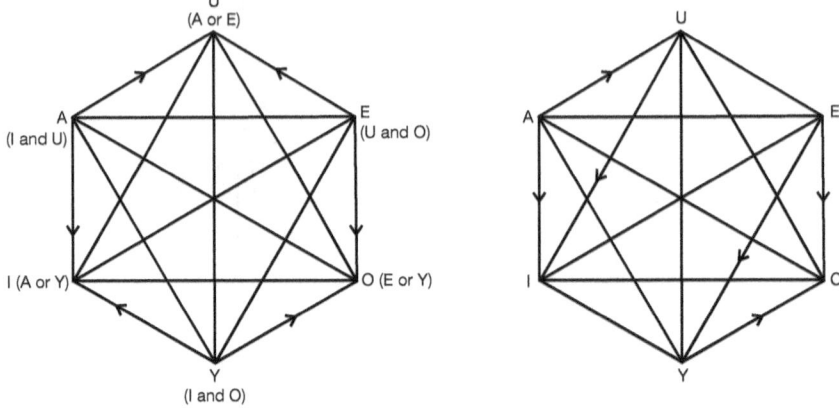

FIGURE 10.5 Blanché's hexagon (*left*), Czezowski's hexagon (*right*).

In both Blanché and Czezowski diagrams, diagonals represent contradiction, but there are differences within the lists of respective relations of subalternation, contrariety, and subcontrariety. We can restrict our attention here to those holding between the relations of subalternation, that is, relations of inference. In Blanché, E implies U and Y implies I, but neither of these inferences holds for Czezowski. Conversely, for Czezowski, U implies I and E implies Y, while neither holds for Blanché.

Czezowski's extension of the singular square as an attempt to capture the logical relations—contradiction, contrariety, subcontrariety, and subalternation—among the positive and negative versions of three types of propositions, singular, particular, and universal, has the 3 × 2 structure of the unity of geometric, arithmetic, and harmonic means that, according to Proclus (Proclus 1970, 55), had been achieved by Eudoxus of Cnidus and that was expressed by Hegel in his treatment of the "ratio of powers." We might also think of it as an attempted diagrammatic representation of the types of judgments found in Hegel's subjective logic.[8] Similarly, it is clear that Czezowski captures some of the important inferential relations that we have seen in Hegel's account of syllogisms in the "Subjective Logic," with such "Hegelian" resonances coming out in the contrasts with Blanché. While Czezowski's U-judgment, "This S is P," will, like Blanché's U, be implied by the A-judgment "All Fs are G," Czezowski, but not Blanché, has I-judgments inferred from U-judgments, repeating Hegel's abstractive inference from "This F is G" to the less determinate "Some F is G."

Most importantly, however, there is a further and deeper way in which Czezowski's account of logical relations echoes Hegel's. For Czezowski, it emerges that these relations among singular, particular, and universal propositions can no longer be considered univocal. They will be defined differently depending on the interpretation of the sentences being related. Czezowski puts this down to the fact that singular propositions are, from a formal point of view, hybrids: in certain contexts they behave logically like universal propositions, in others they behave like particular propositions.[9] We have seen something like this idea in Heyting's intuitionistic logic where an intuitionistic version of Boolean logic can be converted to the more classical Boolean form by invoking some hypothesis about the nature of the world that the reasoning is about. Arthur Prior would later also suggest a similar need for hybridity in logic in order to accommodate both tensed and modal judgments (Blackburn 2006), and this idea would be taken up under the title of "two-dimensional logic" (Humberstone 2004). It is also in accord with the way Hegel had treated the relation of the determinations of singularity and particularity, based on Ploucquet's concepts of exclusive and comprehensive particularity—the modern version, I have argued, of Plato's divided middle term. Consonant with these approaches Czezowski expresses this lack of univocity in logic by the idea that the hexagon is best understood as resulting from the superimposition of three different logical "squares," which might be understood as lying on differently oriented planes within three-dimensional space.[10] In this way, just as Hegel's syllogism is articulated into three figures, Czezowski's logical hexagon similarly fractures into three related logical squares when the duality of judgment forms is taken seriously.

In the introduction we noted Hegel's use of the "triangle of triangles" in his early attempts to give a graphic representation of Plato's syllogism, and the logical hexagon we have arrived at in this chapter exhibits clear parallels. Indeed, like the triangle of triangles, the six-pointed star that results from drawing the diagonals of a hexagon had played a role in a range of religions beyond Judaism with which it is usually associated as the "star" or "shield" of David.[11] In medieval cathedrals it had been used in ways similar to the triangle of triangles to induce a sense of connection with an infinite God, and it was also found in a more secular form in Masonism. The devout Pascal, in the never-to-be-published "Conicorum opus completum," had called the construction involved in his own theorem (with its six points located on a conic section all joined diagonally) the "mystic hexagon."[12] The mathematical importance of Pascal's construction would not be acknowledged until the rebirth of projective geometry in the nineteenth century,[13] but it seems to have been known in the late eighteenth century to thinkers such as Herder and Goethe (Gillies 1941).[14]

Hegel's initial interests in diagrams such as these, shared with the likes of Schelling and Baader, had seemed to be driven by their mystical or

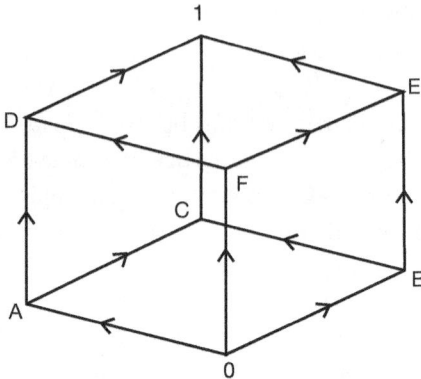

FIGURE 10.6 The hexagon as a perspective on a logical cube.

"theosophical" significance, but even if such an interest had persisted throughout Hegel's life, this does not preclude the idea expressed by Lukács, Harris, and Schneider that they had also come to assume a different significance from an interest in "geometric logic" (Schneider 1975, 139) or concern with "geometric determinacy" (Harris 1983, 185). In the triangle of triangles, the relevant experience would seem to be that of being drawn into the receding spaces suggested by the diminishing size of the triangles—that is, the experience of movement along a third dimension orthogonal to that of the plane in which the diagram was constructed. This is consistent with Hegel's insistence on the three-dimensional and dynamic character of Plato's syllogism in the *Timaeus*. Might it not also suggest that the relation between these three squares of Czezowski's hexagon might be appreciated from a point of view that belongs to a space *not* restricted to the plane of the diagram itself? After all, it becomes apparent while looking at these logical hexagons that one could be looking at a type of transparent logical cube offering different alternative paths through logical space. In figure 10.6, for example, one path can be traced between 0 and 1 via A and D, and another via F and E, each path negotiating logically different squares.

We have finally reached an idea that looks something like a modern analogue of the logic that Hegel had appreciated in Plato's syllogism, the dimensions of which were deemed necessary for thought about the spatiotemporal cosmos. It is now not unusual for the types of opposed logical systems as found in discussions of modal and nonmodal logics, intuitionist and classical logics, and so on to be described as "two-dimensional" (e.g., Humberstone 2004) in the sense of employing two different logical systems. Typically, however, the response to this situation has focused around how to reduce these competing systems of logical axioms to one, the one logical system insisted upon typically being the classical quantified predicate calculus initiated by Frege and Russell. Hegel's formal logic, I have been suggesting, had such a "two-dimensional" character, but he clearly refused to think of these two systems as reducible to one. However, neither did he simply accept the dualism. As in Plato's musically based syllogism, two incommensurable means might be unified by a third without a loss of this underlying incommensurability.

Might he not have thought of his two homologously contrasted types of judgments as appearances resulting from a properly three-dimensional structure with an added dimension being projected onto the two-dimensional plane of the diagram? A positive answer here, I suggest, conforms with central features of his stance toward Kant's transcendental idealism. Kant had accounted for our cognitive grasp of the spatiotemporal features of the world in terms of the dual nonconceptual cognition of intuition, but Hegel had not accepted this absolute cognitive dichotomy between intuitions and concepts. The tridimensionality of space together with the one-dimensionality of time must be somehow represented within the conceptual structure of thought. Kant's own precritical idea of an opposition between two judgment forms marked by different ways of treating negation had provided the starting point for Hegel's reconstruction of Aristotle's syllogism. This had allowed the proper separation of the determinations of singularity and particularity that Aristotle had not been able to achieve, and that Kant had achieved only with the later introduced and problematic intuition-concept distinction. But while drawing upon elements of both Aristotle and Kant, Hegel sought to overcome the limitations of each as expressions of "the understanding," *der Verstand*, and to thereby capture something of Plato's rational syllogism. Comprehending the encompassing logical system as a system of logical life lived out, as is life in general, in the spatiotemporal world gives us a sense of what the limitations of logics of lesser dimensionalities consist in and how their underlying unity might be grasped.

Conclusion:
The God at the Terminus of Hegel's Logic

> Three conceptions are perpetually turning up at every point in every theory of logic. . . . I call them conceptions of First, Second, Third. . . . Such are the materials out of which chiefly a philosophical theory ought to be built in order to represent the state of knowledge to which the nineteenth century has brought us. . . . We can readily foresee what sort of metaphysics would appropriately be constructed from those conceptions. Like some of the most ancient and some of the most recent speculations it would be a Cosmogonic Philosophy.
>
>   C. S. PEIRCE, "The Architecture of Theories"

One might say that Hegel's last words on the nature of syllogisms occurs in the conclusion of the *Philosophy of Spirit*, the final part of the *Encyclopedia of the Philosophical Sciences*, where he refers to the three parts of the system—*The Science of Logic*, the *Philosophy of Nature*, and the *Philosophy of Spirit*—as themselves three "syllogisms" (*E:PS*, §§574–577). What had been under consideration in the *Encyclopedia* had been how the logical structure of the syllogism worked out in the first part, the *Logic*, could be shown to inform the organization of both the natural and human worlds, or nature and spirit, developed in the second and third parts. But the passage concerning the "three syllogisms" at its conclusion hints that this may not really bring this encyclopedic system to a conclusion as had been expected.

It is generally assumed that with the transition from *The Science of Logic* to the *Philosophy of Nature* Hegel's treatment of logic itself has been completed, but Hegel's addition of the "three syllogisms" brings this into question.[1] The *Philosophy of Spirit* had ended with the third form of absolute spirit, philosophy itself, which Hegel characterizes as the "self-thinking idea, the truth aware of itself" and which he labels "the logical" (*das Logische*). And so, ending with logic, the *Encyclopedia* has returned to its beginning, making apparent its structure as a "circle of circles" (*E:L*, §15). However, this seems to have implications for the conception of logic that had meant to be settled at the end of part 1. Hegel now describes logic as universality, but now understood as proven, having concrete contents "in its actuality." As such, "the logical has risen into its pure principle and also into its element" from out of its initial appearance (*E:PS*, §574), an appearance presumably that had been described in *The Science of Logic* as a "realm of shadows" (*SL*, 37; 21:42).

We are then led to consider two further paths through the *Encyclopedia* beyond the one through which we have just passed. These two further journeys beyond the actual one traversed will see logic transitioning to nature via the middle term of spirit, and nature transitioning into spirit via the middle term of logic. The three syllogisms, of course, reproduce the S-P-U, P-S-U, and P-U-S structures of the original treatment of the syllogism and exemplify the pattern of interrelating three means upon which the Platonic syllogism was formed.

Matching the "absolute idea" of *The Science of Logic*, this end point reached is now summed up as "the eternal idea" that "in full fruition of its essence, eternally sets itself to work, engenders and enjoys itself as absolute spirit" (*E:PS*, §577). These are Hegel's final words, followed by his famous quoting of a passage from Aristotle's *Metaphysics* book 12 (1072b18–30) concerning the life of Aristotle's god as a thinking that thinks itself. This dramatic end has attracted considerable discussion, but here I want to focus on the consequence of the positing of the three syllogisms that leads into it—there are apparently two other alternative ways of working through the sequence of the *Encyclopedia* than the one Hegel has offered—alternative pathways just like those that can be traced though the formal syllogism of Peirce. These alternatives cannot fail to have consequences for the understanding of each of those parts, including, of course, Hegel's *Logic*.

Hegel may appeal to Aristotle's god here, but the strongly Platonic construal of the three syllogisms is clearly on display. I suggest that we can here think of Aristotle's god as something like Plato's cosmic animal without a role for Plato's separate "artificer."[2] The result is surely Hegel's reinterpretation of Plato's cosmic animal from the *Timaeus* with its beautiful proportion in which, as in his paraphrase of Plato, "since the middle term has become the first and the last and, conversely, the last and the first have become the middle term, they have then all become one" (*LHP* 2:210; 3:39). Plato's syllogism has the distinctly three-dimensional structure through which thought can move in a way needed to make sense of those two-dimensional diagrams among judgments within syllogisms or among syllogisms themselves observed in the attempts of Peirce, Blanché, and Czezowski. Hegel's wording of the nature of his third syllogism is here striking: it is that of which the earlier syllogisms can be regarded as its "two appearances."

As is often the case with reading Hegel, here the reader's thinking seems to spin out of control. This is surely not the response for which "logicians" standardly aim. Typically, they want to nail down distinctions, get some arrangement right, and "move on." Hegel typically points to these tendencies as characteristics of *der Verstand*, "the understanding," but we must not forget that *das Vernunft*, "reason," never simply bypasses *der Verstand* but manifests itself in the contradictions within which *verständlich* thought gets caught and from which it has to free itself by the redeterminations of its categories. Nevertheless, these "spinning-out-of-control" moments in Hegel often seem closer to *das Mystische* than *das Logischer*, as with the feeling of being drawn into the fractal space of the "triangle of triangles."

Hegel may have a way of distinguishing mysticism or religion from philosophy in terms of the distinction between the type of imagistic *Vorstellungen* to which religion is constrained and the properly "conceptual" medium of philosophy, but here the distinction is not so clear. In a modern context, for an author to end on a seemingly theological or mystical note would be taken as indicating that the work being terminated was of an essentially theological or mystical nature. But as an idealist, Hegel was predominantly interested in the idea of God generally implicated in our mental/spiritual lives, and here it may be instructive to contrast the god invoked at the end of the *Encyclopedia* with the ideas of alternative gods often implicitly smuggled into rival philosophies—for our purposes, the idea of the god embedded within Newton's cosmology.

One thing that Hegel and Baader had in common was an appreciation of the Silesian mystic Jakob Böhme,[3] whose theology had come into stark contrast with Newton's in the context of the English Civil War when Böhme's views attracted many radical republicans. This was seemingly because Böhme, influenced by Neoplatonic models, pictured the cosmos as alive and self-organizing—a picture that had resonated with the democratic and republican aspirations of those of Cromwell's followers who identified as "Behmenists."[4] The theology to which Newton subscribed was the complete antithesis. As committed to the beliefs of the radical anti-trinitarian Arian heresy, Newton denied the divinity of Christ, saw the physical world as governed by the laws legislated by an unequivocally unitary transcendent God, and supported the European monarchies as the local representatives of this divine ruler. Moreover, this theology was not isolated from his natural philosophy.

Space for Newton had to be something rather than nothing, as the so-called nullibilist account of space, found in Descartes, for example, seemed to leave no place in the universe for God. Newton had taken the side of the Cambridge Platonist Henry More, who had argued that spirits were extended nonmaterial substances and that space and time themselves could be thought of as the extension of the nonmaterial absolute, God (Christianson 1984, 248). Thus, in the "General Scholium" of the *Principia* (*Philosophiæ Naturalis Principia Mathematica*), God is described as "eternal and infinite, omnipotent and omniscient, ... he rules all things, and he knows all things that happen or can happen.... By existing always and everywhere he constitutes duration and space" (Newton 2016, 440). As space was an objectively real substance in this way, it made sense to think of its infinite parts as capable of being objectively determined as ordered triples of real numbers as on a cosmic set of Cartesian coordinates. Hence Newton could go on to talk of "each and every particle of space" as being eternal, that is, as being "always," and similarly "each and every indivisible moment of duration is everywhere," and because God *is* space and time "the maker and lord of all things will not be never or nowhere" (440). This omnipresence has a correlate in divine omniscience as brought out at the conclusion of Newton's *Opticks*: "The Organs of Sense are not for enabling the Soul to perceive the Species of Things in its Sensorium, but only for conveying them thither; and God has no need of such Organs, he being every where present to the Things themselves" (Newton 2012, 403–404).

The reference to the god of Aristotle/Plato at the conclusion of Hegel's *Encyclopedia* might be frustrating in its indeterminacy, but the general idea he has in mind becomes immediately obvious when that god is contrasted with Newton's. From Newton's point of view, matter, as dependent on its creator, has no necessary existence: it was within God's power to have *not* created the material world or to have created any number of different ones. Neither does matter have the autonomous power to act: it is an inert, "dead" stuff moved around by a force external to it—the force of gravity—and to the extent that we are made of it, we too are similarly dead stuff moved around by laws decreed by God analogous to the laws decreed by an absolute monarch. The same holds for our capacity to know the world. Because we are made of matter, we are reliant on the sorts of sensory organs of which God has no need.

This was the view criticized by Schelling with his world-soul and by Baader with his *Wärmestoff*, but Hegel had no need to appeal to such quasi-scientific responses to Newton. His response was on a different conceptual level.

In his comparison of Kepler and Newton in the *Philosophy of Nature*, Hegel notes of the latter:

> It is not the assumptions, procedure and results which analysis requires and affords which are questioned here, but the physical worth and the physical significance of its determinations and procedure. It is here that attention should be concentrated, in order to explain why physical mechanics has been flooded by a monstrous metaphysic, which, contrary to both experience and the concept, has its sole source in these mathematical determinations. (*E:PN*, §270, remark, p. 265)

The "monstrous metaphysic" involved, I think it is clear, is the sort of larger picture involving God that Newton makes explicit in passages such as these.

In his years in Berlin Hegel had shown considerable warmth toward Franz von Baader, who had been particularly critical of both Hegel and Schelling for their alleged "Spinozism."[5] Hegel objected to this description of himself and urged that there was not as great a difference between his and Baader's respective stances as Baader had assumed. But while Baader damned Spinozist pantheism, Hegel's hostilities were more directed in the opposite direction. The very idea of the radically transcendent God was to a large extent shared by both Newton and Kant, but, among its other problems, such a theology had struck many of those attracted to the English Civil War or the French Revolution as condemning humans' earthly life to servitude and ignorance. For Hegel, the appropriate philosophical stance on such matters was to raise to conceptual determinacy the revolutionaries' alternative theology cast in its imagistic form of representation that Hegel called *Vorstellungen*. But just as within reason there are contexts for which one form of judgment working with images and analogies is more appropriate than another, within absolute spirit there are contexts in which the response of art or religion will be more appropriate than that of philosophy.

Hegel had found in Kepler a better cosmologist than Newton, and, like Kepler, he found in Plato's overtly mythological thought the kernel of a logic that would be better suited for the lives of free and intelligent this-worldly beings than those found in Aristotle or Kant. As chance would have it, in the early nineteenth century a form of geometry would reemerge to which Kepler had been an important early contributor and which had reconnected with a type of ancient geometrical thought on which Plato himself had drawn. From there, this geometry had entered into a struggle with the more conventional analytic geometry instituted by Descartes and utilized by Newton, and this struggle would continue through the nineteenth century and be reflected in the different paradigms of logic that emerged after Hegel's death. These struggles between arithmetic and geometrical alternatives have continued to the present within both mathematics, logic and physics,[6] and while analytic philosophy had early on proclaimed the "classical" approach of Frege and Russell the victor, this has not been how things have necessarily come to be viewed from within mathematics or its more recent spin-offs, such as computer science. Such a situation may signal a greater relevance for Hegel's approach to logic today than is conventionally acknowledged.

Acknowledgments

I first want to express my gratitude to Robert Pippin for encouragement and guidance in relation to this project from its early days, as well as for extremely helpful feedback on an earlier incarnation. This must extend to the two initially anonymous readers for the University of Chicago Press, who later outed themselves as Dean Moyar and Terry Pinkard. They provided invaluable and detailed critical feedback, both substantive and presentational. Two further people proved essential to the ideas presented here taking shape. Early on, Robert Brandom demonstrated to me and many others that it was possible to consider Hegel's thought in a wider philosophical context than that in which it is often discussed. The lucidity of his powerful interpretations developed over a quarter of a century located Hegel in a space of possibilities that allowed other alternatives to come into view. Coming from a different direction, Norman Wildberger's philosophically acute approach to mathematics and its history helped me to (hopefully) make something of a handful of vague intuitions I had held concerning the possible relevance of ancient geometry for Hegel's logic.

To take Hegel seriously implies taking seriously what Terry Pinkard has described as the "sociality of reason" as the place from which ideas arrive. At times, like that of the recent international pandemic, the social space of reason can seem to recede. The relative isolation provided by the pandemic afforded me a type of holiday during which I could put the more socially engaged side of my thinking on hold and follow up ideas that had been nagging at me for some time. While appearing somewhat foreign to the world of Hegel interpretation in which I had been working, these ideas are ones that had nevertheless presented themselves to me from out of the many crisscrossing conversations on Hegel I had been fortunate to have been part of over the last decades. There would be too many people to thank here, but a list might start with, besides those mentioned above, Mike Beaney, Jay Bernstein, Georg Bertram, Andy Blunden, Brady Bowman, Diego Bubbio, John Burnheim, Marina Bykova, Bruin Christensen, Byron Clugston, Alessandro De Cesaris, Jean-Philippe Deranty, Bill deVries, Cinzia Ferrini, Elena Ficara, Eckart Förster, Sebastian Gardner, Stephen Gaukroger, John Grumley, Johannes Haag, Heikki Ikäheimo, Jim Kreines, Kathy Legge, Giovanna Luciano, Simon Lumsden, David Macarthur, Jakub Mácha, John McDowell, Jake McNulty, Giovanna Miolli, Doug Moggach, Greg Moss, Dalia Nassar, Karen Ng, Julia Peters, Huw Price, Graham Priest, Sebastian Rand, Tom Raysmith, Carl Sachs, Ulrich Schlösser, Sally Sedgwick, Sebastian Sequoia-Grayson, Sebastian Stein, Bob Stern, Plato Tse, Ken Westphal, and Chris Yeomans.

At the University of Chicago Press, Kyle Wagner proved to be the editor every writer hopes for. I am grateful for his wise guidance during the project's realization. At home, Vicki Varvaressos was a bottomless fount of encouragement and love, despite being, for lengthy periods of this book's genesis, in lockdown with a madman.

Notes

Preface

1. Such an attitude has been neatly summed up by Uwe Petersen: "I do not take an exegesis of the writings of Hegel as a key to the development of a theory of dialectic, at least not one that would meet the standards of mathematical logic. Hegel has envisaged the possibility of a new science ('Wissenschaft') which he called *Wissenschaft der Logik* ('Science of Logic'), but he didn't leave us more than vague ideas and wildly exaggerated claims.... To my mind, the impotence of Hegel-scholarship has been sufficiently established in the 180 odd years since his death" (Petersen 2018, 2–3).

2. Again, these were topics with which Hegel was familiar. How to develop this aspect of Leibniz's logical thought had been the subject of a major dispute between Gottfried Ploucquet, the authority on logic at the Tübingen Seminary during Hegel's time there, and the Swiss mathematician Johann Heinrich Lambert.

3. I use "homology" to stand for a local double ratio, $a : b :: c : d$, and homomorphism for the more general system underlying such homologies. Mathematically, a homomorphism is a function between different algebraic structures that preserves the structural properties of the first in the second. See, for example, Anonymous 2008, 4.1.

Introduction

1. Initial reference is to the volume and page numbers of the (sometimes modified) English translation of *Lectures on the History of Philosophy*. The following is to volume and page numbers of the Meiner edition of Hegel, *Vorlesungen über die Geschichte der Philosophie*.

2. In fact, in the early twentieth century the Polish mathematician Waclaw Sierpinski would explore the properties of iterated instances of the embeddings of this figure, now known as the Sierpinski triangle.

3. This does not, of course, preclude that they could have continued to have significance for Hegel as religious representations (*Vorstellungen*). Nothing in Hegel would preclude such things as operating on both levels. In fact, much in his approach would suggest it.

4. Baader had been attracted to Schelling's account of the "world soul" (*Weltseele*) in Schelling's *On the World Soul: An Hypothesis of Higher Physics for Explaining Universal Organism*, published in 1798. Schelling's interest in the notion dated back to notes on Plato's *Timaeus* written in 1794.

5. Seemingly not having had access to Baader's work, Harris had confusingly translated *pythagoräische Quadrat* as "Pythagorean square" (Harris 1983, ch. 4). On the degree to which the *tetraktys* had been employed throughout the Middle Ages, see Hopper 1938.

6. Later, however, he would swing to a religious and political form of conservatism and appears to have played a role in the formation of the "Holy Alliance" between Russia, Prussia, and Austria in 1815 (Betanzos 1998, 67–68).

7. On Baader's complex relationships to German idealist and romantic thought, see Betanzos 1998, introduction and ch. 1.

8. Carnot had been elected to the National Assembly in 1791 and the National Convention in 1792. In 1793, he had become a member of the Committee for Public Safety and by 1794 "had achieved his objective of virtual total control of military affairs" (Gueniffey 1989, 199). He was involved in the overthrow of Robespierre.

9. On Schweikardt, see Ewald 1996, 301. On Hauff's influence, see Halsted 1896, 105.

10. Here the revolutionary work was done by his son, Sadi Carnot, on the basis of his father's work (Gillispie and Pisano 2013, chs. 6–7).

11. Monge's descriptive geometry would eventually appear in the school curriculum as "technical drawing." Descriptive geometry is also called "synthetic" as opposed to "analytic" or "coordinate" geometry.

12. Another book in Hegel's library was Archimedes's works *On the Sphere and Cylinder* and *Measurement of a Circle* (Mense 1993, 670).

13. In their history of Carnot's science, Gillispie and Pisano point out that Carnot had pursued an approach to mechanics in a "geometric or trigonometric" spirit, rather than the algebraic one of Joseph-Louis Lagrange's *Théorie des fonctions analytique* (Gillispie and Pisano 2013, 16). (Lagrange's book was also in Hegel's library (Mense 1993, 686).) In contrast to Lagrange, Carnot focused on the way such "primary bodies" were organized into a finite system. This gave Carnot's mechanics a holistic rather than atomistic approach, as reflected in Hegel's treatment of mechanics in the *Encyclopedia Philosophy of Nature* (*E:PN*, §§253–271).

14. This will be explored further in chapter 3.4.

15. The idea of Greek geometric algebra was taken up and popularized by Thomas Heath in his *History of Greek Mathematics* (Heath 1921, 1:150).

16. During the nineteenth century it would be thought that this alternative to Euclidean geometry also had its origins in Euclid, although in a lost work, Euclid's "Porisms."

17. Links between the logics of Hegel and Grassmann have also been described by the mathematician F. W. Lawvere (Lawvere 1996).

18. Descartes was the first to use the letters "x" and "y" in this way to represent variables.

19. Once again, Hegel possessed a major work by Diophantus, *On the Polygonal Numbers* (Mense 1993, 671).

20. This was the term used by William Kingdon Clifford for his unification of projective geometry, linear algebra, and William Rowan Hamilton's theory of quaternions.

21. The English translation here gives "the analogy or the constant geometrical relationship," which does not capture the specificity of Hegel's more technical reference to Pythagorean doctrine. These issues will be taken up in chapter 3.

Chapter One

1. For example, book 5 of Euclid's *Elements* is usually traced back to the work of Eudoxus of Cnidus, a prominent member of Plato's early Academy, and parts of book 13 to Theaetetus,

NOTES TO PAGES 21–29   237

the subject of Plato's dialogue *Theaetetus*, and, like Eudoxus, an important member of the early Academy. For recent reconstructions of the prehistory of Euclid's *Elements*, see Knorr 1975 and Artmann 1991.

2. Thus Fossheim (Fossheim 2012) argues that Plato's method of division was not meant as a procedure for intellectual discovery but rather as a way of organizing and presenting knowledge already obtained.

3. From Plato's point of view, this would be expressed more by saying that if a being participates in the idea <Greek>, then it thereby participates in the idea <human> and, in turn, in the idea <animal>.

4. The phrase "due measure" seems the most common English translation, but Jowett, for example, gives "the character of the mean," and Fowler "the principle of the mean." To the basic meanings of "measure," "standard or rule," and "mean between two extremes," Liddell and Scott (1882, 957) add the poetic meaning of "metre" as opposed to *melos*, "tune." For an informative account of the archaic uses of the term with noetic rather than physical connotations, see Prier 1976.

5. The Pythagoreans attributed the theorem to their founder, about whom we know next to nothing. In any case, the existence of "Pythagorean triples"—a triple of integers satisfying Pythagoras's theorem, such as 3, 4, 5 and 5, 12, 13, was known to mathematicians in both Babylon and China (van der Waerden 1983, ch 1). The importance of the theorem for the Greeks is the knowledge of its proof.

6. In this case, the ratio is $\sqrt{2}:1$. A simple deduction of the irrationality of $\sqrt{2}$ had been attributed to Euclid in *Elements* book 10, although this is now believed to have been a later interpolation.

7. Szabó discusses the extent of the mathematical knowledge presupposed by this pun in Szabó 1978, ch. 1.9.

8. For a good overview, see Krämer 1990, pt. 1. Krämer attributes the rejection of the doxographical tradition to the influence of Schleiermacher, whose reconstruction of Plato's oeuvre had been influenced by his own romantic views on the relations of philosophy and literary art.

9. The school includes, in Germany, Hans Krämer and Konrad Gaiser, and in Italy, Giovanni Reale. For a synoptic account, see Nikulin 2012.

10. Sayre's book was first published in 1983.

11. Findlay had done important work on Hegel in the 1950s and 1960s (Findlay 1958 and 1963).

12. Krämer also stresses the influence of Plato as understood within the unwritten-doctrines tradition upon Hegel (Krämer 1990, ch. 11).

13. Henry Harris had pointed to the significance of the discovery of incommensurability for Hegel: "Hegel attached great importance, for his own Logic, to the fact that Greek geometers discovered ratios that were not numerically determinate in some of the simplest (most easily intuited) spatial relationships. This was, for him, the fundamental paradigm of the necessary self-transcendence of the Understanding in 'dialectic'" (Harris 1997, 1:118). Significantly, Hegel possessed a work by Johann Wolfgang Müller, the mathematics teacher at the Nuremberg Gymnasium during his years there, giving an analysis of the doctrine of incommensurability as set out in Plato's *Theaetetus*, 147d–148b (Müller 1796; Mense 1993, 673).

14. It is controversial as to what *proton* numbers refer. Possibly rather than to "primes," the reference was to the numbers 1 and 2, which, for the Pythagoreans, were not properly numbers at all but principles from which numbers were generated.

15. A good overview of the scope of Pythagorean arithmetic in the fifth century BCE is given in Knorr 1975, ch. 5.

16. As McKirahan points out about the Pythagorean conception of a point as a "unit in position," it "skips over the facts that geometrical points are different to arithmetical units, and straight lines are determined by two points in a different way from that in which the number 2 is composed of two units" (McKirahan 2010, 100). Heath discusses the way that such "figured numbers" as square, triangular, and oblong numbers were used in Pythagorean calculations (Heath 1921, 1:75–84).

17. This meant, however, that there was no sense to be given to the idea of a number raised to a power *greater* than 3.

18. On this classification, see Nicomachus of Gerasa 1926, 238.

19. This idea persists in Aristotle when he notes that "all these things—numbers, lengths, times, solids—do not constitute a single named item and differ in sort from one another" (Aristotle 1984, *Posterior Analytics*, 74a20–22).

20. In calculus, for $y = x^n$, the differential, $\frac{dy}{dx} = nx^{n-1}$. The differential of a square number is thus linear.

21. The linguistic interpretation construes Aristotle's use of *logos* and *logoi* as "speech," but, as we will see, the word *logos* could equally be translated as "ratio."

22. Here I follow Whitaker (Whitaker 1996, 89), who claims that "Aristotle's own terms, 'singular' [*kath ekaston*] and 'partial' [*en merei*], are used clearly and consistently." Whitaker is critical of the widespread confusion of these terms in English translations of Aristotle that, he claims, started with Aquinas.

23. As suggested earlier, the later introduction of algebra might be seen as providing a model for clarifying this distinction with that between a constant and a variable.

24. Similarly, Henry Harris notes that while Hegel's basic intellectual orientation was toward the cultural history of humankind, he maintained a deep interest in mathematics and physics throughout his life (Harris 1972, 46).

25. Paterson claims that in relation to his stance on geometry Hegel had been "very little influenced" by Schelling despite their shared interest in Neoplatonism (Paterson 2005, 67).

26. See especially the discussion of the relation of arithmetic to geometry in "Remark 1" in the chapter "Quantum" (*SL*, 170–177; 21:196–203). For example, "geometry as such does not *measure* spatial figures . . . but only *compares* them" (170; 21:196) and "the magnitude of the line, and of the other spatial determinations as well, must be taken as number" (171; 21:196).

27. The centrality of such an "indissoluble dialectical relationship—a 'unity of opposites'" operating between continuous and discrete magnitudes for Hegel has been stressed by Bell (Bell 2019, 98–104).

28. As Robin Smith points out about the dialectical context, dialectical arguments proceed by question and answer rather than by a series of assertions (Smith 1993, 338). Aristotle seems to have had in mind Socratic questioning in particular (341–342).

29. For an illuminating account of the senses in which Hegel's logic *was* involved with "form," see Ficara 2021, ch. 5.

30. "In the *Logic* the question is dual: What is being such that it is intelligible? What is the intelligibility of being?" (Pippin 2019, 257).

31. Initial page numbers are to di Giovanni's English translation, although this is sometimes modified. The following reference is to volume and page numbers of the Meiner edition, Hegel, *Gesammelte Werke*.

Chapter Two

1. It is commonly argued that such schematic letters should not be regarded as the "variables" used later in algebra. In Aristotle, schematic letters stand in for definite terms, and are thus replaceable by such terms. Variables, as the sorts of things bound by quantifiers (Dutilh Novaes 2012, 71 and 71n9), were not part of the Greek world.

2. Related to this, Aristotle's use of the word *ekthesis* for the "setting out" of an argument in syllogistic form is taken from the geometrical "setting out" of a proof in relation to points and lines in a figure (Einarson 1936, 161–162).

3. Writing three quarters of a century later, Netz would comment that "while many of his [Einarson's] individual arguments need revision, the hypothesis is sound" (Netz 1999, 15n12).

4. The issues here are complex. Aristotle had identified the "mathematical Pythagoreans" as having made advances in the science of demonstrative reasoning (Aristotle 1984, *Metaphysics*, book 1, ch. 5). But while praising the way the Pythagoreans had used mathematics to forge such an account of reasoning, Aristotle was nevertheless critical of the interpretations they had given to their own work. From his perspective, they conflated two types of knowledge that he carefully distinguished, knowledge of facts, knowledge *to hoti*, and demonstrative knowledge of the reasons for those facts, knowledge *to dioti* (Horky 2013, 3–4; Aristotle 1984, *Posterior Analytics*, 78a22–30). This criticism would spill over into his criticism of Plato, whose views he associated with those of the Pythagorean mathematicians.

5. Szabó would concentrate especially on the prehistory of the key terms *oros* and *diastema* (Szabó 1978, chs. 2.3–2.6).

6. Thus, in "All Athenians are Greeks and some Athenians are philosophers, therefore some Greeks are philosophers," the term "Athenian" is the middle term.

7. There are strong echoes of Plato here, as in the *Philebus* Plato compares the letter or simple unit of writing, *stoicheon*, to the constituent sounds of music (Plato 1997, *Philebus*, 17a–e).

8. In a fragment on music, Plutarch attributes to "Aristotle, the pupil of Plato" the view of harmony as "heavenly, by nature divine, beautiful and inspired" and as having "two means, the arithmetical and the harmonic" (Aristotle 1984, *Fragments*, F 47 R3). Aristotle's most explicit discussion of music is in *Politics* book 8, chs. 5–7, where he engages with Plato's views about the role of music in education in the *Republic*. A much more technical discussion of music that engages with Pythagorean harmony theory is found in *Problems* book 19, although the authenticity of the attribution of this work to Aristotle is contested.

9. There was a further constraint to Archytas's analysis of harmonic intervals besides their being generally drawn from the *tetraktys*. As seen in the ratios corresponding to the octave itself and to the perfect fifth and fourth dividing the octave—2:1, 3:2, and 4:3—the difference between the terms of such ratios must be the *monas*, the fundamental measure for the Pythagoreans. Such ratios, now called "superparticular," were said to be *epimoric*.

10. It is significant that Smith himself seems to have abandoned these claims in later work, adopting a more "geometric" approach to the syllogism following that of Corcoran.

11. The first four of the five Platonic solids are three dimensional "polyhedra" in which the faces are either equilateral triangles (the tetrahedron and icosahedron), right-angled triangles (the octahedron), or squares (the cube). The fifth is the dodecahedron, having twelve regular pentangular faces. Timaeus treats the cosmos as a whole in terms of the dodecahedron. The structure of the Platonic solids had been unraveled by the actual Theaetetus, who features in the

dialogues *Theaetetus*, *Sophist*, and *Statesman*. Later, Kepler would apply a nested structure of these Platonic solids to the solar system.

12. Cf. Euclid: "Between two cube numbers there are two mean proportional numbers, and the cube has to the cube the ratio triplicate of that which the side has to the side" (Euclid 1956, book 8, prop. 12).

13. See, for example, the translator's note 12 to the passage quoted.

14. Calculating the length of the side of a cube of volume x units requires finding the cubed root of x ($^3\sqrt{\ }$ x), but this was beyond the rudimentary algebra available to the Greeks. This problem, associated with Plato, was called the "Delian problem," and the suggestion that the interval needed to be divided by two mean proportionals is associated with the mathematician Hippocrates of Chios. On Archytas's complex three-dimensional geometric solution, see Heath 1921, 1:246.

15. While the idea of the "unlimited" was common to other pre-Socratics such as Anaximander and Anaxagoras, the ubiquity of the limit or "limiter" was innovatory with Philolaus (Graham 2014, 52–53).

16. Thus, drawing on Baader, Eschenmayer had appealed to this mathematical distinction as relevant to that between the mere physics of sound and the associated sensory quality of its reception. With this he pressed upon Schelling the importance of mathematics for natural philosophy (Eschenmayer 2020).

17. In fact, dividing the octave at the geometric mean produces what is thought to be the *most* dissonant interval, the *tritone*, an interval favored in the scores of many horror movies.

18. That is, $m_A(a,b) = \frac{a+b}{2}$. This is usually what is meant by the term "average."

19. $m_H(a,b) = \frac{2ab}{a+b}$.

20. The same point has been made by Knorr in relation to Archytas's use of *analogia* in that Archytas "refers to each of the three progressions—the arithmetic, geometric and harmonic—as analogia; but only the geometric is a 'proportion' in the strict sense" (Knorr 1975, 219). More recently, Borzacchini has described Philolaus's use of "ratio" as reflecting an early phase of the development of the notion "when *logos* meant just a vaguely characterized relation between two numbers somehow connected with its music-theoretic actualization as *diastima* characterized as both a pair of tones and a pair of extremes on the canon" (Borzacchini 2007, 283).

21. It was this single *geometric* mean that came to be known among the geometers as "*the* mean proportional."

22. As Euclid shows (Euclid 1956, book 13, prop. 8), the Golden Ratio actually characterizes the divisions of the diagonals of a regular pentagon—those diagonals forming the Pythagoreans' "pentagram."

23. Heath, for example, attributes book 5 of Euclid's *Elements* to Eudoxus (Euclid 1956, 2:112–113).

24. For the last, Jowett has "perception of shadows." What is perceived in *eikasia* is an *eikon*, the origin of the English word "icon."

25. Later, Aristotle would make it clear that the figures were not themselves the geometer's objects but "what is made clear through them" (Aristotle 1984, *Posterior Analytics*, 76b39–77a2).

26. Aristotle had discussed how the Pythagoreans thought of numbers as objects whereas for him they were not objects but properties of objects (Horky 2013, 30–34).

27. To avoid confusion, I will use "Platonistic" to refer to the ideas of the conventional Plato of the middle dialogues.

28. There is an important difference here from the other well-known sequence from *Republic* chapter 10 concerning the idea of the bed, an actual bed, and the painting of a bed. While the actual bed was a sensible object, the mathematical objects of *dianoia* are supersensuous.

29. For a general discussion of the history of the perception of the problem and responses to it, see especially Smith 1996, 31 and 40–43 and Echterling 2018, 2–5.

30. A similar "reduction" is found in Proclus, whom Hegel presumably follows in this instance.

31. Proclus seems to have been the first to associate this ratio with Plato (Heath 1921, 1:323), and there has been debate among classical scholars as to whether Plato would have been aware of the construction of the Golden Ratio. (For a survey, see Dreher 1990.)

32. Which of the realms is to be regarded as represented by the larger segment, and which by the smaller, is not specified in Plato's text, and so the choice is up to the interpreter.

33. Des Jardins is also one of the few interpreters to take seriously the fact that the Plato's Divided Line combines arithmetic and geometric means (Des Jardins 1976, 491–492).

Chapter Three

1. These ratios, it will turn out, were not really ratios in the conventional sense.

2. This term, rendered as "magnitude" in di Giovanni's translation, could equally be translated "quantity," but as Hegel reserves *Quantität* for the subcategory, I will follow di Giovanni in retaining "magnitude" for the parent category. It must be remembered, however, that "magnitude" is not here being used to express continuous magnitudes in contrast to discrete multitudes. It is meant to cover both.

3. Hegel's *Aufhebung* from the verb *aufheben* presents a particular difficulty for finding an English equivalent. While that which is *aufgehoben* is superseded or negated, it is done in such a way that it is nevertheless retained as a determination within the sense of that which has superseded it.

4. One might add, of course, the pebbles allegedly used by the early Pythagoreans to construct diagrammatic numbers, whence the term "calculus."

5. As with many aspects of Hegel's *Logic*, illumination here can be provided by W. E. Johnson, who, in his inquiry into logic, raised the ontological status of the category "thing"—a category, he suggests, that is more general than that of substance (Johnson 1921, ch. 9, §1). It would be a limitation of Aristotelian thought for Hegel that these categories of thing and substance were identified.

6. For example, from the claim in the *Prolegomena to Any Future Metaphysics*, where he writes that "geometry bases itself on the pure intuition of space. Even arithmetic forms its concepts of numbers through successive addition of units of time" (Kant 1997, §10).

7. In the context of the discussion of the schematism in the *Critique of Pure Reason*, geometry is seen as grounded in the relations given exclusively by outer sense. While arithmetic utilizes the temporal relations grounded in inner sense, number nevertheless reflects "the unity of the synthesis of the manifold of a homogeneous intuition in general," suggesting a reliance on the combined intuitions of space and time found in outer experience (Kant 1998, A142–3/B182). The directionality peculiar to time might be correlated with the role of order in mathematics that would come to be emphasized in the nineteenth century.

8. Later, Hegel would, in the Greek way, link quantities raised to higher powers to the magnitudes of geometrical areas and volumes.

9. That is, Hegel seems to be appealing to the ambiguity of the distinction between what would now be discussed as a set (the amount) and its members (the units)—a distinction that would of course become central to the foundations of mathematics in the late nineteenth century.

10. This modern notation for expressing a number, n, to the power of p, as in n^p, had been introduced by Descartes (Descartes 1954, 2).

11. There was no place for negative numbers, fractions, or exponents in the modern sense in Greek mathematics.

12. For example, Hegel says of "the raising to a power, the extraction of a root; also the treatment of exponential magnitudes and logarithms" that "the interest and the effort of all these operations lie solely in the relations based on powers. . . . Together they constitute a system of the treatment of powers" (SL, 237; 21:275–276).

13. Napier had apparently learned of their use from the astronomer (and for a time, Kepler's employer) Tycho Brahe (Pierce 1977, 23).

14. Logarithms were soon transferred to the base 10, and then, in the eighteenth century to base "e," this being a constant defined by Euler (an irrational number, 2.71828 . . .), giving a form most suited to the calculation of growth within natural systems. On the history of this development, see especially Cajori 1903.

15. In fact, the subsequent history of the Western "diatonic" scale has the complete scale divided into twelve equal semitones that form a logarithmic progression. Some musicians still insist, however, on the Pythagorean fourth and fifth being purer consonant intervals because of harmonic overtones lost in the modern scale.

16. For a recent similar account of the interplay of practices of counting and reckoning at the origin of mathematics see Ferreirós 2016, ch. 2.4.

17. In arithmetic, the order in which individual operations are performed is generally irrelevant. Using brackets to indicate the order in which both addition and multiplication are performed, $4 + (3 + 2) = (4 + 3) + 2$ and $4 \times (3 \times 2) = (4 \times 3) \times 2$. With this, these individual functions are said to be associative. When these functions are mixed, however, the order matters. For example, $4 + (3 \times 2) \neq (4 + 3) \times 2$. Here, multiplication is said to "distribute over" addition, such that $4 \times (3 + 2) = (4 \times 3) + (4 \times 2)$ while $4 + (3 \times 2) \neq (4 + 3) \times 2$. Finally, the order in which numbers are added or multiplied is standardly not relevant: $4 + 3 = 3 + 4$ and $4 \times 3 = 3 \times 4$. Here, addition and multiplication are said to be commutative.

18. Russell could be a proponent of such an arithmetization of geometry only because he had incorporated the idea of order as intrinsic to arithmetic itself. Thus, he also attempted to account for the idea of continuous magnitudes in terms of the notion of order: "*Continuity* applies to series (and only to series) whenever these are such that there is a term between any two given terms" (Russell 1903, 193). This led him to reject the traditional opposition of discrete and continuous. For example, the rational numbers, while discrete, form a continuous series in this respect. Around this time C. S. Peirce would fiercely oppose any idea of the reduction of continuous to discrete magnitudes.

19. The basic meaning of "exponent" is the number of times a term needs to be multiplied by itself to reach a certain value. Hence the power to which a number is raised is also called the "exponent." Hegel uses "exponent" in the former sense as the exponent of a ratio, but uses *Potenz* (power) in the later sense.

20. Or, one might say, unit and number of units. This idea of ratio effectively starts with Euclid's definitions 1 to 3 in book 5.

21. It will be remembered that Hegel's unit/amount distinction has something of the modern element/set distinction.

22. Ast was for a few years a contemporary of Hegel at Jena.

23. Arithmology was a distinct form of Pythagorean revival from the first century BCE that focused on the mathematical doctrines of Archytas and others from around the time of Plato. See especially Zhmud 2019. Knorr points to the relevance of these two books in providing the historical context for the way the theory of means had been continued in post-Euclidean geometry with its debt to Eudoxus (Knorr 1986, 213–218). This was the tradition inherited by Proclus.

24. Plato had been critical of Archytas's restriction of mathematical relationships to empirical phenomena such as musical harmonies or the movements of the planets. Properly regarded, mathematics for Plato was "pure"—it investigated the mathematical objects themselves. Even consonance and dissonance, it would seem, can hold among the ideal numbers themselves (Plato 1997, *Republic*, 531c; Klein 1968, 52).

25. It needs to be kept in mind here that Iamblichus's number line is running in the inverse direction to the conventional left-to-right orientation.

26. This, he argues, opposes different conceptions of infinity. The left-hand branch is the typically "potential" infinite familiar from Aristotle, but the right-hand branch, because packed into a finite space, suggests an "actual" infinite (Borzacchini 2007, 290).

27. Aristotle had distinguished his use of *dynamis* (potential or capacity) from this geometrical use, treating the latter as a metaphor (Aristotle 1984, *Metaphysics*, 1019b28–30).

28. As noted earlier, Eschenmayer also employed the distinction between arithmetic and geometric series.

29. Hegel here touches on an issue prominent at the time—that of Goethe's project of finding a particular plant that made manifest the universal essence of all plants, the proto-plant or *Urpflanze*.

30. Proclus is here continuing Archytas's use of *analogia*, "proportionals," which are not proportions as standardly conceived.

31. Similar summaries are to be found in Heath 1921, 2:86–89 and Knorr 1986, 212–219.

32. According to Szabó, the "terms" (*oroi*) defining a ratio had first referred to points on the duodecimally divided canon of the monochord, providing a type of "coordinate" like Descartes' later system. Later, however, they came to stand for the lengths of the strings divided by the bridge, that is, continuous rather than discrete magnitudes (Szabó 1978, ch. 2.6).

33. In 1827 August Möbius introduced the idea of a "division ratio" (*Teilungsverhältnis*) for this type of division of a line segment (Struik 1953, 13).

34. Remember that "$a - x$" is really an arithmetic correlate of a continuous magnitude. It could, therefore, have an irrational value.

35. Consider, for example, the double ratio $\frac{x-a}{b-x} = \frac{a}{x}$. Multiplying each side by both denominators will give the equation, $x^2 - ax = ab - ax$, which reduces to $x^2 = ab$ making x the geometric mean of a and b. Nicomachus explicitly links the need for two middle terms in an "even-times even" series to Plato's argument in the *Timaeus* for the need for two middle terms when unifying the parts of a three-dimensional solid (Nicomachus 1926, book 2, ch. 24).

36. Multiplying both sides of $\frac{x-a}{b-x} = \frac{a}{b}$ by the two denominators, $b - x$ and b, results in the equation $bx - ab = ab - ax$, which reduces to $x = \frac{2ab}{a+b}$, which, by definition, is the harmonic ratio.

37. Significantly, the first "subcontrary to the geometric" ($x : a$), as had been suggested by Proclus, turns out to be equivalent to the Golden Ratio.

38. See Pappus's diagram showing the interrelation of the three musical means in Thomas 1941, 2:569.

39. This had been made explicit by Möbius with his idea of the division ratio.

40. It has to be remembered that the relation could not be expressed in this numerical way in Greek geometry because of the lack of negative numbers.

41. Lasserre's description of Plato here is questionable, as Plato criticized Archytas's limitations of the significance of the "harmonies" between numbers to the empirical fields of music and cosmology (Klein 1968, 52).

42. Authorship of this work is contested. It is commonly attributed to Philippus of Opus, a member of the Academy and follower of Plato (Borzacchini 2007, 280–281).

43. The present English name "cross-ratio" was only introduced at the end of the nineteenth century by the English mathematician/philosopher William Clifford.

44. When one becomes familiar with projective geometry, many of its features start to look distinctly Hegelian. In the twentieth century, for example, projective geometry would be taken up by followers of the Goethe-inspired spiritual movement led by Rudolf Steiner (see, for example, Whicher 1971). Here, parallels were grasped between the transformational structures of projective geometry and Goethe's distinctive approach to sciences such as comparative anatomy and biology with their focus on homologous structures.

45. One could point to a variety of books in Hegel's library attesting to a quite specialist knowledge in these matters. For example, books on trigonometry, the principles behind the use of logarithms, the role of incommensurability in Plato's *Theaetetus*, and so on (Mense 1993).

46. It will turn out that this doubling of the significance of each dimension is correlated with Eudoxus's extension of the three Archytan means to six.

47. On Kant's dual criticisms here of Leibniz's *analysis situs* and his relativistic conception of space, see Storrie 2013.

48. Thus, he would appeal to the existence of incongruent counterparts in the *Inaugural Dissertation* of 1770, the *Prolegomena to Any Future Metaphysics* of 1783 (Kant 1997, §13), and in the *Metaphysical Foundations of Natural Science* of 1786 (Kant 1985, 22–23).

49. "Quaternions," discovered by Hamilton in the 1840s, are vectors considered as existing in four-dimensional space, three of the coordinates of which are considered imaginary rather than real. The use of quaternions proved useful in physics.

50. Again, Kant had anticipated the idea of oriented three-dimensional volumes with his observations on so-called incongruent counterparts (Kant 1992b, 368–371).

Chapter Four

1. Schelling does not mention geometry in this essay, but in the follow-up essay in 1802 (Schelling 2001b) the geometric model for philosophical method is made explicit.

2. Kant's implicitly vector-based "phorometric" analysis in *Metaphysical Foundations of Natural Science* of 1786 (Kant 1985, pt. 2; Friedman 2013, ch. 5) would thereby become a popular starting point for such *Naturphilosophen* as Baader and Schelling.

3. Eschenmayer's diagram is reproduced and discussed in Holland 2019, 119 and Châtelet 2000, ch. 3.4.

4. On the surprising extent to which the *Naturphilosophen* had employed this imagery of the lever, see Holland 2019, ch. 3.

NOTES TO PAGES 90-95   245

5. Schelling thus seems to adhere to Kant's conception of an asymmetrical relation of geometry and arithmetic that follows from making time the exclusive dimension of pure intuition of inner sense, while things of the external world are grasped in terms of both dimensions. As Wood points out, Fichte too had given a foundational role to geometry over arithmetic (Wood 2012, 35). It would seem that Schelling had used this priority to reverse Fichte's relation of subjectivity and objectivity, assigning subjectivity now to the derivative science of arithmetic.

6. According to Sans, Hegel would not start opposing the inherence relation to the subsumption relation until 1808 in logic texts used during his period as high school teacher in Nuremberg (Sans 2004, 97–98).

7. We have noted the works of Carnot in his possession. For Lagrange's *Théorie des fonctions analytiques*, Hegel possessed a 1798 German translation of the 1797 edition as well as a revised 1813 edition in the original French (Mense 1993, 686). He also possessed Lagrange's *Traité de la résolution des équations numériques* (679). His was clearly an ongoing interest.

8. While study of the four conic sections—circle, ellipse, parabola, and hyperbola—had been introduced in antiquity by Apollonius, according to Del Centina (Del Centina 2016, 567–568), the four conics had, up until Kepler, been treated separately.

9. The principle of continuity would later be given an algebraic form with the idea of continuous functions. This idea would become a central notion of the discipline of topology, yet another branch of mathematics inspired by Leibniz's *analysis situs*.

10. While Hegel writes, "dass vermöge des Gesetzes der Stätigkeit die verschwindenden Grössen noch das Verhältniss, aus dem sie herkommen, ehe sie verschwinden, behalten," Hauff's wording is "das *Gesetz der Stetigkeit* es sey, vermöge dessen die verschwindenden Grössen noch in demselben Verhältnisse bleiben, dem sie, vor dem Verschwinden, sich stuffenweise näherten."

11. In a later, expanded edition of the work first published in 1813, Carnot would emphasize that the infinitesimals of calculus were simply an extension of Descartes's analytic approach, being an application of his method of indeterminate quantities (Carnot 1839, 150).

12. In their account of Hegel's interpretation of calculus (Kaufmann and Yeomans 2017), Kaufmann and Yeomans build on Hegel's treatment of ratios as mathematical objects that are more fundamental than their numerical constituents, as well as the crucial role played by variables in the concept of the differential. However, they see Hegel here as following Lagrange in adopting an algebraic orientation, from the perspective of which Carnot is being criticized. Thus, they claim, Hegel "establishes algebra's primacy over geometry, which is the approach of modern mathematics" (Kaufmann and Yeomans 2017, 382). But while Hegel's position isn't that of Schelling, neither is it the reversal of it, affirming "algebra's primacy over geometry." Hegel follows Carnot in his alternative algebraization of geometry to the reductive project of analytic geometry informing Lagrange's work.

13. Playfair also appealed to the ancient sense of "analysis" as given in the regressive or "problems" approach to geometric method, proceeding from a fact to its conditions (Ackerberg-Hastings 2002, 53–54), a sense altered by Descartes, who gave it an arithmetically based algebraic meaning.

14. In 1806, Jean-Robert Argand would suggest a geometric interpretation for the imaginary number $\sqrt{-1}$. Gilles Châtelet considers Argand here in relation to the considerations of directionality introduced by Kant (Châtelet 2000, 82–88). An interpretation of *i* within the framework of linear algebra would follow from the idea of areas with negatively valued magnitudes due to their orientation, such that the side of a square of area –1, for example, would have magnitude

√−1. Complex numbers, consisting of a pair of real and imaginary numbers, would be central to William Rowan Hamilton's theory of "quaternions" developed in the 1840s that would be absorbed into linear algebra by both Benjamin Peirce and William Clifford in the 1870s. These would play a crucial role in understanding the interaction of vectors in three-dimensional space.

15. It is now generally acknowledged that while these authors were not innovative mathematicians themselves, they nevertheless had preserved reasonably faithfully these major developments from earlier periods of Greek mathematics.

16. The double ratio can be proved for the circle by the use of a few simple theorems from Euclid's *Elements* plus Pythagoras's theorem. See Field and Gray 1987, 4–8.

17. It can be intuitively appreciated that Apollonius's construction is a special case of Pappus's (or Pappus's a generalization of that of Apollonius). If the angle AGC of figure 4.3 is increased, points C and E will gradually converge to meet at that point where the line CG becomes a tangent to the circle. At that point, the lines CD and CE become a single line intersecting the diameter of the circle at a right angle, producing Apollonius's figure.

18. The twentieth-century geometer Harold Coxeter would sum up the relation as follows: "Plane projective geometry may be described as the study of geometrical properties that are unchanged by 'central projection,' which is essentially what happens when an artist draws a picture of a tiled floor on a vertical canvas. The square tiles cease to be square, as their sides and angles are distorted by foreshortening; but the lines remain straight, since they are sections (by the picture-plane) of the planes that join them to the artist's eye" (Coxeter 1987, 3).

19. Thus, if one takes Leibniz's project as inspired by projective geometry, one sees the error in the claim made by the editors of Kant's precritical essays that "Leibniz utterly fails to recognize that the two triangles ABC and DEF are, in fact, not congruent at all" (Walford and Meerbote 1992, lxx).

20. According to Coolidge, this "projective invariance" of the cross-ratio had been appreciated in ancient times (Coolidge 1934, 217–218).

21. There is a strong suggestion of this in Hegel's claim in support of Kepler that free motion requires "two determinations," as in the ellipse with its two foci, rather than one, as in the circle with its one center. From Kepler's thesis of the unity among the four conic sections, just as the parabola has two foci, with one at infinity, the circle also has two, but in the case of the circle, the two foci overlap. The circle is thus a particular instance of the ellipse.

22. Indeed, this student had withdrawn an earlier thesis on descriptive geometry in relation to Apollonius, and the withdrawn thesis was also in the possession of Hegel. For a professor of Hegel's status to have kept such works in his library surely testifies to an interest in their contents.

23. It might be said that for Grassmann both "scalars" and directed magnitudes are capable of "inverses" in the sense in which Hegel uses this notion.

24. Among other things, this simplifies the idea of subtraction between vectors as $\overrightarrow{AB} - \overrightarrow{CD} = \overrightarrow{AB} + (\overrightarrow{CD}, -1)$.

25. The English mathematician Clifford had been a friend of C. S. Peirce since 1870, and his work would be significant for Peirce's logic. Clifford's expansion of Grassmann's linear algebra to incorporate Hamilton's theory of quaternions was published in the first volume of the *American Journal of Mathematics* in 1878.

26. For a relatively nontechnical account of his approach to vector multiplication, see Clifford 1886, ch. 4, especially §15. Benjamin Peirce had also incorporated quaternions into linear algebra but seemed to have been ignorant of Grassmann's work.

27. An operation '∗' is commutative if $A * B = B * A$, and anticommutative if $A * B = -B * A$.

28. By the time Grassmann came to write *Linear Extension Theory*, projective geometry had become familiar via the work of former students of Monge and Carnot such as Jean-Victor Poncelet. On the basis of Poncelet's work, Grassmann had reconstructed the cross-ratio using vectors (Grassmann 1995, 259–268). While the details here are complex, it would seem that the anticommutativity of multiplication in linear algebra (in Grassmann's external product and Clifford's wedge product) was reflected in the negative sign of the harmonic cross-ratio. Later developments of projective geometry would indeed restore the three-dimensional framework within which the two-dimensional diagrams of Desargues and Carnot could be understood.

29. In the modern guitar, for example, the frets are spaced according to a logarithmic scale base 2, such that with each semitone the frequency of the note produced is increased by the ratio of $^{12}\sqrt{2} : 1$.

Chapter Five

1. The term (although not used there) comes from Kant's comparison of his own method to that of Copernicus in the Preface to the second edition of the *Critique of Pure Reason* (Kant 1998, Bxvii and xxii, note).

2. The development of this type of mathematics would be a part of the transformation that led the discipline beyond the conception of the science of quantity to include relations of order—the centrality of which would be emphasized by Russell at the end of the century (Russell 1901 and 1903, pt. 4). Leibniz is commonly discussed as broaching the idea of an ordered set; see, for example, the entry "Partially ordered sets," in the European Mathematical Society's *Encyclopaedia of Mathematics*, https://www.encyclopediaofmath.org/index.php/Partially_ordered_set.

3. Glashof continues: "Leibniz of course did not put his ideas into the modern framework of syntax/semantics interplay of the Tarski type ... but in hindsight it has been a big step in that direction" (Glashoff 2010, 263).

4. For example, the law of "commutivity" states that whether a is added to b or b is added to a makes no difference to the result.

5. Group theory was effectively created by the French mathematician Évariste Galois in 1832. Importantly, it would be applied to geometry by Felix Klein in the 1870s so as to differentiate the various kinds of geometry according to what was treated as invariant in them (Klein 1893). For a historical account of the development of group theory, see Wussing 1984.

6. The background of the development of abstract algebra in Britain and its link to algebraic logic will be explored in chapter 8.

7. Leibniz was not the first to suggest the "duodecimal" system. On the history of this notion, see Zacher 1973.

8. In set theory the "new" number zero would be represented by the "empty set," a set with definite properties, such as being a subset of any other set. This would be significant within the logic of the algebraic Aristotelians.

9. A stroke had prevented Ploucquet from actually teaching during Hegel's years at Tübingen, and the teaching in logic was done by one of his followers using Ploucquet's text (Ploucquet 2006). Hegel had Ploucquet's major works in logic in his library at Berlin (Mense 1993, 686).

10. "Strict analogy" here suggests isomorphic equivalence. It is being argued here that this relation for Hegel was weaker, more homology as an expression of a systematic homomorphism.

11. Cf. "Aristotle himself seems to have followed the way of ideas (*viam indealem*), for he says that animal is in man, namely a concept in a concept; for otherwise men would be among animals (*insint animalibus*)" (Leibniz 1966, 120).

12. Hegel mentions Lambert in *The Science of Logic*, specifically in relation to the project of giving a mathematical notation to logic "based on lines, figures and the like" (*SL*, 544; 12:47). The context is a discussion of the inadequacy of such mathematical notation to capture properly logical relations, but it is clear that Hegel's critique is directed to the assumption that properly logical relations can be represented by a wholly uninterpreted syntax. Thus, he alludes to the dependence of such constructed languages on natural language (545–546; 12:48).

13. Kant himself had, in 1755, put forward a superficially similar picture of the cosmos in his anonymously published *Universal Natural History and Theory of the Heavens*. However, Kant's more evolutionary account is now considered more modern than Lambert's, whose view was premised on a teleological notion that God had designed the universe in such a way that it would support life and the mind throughout its extent.

14. The first expression of topology is thus commonly taken to be Euler's solution to the problem concerning the seven bridges of Königsberg. Is it possible, it was asked, to go for a walk in Königsberg and, crossing each of its seven bridges only once, end up where one started? Euler showed it was not.

15. Thus, Aristotle disputed the idea that there was any empty space beyond the edge of the cosmos. There was simply nothing—not something that we can think of as empty space.

16. Kepler had applied Apollonius's theory of conics to the field of optics. Conic sections, he argued, have two foci, but in the case of the parabola, one lies on the axis of the curve "at an infinite distance from the first" (Field and Gray 1987, 187).

17. As emphasized by Stepelevich (Stepelevich 1998), Hegel's attitude to geometry was consistent with the idea of non-Euclidean geometry.

18. This issue is now discussed under the idea of "logical infallibility" and would come to be used by intuitionistic logicians against the use of the classical laws of logic.

19. And yet in a later part of the text, Hegel seems to imply that Ploucquet himself had similarly aspired to a universal characteristic (*SL*, 608; 12:110).

20. As he reports in his letter to Niethammer of December 14, 1808 (*Brf*, 489).

21. In Hegel's time, the benefits of such alienations of the commonplace were promoted by romantic philosophers and literary theorists.

22. The story was related by Aristotle's student, the music theorist Aristoxenus (Aristoxenus 1902, 187).

23. It will be remembered that Hegel does not treat mathematics in terms of the distinction "pure" and "applied." There is no eternal "Platonic" realm of mathematical objects—what counts as a mathematical object, a number, for example, evolves historically under the pressure of the need to resolve contradictions generated in the extension of calculative practices.

Chapter Six

1. On the new way of conceiving of individuals as universals in the medieval period, see Tarlazzi 2017.

2. In a late unpublished paper Leibniz had written in relation to the logical properties of a singular proposition, "Should we say that a singular proposition is equivalent to a particular and

to a universal proposition? Yes, we should" (Leibniz 1966, 115). This aspect of Leibniz's approach has been brought out clearly by Fred Sommers and George Englebretsen (Sommers 1982, 15–21; Englebretsen 1988).

3. As has been indicated by Michael Franz, Ploucquet's distinction would undermine the traditional theory of judgments as expressed in the "square of opposition" (Franz 2005, 99), giving the lie to Leibniz's belief that the reciprocity of intensional and extensional interpretations of judgments could be purchased without loss or that a strict analogy existed between concepts and propositions. This same dialectic, as we will see, would play out when algebraic logic was reinvented in the nineteenth century.

4. Robert Brandom (Brandom 1994, 79–80) would later repeat this criticism of the way that philosophers prior to Kant had conceived of judgment as a form of classification, prompting his own solution of judgment as being conceived fundamentally as a "move in a language game" involving the asking for and giving of reasons for asserted propositions.

5. For example, while a version of this distinction between separate judgment forms employing internal and external negation would appear in the *Prolegomena for Any Future Metaphysics* as a distinction between "judgments of perception" and "judgments of experience," Kant would apparently abandon this in the second edition of the *Critique of Pure Reason*. Later still, in the context of the *Critique of the Power of Judgment*, an internally negated pair of contrary concepts would reappear between the beautiful and ugly showing some continuity with Kant's earlier treatment of these terms in the precritical period, but this would be at the expense of judgments of taste being properly cognitive (Kant 2000, §5).

6. This may be regarded as the consequence of the univocity of the middle term of Aristotle's syllogistic. When implication is conceived as class inclusion, there is nothing preventing its iteration such that more than two premises can be found in a syllogism.

7. Leibniz's own endorsement of the *characteristica universalis* and its "algebraic" logic was not itself as straightforward as is usually assumed, as seen in his thoughts about an alternative *analysis situs*.

8. I will follow convention in using the phrase "the calculus" to capture the inversely linked techniques of differential and integral calculus in this way.

9. This is the law that the attractive force between bodies is directly proportional to the product of their masses and inversely proportional to the square of their distance from each other, $F = m_1 m_2 / d^2$. See also *E:PN*, §270, remark and addition, pp. 263–281.

10. This was the accepted view at the time, as it is now. However, Cinzia Ferrini has raised the possible relevance for Hegel of criticisms made of Newton in the 1720s by the French Jesuit mathematician Louis Bertrand Castel (Ferrini 1994).

11. The paragraph is concerned with mathematics as dealing with "magnitude alone" abstracting from dimensions of space that have been differentiated by "the concept." The following paragraph commences: "Immanent, so-called pure mathematics *also* . . ." (*Phen*, §§45–46, emphasis added).

12. On the important role played by the principle of continuity in the development of projective geometry after Carnot, see Nagel 1939, §§16–23.

13. This was a revised version of Carnot's *Essai sur les machines en général* from 1783.

14. Hegel singles out the way that the analysts had attempted to separate out the framework of the calculus from the types of physical application in which it had been applied—an attitude conflicting with his refusal to separate "pure" and "applied" mathematics—and in the second remark turns to "the purpose of differential calculus deduced from its application."

15. Famously, in May 1832 the twenty-year-old Évariste Galois had sat up through the night so as to set out in a letter to a friend his theory of groups. He did this because the next morning he would face an opponent in a duel and feared being killed. Indeed, he would be wounded and, a day later, would die.

16. The implication is that, in contrast, Newton abstracts away from concrete singulars of perception to those abstract particulars subsumable under laws.

17. For example, according to Kepler's second law, a line segment joining a planet to the sun is said to sweep out equal areas during equal intervals of time, such that an accumulation of successive areas is related to an accumulation of qualitatively different linear magnitudes, those of time. While the quantities of distances, times, and so on can be measured, there are no directly measurable "quantities" of gravity.

18. This aspect of Hegel's critique is perspicuously presented by Brigitte Falkenburg (Falkenburg 1998).

19. In a similar spirit, Wittgenstein would later express the need for friction with the imperative, "Back to rough ground" (Wittgenstein 1953, §107).

20. That all the terms of the syllogisms in this figure are predicates is indicated in Hegel's way of representing them as having universals in all positions, U-U-U. Abstract universals of this kind can only be predicates.

21. It will be remembered that to be a judgment, the subject and predicate terms must be determined as different determinations. As the components of the mathematical syllogism are no longer proper judgments, it is not a proper syllogism.

22. In the case of a conditional, "if p then q," this compound proposition must be able to be regarded as true or false independently of the question of the actual existence of those "thirds" belonging or not to the relevant classes involved. "If Sherlock Holmes is a detective, then he investigates the causes of certain strange happenings" needs to be able to be true despite the fact that there is no worldly thing picked out by the name Sherlock Holmes.

Chapter Seven

1. As is the case, for example, with the well-known "All humans are mortal; Socrates is a human; therefore, Socrates is mortal."

2. "Nor can one understand through perception. . . . for one necessarily perceives singulars [*kath ekaston*] whereas understanding comes by being familiar with the universal" (Aristotle 1984, *Posterior Analytics*, 87b 28–39).

3. Significantly, while this series can be continued in both ascending and descending directions, the direction involved changes the relation of the inference to the faculty of reason itself (A331/B338). We will see Peirce capitalize on the significance of the direction of the inference in chapter 8.2.

4. The verb *kategoreo* had the primary legal meaning of "to speak against someone or accuse them of something." In this context it becomes simply something *said of* something or someone. The English *predicate* similarly contains the Latin root for "say," *dicere*.

5. In the seventeenth century, for example, diagrams capturing containment relations were employed by Leibniz himself (Moktefi and Shin 2012, 616), and in the eighteenth century, similar diagrams were used by Leonhard Euler, after whom they were named. However, the first person to have used such diagrams in that century seems to have been the logic master at Tübingen during Hegel's time there, Gottfried Ploucquet, in his *Fundamenta philosophiae speculativae* in 1759.

Moreover, this fact had been brought into wider focus at the time by a public precedence dispute that had broken out between Ploucquet and the mathematician Johann Heinrich Lambert (Lemanski 2017, 59). This dispute in fact went beyond the issue of precedence to that of the relation of such diagrams to the project of developing Leibniz's logic, the project within which Ploucquet and Lambert were the two major eighteenth-century figures (Lu Adler 2017, 42).

6. Paterson traces Hegel's views here to Proclus. Paterson 2005, 79–81.

7. For a general account of the square and its later transformations, see Parsons 2017.

8. We will return to these alternative renderings of the last form below.

9. In modern logic, subalternation from A to I would *not* be taken to be a valid inference, given the reinterpretation of the meaning of the judgment forms involved. Thus, post-Russell, Aristotle would be accused of giving universal affirmative judgments "existential purport," a property they do not have because, according to classical predicate calculus, they should be properly understood as conditionals.

10. The notion of subcontrariety, it will be remembered, had come from early Greek geometry, where it referred to similar but "inverted" triangles and had been linked specifically to the "harmonic" division of an interval.

11. This seems to be the basis of the puzzling feature of Aristotelian *pragmata*, often thought of as "states of affairs" that, in contrast to their modern equivalents, can actually be false. See, for example, Crivelli 2004, 4.

12. According to Arthur Prior, the idea of timelessly true or false propositions only started to become the dominant view in the nineteenth century, and it was not until the turn of the twentieth century that it became the standard view (Prior 1957, 116). In particular, it would be championed by Russell. Later, Prior himself would revive a form of logic for such "tensed" sentences (Prior 1967).

13. This indeterministic conception of future as opposed to past states of affairs was to become an object of debate between later Peripatetics, who affirmed a type of libertarian indeterminism about the future, and the Stoics who defended causal determinism and a type of compatibilism. In modern logic, judgments of indeterminate truth-value would be permitted by intuitionistic logic, in contrast to Boolean logic, in which all propositions have a determinate truth-value.

14. In this way, Aristotle is sometimes described as having a "two-sided" potestative account of the modality of actions that are "up to us" (e.g., Malink 2016), an aspect of Aristotle's account of modality that importantly separated it from the determinist consequences of Stoic propositional logic that adhered to the principle of bivalence.

15. Here there is a straightforward equality between the two instances of the middle term. Such "advances along the line of *equality*," as Hegel points out in the *Phenomenology*, constitute just "what is formal in mathematical convincingness" (*Phen*, §45).

16. This is effectively the Stoics' *modus ponens* ("If something is human it is mortal" and "Gaius is human" therefore "Gaius is mortal") expressed in the form of a syllogism with a judgment with a universally quantified subject as major premise.

17. I have argued for the parallels between Hegel's judgment of the concept and Kant's judgment of taste in Redding 2007, ch. 6.

18. If we read the judgments involved as having the normal subject-predicate word order, Hegel seems to have reversed Aristotle's second and third figures. We will return to this below in chapter 10.

19. In Hegelian terms, we might say that Brandom's inferential space, conceived along more Fregean lines, will be the space of understanding rather than the space of reason.

20. In this case it would be a false judgment, but a judgment, nevertheless. Were all roses red, it might be said that "the rose as such is red," in just the way it can be correctly said that "the rose as such is a plant."

21. Questions of truth or falsity here, we might say, depend upon whether the subject does or does not "measure up to" what is said in the predicate.

22. Kant, of course, has a different reason for why we humans cannot reach this goal, and while Hegel is in some sense on the side of Kant here, he is critical of the intelligibility of the very idea of the project of which Kant thinks we humans are incapable.

23. Cf. "Spirit is in itself the movement which is cognition—the transformation of that former *in-itself* into *for-itself*, of *substance* into *subject*, of the object of *consciousness* into the object of *self-consciousness*, i.e., into an object that is just as much sublated, or into the *concept*. This transformation is the circle returning back into itself, which presupposes its beginning and reaches its beginning only at the end" (*Phen*, §802).

Chapter Eight

1. For an overview, see Houser 1994.

2. There are now, of course, many works on the Fregean revolution in logic and its philosophical consequences. For a clear overview, see, for example, Beaney 1996.

3. Boole had been unaware of Leibniz's earlier work when writing *Laws of Thought*.

4. In this respect Schröder would be an exception, taking the side of Frege's universalism in advocating a doctrine of universal language he called "pasigraphy" (Peckhaus 2014). Nathan Houser has presented Peirce's response to the logicist claim that logic must ground mathematics as follows: "If there has to be a science of reasoning before reasoning can be legitimately employed, then there can be no science at all. Even a science of reasoning must be developed by reasoning" (Houser 1997, 12).

5. Johnson would repeat this view three decades later. "This necessary recourse to ordinary language in developing a deductive system shows that direct attention to meanings, presented linguistically, is entailed in the intelligent following of even a professedly symbolic exposition. . . . If the symbolic language is so constructed that a minimum of interpretation clauses is required, then there is a corresponding minimum in the extent to which actual thinking is involved. But, however few interpretation clauses are required, the intelligent use of symbolic formulae cannot be reduced to a merely mechanical process" (Johnson 1922, 45).

6. In a sense, this might be thought of as a stance for which Kurt Gödel later offered a proof. Findlay, who had published in *Mind* one of the first general philosophical accounts of Gödel's theorem (Findlay 1942), believed Gödel's approach had been anticipated by Hegel (Findlay 1963, ch. 13, 221–222). Findlay's willingness to go against the grain and make these sorts of connections was shared by Henry Harris: "Hegel himself would certainly have been deeply interested by many developments in modern mathematics—beginning with Cantor's mathematics of the infinite. We ought to keep an open mind about how he would regard the attempts to formalize his own logic" (Harris 1997, 1:118).

7. Up to this time, British mathematicians had largely relied upon Newton's more geometrical and physically interpreted framework.

8. This was the case at least in theory. In *The Mathematical Analysis of Logic* Boole refers to "the Universe . . . as comprehending every conceivable class of objects whether actually existing or not" (Boole 1847, 14), making his "Universe" effectively the totality of possible worlds, much like Leibniz.

9. In terms of the structures of abstract algebra developed during the nineteenth century, a Boolean algebra would count as a "field," an extension of the idea of a "group" in which elements of an underlying set were subject to two different binary operations distinguished as product and sum, respectively.

10. Boole's use of multiplication here was much like Leibniz's use of conceptual addition, such that while Leibniz had it that "A ⊕ A = A," in Boole a similar law is expressed as $xx = x$, or as he writes it "$x^2 = x$." Boole called this "the index law." Later, Benjamin Peirce named it the law of idempotence.

11. The logical interpretation of this would prove contentious, however.

12. That is, *not (p or q) = not p and not q*, while *not (p and q) = not p or not q*. On the extensive dualities of algebraic logic, see, for example, Demey and Smessaert 2022.

13. Boole himself did not intend such a sentence to be read as predicating a verb (shines) of an object (the sun). Rather, his conception of a sentence is more like Aristotle's, in which subject and predicate terms are joined by the copula "is," with the apparent verb "shines" being elliptical for "is a shining thing." In this sense, in his proto-set-theoretical approach, relations of inclusion predominated over those of order.

14. These relations are difficult to tie down. The *de-dicto* proposition could also be thought to be what the *dictum* referred to was *about*. Thus, *de-dicto* could also be understood as *de-facto*.

15. Boole's way of conveying exactly what he means by this point is far from clear: "I do not hereby affirm that the relation between these propositions is, like that which exists between the facts which they express, a relation of causality, but only that the relation among the propositions so implies, and is so implied by, the relation among the facts, that it may for the ends of logic be used as a fit representative of that relation" (Boole 1854, 38).

16. What would come to be the standard analytical account after Russell would be to treat the conditional as an assertion that is conjoined to a further premise and issues in a conclusion by the rule of *modus ponens*: the assertion of the compound "if p then q" is conjoined to the assertion "p" and from the conjunction is derived the assertion "q." But Russell was not the only person to address these issues, and writers within the algebraic tradition had also sought to eliminate the unclarities and confusions they found in Boole.

17. Famously, C. I. Lewis would argue that this simply is not what the word "implies" means (Lewis 1912; 1918, ch. 4). If a implies b, there must be some connection between them, but on Russell's analysis, "5 is an even number" is supposed to imply "two plus two equals four," because the first sentence, as false, implies any sentence.

18. Boole required the exclusive sense in order to maintain the arithmetical law of addition that stated (in arithmetic modular 2) that $x + x = 0$.

19. The term *Entfremdung* Hegel employs here is the same term employed metaphysically for the alienation or externalization of ideal entities into incommensurable concrete objectivity—the alienation of "the Idea" into nature or the alienation of an individual's intention into objectivity in work.

20. The possession of such "inverses" had become described as one of the defining feature of "groups" and "fields" in abstract algebra. The significance of such inverses for Hegel has been noted above in chapter 3.1.

21. In fact, "exponentiation" would later be reintroduced in the approach of "linear logic" to provide a nonderived model for the relation of logical consequence. See below, section 8.5.

22. Traditionally a function was understood as something like a rule-governed operation performed on numbers, but a more formal interpretation in terms of set theory would develop.

From this perspective, a function would be understood as an abstract "mapping" between elements of Platonistically conceived sets rather than an activity performed by a subject.

23. A proposition could be thought of as being "mapped" to one of the two truth-values considered as the two members of a set, later called the "Boolean" set, true and false, respectively.

24. On the relevance of linear algebra for Peirce's logic, see, for example, Brunning 1991.

25. On the basis of these innovations Peirce is thus now regarded as one of the founders of a twentieth-century branch of mathematics that investigates the properties of such "partially-ordered sets" or "posets" (Brady 2000, chs. 2 and 3). While there are many examples of posets, the notion is commonly illustrated by the example of the two-placed relation "x is a divisor of y" applied to natural numbers, an example that takes us back to Leibniz's arithmetic conception of the composition of concepts and from there all the way back to Plato's philosophical arithmetic. For the numbers 2 and 6, that 2 divides 6 exemplifies transitivity (if 2 divides 6 and 6 divides 12, then 2 divides 12), reflexivity (2 divides itself) and anti-symmetry (6 does not divide 2 and would only divide it if it equaled 2).

26. In 1885, Peirce would draw on a paper published by his student O. H. Mitchell in Peirce et al. 1883, a volume that Peirce had himself edited.

27. Peirce's signs "Σ" and "Π" play the equivalent roles within his system to the existential ("$\exists$") and universal ("$\forall$") quantifiers of classical predicate calculus stemming from Frege and Russell.

28. Such modal operators, together with the negation operator, would generate four basic modal judgment types—judgments that were possibly true (in Lewis's formalism, $\Diamond p$) and those that were not possibly true ($\sim \Diamond p$), those that were necessarily true ($\Box p$) and those that were not necessarily true ($\sim \Box p$).

29. These, of course, are not mutually exclusive. If a proposition p is certain, then it is true.

30. It might be objected that MacColl's "certain" here is not a properly modal notion but an epistemological one, and that interpreted as "necessary" it means some sort of subjective epistemic necessity rather than objective modal necessity. While this is taken to be a standard distinction in analytic discussions, I suggest that from the point of view of intensional logics more compatible with idealism this distinction will not be clear-cut.

31. Russell points out that he had earlier believed that Peano had been responsible for this shift in the focus of logic, but now acknowledges that this breakthrough had been made by MacColl as early as 1878 (Russell 1906, 255n1).

32. Indeed, there is a point to MacColl's complaint here, given that the concept of "identity" adopted in the new Frege-Russell logic was something like that earlier proposed by Leibniz's theory of the "identity of indiscernibles." For Leibniz, to capture the idea of a thing persisting though changes of its properties and relations required building the thing's entire history into its "complete concept," it becoming a necessary part of Caesar's identity as Caesar that he crossed the Rubicon, for example.

33. Johnson did important work on probability and influenced the economist John Maynard Keynes.

34. For example, "we may characterize a certain child by the adjective 'liking a certain book,' or a certain book by the adjective 'pleasing a certain child'" (Johnson 1921, 203).

35. Extending subject terms to propositions would thus accommodate MacColl's treatment of modal judgments.

36. Thus, "the substantive proper seems to coincide with the category 'existent'" (Johnson 1921, xxxv).

37. Corresponding to this, for Frege, such judgments are primarily "about" the descriptive concepts involved. What is here asserted of such a concept is that it is satisfied or instantiated by some object.

38. For a clear account, see Prior 1949.

39. Thus, Johnson distinguishes the most basic and indeterminate relation that can exist between things as "otherness" rather than difference. The relations among determinates of a determinable are ones of difference, but in contrast, the relation between color and shape qua determinables is one of "otherness."

40. In general, the distinction singular-particular is not commonly found in the British logical tradition, and following the more "British" usage, Johnson employs "particular" to encompass what for Hegel would be both singulars and particulars. Thus, Johnson uses "particular" "not to apply to quasi-substantives, but to be restricted to substantives proper, i.e. existents, or even more narrowly to occurrents" (Johnson 1922, xiii). We may think of Johnson's terminological distinction between determinate and determinable adjectives as an attempt to establish within the more general category of "particularity" a distinction akin to Hegel's singular-particular distinction. In this sense, Johnson's usage is more like Ploucquet's, with his distinction between "exclusive" and "comprehensive" particularity.

41. Thus, Frege has a sign for assertion, '⊢,' but no equivalent sign for denial.

42. This is a logical feature they would share with Heyting and other "intuitionists."

43. It was also meant as alternative to the "formalism" of David Hilbert for whom the truths of mathematics expressed the set of rules, akin to the rules of a game, according to which finite strings of symbols were to be manipulated.

44. On the idealist features of Brouwer's mathematics, see Detlefsen 1998.

45. Brouwer worked in a mathematical discipline that was another to have claimed the mantel of Leibniz's proposed *analysis situs*—topology. For a helpful account of Brouwer's philosophy of mathematics, see van Atten 2020.

46. This did not mean that the laws of excluded middle or double negation elimination were refuted, however: they were regarded as neither affirmed nor denied, and so could thereby be introduced separately as additional axioms. This would affect the way negation was understood by Heyting.

47. In one of Brouwer's examples ($\sim p \supset (p \supset 1 = 2)$).

48. (C and D) implies C *and* (C and D) implies D.

49. As can be appreciated in figure 8.1, disjunctive nodes are inversions of conjunctive ones, again expressing the duality of these logical connectives.

50. The terms "edge" and "vertex" suggest these diagrams are to be read as three-dimensional figures, with figure 8.1 representing a type of transparent cube. Below (section 10.2), we will raise the question of what it might be to think of these diagrams as three-dimensional structures—an interpretation more in line with Hegel's understanding of Plato's logic of the three-dimensional world.

51. C. S. Peirce has been described as the inventor of the idea of lattices (Birkhoff 2020). Influenced by the work of Clifford and others, Peirce went on to develop his own diagrammatic representations of such structures, but they have not generally been taken up.

52. The values for true and false are sometimes represented by the signs '⊤' (top) and '⊥' (bottom), respectively.

53. A semilattice has one binary operation rather than Boole's two (i.e., "addition" and "multiplication"), leading it to model logical relations among the propositions differently. The algebra

of Leibniz's logic is described as a semilattice in both Swoyer (1994, 24–25) and Malink and Vasudevan (2016, §3.1).

54. For an account that stresses the role played by Peirce in Gentzen's forms of proof, see Anellis and Abeles 2016.

55. Linear logic was introduced by the French logician Jean-Yves Girard in 1987. A general, but still technical account is to be found in Di Cosmo and Miller 2019. The results of linear logic have been applied in linguistic theory in an attempt to capture the different inferential connotations carried by words in natural languages.

56. Thus, the expression "$c \leq (a \supset b)$" (the conditional, "if a then b" is a consequence of the truth of c) is introduced as equivalent to "$(c \wedge a) \leq b$" (read as the conjoint truths of c and a imply b). In general terms, if the truth of b depends on the truths of both a and c, then given c, it can be said that "if a then b." In this way the conditional has been introduced independently of negation. This equivalence has played an important role in the development of computer science, where it is referred to as the "Curry-Howard isomorphism."

57. Of course, general parallels between the thought of Peirce and Hegel have been noted. See, for example, Stern 2013.

Chapter Nine

1. Between the Jena and Heidelberg versions of the system, Hegel had underlined the importance of the circularity that runs through his system with a name change from "system" to "encyclopedia" (*Enzyklopädie*) with its connotations of "circle." Each part of philosophy would now be described as "a philosophical whole, a circle coming to closure within itself, but in each of its parts the philosophical idea exists in a particular determinacy or element [*einer besonderen Bestimmtheit oder Elemente*]. The individual circle [*einzelne Kreis*], simply because it is itself a totality, also breaks through the boundary of its element and founds a further sphere. The whole thus presents itself as a circle of circles" (*E:L*, §15).

2. We might perhaps think of the homomorphism of Hegel's two judgment types as underlying the intuition of those "redundancy theorists" of truth who, in focusing on the fact that a Boolean secondary judgment such as "It is true that the sky is blue" seems to say no more than the primary judgment "The sky is blue," draw the conclusion that the predicate "true" is redundant. Significantly, Frank Ramsay, to whom the theory is often attributed, had been a student of Johnson and a supporter of his logic (Ramsay 1922).

3. Hegel gives the examples "This plant is curative," "This instrument is useful," and "This punishment works as a deterrent" (*E:L*, §174, addition).

4. We might think of how the discovery of such relative properties in science is contingent on a type of disinterpretation of qualities that have already been attributed to objects. According to Foucault, in the sixteenth century walnuts were considered to cure headaches because they resembled little brains (Foucault 1970, 25). The transition to the new way of thinking of a property like "curativeness" might be found in Descartes's criticism of the habit that "when we discover several resemblances between two things, to attribute to both equally, even on points in which they are in reality different, that which we have recognized to be true of only of them" (Descartes, *Rules for the Direction of the Mind*, quoted in Foucault 1970, 51). "Cartesian doubt" might be considered as a way of stripping objects of their meanings in order that new meanings might be discovered.

5. In discussing Kepler's third law in the *Encyclopedia Philosophy of Nature* Hegel notes that "the greatness of this law consists in its presentations of the *rationality of the matter* with such simplicity and immediacy. In the Newtonian formula however, it is transformed into a law applied to the *force* of gravity, and so shows how *reflection* which fails to get to the bottom of things can distort and pervert the truth" (*E:PN*, §270, remark, p. 269).

6. Carnot, we are told, was proud of his "distinction between what he called impelling forces ('forces-sollicitantes') and resisting forces ('forces-resistantes')" that could not be reduced to "a metaphysical differentiation between cause and effect" but determined "merely by the geometry of the system" (Gillispie and Pisano 2013, 22).

7. This had been at the heart of Aristotle's criticism of Plato's appeal to "collection" in the process of collection and division, as it had been central to the nominalists' criticism of judgments about Aristotelian kinds.

8. This reversal in turn creates the need for two more principles that "may be regarded as inverse to the Applicative and Implicative principles respectively"—the Counter-applicative and Counter-implicative principles. For example, in relation to the former, "when we are justified in passing from the assertion of a predication about some *one* given to the assertion of the same predication about some other, then we are also justified in assertion the same predication about *every*" (Johnson 1922, 28). The invertibility of the order implicit in directionality is once again crucial.

9. This all depends on treating syllogisms as having a fundamental diagrammatic dimension (Peirce 2010, 20) and the analysis of syllogisms as depending on the observation of such diagrams (47). The idea of moving through syllogistic structures via different paths exemplifies what Peirce describes as "making experiments upon diagrams and the like and . . . observing the results" and which constitutes the "very life of mathematical thinking" (40).

10. Thus, in figure 4.4, the line GHI is the line of the intersection of the planes upon which the triangles lie. As points common to both planes, G, H, and I must fall on that line.

11. It is as if the judge comes to say to herself, "I feel this way and I feel it *because* of the way the house is put together."

12. I have argued elsewhere (Redding 2007, ch. 4.2) that a certain convergence among the views of Peirce, Hegel, Kant, and Leibniz in relation to this form of nondemonstrative inference could be traced to a way of reading Aristotle's logic found in the Renaissance philosopher Jacobo Zabarella, who himself seems to have been influenced by the ancient "problems" approach to geometry.

13. This analogical inference could not be reduced to a three-termed geometric sequence because this form of inference was considered to have its application across a genus.

14. The principle involved seems to be something like that of the "principle of continuity" utilized by Kepler and Leibniz.

15. This would importantly separate Hegel from Schelling, for whom religious imagery and the conceptual relations of philosophy were on the same level.

16. Concerning the judgment with this newly determined subject term, he later adds, "This combination, implicit and explicit, constitutes the basis of a new judgment—*the judgment of necessity*" (*SL*, 575; 12:77).

17. Hegel treats the judgment of necessity as the third judgment type after the judgment of existence and judgment of reflection. However, I think it makes more sense to treat the first two judgment types as belonging to the one cycle as its ascending and descending phases.

18. In Johnsonian terms, we might regard the initial subject of this type of judgment as at best "quasi-substantival."

19. This type of approach is particularly emphasized by Brandom. See, for example, Brandom 2009, pt. 1.

20. Exceptions to the general reluctance to read Hegel's political theory in the light of the notion of value are Dean Moyar (Moyar 2021) and Jean-Philippe Deranty (Deranty 2005). Terry Pinkard had also stressed the need for a place for value in Hegel's account of nature, undercutting the tendency for "normativity" to be opposed to nature by being exclusively identified with the realm of spirit (Pinkard 2012).

21. "This man is sitting" said of Socrates asserts of Socrates that he is sitting but presupposes that he, as a man, is both rational and an animal.

22. It will be remembered that action for Aristotle is characterized by this singularity, which is why practical reason is for him not demonstrative but relies on analogical ways of seeing: seeing A as having a property B in a way that is analogous to the way in which another object C has the property D.

23. We will return to the objects of judgments of the concept as Platonic *paradigmata* in chapter 9.

24. In the second half of the twentieth century, such "subject-placing" indexical judgments that Russell had ruled out as judgments would come to be thought by many to play a noneliminable role in cognitive life.

25. In Ng 2020, Karen Ng explores the notion of logical life in Hegel by examining it in the context of natural life qua immediate form of the Idea in chapter 1 of section 3 of book 3 of *The Science of Logic*. This context, I suggest, provides a type of retrospective justification for treating the three syllogistic figures of the subjective logic as moments of a more formally conceived "logical life."

Chapter Ten

1. Or, more properly, "E," "B," and "A" correlating with *Einzelheit, Besonderheit*, and *Allgemeinheit*.

2. Hegel insists that when the subject and predicate places are occupied by the same determination a degenerate type of judgment results, such as is found in the degenerate propositions of Leibniz's universal characteristic, which are composed entirely of universals.

3. Blanché had specifically invoked the hexagon in opposition to von Wright's treatment of deontic logic (von Wright 1951).

4. A similar square is suggested in Aristotle, *De Interpretatione*, 21b10ff and *Prior Analytics*, 32a18–28.

5. Such an interpretation of "contingently p" as "not impossibly p and not necessarily p" had been independently introduced into modal discussions around the same time by Montgomery and Routley (Montgomery and Routley 1966). In fact, a similar idea is found in Aristotle's *Prior Analytics*, book 1, chapter 13 (32a18–21)—a section generally regarded as pertaining to Aristotle's modal logic—where it is discussed as "two-sided possibility" and opposed to one-sided possibility, which is equated simply with the denial of impossibility (Malink 2016).

6. Blanché's logical hexagon would be linked to Goethe's color theory (Goethe 1988, section VII, Physics) by a number of nonclassical logicians (see, for example, Béziau 2017).

7. I have altered the orientation of Czezowski's hexagon to allow easier comparison with Blanché's. Czezowski gives the following key to the diagram (Czezowski 1955, 393):

Judgment types: A: universal positive, E: universal negative, U: singular positive, Y: singular negative, I: particular positive, O: particular negative.
Logical relations: Subalternation: A-U, U-I, A-I, E-Y, Y-O, E-O; Contrariety: A-E, E-U, A-Y; Subcontrariety: I-O, O-U, I-Y; Contradiction: A-O, E-I, U-Y.

8. Of course, Hegel was not on the radar of many logicians during the twentieth century, and Czezowski could hardly be expected to recognize that he was, effectively, retracing some of the consequences of Hegel's own attempts to integrate Aristotle-styled singular and modal squares of his practical logic with the traditional square of his official demonstrative logic.

9. George Englebretsen (Englebretsen 1986) explores this aspect of Czezowski's logic in relation to the proposal for "wild quantity" put forward by the twentieth-century algebraic logician Fred Sommers (Sommers 1982). Sommers's idea of "wild quantity" is, I suggest, like the idea of "hybrid logics," another expression of Plato's split middle term.

10. The first is the traditional square, with corners A E I O, and the second and third squares are formed by sides representing implication relations stretching from U- and Y-propositions to various other vertices, resulting in the squares U E Y I and A Y O U, respectively.

11. It is thus found in medieval Christianity as well as Islamic and Hindu religions.

12. Pascal's theorem, a generalization of a theorem found in Pappus, is known about because the manuscript had been examined by Leibniz after Pascal's death. For the history, see Del Centina 2020.

13. Both Poncelet in 1822 and Chasles in 1836 would emphasize the importance of Pascal's "mystic hexagram" for geometry (Del Centina 2020, 491).

14. Leibniz's letter to Pascal's sister together with other works of Pascal had been published in 1779 (Del Centina 2020, 470).

Conclusion

1. Hegel had added these to the 1827 and 1830 editions.

2. In any case, besides whatever theological dimension this passage conveys, as Ermylos Plevrakis has argued, Hegel's Aristotelian *theos* might also be seen as representing a "metascientific contextualization of all (philosophical) sciences" (Plevrakis 2020, 84).

3. Baader has been described as responsible for Hegel's attraction to Böhme (Betanzos 1998, 54).

4. On the widespread following that Böhme's writings had attracted among the radical Protestant sects during the English Civil War, see Hutin 1960, ch. 3.

5. In the 1827 Preface to the *Encyclopedia of the Philosophical Sciences*, Hegel would reply to these criticisms in an amicable way, playing down the disagreements about religion assumed by Baader.

6. Toward the end of the twentieth century Clifford's geometric algebra was revived by David Hestenes to provide a unified mathematical language for the expression of modern physics. See, for example, Hestenes and Sobczyk 1984.

Bibliography

Abeles, Francine F. 2014. "Nineteenth-Century British Logic on Hypotheticals, Conditionals, and Implication." *History and Philosophy of Logic* 35, no. 1: 24–37.
Ackerberg-Hastings, Amy. 2002. "Analysis and Synthesis in John Playfair's *Elements of Geometry*." *British Journal for the History of Science* 35, no. 1 (March): 43–72.
Andersen, Kirsti. 2007. *The Geometry of an Art: The History of the Mathematical Theory of Perspective from Alberti to Monge*. New York: Springer.
Anellis, Irving H. 2011. "MacColl's Influences on Peirce and Schröder." *Philosophia Scientiae* 15, no. 1 (April): 97–128.
Anellis, Irving H., and Francine F. Abeles. 2016. "The Historical Sources of Tree Graphs and the Tree Method in the Work of Peirce and Gentzen." In *Modern Logic 1850–1950*, ed. F. F. Abeles and M. E. Fuller, 35–97. Basel: Springer.
Angelelli, Ignacio. 1990. "On Johannes Raue's Logic." In *Leibniz' Auseinandersetzung mit Vorgängern und Zeitgenossen*, ed. Ingrid Marchlewitz and Albert Heinekamp, 184–190. Stuttgart: Franz Steiner Verlag.
Anonymous. 2008. "Introduction—I.3. Some Fundamental Mathematical Definitions." In *The Princeton Companion to Mathematics*, 16–48. Princeton, NJ: Princeton University Press.
Aristotle. 1984. *The Complete Works of Aristotle: The Revised Oxford Translation*. Ed. Jonathan Barnes. Princeton, NJ: Princeton University Press.
Aristotle. 1989. *Prior Analytics*. Trans., with introduction, notes, and commentary, Robin Smith. Indianapolis: Hackett.
Aristoxenus. 1902. *The Harmonics of Aristoxenus*. Ed., with translation, notes, introduction, and index of words, Henry S. Macran. Oxford: Clarendon Press.
Artmann, Benno. 1991. "Euclid's *Elements* and Its Prehistory." *Apeiron* 24, no. 4 (October): 1–47.
Ashworth, E. Jennifer. 2017. "Medieval Theories of Analogy." In *The Stanford Encyclopedia of Philosophy* (Fall 2017 ed.), ed. Edward N. Zalta. https://plato.stanford.edu/archives/fall2017/entries/analogy-medieval/.
Astroh, Michael, and Stephan Read. 1998. "Introduction" to *Hugh MacColl and the Tradition of Logic*. *Nordic Journal of Philosophical Logic* 3, no. 1 (December): ii–vi.
Baader, Franz. 1798. *Über das pythagoräische Quadrat in der Natur oder die vier Weltgegenden*. Tübingen: Cotta.

Barbera, André. 1984a. "The Consonant Eleventh and the Expansion of the Musical Tetractys: A Study of Ancient Pythagoreanism." *Journal of Music Theory* 28, no. 2 (Autumn): 191–223.

Barbera, André. 1984b. "Placing *Sectio Canonis* in Historical and Philosophical Contexts." *Journal of Hellenic Studies* 104: 157–161.

Barbin, Évelyne, Marta Menghini, and Klaus Volkert, eds. 2019. *Descriptive Geometry, the Spread of a Polytechnic Art: The Legacy of Gaspard Monge*. Cham: Springer Nature.

Barker, Andrew, ed. 1989. *Greek Musical Writings*. Vol. 2, *Harmonic and Acoustic Theory*. Cambridge: Cambridge University Press.

Barker, Andrew. 1991. "Three Approaches to Canonic Division." *Apeiron* 24, no. 4 (March): 49–83.

Barker, Andrew. 2007. *The Science of Harmonics in Classical Greece*. Cambridge: Cambridge University Press.

Basso, Paola. 2010. "Lambert, Johann Heinrich (1728–1777)." In *The Dictionary of Eighteenth-Century German Philosophers*, ed. Heiner F. Klemme and Manfred Kuehn, 451–455. London: Continuum.

Beaney, Michael. 1996. *Frege Making Sense*. London: Bloomsbury Academic.

Beiser, Frederick. 2005. *Hegel*. New York: Routledge.

Bell, John L. 2019. *The Continuous, the Discrete, and the Infinitesimal in Philosophy and Mathematics*. Berlin: Springer.

Berkeley, George. 1996. *The Analyst*. In *From Kant to Hilbert: A Source Book in the Foundations of Mathematics*, ed. W. Ewald, 1:60–92. Oxford: Oxford University Press.

Betanzos, Ramón J. 1998. *Franz von Baader's Philosophy of Love*. Ed. Martin M. Herman. Vienna: Passagen Verlag.

Béziau Jean-Yves. 2017. "A Chromatic Hexagon of Psychic Dispositions." In *How Colours Matter to Philosophy*, ed. M. Silva, 273–288. Cham: Springer.

Billington, James H. 1980. *Fire in the Minds of Men: Origins of the Revolutionary Faith*. Boston: Basic Books.

Birkhoff, Garrett. 2020. "Lattice (mathematics)." *Access Science*. https://doi.org/10.1036/1097-8542 .373200.

Blackburn, Patrick. 2006. "Arthur Prior and Hybrid Logic." *Synthese* 150, no. 3 (June): 329–372.

Blanché, Robert. 1966. *Structures intellectuelles: Essai sur l'organisation systématique des concepts*. Paris: Vrin.

Bobzien, Susanne. 1997. "Stoic Conceptions of Freedom and Their Relation to Ethics." *Bulletin of the Institute of Classical Studies*, Supplement, no. 68: 71–89.

Bobzien, Susanne. 2020. "Ancient Logic." In *The Stanford Encyclopedia of Philosophy* (Summer 2020 ed.), ed. Edward N. Zalta. https://plato.stanford.edu/archives/sum2020/entries /logic-ancient/.

Bochenski, I. M. 1961. *A History of Formal Logic*. Trans. and ed. Ivo Thomas. Notre Dame: University of Notre Dame Press.

Boole, George. 1847. *The Mathematical Analysis of Logic, Being an Essay towards a Calculus of Deductive Reasoning*. Cambridge: Macmillan, Barclay and MacMillan.

Boole, George. 1854. *An Investigation of the Laws of Thought, on Which Are Founded the Mathematical Theories of Logic and Probabilities*. London: Macmillan and Co.

Borzacchini, Luigi. 2007. "Incommensurability, Music, and Continuum: A Cognitive Approach." *Archive for the History of Exact Sciences*, 61, no. 3 (May): 273–302.

Bos, H. J. M. 1980. "Newton, Leibniz, and the Leibnizian Tradition." In *From the Calculus to Set Theory, 1630–1910: An Introductory History*, ed. I. Grattan Guinness, 49–93. Princeton, NJ: Princeton University Press.

Bosley, Richard. 2013. "The Geometry of Diagrams and the Logic of Syllogisms." In *Visual Reasoning with Diagrams, Studies in Universal Logic*, ed. A Moktefi and S.-J. Shin, 19–31. Basel: Springer.

Bowman, Brady. 2013. *Hegel and the Metaphysics of Absolute Negativity*. Cambridge: Cambridge University Press.

Boyce Gibson, A. 1955. "Plato's Mathematical Imagination." *Review of Metaphysics* 9, no. 1 (September): 57–70.

Boyer, Carl B. 1959. *The History of Calculus and Its Conceptual Development*. Mineola, NY: Dover.

Brady, Geraldine. 2000. *From Peirce to Skolem: A Neglected Chapter in the History of Logic*. Amsterdam: Elsevier.

Brandom, Robert. 1994. *Making It Explicit: Reasoning, Representing, and Discursive Commitment*. Cambridge, MA: Harvard University Press.

Brandom, Robert B. 2008. *Between Saying and Doing: Towards an Analytic Pragmatism*. Oxford: Oxford University Press.

Brandom, Robert. 2009. *Reason in Philosophy. Animating Ideas*. Cambridge, MA: Harvard University Press.

Brandom, Robert. 2019. *A Spirit of Trust: A Reading of Hegel's Phenomenology*. Cambridge, MA: Harvard University Press.

Brumbaugh, Robert. 1954. *Plato's Mathematical Imagination: The Mathematical Passages in the Dialogues and Their Interpretation*. Bloomington: Indiana University Press.

Brumbaugh, Robert S. 1989. *Platonic Studies in Greek Philosophy: Form, Arts, Gadgets, and Hemlock*. Albany: State University of New York Press.

Brunning, Jacqueline. 1991. "C. S. Peirce's Relative Product." *Review of Modern Logic*, 2, no. 1 (September): 33–49.

Burkert, Walter. 1972. *Lore and Science in Ancient Pythagoreanism*. Trans. E. L. Minar Jr. Cambridge, MA: Harvard University Press.

Burnyeat, M. F. 2000. "Plato on Why Mathematics Is Good for the Soul." *Proceedings of the British Academy* 103 (January): 1–81.

Cajori, Florian. 1903. "History of the Exponential and Logarithmic Concepts, I and II." *American Mathematical Monthly* 20, no. 1 (January): 5–14 and no. 2 (February): 35–47.

Cantù, Paola. 2010. "Aristotle's Prohibition Rule on Kind-Crossing and the Definition of Mathematics as a Science of Quantities." *Synthese* 174, no. 2 (May): 225–235.

Carnot, L. N. M. 1797. *Réflexions sur la métaphysique du calcul infinitésimal*. Paris: Chez Duprat.

Carnot, L. N. M. 1800. *Betrachtungen über die Theorie der Infinitesimalrechnung*. Trans. Johann Karl Friedrich Hauff. Frankfurt am Main: Jägerschen Buchhandlung.

Carnot, L. N. M. 1801. *De la corrélation des figures de géométrie*. Paris: Chez Duprat, Libraire pour les Mathématiques.

Carnot, L. N. M. 1803a. *Géométrie de position*. Paris: Chez Duprat.

Carnot, L. N. M. 1803b. *Principes fondamentaux de l'équilibre et du mouvement*. Paris: Deterville.

Carnot, L. N. M. 1839. *Réflexions sur la métaphysique du calcul infinitésimal*. 3rd ed. Paris: Bachelier Imprimeur-Libraire.

Chasles, M. 1837. *Aperçu historique sur l'origine et le développement des méthodes en géométrie*. Brussels: M. Hayez, Imprimeur d L'Académie Royale.

Châtelet, Gilles. 2000. *Figuring Space: Philosophy, Mathematics, and Physics.* Trans. Robert Shore and Muriel Zagha. Dordrecht: Kluwer.

Christianson, Gale E. 1984. *In the Presence of the Creator: Isaac Newton and His Times.* New York: The Free Press.

Clifford, William Kingdon. 1878. "Applications of Grassmann's Extension Algebra." *American Journal of Mathematics* 1, no 4: 350–358.

Clifford, William Kingdon. 1886. *The Common Sense of the Exact Sciences.* 2nd ed. London: Kegan Paul, Trench, and Co.

Cohen, S. Marc. 2016. "Aristotle's Metaphysics." In *The Stanford Encyclopedia of Philosophy* (Winter 2016 ed.), ed. Edward N. Zalta. https://plato.stanford.edu/archives/win2016/entries/aristotle-metaphysics/.

Coolidge, J. T. 1934. "The Rise and Fall of Projective Geometry." *American Mathematical Monthly* 41, no. 4 (April): 217–228.

Corcoran, John. 2003. "Aristotle's *Prior Analytics* and Boole's *Laws of Thought*." *History and Philosophy of Logic* 24, no. 4: 261–288.

Correia, Manuel. 2017. "Aristotle's Squares of Opposition." *South American Journal of Logic* 3, no. 1 (July): 1–14.

Cortese, Joào Figueirdo Nobre. 2015. "Infinity between Mathematics and Apologetics: Pascal's Notion of Infinite Distance." *Synthese* 192, no. 8 (August): 2379–2393.

Couturat, Louis. 1901. *La logique de Leibniz, d'après des documents inédits.* Paris: Félix Alcan.

Couturat, Louis. 1903. *Opuscules et fragments inédits de Leibniz: Extraits de la Bibliothèque royale de Hanovre.* Paris: Félix Alcan.

Coxeter, H. S. M. 1987. *Projective Geometry.* New York: Springer.

Craig, E., and M. Hoskin. 1992. "Hegel and the Seven Planets." *Journal for the History of Astronomy* 23, no. 3 (August): 208–210.

Crivelli, Paolo. 2004. *Aristotle on Truth.* Cambridge: Cambridge University Press.

Czezowski, Tadeusz. 1955. "On Certain Peculiarities of Singular Propositions." *Mind* 64, no. 255 (July): 392–395.

Del Centina, Andrea. 2016. "On Kepler's System of Conics in *Astromomiae pars optica*." *Archive for History of Exact Sciences* 70, no. 6 (November): 567–589.

Del Centina, Andrea. 2020. "Pascal's *Mystic Hexagram*, and a Conjectural Restoration of His Lost Treatise on Conic Sections." *Archive for History of Exact Sciences* 74, no. 5 (September): 469–521.

Demey, Lorenz, and Hans Smessaert. 2022. "Duality in Logic and Language." In *The Internet Encyclopedia of Philosophy.* https://iep.utm.edu/dual-log/.

Deranty, Jean-Philippe. 2005. "Hegel's Social Theory of Value." *Philosophical Forum* 36, no. 3 (August): 307–331.

De Risi, Vincenzo. 2007. *Geometry and Monadology: Leibniz's "Analysis Situs" and Philosophy of Space.* Basel: Birkhäuser.

De Risi, Vincenzo. 2018. "Analysis Situs, the Foundations of Mathematics, and a Geometry of Space." In *The Oxford Handbook of Leibniz,* ed. Maria Rosa Antognazza, 247–258. Oxford: Oxford University Press.

Descartes, René. 1954. *The Geometry of Rene Descartes, with a Facsimile of the First Edition.* Trans. David E. Smith and Marcia L. Latham. New York: Dover Publications. Originally published 1637.

Des Jardins, Gregory. 1976. "How to Divide the Divided Line." *Review of Metaphysics* 29, no. 3 (March): 483–496.

Detlefsen, Michael. 1998. "Constructive Existence Claims." In *The Philosophy of Mathematics Today*, ed. Matthias Schirn, 307–335. Oxford: Clarendon Press.

D'Hondt, Jacques. 1968. *Hegel secret: Recherches sur les sources cachées de la pensée de Hegel*. Paris: Presses Universitaires de France.

Di Cosmo, Roberto, and Dale Miller. 2019. "Linear Logic." In *The Stanford Encyclopedia of Philosophy* (Summer 2019 ed.), ed. Edward N. Zalta. https://plato.stanford.edu/archives/sum2019/entries/logic-linear/.

Dieudonné, Jean. 1985. *History of Algebraic Geometry: An Outline of the History and Development of Algebraic Geometry*. Trans. Judith D. Sally. Monterey, CA: Wadsworth.

Di Giovanni, George. 2021. "Determination (*Bestimmung*)." In *The Cambridge Kant Lexicon*, ed. Julian Wuerth, 145–146. Cambridge: Cambridge University Press.

Dorier, Jean-Luc. 1995. "A General Outline of the Genesis of Vector Space Theory." *Historia Mathematica* 22, no. 3 (August): 227–261.

Dreher, John Paul. 1990. "The Driving Ratio in Plato's Divided Line." *Ancient Philosophy* 10, no. 2 (Fall): 159–172.

Durkheim, Émile, and Marcel Mauss. 1903. "Essai sur quelques formes primitives de classification." *L'Année Sociologique* 6: 1–72.

Dutilh Novaes, Catarina. 2012. *Formal Languages in Logic: A Philosophical and Cognitive Analysis*. Cambridge: Cambridge University Press.

Echterling, Terry. 2018. "What Did Glaucon Draw? A Diagrammatic Proof for Plato's Divided Line." *Journal of the History of Philosophy* 56, no. 1 (January): 1–15.

Einarson, Benedict. 1936. "On Certain Mathematical Terms in Aristotle's Logic: Parts I and II." *American Journal of Philology* 57, no. 1: 33–54 and 57, no. 2: 151–172.

Englebretsen, George. 1986. "Czezowski on Wild Quantity." *Notre Dame Journal of Formal Logic* 27, no. 1 (January): 62–65.

Englebretsen, George. 1988. "A Note on Leibniz's Wild Quantity Thesis." *Studia Leibnitiana* 20, no. 1: 87–89.

Eschenmayer, A. C. A. 2020. "Spontaneity = World Soul, or the Highest Principle of Philosophy of Nature." In Benjamin Berger and Daniel Whistler. *The Schelling-Eschenmayer Controversy, 1801: Nature and Identity*, 17–45. Edinburgh: Edinburgh University Press.

Euclid. 1956. *The Thirteen Books of Euclid's Elements*. Trans. from the text of Heiberg, with introduction and commentary, Sir Thomas L. Heath. 3 vols. New York: Dover.

Euclid. 1975. "An Annotated Translation of Euclid's 'Division of a Monochord,'" trans. Thomas J. Mathiesen. *Journal of Music Theory* 19, no. 2 (Autumn): 236–258.

Ewald, William, ed. 1996. *From Kant to Hilbert: A Source Book in the Foundations of Mathematics*. 2 vols. Oxford: Oxford University Press.

Falkenburg, Brigitte. 1998. "How to Save the Phenomena: Meaning and Reference in Hegel's Philosophy of Nature." In *Hegel and the Philosophy of Nature*, ed. Stephen Houlgate, 97–136. Albany: State University of New York Press.

Ferguson, Kitty. 2010. *Pythagoras: His Lives and the Legacy of a Rational Universe*. London: Icon.

Ferreirós, José. 2016. *Mathematical Knowledge and the Interplay of Practices*. Princeton, NJ: Princeton University Press.

Ferrini, Cinzia. 1994. "On Newton's Demonstration of Kepler's Second Law in Hegel's *De Orbitis Planetarum* (1801). *Philosophia Naturalis* 31: 150–170.

Ficara, Elena. 2021. *The Form of Truth: Hegel's Philosophical Logic*. Berlin: Walter de Gruyter.

Fichte, J. G. 1994. "An Attempt at a New Presentation of the *Wissenschaftslehre* (1797/98): First Introduction." In *Introductions to the Wissenschaftslehre and Other Writings (1797–1800)*, ed. and trans. Daniel Breazeale, 1–35. Indianapolis: Hackett.

Field, J. V., and J. J. Gray. 1987. *The Geometrical Works of Girard Desargues*. New York: Springer Verlag.

Findlay, John N. 1942. "Goedelian Sentences: A Non-Numerical Approach." *Mind* 51, no. 203 (July): 259–265.

Findlay, John N. 1958. *Hegel: A Re-examination*. London: Routledge.

Findlay, John N. 1963. "The Contemporary Relevance of Hegel." In *Values and Intentions: A Study in Value Theory and Philosophy of Mind*, 217–231. London: George Allen and Unwin.

Findlay, John N. 1970. "Towards a Neo-neo-Platonism." In *Ascent to the Absolute: Metaphysical Papers and Lectures*, 248–267. London: George Allen and Unwin.

Findlay, John N. 1974a. "Hegelianism and Platonism." In *Hegel and the History of Philosophy: Proceedings of the 1972 Hegel Society of America Conference*, ed. Joseph J. O'Malley, K. W. Algozin, and Frederick G. Weiss, 62–76. The Hague: Martinus Nijhoff.

Findlay, John N. 1974b. *Plato: The Written and Unwritten Doctrines*. London: Routledge.

Findlay, John N. 1983. "Plato's Unwritten Dialectic of the One and the Great and Small." *Society for Ancient Greek Philosophy Newsletter* 113. https://orb.binghamton.edu/sagp/113.

Fisher, Jeffrey J. 2018. "Measurement and Mathematics in Plato's *Statesman*." *Ancient Philosophy* 38, no. 1: 69–78.

Förster, Eckart. 2012. *The Twenty-Five Years of Philosophy: A Systematic Reconstruction*. Trans. Brady Bowman. Cambridge, MA: Harvard University Press.

Fossa, John A., and Glenn W. Erickson. 2005. "The Divided Line and the Golden Mean." *Revista Brasileira de História de Matemática* 5, no. 9 (September): 59–77.

Fossheim, Hallvard. 2012. "Division as a Method in Plato." In *The Development of Dialectic from Plato to Aristotle*, ed. Jakob L. Fink, 91–114. Cambridge: Cambridge University Press.

Foucault, Michel. 1970. *The Order of Things: An Archaeology of the Human Sciences*. Trans. Alan Sheridan. London: Tavistock.

Francoeur, L. B. 1807. *Traité élémentaire de mécanique*. 4th ed. Paris: Klostermann.

Franz, Michael. 2005. "Gottfried Ploucquets Urteilslehre in Rahmen der Logikgeschichte des 18. Jahrhunderts." *Zeitschrift für philosophischen Forschung* 59, no. 1: 95–113.

Frege, Gottlob. 1960. "A Critical Elucidation of Some Points in E. Schröder's *Vorlesungen über die Algebra der Logik*," trans. Peter Geach. In Peter Geach and Max Black, *Translations from the Philosophical Writings of Gottlob Frege*, 86–106. Oxford: Blackwell.

Frege, Gottlob. 1979. "Boole's Logical Calculus and the Concept-Script." In *Posthumous Writings*, ed. Hans Kermes, Friedrich Kambartel, and Friedrich Kaulbach, trans. Peter Long and Roger White, 9–46. Oxford: Blackwell.

Frege, Gottlob. 1980. *Philosophical and Mathematical Correspondence*. Ed. G. Gabriel, H. Hermes, F. Kambartel, C. Thiel, and A. Veraart. Abridged for the English edition by B. McGuinness and trans. H. Kaal. Oxford: Blackwell.

Frege, Gottlob. 1997. "Begriffsschrift." In *The Frege Reader*, ed. Michael Beaney, 47–78. Oxford: Blackwell.

Friedman, Michael. 2013. *Kant's Construction of Nature: A Reading of the "Metaphysical Foundations of Natural Science."* Cambridge: Cambridge University Press.

Gallie, W. B. 1964. "Essentially Contested Concepts." In *Philosophy and the Historical Understanding*, 157–191. London: Chatto and Windus.

Gibson, Sophie. 2005. *Aristoxenus of Tarentum and the Birth of Musicology*. New York: Routledge.
Gillies, Alexander. 1941. "The Macrocosmos-Sign in Goethe's 'Faust' and Herder's Mystic Hexagram." *Modern Language Review* 36, no. 3 (July): 397–399.
Gillispie, Charles Colston, and Raffaele Pisano. 2013. *Lazare and Sadi Carnot: A Scientific and Filial Relationship*. 2nd ed. Dordrecht: Springer.
Glashoff, Klaus. 2010. "An Intensional Leibniz Semantics for Aristotelian Logic." *Review of Symbolic Logic* 3, no. 2 (June): 262–272.
Goethe, Johann Wolfgang von. 1988. *Scientific Studies*. Ed. and trans. Douglas Miller. Princeton, NJ: Princeton University Press.
Gouvêa, Fernando Q. 2008. "From Numbers to Number Systems." In *The Princeton Companion to Mathematics*, 77–83. Princeton, NJ: Princeton University Press.
Graham, Daniel W. 2014. "Philolaus." In *A History of Pythagoreanism*, ed. Carl A. Huffman, 46–68. Cambridge: Cambridge University Press.
Grant, Edward. 1981. *Much Ado about Nothing: Theories of Space and Vacuum from the Middle Ages to the Scientific Revolution*. Cambridge: Cambridge University Press.
Grassmann, Hermann. 1995. *A New Branch of Mathematics: The Ausdehnungslehre of 1844, and Other Works*. Trans. Lloyd C. Kannenberg. Foreword by Albert C. Lewis. Chicago: Open Court.
Gray, Jeremy. 2007. *Worlds Out of Nothing: A Course in the History of Geometry in the 19th Century*. London: Springer.
Gueniffey, Patrice. 1989. "Carnot." In *A Critical Dictionary of the French Revolution*, ed. Francois Furet and Mona Ozouf, trans. Arthur Goldhammer, 197–203. Cambridge, MA: Harvard University Press.
Halsted, George Bruce. 1896. "Subconscious Pangeometry." *The Monist* 7, no. 1 (October): 100–106.
Harris, H. S. 1972. *Hegel's Development I: Towards the Sunlight, 1770–1801*. Oxford: Clarendon Press.
Harris, H. S. 1983. *Hegel's Development: Night Thoughts (Jena 1801–1806)*. Oxford: Oxford University Press.
Harris, H. S. 1997. *Hegel's Ladder*. 2 vols. Indianapolis: Hackett.
Hauff, Johan Karl Friedrich. 1800. "Vorrede des Übersetzers" [Translator's preface] to L. N. M. Carnot, *Betrachtungen über die Theorie der Infinitesimalrechnung*. Trans. Johann Karl Friedrich Hauff. Frankfurt am Main: Jägerschen Buchhandlung.
Heath, T. L. 1896. *Apollonius of Perga: Treatise on Conic Sections*. Edited in modern notation with introductions including an essay on the earlier history of the subject. Cambridge: Cambridge University Press.
Heath, T. L. 1897. *The Work of Archimedes*. Edited in modern notation with introductory chapters by T. L. Heath. Cambridge: Cambridge University Press.
Heath, T. L. 1910. *Diophantus of Alexandria: A Study in the History of Greek Algebra*. 2nd ed. Cambridge: Cambridge University Press.
Heath, T. L. 1921. *A History of Greek Mathematics*. 2 vols. Oxford: Clarendon Press.
Heath, T. L. 1949. *Mathematics in Aristotle*. Oxford: Oxford University Press.
Hestenes, David, and Garret Sobczyk. 1984. *Clifford Algebra to Geometric Calculus: A Unified Language for Mathematics and Physics*. Dordrecht: Springer.
Heuser, Marie-Luise. 2011. "The Significance of *Naturphilosophie* for Justus and Hermann Grassmann." In *Hermann Graßmann from Past to Future: Graßmann's Work in Context (Graßmann*

Bicentennial Conference, September 2009), ed. Hans-Joachim Petsche, Albert C. Lewis, Jörg Liesen, and Steve Russ, 49–60. Basel: Springer.

Hoffmann, Michael. 2010. "'Theoric Transformations' and a New Classification of Abductive Inferences." *Transactions of the Charles S. Peirce Society* 46, no. 4 (Fall): 570–590.

Holland, Jocelyn. 2019. *The Lever as Instrument of Reason: Technological Constructions of Knowledge around 1800*. London: Bloomsbury.

Hopper, Vincent Foster. 1938. *Medieval Number Symbolism: Its Sources, Meaning, and Influence on Thought and Expression*. New York: Columbia University Press.

Horky, Phillip Sidney. 2013. *Plato and Pythagoreanism*. Oxford: Oxford University Press.

Horn, Laurence. 2017. "The Singular Square: Contrariety and Double Negation from Aristotle to Homer." In *Formal Models in the Study of Language: Applications in Interdisciplinary Contexts*, ed. J. Blochowiack, C. Grisot, S. Durrleman, and C. Laenzlinger, 143–179. Berlin: Springer.

Houlgate, Stephen. 2006. *The Opening of Hegel's "Logic": From Being to Infinity*. West Lafayette: Purdue University Press.

Houlgate, Stephen. 2014. "Hegel on the Category of Quantity." *Hegel Bulletin* 35, no. 1 (May): 16–32.

Houser, Nathan. 1994. "Algebraic Logic from Boole to Schröder, 1840–1900." In *Companion Encyclopedia of the History and Philosophy of the Mathematical Sciences*, ed. Ivor Grattan-Guinness, 600–616. Abingdon: Taylor and Francis.

Houser, Nathan. 1997. "Peirce as Logician." In *Studies in the Logic of Charles Sanders Peirce*, ed. Nathan Houser, Don D. Roberts, and James Van Evra, 1–22. Bloomington: Indiana University Press.

Høyrup, Jens. 2017. "What Is 'Geometric Algebra,' and What Has It Been in Historiography?" *AIMS Mathematics* 2, no. 1: 128–160. https://doi.org/10.3934/Math.2017.1.128.

Humberstone, Lloyd. 2004. "Two-Dimensional Adventures." *Philosophical Studies* 118, nos. 1–2 (March): 17–65.

Hutin, Serge. 1960. *Les disciples anglais de Jacob Boehme aux XVIIe et XVIIIe siècles*. Paris: Éditions Denoël.

Iamblichus. 1988. *The Theology of Arithmetic*. Trans. Robin Waterfield with a foreword by Keith Crichlow. Grand Rapids, MI: Phanes Press.

Jaki, Stanley L. 1976. "Introduction" to Johann Heinrich Lambert, *Cosmological Letters on the Arrangement of the World-Edifice*. Edinburgh: Scottish Academic Press.

Johnson, W. E. 1892. "The Logical Calculus, Parts I, II, and III." *Mind*, n.s., 1, no. 1: 3–30; 1, no. 2: 235–250; 1, no. 3: 340–357.

Johnson, W. E. 1921. *Logic: Part I*. Cambridge: Cambridge University Press.

Johnson, W. E. 1922. *Logic: Part II, Demonstrative Inference: Deductive and Inductive*. Cambridge: Cambridge University Press.

Jourdain, P. E. B. 1914. "Preface" to Louis Couturat, *The Algebra of Logic*, i–v. Chicago: Open Court.

Kant, Immanuel. 1985. *Philosophy of Material Nature: The Complete Texts of Prolegomena to Any Future Metaphysics That Will Be Able to Come Forward as Science and Metaphysical Foundations of Natural Science*. Trans. Paul Carus and James W. Ellington. Indianapolis: Hackett.

Kant, Immanuel. 1992a. "Attempt to Introduce the Concept of Negative Magnitudes into Philosophy (1763)." In *Theoretical Philosophy, 1755–1770*, trans. and ed. David Walford in collaboration with Ralf Meerbote, 207–241. Cambridge: Cambridge University Press.

Kant, Immanuel. 1992b. "Concerning the Ultimate Ground of the Differentiation of Directions in Space (1768)." In *Theoretical Philosophy, 1755–1770*, trans. and ed. David Walford in collaboration with Ralf Meerbote, 365–372. Cambridge: Cambridge University Press.
Kant, Immanuel. 1992c. *The Jäsche Logic*. In *Lectures on Logic*, trans. and ed. J. Michael Young, 521–640. Cambridge: Cambridge University Press.
Kant, Immanuel. 1997. *Prolegomena to Any Future Metaphysics That Will be Able to Come Forward as Science*. Trans. and ed. Gary Hatfield. Cambridge: Cambridge University Press.
Kant, Immanuel. 1998. *Critique of Pure Reason*. Ed. and trans. Paul Guyer and Allen W. Wood. Cambridge: Cambridge University Press.
Kant, Immanuel. 2000. *Critique of the Power of Judgment*. Ed. Paul Guyer and trans. Paul Guyer and Eric Matthews. Cambridge: Cambridge University Press.
Kates, Gary. 1985. *The Cercle Social, the Girondins, and the French Revolution*. Princeton, NJ: Princeton University Press.
Kaufmann, Ralph M., and Christopher Yeomans. 2017. "Hegel on Calculus." *History of Philosophy Quarterly* 34, no. 4 (October): 371–389.
Kaulbach, Friedrich. 1973. "Das copernicanische Prinzip und die philosophische Sprache bei Leibniz." *Zeitschrift für philosophische Forschung* 27, no. 3 (July–September): 333–347.
Klein, Felix. 1893. "A Comparative Review of Recent Researches in Geometry" (A Translation by M. W. Haskell of *Vergleichende Betrachtungen über neuere geometrische Forschungen* [1872]). *Bulletin of the New York Mathematical Society* 2, no. 10 (July): 215–249.
Klein, Jacob. 1968. *Greek Mathematical Thought and the Origin of Algebra*. Trans. Eva Brann. Cambridge, MA: MIT Press.
Klein, Jacob. 1985. "The Concept of Number in Greek Mathematics and Philosophy." In *Jacob Klein: Lectures and Essays*, ed. Robert B. Williamson and Elliott Zuckerman, 43–52. Annapolis: St. John's College Press.
Knorr, Wilbur Richard. 1975. *The Evolution of Euclidean Elements*. Dordrecht: Reidel.
Knorr, Wilbur Richard. 1986. *The Ancient Tradition of Geometric Problems*. Boston: Birkhäuser.
Krämer, Hans Joachim. 1990. *Plato and the Foundations of Metaphysics: A Work on the Theory of the Principles and Unwritten Doctrines of Plato with a Collection of the Fundamental Documents*. Ed. and trans. John R. Catan. Albany: State University of New York Press.
Kreines, James. 2015. *Reason in the World: Hegel's Metaphysics and Its Philosophical Appeal*. New York: Oxford University Press.
Kripke, Saul A. 1972. *Naming and Necessity*. Cambridge, MA.: Harvard University Press.
Kuhn, Thomas. 1962. *The Structure of Scientific Revolutions*. Chicago: University of Chicago Press.
Lambert, Johann Heinrich. 1976. *Cosmological Letters on the Arrangement of the World-Edifice*. Trans., with an introduction and notes, Stanley L. Jaki. Edinburgh: Scottish Academic Press.
Lasserre, François. 1964. *The Birth of Mathematics in the Age of Plato*. London: Hutchinson.
Lawvere, F. William. 1996. "Unity and Identity of Opposites in Calculus and Physics." *Applied Categorical Structures* 4, nos. 2–3 (June): 167–174.
Leibniz, G. W. 1966. *Logical Papers: A Selection Translated and Edited with an Introduction by G. H. R Parkinson*. Oxford: Oxford University Press.
Leibniz, G. W. 1989a. *Philosophical Essays*. Trans. and ed. Roger Ariew and Daniel Garber. Indianapolis: Hackett.
Leibniz, G. W. 1989b. *Philosophical Papers and Letters: A Selection Translated and Edited, with an Introduction by Leroy E. Loemker*. 2nd ed. Dordrecht: Kluwer.

Leibniz, G. W. 1996. *New Essays on Human Understanding*. Trans. and ed. Peter Remnant and Jonathan Bennett. Cambridge: Cambridge University Press.

Leibniz, G. W. 1998. *Philosophical Texts*. Trans. and ed. R. S Woolhouse and Richard Francks. Oxford: Oxford University Press.

Leibniz, G. W. 2006. *Philosophischer Briefwechsel*. Ed. Leibniz-Forschungsstelle der Universität Münster. Berlin: Akademie Verlag.

Lemanski, Jens. 2017. "Periods in the Use of Euler-Type Diagrams." *Acta Baltica Historiae et Philosophiae Scientiarum* 5, no. 1 (Spring): 50–69.

Lenzen, W. 1990. *Das System der leibnizschen Logik*. Berlin: Walter de Gruyter.

Lenzen, W. 2004. "Leibniz's Logic." In *Handbook of the History of Logic*, vol. 3, *The Rise of Modern Logic: From Leibniz to Frege*, ed. Dov M. Gabbay and John Woods, 5–92. Amsterdam, Elsevier.

Leuer, Dennis Osborn. 1976. "Life and Works of Franz von Baader." PhD thesis, University of Oxford. Oxford University Research Archive. https://ora.ox.ac.uk/objects/uuid:a75f97cc-8968-40ad-8529-25f6e48396e5.

Lewis, Albert C. 1977. "H. Grassmann's 1844 *Ausdehnungslehre* and Schleiermacher's *Dialektik*." *Annals of Science* 34, no. 2: 103–162.

Lewis, C. I. 1912. "Implication and the Algebra of Logic." *Mind* 21, no. 84 (October): 522–531.

Lewis, C. I. 1918. *A Survey of Symbolic Logic*. Berkeley: University of California Press.

Lewis, C. I., and C. H. Langford. 1932. *Symbolic Logic*. New York: Century.

Liddell, Henry George, and Robert Scott. 1882. *Greek-English Lexicon*. 7th ed. New York: Harper and Brothers.

Lloyd, G. E. R. 1966. *Polarity and Analogy: Two Types of Argumentation in Early Greek Thought*. Cambridge: Cambridge University Press.

Lu Adler, Huapang. 2017. "From Logical Calculus to Logical Formality: What Kant Did with Euler's Circles." In *Kant and His German Contemporaries*, vol. 1, *Logic, Mind, Epistemology, Science, and Ethics*, ed. Corey W. Dyck and Falk Wunderlich, 35–55. Cambridge: Cambridge University Press.

Lukács, György. 1975. *The Young Hegel*. Trans. R. Livingstone. London: Merlin.

Łukasiewicz, Jan. 1953. "A System of Modal Logic." *Proceedings of the XIth International Congress of Philosophy* 14: 82–87.

Łukasiewicz, Jan. 1957. *Aristotle's Syllogistic from the Standpoint of Modern Formal Logic*. Oxford: Oxford University Press.

MacColl, Hugh. 1906. *Symbolic Logic and Its Applications*. London: Longmans, Green.

MacColl, Hugh. 1907. "Symbolic Logic (a Reply)." *Mind* 16, no. 63 (July): 470–473.

Malink, Marko. 2016. "Aristotle on One-Sided Possibility." In *Logical Modalities From Aristotle to Carnap: The Story of Necessity*, ed. Max Cresswell, Edwin Mares, and Adriane Rini, 29–49. Cambridge: Cambridge University Press.

Malink, Marko, and Anubav Vasudevan. 2016. "The Logic of Leibniz's *Generales Inquisitiones de Analysi Notionum et Veritatum*." *Review of Symbolic Logic* 9, no. 4 (December): 686–751.

Marciszewski, Witold, and Roman Murawski. 1995. *Mechanization of Reasoning in a Historical Perspective*. Amsterdam: Ripodi.

Markowsky, George. 1992. "Misconceptions about the Golden Ratio." *College Mathematics Journal* 23, no. 1 (January): 2–19.

Martin, Christopher J. 1991. "The Logic of Negation in Boethius." *Phronesis* 36, no. 3 (January): 277–304.

Martinez, Alberto A. 2006. *Negative Math: How Mathematical Rules Can Be Positively Bent.* Princeton, NJ: Princeton University Press.
McDowell, John H. 2003. "The Apperceptive I and the Empirical Self: Toward a Heterodox Reading of 'Lordship and Bondage.'" *Hegel Bulletin* 24, nos. 1–2: 1–16.
McKirahan, Richard. 1992. *Principles and Proofs: Aristotle's Theory of Demonstrative Science.* Princeton, NJ: Princeton University Press.
McKirahan, Richard D. 2010. *Philosophy before Socrates: An Introduction with Texts and Commentary.* 2nd ed. Indianapolis: Hackett.
Mense, André. 1993. "Hegel's Library: The Works on Mathematics, Mechanics, Optics, and Chemistry." In *Hegel and Newtonianism*, ed. M. J. Perry, 669–709. Dordrecht: Kluwer.
Mesnard, J. 1978. "Leibniz et les papiers de Pascal." In *Leibniz à Paris (1672–1676)*, ed. A. Heinekamp and D. Metter, 45–58. Wiesbaden: Franz Steiner Verlag.
Moktefi, Amirouche, and Sun-Joo Shin. 2012. "A History of Logic Diagrams." In *Logic: A History of Its Central Concepts*, ed. D. M. Gabbay, F. J. Pelletier, and J. Woods, 611–682. Amsterdam: North-Holland.
Monge, Gaspard. 1799. *Géométrie descriptive: Leçons données aux École normales, L'An 3 de la République.* Paris: Baudouin.
Montgomery, H., and R. Routley. 1966. "Contingency and Non-contingency Bases for Normal Modal Logics." *Logique et Analyse* 9, nos. 35–36 (December): 318–328.
Moschovakis, J. R. 2009. "The Logic of Brouwer and Heyting." In *The Handbook of the History of Logic*, ed. D. Gabbay, 5:77–125. Amsterdam: Elsevier.
Moyar, Dean. 2021. *Hegel's Value: Justice as the Living Good.* Oxford: Oxford University Press.
Müller, Johann Wolfgang. 1797. *Commentar über zwei dunkle mathematische Stellen in Plato's Schriften, wovon die eine im Theätet, die andere im Meno vorkommt.* Nuremberg: Georg Paul Pech.
Nagel, Ernest. 1939. "The Formation of Modern Conceptions of Formal Logic in the Development of Geometry." *Osiris* 7: 142–223.
Nagel, Ernest. 1979. "'Impossible Numbers': A Chapter in the History of Modern Logic." In *Studies in the History of Ideas*, vol. 3, *Teleology Revisited and Other Essays in the Philosophy and History of Science*, 166–194. New York: Columbia University Press. Originally published 1935.
Netz, Reviel. 1999. *The Shaping of Deduction in Greek Mathematics: A Study in Cognitive History.* Cambridge: Cambridge University Press.
Newton, Isaac. 2012. *Opticks: Or, A Treatise of the Reflections, Refractions, Inflections, and Colours of Light.* Based on the Fourth Edition, London, 1730. New York: Dover.
Newton, Isaac. 2016. *The Principia: The Authoritative Translation; Mathematical Principles of Natural Philosophy.* Trans. I. Bernard Cohen and Anne Whitman, with Julia Budenz. Berkeley: University of California Press.
Ng, Karen. 2020. *Hegel's Concept of Life: Self-Consciousness, Freedom, Logic.* Oxford: Oxford University Press.
Nicomachus of Gerasa. 1926. *Introduction to Arithmetic.* Trans. Martin Luther D'Ooge, with studies in Greek arithmetic by Frank Egleston Robins and Louis Charles Karpinski. New York: Macmillan.
Nikulin, Dmitri. 2012. *The Other Plato: The Tübingen Interpretation of Plato's Inner-Academic Teachings.* Albany: State University of New York Press.
Ockham, William of. 1980. *Ockham's Theory of Propositions: Part II of the Summa Logicae.* Trans. Alfred J. Freddoso and Henry Schuurman. Notre Dame: University of Notre Dame Press.

Otte, Michael. 2011. "Justus and Hermann Grassmann: Philosophy and Mathematics." In *Hermann Graßmann from Past to Future: Graßmann's Work in Context (Graßmann Bicentennial Conference, September 2009)*, ed. Hans-Joachim Petsche, Albert C. Lewis, Jörg Liesen, and Steve Russ, 61–70. Basel: Springer.

Pappus of Alexandria. 1941. "Problems and Theorems." In *Greek Mathematical Works*, vol. 2, *Aristarchus to Pappus*, ed. and trans. Ivor Thomas, 566–571. Cambridge, MA: Harvard University Press.

Parsons, Terence. 2017. "The Traditional Square of Opposition." In *The Stanford Encyclopedia of Philosophy* (Summer 2017 ed.), ed. Edward N. Zalta. https://plato.stanford.edu/archives/sum2017/entries/square/.

Paterson, Alan L. T. 2005. "Hegel's Early Geometry." *Hegel-Studien* 39/40: 61–124.

Patzig, Günther. 1968. *Aristotle's Theory of the Syllogism: A Logico-Philosophical Study of Book A of the "Prior Analytics."* Trans. J. Barnes. Dordrecht: Reidel.

Peckhaus, Volker. 1999. "Hugh MacColl and the German Algebra of Logic." *Nordic Journal of Philosophical Logic* 3, no. 1 (December): 17–34.

Peckhaus, Volker. 2014. "Ernst Schröder on Pasigraphy." *Revue d'Histoire des Sciences* 67, no. 2 (July–December): 207–230.

Peirce, Benjamin. 1881. "Linear Associative Algebra." *American Journal of Mathematics* 4: 97–229.

Peirce, C. S. 1870. "Description of a Notation for the Logic of Relatives, resulting from an Amplification of the Conceptions of Boole's Calculus of Logic." Reprinted in *Writings of Charles S. Peirce: A Chronological Edition*, vol. 2, *1867–1871*, ed. Edward C. Moore, Max H. Fisch, Christian J. W. Kloesel, Don D. Roberts, and Lynn A. Ziegler, 359–432. Bloomington: Indiana University Press, 1984.

Peirce, C. S. 1885. "On the Algebra of Logic: A Contribution to the Philosophy of Notation." Reprinted in *Writings of Charles S. Peirce: A Chronological Edition*, vol. 5, *1884–1886*, ed. Christian J. W. Kloesel, 258–291. Bloomington: Indiana University Press, 1993.

Peirce, C. S. 1992. *The Essential Peirce: Selected Philosophical Writings*. Vol. 1, *1867–1893*. Ed. Nathan Houser and Christian Kloesel. Bloomington: Indiana University Press.

Peirce, C. S. 1998. *The Essential Peirce: Selected Philosophical Writings*. Vol. 2, *1893–1913*. Ed. The Peirce Edition Project. Bloomington: Indiana University Press.

Peirce, C. S. 2010. *Philosophy of Mathematics: Selected Writings*. Ed. Matthew E. Moore. Bloomington: Indiana University Press.

Peirce, C. S., Alan Marquand, Christine Ladd-Franklin, O. H. Mitchell, and Benjamin Ives Gilman. 1883. *Studies in Logic*. Boston: Little, Brown.

Petersen, Uwe. 2018. "The Logical Foundation of Dialectic—A Short Outline." *Academia.edu*. https://www.academia.edu/37662548/THE_LOGICAL_FOUNDATION_OF_DIALECTIC_A_SHORT_OUTLINE.

Petsche, Hans-Joachim. 2009. *Hermann Grassmann: Biography*. Basel: Birkhäuser.

Pierce, R. C. 1977. "A Brief History of Logarithms." *Two-Year College Mathematics Journal* 8, no. 1 (January): 22–26.

Pinkard, Terry. 2000. *Hegel: A Biography*. Cambridge: Cambridge University Press.

Pinkard, Terry. 2012. *Hegel's Naturalism: Mind, Nature, and the Final Ends of Life*. Oxford: Oxford University Press.

Pippin, Robert. 2019. *Hegel's Realm of Shadows: Logic as Metaphysics in "The Science of Logic."* Chicago: University of Chicago Press.

Plato. 1997. *Complete Works*. Ed., with introduction and notes, John M. Cooper. Indianapolis: Hackett.
Plevrakis, Ermylos. 2020. "The Aristotelian *Theos* in Hegel's *Philosophy of Mind*." *Hegel Bulletin* 41, no. 1 (April): 83–101.
Ploucquet, Gottfried. 2006. *Logik*. Ed. and trans., with an introduction, Michael Franz. Hildesheim: Georg Olms.
Popper, Karl R. 1962. *Conjectures and Refutations: The Growth of Scientific Knowledge*. New York: Basic Books.
Porphyry. 2006. *Introduction*. Trans., with an introduction and commentary, Jonathan Barnes. Oxford: Clarendon Press.
Porubský, Štefan. 2010. "Prosthaphaeresis—a Forgotten Algorithm." In *Kepler's Heritage in the Space Age (400th Anniversary of Astronomia nova)*, ed. Alena Hadravová, Terence J. Mahoney, and Petr Hadrava, 63–77. Prague: National Technical Museum in Prague.
Posch, Thomas. 2011. "Hegel and the Sciences." In *A Companion to Hegel*, ed. Stephen Houlgate and Michael Baur, 177–202. Chichester: Wiley-Blackwell.
Pozzo, Roberto. 2010. "Gottfried Ploucquet." In *The Dictionary of Eighteenth-Century German Philosophy*, ed. Heiner F. Klemme and Manfred Kuehn, 2:899–903. London: Continuum.
Prier, Raymond Aldoph. 1976. "Some Thoughts on the Archaic Use of Metron." *Classical World* 70, no. 3 (November): 161–169.
Priest, Graham. 1989/1990. "Dialectic and Dialethic." *Science and Society* 53, no. 4 (Winter): 388–415.
Prior, Arthur N. 1949. "Categoricals and Hypotheticals in George Boole and His Successors." *Australasian Journal of Psychology and Philosophy* 27, no. 3: 171–196.
Prior, Arthur N. 1957. *Time and Modality, being the John Locke Lectures for 1955–1956 Delivered in the University of Oxford*. Oxford: Oxford University Press.
Prior, Arthur N. 1967. *Past, Present, and Future*. Oxford: Clarendon Press.
Proclus. 1970. *A Commentary on the First Book of Euclid's "Elements."* Trans., with introduction and notes, Glenn R. Morrow. Princeton, NJ: Princeton University Press.
Ramsay, Frank. 1922. Review of W. E. Johnson's *Logic: Part II*. *New Statesman* 19: 469–70.
Redding, Paul. 1996. *Hegel's Hermeneutics*. Ithaca: Cornell University Press.
Redding, Paul. 2007. *Analytic Philosophy and the Return of Hegelian Thought*. Cambridge: Cambridge University Press.
Redding, Paul. 2009. *Continental Idealism: Leibniz to Nietzsche*. London: Routledge.
Redding, Paul. 2015. "An Hegelian Solution to a Tangle of Problems Facing Brandom's Analytic Pragmatism" *British Journal for the History of Philosophy* 23, no. 4: 657–80.
Rescher, Nicholas. 1954. "Leibniz's Interpretation of His Logical Calculi." *Journal of Symbolic Logic* 19, no. 1 (March): 1–13.
Robin, Léon. 1908. *La théorie platonicienne des idées et des nombres d'après Aristote*. Paris: F. Alcan.
Rorty, Richard. 1967. *The Linguistic Turn: Essays in Philosophical Method*. Chicago: University of Chicago Press.
Rorty, Richard. 1979. *Philosophy and the Mirror of Nature*. Princeton, NJ: Princeton University Press.
Rorty, Richard. 1982. *Consequences of Pragmatism*. Brighton: Harvester Press.
Rose, Lynn E. 1968. *Aristotle's Syllogistic*. Springfield, IL: Charles C. Thomas.

Russell, Bertrand. 1897. *An Essay on the Foundations of Geometry*. Cambridge: Cambridge University Press.
Russell, Bertrand. 1901. "On the Notion of Order." *Mind* 10, no. 37 (January): 30–51.
Russell, Bertrand. 1903. *The Principles of Mathematics*. Cambridge: Cambridge University Press.
Russell, Bertrand. 1905. "On Denoting." *Mind* 14, no. 56 (October): 479–493.
Russell, Bertrand. 1906. "Symbolic Logic and Its Applications, by Hugh MacColl: Review." *Mind* 15, no. 58 (April): 255–260.
Salamone, Maria Antonietta. 2019. "The Two Supreme Principles of Plato's Cosmos—the One and the Indefinite Dyad—the Division of a Straight Line into Extreme and Mean Ratio, and Pingala's Matrameru." *Symmetry* 11, no. 1 (January): 1–13.
Sans, Georg. 2004. *Die Realisierung des Begriffs: Eine Untersuchung zu Hegels Schlusslehre*. Berlin: Akademie Verlag.
Sayre, Kenneth. 2005. *Plato's Late Ontology—A Riddle Resolved*. With a new introduction and the essay "Excess and Deficiency at *Statesman* 283C–285C." Las Vegas: Parmenides Publishing.
Schelling, F. W. J. 1967. "Über die Construction in der Philosophie." In F. W. J. Schelling and G. W. F. Hegel, *Kritisches Journal der Philosophie* (1802–1803), 1–2: 26–61. Hildesheim: Georg Olms.
Schelling, F. W. J. 1994. *Timaeus (1794): Zur Bedeutung der Timaeus-Handschrift für Schellings Naturphilosophie*. Ed. Hartmut Buchner and Hermann Krings. Stuttgart-Bad Canstatt: Frommann-Holzboog.
Schelling, F. W. J. 2001a. "Presentation of My System of Philosophy (1801)," trans. Michael G. Vater. *Philosophical Forum* 32, no. 4 (winter): 339–371.
Schelling, F. W. J. 2001b. "Further Presentations from the System of Philosophy (1802)," trans. Michael G. Vater. *Philosophical Forum* 32, no. 4 (winter): 373–397.
Schneider, Helmut, 1975. "Anfänger der Systementwicklung Hegels in Jena." *Hegel-Studien* 10: 133–171.
Schröder, Ernst. 1890–1905. *Vorlesungen über der Algebra der Logik (Exakte Logik)*. 3 vols. Leipzig: B. G. Teubner.
Schubring, Gert. 2005. *Conflicts between Generalization, Rigor, and Intuition: Number Concepts Underlying the Development of Analysis in 17–19th Century France and Germany*. New York: Springer.
Shorey, Paul. 1924. "The Origin of the Syllogism." *Classical Philology* 19, no. 1 (January): 1–19.
Smith, Nicholas D. 1996. "Plato's Divided Line." *Ancient Philosophy* 16, no. 1: 25–46.
Smith, Robin. 1978. "The Mathematical Origins of Aristotle's Syllogistic." *Archive for History of Exact Sciences* 19, no. 3 (October): 201–210.
Smith, Robin. 1993. "Aristotle on the Uses of Dialectic." *Synthese* 96, no. 3 (September): 335–358.
Sommers, Fred. 1982. *The Logic of Natural Language*. Oxford: Oxford University Press.
Stelzner, Werner. 1999. "Context-Sensitivity and the Truth-Operator in Hugh MacColl's Modal Distinctions." *Nordic Journal of Philosophical Logic* 3, no. 1 (December): 91–118.
Stenzel, Julius. 1924. *Zahl und Gestalt bei Platon und Aristoteles*. Leipzig: B. G. Teubner.
Stepelevich, Lawrence S. 1998. "Hegel's Geometric Theory." In *Hegel and the Philosophy of Nature*, ed. Stephen Houlgate, 71–96. Albany: State University of New York Press.
Stern, Robert. 2013. "An Hegelian in Strange Costume? On Peirce's Relation to Hegel, I and II." *Philosophy Compass* 8, no. 1 (January): 53–62 and 63–72.
Storrie, Stefan. 2013. "Kant's 1768 Attack on Leibniz' Conception of Space." *Kant-Studien* 104, no. 2 (June): 145–166.

Striker, Gisela. 2009. Aristotle, *Prior Analytics Book 1*. Trans., with an introduction and commentary, Gisela Striker. Oxford: Clarendon Press.

Struik, Dirk J. 1953. *Lectures on Analytic and Projective Geometry*. Cambridge, MA: Addison Wesley.

Swoyer, Chris. 1994. "Leibniz's Calculus of Real Addition." *Studia Leibnitiana* 26, no. 1: 1–30.

Szabó, Árpád. 1978. *The Beginnings of Greek Mathematics*. Reidel: Springer.

Tarlazzi, Caterina. 2017. "Individuals as Universals: Audacious Views in Early Twelfth-Century Realism." *Journal of the History of Philosophy* 55, no. 4 (October): 557–581.

Tarski, Alfred. 1954. "Contributions to the Theory of Models, I and II." *Indagationes Mathematicae* 57: 572–581 and 582–588.

Thomas, Ivor, ed. and trans. 1939–1941. *Greek Mathematical Works*. 2 vols. Cambridge, MA: Harvard University Press.

Van Atten, Mark. 2020. "Luitzen Egbertus Jan Brouwer." In *The Stanford Encyclopedia of Philosophy* (Spring 2020 ed.), ed. Edward N. Zalta. https://plato.stanford.edu/archives/spr2020/entries/brouwer/.

Van der Waerden, B. L. 1983. *Geometry and Algebra in Ancient Civilizations*. Berlin: Springer-Verlag.

Venn, John. 1881. *Symbolic Logic*. London: Macmillan.

Von Fritz, Kurt. 1945. "The Discovery of Incommensurability by Hippasus of Metapontum." *Annals of Mathematics*, second series, 46, no. 2 (April): 242–264.

Von Wright, G. H. 1951. "Deontic Logic." *Mind* 60, no. 237 (January): 1–15.

Walford, David, and Ralf Meerbote. 1992. "Introduction to the Translations." In Immanuel Kant, *Theoretical Philosophy, 1755–1770*, trans. and ed. David Walford in collaboration with Ralf Meerbote, xlix–lxxxi. Cambridge: Cambridge University Press.

Whicher, Olive. 1971. *Projective Geometry: Creative Polarities in Space and Time*. Forrest Row: Rudolf Steiner Press, 1971.

Whitaker, C. W. A. 1996. *Aristotle's De Interpretatione: Contradiction and Dialectic*. Oxford: Clarendon Press.

Wittgenstein, Ludwig. 1922. *Tractatus Logico-Philosophicus*. Trans. C. K. Ogden. London: Routledge & Kegan Paul.

Wittgenstein, Ludwig. 1953. *Philosophical Investigations*. Trans. G. E. Anscombe. Oxford: Blackwell.

Wolff, Michael. 1999. "On Hegel's Doctrine of Contradiction," trans. E. Flynn and K. R. Westphal. *Owl of Minerva* 31, no. 1 (Fall): 1–22.

Wood, David. W. 2012. *Mathesis of the Mind: A Study of Fichte's Wissenschaftslehre and Geometry*. Fichte-Studien, Supplement, vol. 29. Amsterdam: Rodopi.

Wussing, Hans. 1984. *The Genesis of the Abstract Group Concept: A Contribution to the History of the Origin of Abstract Group Theory*. Trans. Abe Shenitzer. Mineola, NY: Dover.

Zacher, Hans J. 1973. *Die Hauptschriften zur Dyadik von G. W. Leibniz: Ein Beitrag zur Geschichte des binären Zahlensystems*. Frankfurt: Vittorio Klostermann.

Zhmud, Leonid. 2019. "From Number Symbolism to Arithmology." In *Zahlen- und Buchstabensysteme im Dienste religiöser Bildung*, ed. L. Schimmelpfennig, 25–45. Tübingen: Seraphim.

Index

algebra: abstract, 138, 195, 247n6, 253n9, 253n20; analytic reduction of geometry to, x, xii, 82, 213; application to logic by Boole and post-Booleans, 112, 132, 169–190; application to logic by Leibniz, xii, 16, 36, 83, 108–115, 128; criticisms of the empty abstractions of, 95, 141; development in early modern Europe, 11–12, 95–96, 133; "disinterpretational theory" of, 171; distinction between constants and variables in, 94, 128, 238n23, 239n1; group theory in, 138, 195, 247n5, 250n15; linear, 9, 11, 84, 102–105; non-Greek provenance of, 11–12, 36; nonreductionistically conceived relations with geometry, 91–92, 95, 117–118 (*see also* geometric algebra); role of abstraction within, 12, 112, 171–172, 175; treatment of functions within, 64–65, 176–177, 235n3, 253–254n22

analogy, 15; Aristotle's metaphorical and nonmetaphorical forms of, 15, 44, 158; Hegel's inference by, 201–204, 218–219. *See also* proportion or analogy

analysis situs, or analysis of situation. *See under* Leibniz

analytic (or coordinate) geometry: as application of algebra to geometry, x–xii, xiv; dependence of infinitesimal calculus upon, 132, 134, 245n11; Leibniz's *analysis situs* as alternative to, 9, 82, 109, 117; projective geometry as alternative to, xi, 96–99; reduction of continuous to discrete magnitudes within, 9, 82, 84, 118

analytic philosophy, ix–x, xii; privileged role of Fregean logic within, ix–x, 169, 232

Andersen, Kristin, 120

Apollonius of Perga, 10, 51, 80, 246n22; construction of harmonic section by, 97–99, 246n17;
treatment of conic sections by, 96, 100, 245n8, 248n16

Apuleius, 155

Archimedes of Syracuse, 10, 51, 64, 133–137, 236n11; method of exhaustion of, 134–136

Archytas of Tarentum, 44; music theory of, 48–51, 74–75, 239n9; nonstandard interpretation of proportion (*analogia*) by, 50–51, 240n20, 243n30; renaming of subcontrary mean to harmonic mean by, 75

Argand, Jean-Robert, 245n14

Aristotle: attitude to Pythagoreans of, 30–31, 158; approach to conceptual measure by, 36–37, 44–45, 149–150; *Categories*, 39, 159; conception of possibility of, 127; criticisms of Plato by, 22, 27–29, 239n4; ethical doctrine of "the mean" of, 14; on future contingent propositions, 159; *Metaphysics*, 229; *Nicomachean Ethics*, xiii, 14, 23, 38, 72; *Posterior Analytics*, 33, 38, 148, 160, 207; *Prior Analytics*, 33–34, 38, 40, 43–44, 189; reinterpretation of Plato's "ideas" by, 22; theology of, 229, 231; theory of metaphor of, 15, 44, 158; use of the musical means by, xiii–xiv, 14–15, 23, 43, 45, 50–51, 72, 80, 159

Aristotle's syllogism, 32–35; ambiguous treatment of singularity in, 34–35, 37–38, 157–160, 206; conflation of intension and extension within, 37, 151, 156; definition of, 33; dialectical variant of, 38, 147, 207; geometric and diagrammatic features of, 33, 42–43, 152–155, 198; inference as iteration of containment relations within, 33–34, 143, 149, 152, 249n6; influence of Plato on, 21–22, 38, 148; linguistic dimensions of, 21, 33–34; musical origins of, 16, 43–45, 148, 198, 239n2; role of contrariety within, 160; role of

Aristotle's syllogism (*cont.*)
geometric mean within, 149, 160; role of perfect or complete syllogism within, 32–34, 44, 172, 215–216; three figures of, 33, 43, 143, 215–218
Aristoxenus, 45, 248n22
arithmetic: binary, 112–113, 140; Hegel's account of development of, 59–65; Plato's "philosophers' arithmetic," 12, 23, 77, 109, 132, 254n25; purported "logicist" grounding of, 15–16, 170, 252n4; Pythagorean approach to, 24, 26, 16, 23, 67, 237n15, 238n16; relation to geometry (*see under* geometry)
arithmetical operations, 111–112, 172, 176, 189–190, 252n9, 252n10; associative, 242n17; commutative, 104, 242n17, 246n27, 247n28, 247n4; logical analogues of, 111–112, 172, 174–175, 195, 253n18
arithmetic mean: definition of, 49, 240n18; harmonic correlation with the perfect fifth (*diapente*), 49; role in Aristotle's theory of justice, 14, 157; role in Golden Ratio and Plato's Divided Line, 52–55; role in musical *tetraktys* and harmonic cross-ratio, 74–76, 98, 80; role in structure of Plato's cosmic animal, 47–48, 148. *See also* musical means of Pythagorean mathematics

Baader, Franz von: appeal to Pythagorean *Quadrat* of, 4–5; *On the Pythagorean Tetrad in Nature*, 4, 89; philosophical and political views of, 4–5, 13, 70, 81, 89, 236n6; relations to Hegel and Schelling, 5–6, 230–232, 236n7, 259n3, 259n5
Barker, Andrew, 25
Becker, Oscar, 26
Bell, John, 92, 126, 238n27
Berkeley, Bishop George, 92, 136
Billington, James, 5
Blanché, Robert, logical hexagon of, 220–224, 258n3, 258n6
Boethius, 155–156
Böhme, Jacob, 230, 259n3, 259n4
Boole, George, 169, 171–176, 252n3; *An Investigation of the Laws of Thought*, 169, 172, 252n2; *The Mathematical Analysis of Logic*, 172, 252n8; rediscovery of algebraic logic by, 109, 169; relation to the Cambridge "analytic society" 171–172
Boole's algebraic logic: Aristotelian features of, 109, 169, 171, 182; binary arithmetic of, 36, 112–113, 172; component term and propositional logics within, 173; duality within, 171, 173, 180, 255n49; interpretation of truth and falsity within, 172, 180, 189, 251n13; limitations of, 113–114, 171, 174, 175–178, 253n16; parallels with Hegel's logic, 163, 173–174; primary and secondary propositions within, 163, 173–174, 180, 253n13, 256n2; set-theoretical aspects of, 109–110, 172–173, 254n23; symbols of as uninterpreted, 172; use of arithmetical operations within, 111, 172–174, 190, 195, 253n10, 253n18, 255–256n53
Borzacchini, Luigi, 24, 69
Bowman, Brady, 10, 79, 123
Boyer, Carl; 92
Brandom, Robert, ix–xiii, xiv–xv; employment of notion of "global isomorphism" by, x, xii, 49; Fregean assumptions of, 207–208, 251n19; "inferentialist" interpretation of Hegel's logic by, 163, 249n4, 258n19; Sellarsian aspects of, ix–x; strong inferentialist semantics of, xi
Brouwer, L. E. J., 186–187, 255n45; influence of idealism on, 186–187, 255n45; intuitionist mathematics of, 186–187, 255n44, 255n47; rejection of law of excluded middle and proof by contradiction by, 187; rejection of "logicist" grounding of mathematics by, 187
Burnyeat, Miles, 158

calculus: of concepts, 109, 111, 121; infinitesimal (*see* infinitesimal calculus); origins of the term, 241n4; of predicates, 15; of propositions, 36, 110, 113; of vectors, 103
Cambridge analytic society, 171
Carnot, Lazare: approach to mechanics of, 8, 133, 136, 194, 197, 236n13, 249n13, 257n6; complete quadrilateral of, 80, 98; *De la corrélation des figures de géométrie*, 6, 8, 79, 80, 94; doctrine of auxiliary or nonexecuatable magnitudes of, 94, 141, 165, 194; Hegel's familiarity with, 6–8, 92–94; *Géométrie de position*, 9, 80; influence of Leibniz's *analysis situs* upon, xii, 16; interpretation of infinitesimal magnitudes by, 92–94, 136, 165, 245n11; practical outlook of, 8; projective geometry (or geometry of position) of, 8–10, 13, 15, 79–82; *Réflexions sur la métaphysique du calcul infinitésimal*, 6, 8, 92, 94; role in French Revolution, xi, 6, 236n8
Carnot, Sadi, 236n10
Cart, Jean-Jacques, 7
characteristica universalis. See under Leibniz's algebraic logic
Chasles, Michel, 65–66, 153, 259n13
chirality, or handedness, 82–83. *See also* incongruent counterparts
Clarke, Samuel, 119
Clifford, William Kingdon; development of vector calculus by, 104, 190, 245–246n14, 247n28, 259n6; influence on C. S. Peirce of, 84, 246n25, 255n51
concepts: containment relations among, 33, 110–111, 114, 150, 162, 173; disinterpretation and reinterpretation of, 170–171, 175, 180, 192, 256n4; incommensurability between, 25–26, 35;

INDEX 279

intension-extension distinction, 37, 109–110, 114, 152–153
conditionals: Boole's interpretation of, 173–174, 253n15; Heyting's interpretation of, 189, 256n56; Johnson's interpretation of, 184; Russell's interpretation of, 174, 253n16; ontological implications of, 250n22; universal judgments interpreted as, 251n9
contradiction: as generated in Hegel's logic, 59, 124, 129, 230; proof by contradiction (reductio ad absurdum), 187; relation to contrariety and incompatibility, 156, 186, 221–222; role in logical hexagons, 224, 259n7; role in propositional logic, 155; role in squares of opposition, 155–158, 220
contrariety: in Aristotle's logic, 159–160; association with opposed directionality, 95; contrary pairs of Pythagoreanism, 30–31, 221–222; in Hegel's judgments of existence, 157, 160–161, 186; in Hegel's judgment of the concept, 161, 181; in Kant's aesthetic judgments, 249n5; in logical hexagons, 224; in Łukasiewicz's modal square, 220; in MacColl's modal logic, 181; relation to contradiction, 156, 186, 221–222; in squares of opposition, 155–158; strong (oppositional) versus weak, 222
Cook Wilson, John, 26
Coxeter, Harold, 246n18
cross-ratio relation: as central invariant of nineteenth-century projective geometry, 8, 100, 121, 151, 244n43, 246n19, 247n28; harmonic cross-ratio, 6, 8, 16, 80, 96, 98, 100, 121, 217; identification with Plato's "most beautiful bond" via musical *tetraktys*, 6, 80, 141, 143; logical analogues of, 141, 143; use in military engineering, 100. *See also* musical *tetraktys*
Czezowski, Tadeusz, 222, 229, 259n8, 259n9; logical hexagon of, 223–226, 259n7; parallels to Hegel's logic in, 223–225

Delian problem, 240n14
De Morgan, Augustus, 112, 171, 177
De Morgan's laws, 173
Deranty, Jean-Philippe, 258n20
Desargues, Girard, xi, 80, 109, 121, 247n28; projective geometry of, 96–100, 120, 165
Desargues's Theorem, 98–100, 202
Descartes, René: analytic geometry of, x–xi, 66, 82, 118; and the "subjectivity" of modern philosophy, 108–109; appeal to the "real" numbers by, 35–36, 119; Desargues's opposition to, 97; *La Géométrie*, 96; introduction of power notation, 242n10; use of variables in geometry, 12, 236n18
Des Jardins, Gregory, 55, 241n33
d'Hondt, Jacques, investigations of Hegel's links to J. K. F. Hauff by, 7

Diophantus of Alexandria, 12, 236n19
directionality: in Grassmann's vector analysis, 103–104; in Schelling's Constructed Line, 151; Kant on the significance of for negative magnitudes, 80–82; of spatial dimensions in Kant's philosophy, 185, 220; significance for logic and logic diagrams of, 151, 198–201, 217–218, 222, 250n3, 257n8; significance for mathematics of, 76, 95, 98, 103, 218, 241n7, 245n13
division of line segments, 73, 97–98; internal and external forms of, 75–76, 80, 97–98, 143, 217; logical analogue of, 164, 217
division of musical intervals, 14, 25, 43–45, 48–50
duality. *See* principle of duality
Durkheim, Émile, and Marcel Mauss, 221

École Polytechnique, xi, 8, 136
Einarson, Benjamin, 16, 43–44, 148, 198
Englebretsen, George, 248–249n2, 259n9
Eschenmayer, Adolf Karl August: criticism of Schelling's understanding of mathematics, 70, 88, 240n16; relevance of arithmetic and geometric series for, 48; relevance of power series for, 70, 88–89
Eschenmayer's diagram, 88–89
Euclid, 50, 80, 237n6; *Elements*, 3, 12, 21, 24, 36, 236–237n1; on the Golden Ratio, 52, 57, 240n22; parallel postulate of, 101, 120; *Porisms*, 97, 236n16
Euclidean geometry, 9–10, 16, 43, 118; approach to ratio and proportion within, 50–51, 57, 67–68, 148; axiomatic method within, 11–12, 89, 112, 118; differences to projective geometry, 8, 93, 96, 100–101, 115; influences of Pythagorean music theory on, 43; proof structures within, 21, 237n5. *See also* geometric algebra
Eudoxus of Cnidus, 51, 60; contributions to Euclid's *Elements*, 52, 67, 71, 236–237n1, 240n23; expansion of the three Archytan musical means by, 73–75, 220, 224, 244n46; geometric innovations of, 17, 35, 77, 84, 132–133, 243n23; influence of on Aristotle's logic, 77; treatment of ratios of continuous magnitudes by, 35, 67, 71, 84, 153–154
Euler, Leonard: containment diagrams of, 250n5; invention of topological science of *geometria situs* by, 118, 219, 248n14; postulation of natural logarithms by, 121, 242n14; role in the development of algebra, 170

Fermat, Pierre de, analytic geometry of, 9, 82, 118
Fichte, Johann Gottlieb, 87–90, 106, 245n5; absolute ego of, 89
Findlay, John N., 27, 29, 237n11, 252n6; thesis of the relevance of Neoplatonism for Hegel, 27, 29
Francoeur, Louis-Benjamin, 136

Frege, Gottlob, 169; *Begriffsschrift*, 177; criticism of Boolean logic by, 113–114, 169, 171, 181; influence on analytic philosophy of, x, xii, 208; postulation of a universal logical language by, 123, 170, 190; propositions as fundamental logical unit for, 177; replacement of subject-predicate by function-argument relation by, 176–177; role in the development of modern "classical" predicate calculus of, 15, 169; treatment of negation by, 255n41. *See also* modern "classical" predicate calculus

French Revolution, xi, 232; Carnot's role in, 6; Hegel's interest in, 6; revival of Pythagoreanism during, 4, 52, 58

Galois, Évariste, 138, 247n5, 250n15

geometric algebra, 9–10, 152–154, 236n15; modern revivals of, 11–12, 16, 82, 104, 110, 173, 236n20, 259n6; role of Eudoxus in development of, 35, 67

geometric logic, 3, 6, 122

geometric mean, xiv, 47–49, 74; definition of, 48–49; harmonic correlation with the octave, 48–49; role in Aristotle's account of justice, 14–15, 157; role in Aristotle's logic, 148–149, 152; role in Plato's Divided Line, 52, 241n33; role in the Golden Ratio, 52–55, 71; role in the musical *tetraktys*, 14, 45, 49–50; role in the structure of Plato's cosmic animal, 15, 47–48. *See also* musical means of Pythagorean mathematics

geometry: analytic (*see* analytic [or coordinate] geometry); arithmetic, relation to, 24, 29, 36–37, 65–66, 88–92, 109, 117–120, 238n26; Euclidean (*see* Euclidean geometry); non-Euclidean forms of, 7, 101, 120, 187, 248n17; problems-based approaches to, 97, 257n12; projective (*see* projective geometry); role of congruence within, 9, 83–84; synthetic (or descriptive) forms of, xi, 8, 96, 102, 236n11, 246n11; three-dimensional (or stereometric) 9–10

Girard, Jean-Yves, 255n55

Goethe, Wolfgang von, 243n29, 244n44

Golden Ratio (or division in extreme and mean ratio), 71–72, 240n22, 241n31; as combining arithmetic and geometric means, 51–52, 55, 71–72; Euclid's treatment of, 52; as manifested in the Pythagorean pentagram, 240n22; popular enthusiasm for, 52; purported role in Plato's Divided Line, 51–56, 71; purported role in Plato's "most beautiful bond," 51

Grassmann, Herman, 102, 118, 247n28; influence of idealist and romantic philosophy on, 101–102; influence of Leibniz's *analysis situs* on, 16, 83; linear extension theory (vector calculus) of, 9–10, 11, 13, 16, 103–104; purported links to Hegel, 11, 101, 236n16; role of directed magnitudes for, 12–13, 81–82, 84

Grassmann, Justus, 102

Hamilton, William Rowan, 84, 236n20, 244n49, 245–246n14

harmonic mean, 50–51, 71, 74; correlation with perfect fourth (*diatessera*), 49; definition of, 49, 240n19; originally called the subcontrary mean, 75. *See also* musical means of Pythagorean mathematics

Harris, Henry S., 2, 6, 226, 236n5, 237n13, 238n24, 252n6

Hasse diagrams, 188–189, 222. See also lattice and semilattice structures

Hauff, J. K. F., 7, 93; mathematical career of, 7, 120, 236n9; purported links to Hegel, 5, 7, 245n10; scientific translations by, 7

Hegel: as aligned with the "unwritten doctrines" school of Plato interpretation, 29; attitude toward Aristotle's ontology of kinds, 207, 211; as critical of central assumptions of analytic philosophy, xii; critique of "ladder" imagery in relation to thought, 165–166, 192; *The Difference between Fichte's and Schelling's System of Philosophy*, 87; doctrine of absolute identity or "identity in difference," xiii, 1, 107, 195, 199; *Encyclopedia of the Philosophical Sciences*, 166, 228, 259n5; familiarity with Pythagorean doctrines, 48, 79; on formal logic, 40, 121–123, 147, 213, 238n29, 252n6; on incommensurable magnitudes, 92–94, 124–125, 134, 136–137, 237n13; interest in mathematics of, x, 3, 6, 9, 10, 92–93, 123, 126, 238n24, 252n6; interest in mysticism and theosophy of, 3–4, 8, 225–226, 230–232; interest in the French Revolution of, 5–6; *Lectures on the History of Philosophy*, 1, 48, 54, 60, 147, 235n1; logic of (*see* Hegel's formal syllogism; Hegel's ontological syllogism; Hegel's subjective logic); on mathematics, 91, 123–125; on Newton's mechanics, 138–139, 196–197, 205–206; notion of alienation/externalization, 123, 175, 253n19; *On the Orbits of the Planets*, 3, 91, 133, 136, 138; *Phenomenology of Spirit*, ix, xiv, 106, 115, 134, 163; *Philosophy of Nature*, 102, 136, 138, 207, 228, 231, 236n13, 257n5; *Philosophy of Right*, ix; *Philosophy of Spirit*, 228; recognition-based theory of self-consciousness of, 106–107, 140, 212; on the relation of geometry to arithmetic, 91–92, 118, 124; relation to Kant's philosophy, 129–130, 185, 208, 211, 227; on the role of empirical experience in natural science, 3, 138, 196–199, 205–206

Hegel's formal syllogism: role of order of terms within, 216–220; syllogism of analogy, 201, 203–204, 218–219; syllogism of existence, 161, 216–218; syllogism of induction, 197–201, 203;

INDEX

syllogism of reflection, 203, 217–218; syllogistic figures within, 161–162; tripartite structure of, 161

Hegel's library, 6: works on ancient mathematics, 6, 68–69, 79, 136, 236n12, 236n19, 237n13, 244n45, 246n22; works on modern mathematics and mechanics, xii, 6, 8, 65, 92–93, 102, 236n13, 237n13, 245n7

Hegel's ontological syllogism: as concrete logical life, 212, 217; imagery of "circle of circles" for, 166, 191, 228, 256n1; Hegel's system as three syllogisms, 228–230; imagery of "triangle of triangles" for, 2–4, 77, 165, 225–226; relation to Plato's rational syllogism of, 41–42, 46–48, 148, 151–152, 157, 195

Hegel's subjective logic: cycles of conceptual redetermination within, 166–167, 176, 191–193, 195; distinction between "singularity" and "particularity" within, 39–41, 153; duality of judgment and predication within, xii, 130, 151; judgment forms within (*see* judgments in Hegel's logic); role of disinterpretation (abstraction) and reinterpretation (concretion) of concepts within, 192–195, 218–219

Hegel's triangle of triangles, 2–3, 36, 77, 165; effect on the viewer of, 2, 225–226, 230; fractal features of, 2, 235n2; similarities to circle of circles, 166, 191

Hestenes, David, 259n6

Heyting, Arend, 17, 163, 186, 192; intuitionistic logic of, 186–190; parallels to Hegel's logic, 190, 194–195, 200, 225; rejection of law of excluded middle and indirect proof by, 187, 189, 255n46; treatment of negation by, 187, 189, 255n46

Hippasus of Metapontum, 24, 26

Hippocrates of Chios, 240n14

Hölderlin, Friedrich, 5

Holy Trinity, 2

homology/homomorphism, xiii, 194–195, 135n3, 247n10; as applied to judgment forms, 194–195; difference to isomorphism, xiii

Horn, Laurence, 223

Houlgate, Stephen, 39, 66

hybrid logics, 225, 259n9

Iamblichus of Chalcis, 49, 51, 69, 72–73, 77–78, 79, 97, 243n25

incommensurable magnitudes, xiv, 13, 35, 49, 55, 70–71, 76, 83; Greek discovery of, xiii, 14, 24–26, 31, 42, 77–78, 124, 135–136; Hegel's concern with, 92–94, 124–125, 134, 136–137, 237n13; Hegel's logical analogues of, 15, 28, 37–38, 56, 139, 207, 227, 244n45, 253n19

incongruent counterparts, Kant's concept of, 82–83, 100, 104, 244n48, 244n50

inference: abductive, 18, 201–203, 213–217; by analogy, 201, 204, 218; deductive, 21–22, 33–34, 199–200, 201, 213–218, 252n5; inductive, 18, 197–205, 213–219; relation to implication, 174, 184, 199–200; as transitivity of containment relation, 33–34, 44–45, 110–111, 149, 162

infinitesimal calculus, xi, 118, 130, 132–133; ancient Greek roots of, 8–9, 133–136; Hegel's attitude to, 8–9, 31, 60, 92, 96, 101, 132, 136–139, 140–141, 144, 249n8

infinitesimal magnitudes, 8; Berkeley's criticism of, 92, 136; Carnot's interpretation of, 92–94, 136, 165, 245n11; Hegel's interpretation of, 92–94, 136

intension-extension distinction. *See under* concepts

inversion: arithmetical forms of, 64–65, 67–71, 84, 151, 176, 253n20; geometrical forms of, 71, 75, 80–81; logical forms of, 107, 126, 163, 165, 194, 214–216, 255n49, 257n8

isomorphism: Brandom's notion of global isomorphism of algebra and geometry, x, xii–xiii, 49; versus homomorphism, xiii

Jacoby, Friedrich Heinrich, 10

Jevons, William Stanley, 175–176

Johnson, William Ernest, 182, 254n33, 255n39, 256n2, 258n18; algebraic logic of, 132, 163, 182–186, 187, 190; criticisms of logic as a universal language by, 123, 170, 175, 252n5; determinable-determinate distinction in, 142, 184–186, 193, 199, 255n39; on induction, 199–205; inference-implication relation in, 184; logical parallels to Hegel's logic in, 170, 184–186, 191–193, 196–201, 203–206, 241n5, 255n40; on relational predicates, 182–184; reliance of contradiction on contrariety for, 186

judgments: *de dicto*, 151, 174; *de facto*, 193, 253n14; *de re*, 141, 151, 163, 166, 194–195, 206; indexical and nonindexical, 165, 183, 194, 258n24; primary and secondary, 173–174, 180, 184, 256n2

judgments in Hegel's logic: absolute content of, 166, 194; of the concept, 139, 160–164, 181, 201–202, 251n17, 258n23; dual, mutually presupposing qualitative and quantitative forms of, xii, 130, 151, 165–166; of existence, 139, 141–142, 163–165; as implicit syllogisms, 160–163, 181, 212; infinite, 142, 144, 194; of necessity, 193, 207, 257n16, 157n17; of reflection, 141, 164–165, 193, 196–197, 257n17

Kant, Immanuel: "Attempt to Introduce the Concept of Negative Magnitudes into Philosophy," 12, 81, 102, 150; concept-intuition distinction of, 83, 167, 184–185, 227; "Concerning the Ultimate Ground of the Differentiation of Directions in Space," 81–83; the "Copernican revolution" of, x, 96, 109, 122, 195–196, 247n1; critique of

Kant, Immanuel (cont.)
  Leibniz by, 113–114, 117, 122, 126, 128–130, 132, 244n47, 246n19; *Critique of Pure Reason*, 117, 130, 150, 241n7, 246n7, 247n1, 249n5; *Critique of the Power of Judgment*, 162, 249n5; dependence of appearance on concepts, 40; doctrine of incongruent counterparts by, 82–83, 104, 244n48; on empirical and transcendental dimensions of self-consciousness, 106–107; *Groundwork of the Metaphysics of Morals*, 211; *The Jäsche Logic*, 126; on Leibniz's *analysis situs*, 82, 120; on mathematics, 16, 60–62, 89–91, 94, 186, 245n5; notion of intensive magnitude in, 202, 205; *Prolegomena to Any Future Metaphysics*, 241n6, 244n48, 249n5; proto-vectorial idea of directed line segments of, 12–13, 80–84, 88, 102–105, 244n2; role of normativity in philosophy for, 208, 211; subjectivist stance of, 87; transitional precritical philosophy of, 11–13, 129–130, 132, 185, 227
Kant's logic: aesthetic judgments in, 162, 249n5, 251n17; early postulation of dual judgment forms in, 130, 132; general versus transcendental, 129, 157; relevance of concept-intuition distinction for, 130, 142, 156–157
Kästner, Abraham Gotthelf, 95
Kaulbach, Friedrich, 109
Kepler, Johannes, 64; anticipation of projective geometry by, xiii, 245n8, 248n16; geometrically based cosmology of, xiv, 133–134, 205, 246n21, 250n17; Hegel's championing of, xi, 3, 9, 136, 138–139, 231–232, 257n5; Platonism of, 79, 239–240n11; principle of continuity in, 93, 101, 136, 165, 219, 257n14; use of points at infinity in, 120, 165
Kepler's laws, 250n17, 257n5
Klein, Felix, 247n5
Klein, Jacob, 26, 31
Knorr, Wilbur, 240n20, 243n23
Krämer, Hans, 29, 237n8, 237n12
Kreines, James, 39
Kripke, Saul, 179

Lagrange, Joseph-Louis, 9, 137; algebraic interpretation of calculus by, 9, 133, 136, 171, 196, 245n12
Lagrangian mechanics: Hegel's criticism of, 9, 136–137; Hegel's familiarity with, 92–93, 245n7
Lambert, Johann Heinrich, 13, 115; as advancing Leibniz's idea of *analysis situs*, 17, 121–122; challenge to Euclid's parallel postulate by, 120; contributions to projective geometry of, 115, 120–121; cosmology of, 115–117; dispute with Ploucquet, 17, 115, 121, 235n2, 250–251n5; Hegel's criticisms of, 122–123, 248n12; "hyper-Copernicanism" of, 116–117; idea of hierarchy of languages by, 116–117, 122, 141, 165; idea of universal geometric logical language of, 120–122, 170
Laplace, Pierre-Simon, 7
lattice and semilattice structures, 110, 255–256n53; diagrammatic presentations of ("Hasse diagrams"), 189, 223; Leibniz's anticipation of, 110, 114–115; Peirce as inventor of, 255n51. *See also* Hasse diagrams; partially ordered sets (posets)
Leibniz, Gottfried Wilhelm: congruent triangles of, 100, 104–105, 246; "Copernican" and "hyper-Copernican" approach of, 108–109, 116–117, 122, 132, 140–141; *Discourse on Metaphysics*, 109, 140; epistemic ladder imagery in, 140–141, 150, 166, 192; "General Inquiries about the Analysis of Concepts and of Truths," 109, 111; infinitesimal calculus of, 8, 92, 130, 132–133; intensional-extensional distinction in, 126–128, 130, 150, 249n3; as introducing modern formal logic, 12, 21, 40, 139; law of continuity of, 93, 257n14; links to projective geometry, 109, 120, 259n12; *New Essays on the Human Understanding*, 114, 129; "On Contingency," 141; on part-whole and container-contained distinctions, 114–115, 178; on perspective (*point de vue*), 140–142, 165; principle of sufficient reason for, 140–141; proposal for an *analysis situs* by, xii, 9, 13, 16–17, 82–84, 109, 117–120; relational conception of space of, 119; revival of Pythagorean notion of "monad" by, 36–37, 112; status of possibility for, 127, 130, 252n8
Leibniz's algebraic logic, 109–115, 126, 129–132, 149–150; *characteristica universalis* within, 84, 112, 121–122, 132, 140, 142, 170, 258n2; containment relations among concepts within, 114–115, 150, 173, 250–251n5; logical calculus (calculus ratiocinator) of, 121, 131, 132, 142–144, 170; numerical model of inference relations within, 32, 36, 110–113, 254n32; parallels to Boole's logic, 171–172; relation between class and propositional logics within, 113–114, 152, 157; relations between intensional and extensional judgments within, 126, 129–131; role of the notion of order within, 110, 114–115, 255–256n53; treatment of singular propositions within, 248–249n2; use of binary number system within, 112, 140, 171, 247n7
Lenzen, Wolfgang, 109–111, 113, 127, 129–131, 144
Lévi-Strauss, Claude, 221
Lewis, C. I., criticism of Russell's material implication, 253n17
logarithmic progression in the modern musical scale, 105, 194, 242n15, 247n29
logarithms: Hegel's interest in, 64–65, 242n12, 244n45; history of, 64–65; relation to exponential powers, 64–65

INDEX

logic: abstraction and generality within, 128, 142, 144, 152, 166, 175, 177, 192–195, 206; algebraic, xii, 12, 16, 36, 40, 110–115, 121, 142, 169–190; classical versus nonclassical, ix, 15, 187, 195; conceptions of the role of mathematics within, 169–170; dialectical, 38, 147; formal or mathematical, 1, 32, 107, 147, 156, 170–171, 179, 235n1; Fregean and Russellian (*see* modern "classical" predicate calculus); as God's language, 117, 122, 248n18; intuitionistic, 186–190, 193–195, 248n18, 251n13; linear, 190, 256n55; proposed universal language for, 13, 15, 122, 132, 170, 190, 252n4; propositional, 36, 127–128, 143, 155–156, 159, 184, 205, 251n14; of reason, 17, 197; relation of term to propositional logics, 113–114, 129–131, 144, 157, 171, 173, 180, 200; syllogistic (*see* Aristotle's syllogism; Hegel's formal syllogism); term (or class), ix, 113–114, 131, 172–173, 177–179, 249n6; three-dimensional, 15, 18, 30, 143, 225–227, 229, 255n50; two-dimensional, 15, 225–227; of the understanding, 40, 43, 147–148, 227, 230
logical calculi: of classes or concepts, 109, 111, 121; of propositions, 36, 110, 113
logical mean or middle term: doubled or split versus univocal, 47, 55–56, 105, 160, 202–203, 208; as modeled on means in music, 43
logical negation: as driving abstraction, 165; external or propositional, 130–131, 166, 186, 193, 121–122; internal or term, 130–131, 156–157, 164; oppositional (strong contrariety), 160–161, 181, 220–222
logic diagrams: of containment (Euler), 121, 152–154, 250n5; Hasse diagrams, 188–189, 222; logical cube, 226, 255n50; logical hexagon, 18, 220–226, 258n3, 258–259n6, 259n7; logical square (square of opposition), 155–158, 220–223
Łukasiewicz, Jan, 220, 223

MacColl, Hugh, 179; attitude to propositional logic, 132, 180, 254n31; as critic of universal logical language, 180; dispute with Russell, 174, 181–182, 254n32; on judgment types, 180–181; modal contraries in, 181, 220; modal logic of, 179–182, 254nn30–31; parallels to Hegel's logic in, 179; *Symbolic Logic and Its Applications*, 180
MacLaurin, Colin, 95
magnitudes: absolute versus signed, 81, 105, 160; continuous and discrete, 66, 69, 71, 82, 242n18; division into kinds, 14, 31–32, 62, 112, 137; incommensurable (*see* incommensurable magnitudes); infinitesimal (*see* infinitesimal magnitudes); negative, 12–13, 81, 92, 95, 98, 103, 129; redetermination in dialectical development of mathematical practice, 26, 35, 124
mathematics: Babylonian, 21; Greek, 112; Egyptian, 21; Indian-Arabic, 12, 36; pure versus applied, 8, 39, 62, 90, 248n23, 249n14; relation of philosophical method to, 25, 89–90; role in education in Plato's *Republic*, 25; structural approaches to, 59, 76, 95, 117. *See also* algebra; arithmetic; Euclidean geometry; geometric algebra; projective geometry; vector analysis
McDowell, John, 106
mean proportional. *See* proportion or analogy
medieval nominalism, 17, 38, 127, 153, 178, 198
Möbius, Augustus, 243n33, 244n39
modern "classical" predicate calculus: analytic philosophy's commitment to, ix–x, 169, 232; role of concepts of truth and falsity within, 159, 181–182, 186; treatment of negation within, 186, 221–222, 255n41; treatment of relations within, 176–179, 182–183; as universal logical language, 15–16, 170, 190, 227. *See also* Frege, Gottlob; Russell, Bertrand
monas/monad. *See* Pythagorean monas/monad
Monge, Gaspard: as head of the École Polytechnique, xi, 136; reintroduction of descriptive geometry, 8, 236n11
monochord, 45, 48–49
More, Henry, 230
Moyar, Dean, 258n20
Müller, Johann Wolfgang, 65, 237n13
musical means of Pythagorean mathematics, 47–52, 57, 71; complementarity of arithmetic and harmonic means within, 49; conceptions of the unity among, 51, 79–80, 84, 191–192, 224, 227; Eudoxus's extension of, 73–77, 220; incommensurability among, 70–71; relation to Hegel's rational syllogism, xiv, 37, 207. *See also* arithmetic mean; geometric mean; harmonic mean
musical *tetraktys*: identification with Plato's "most beautiful bond," 6, 49; as instance of the harmonic cross-ratio, 6, 80, 98; role of Pythagorean musical means within, 14, 45, 76. *See also* cross-ratio relation
"music of the spheres" thesis, xiv, 44, 77, 243n24, 244n38
music theory: ancient, xii, 11, 14, 44–45, 49–50, 65; modern, 105–106, 242n15, 247n29; as source of Aristotle's logical terminology, 43–44

Newton, Issac: conception of absolute space of, 119; employment of vectors by, 103; Hegel's attitude to, xi, 31, 133–134, 138–139, 197; and the infinitesimal calculus, 8, 93, 118, 132–133, 135–136; *Naturalis Principia Mathematica*, 118, 133; Newtonian mechanics, 9, 60, 204–205; reliance on Greek geometry of, 135–136; theological views of, 119, 230–232
Newton's laws, 133; as purportedly explaining Kepler's laws, xi, 3, 133–134, 136, 205

Ng, Karen, 258n25
Nicomachus of Gerasa: Hegel's access to doctrines of, 6, 68–69, 79–80; *Introduction to Arithmetic*, 6, 69, 73, 161; notion of "most perfect proportion" by, 49–50, 96, 141, 149, 157, 217, 243n35; Pythagorean mathematics of, 51, 57, 69, 71–72, 77–81, 84
numbers: auxiliary, 136, 141, 194; cardinal and ordinal, 66; figured or figurative, 3, 29–31, 69, 112, 137, 238n16; fractions, 30, 69, 74, 242n11; Hegel's conception of, 61–65, 123–124; imaginary and complex, 60, 95, 161, 245–246n14; "impossible," 95, 127, 161, 165; infinite, 66; infinitesimal, 8, 92–94, 96, 136, 165, 194, 245n11; irrational, xiii, 66, 134, 242n14; mysticism concerning, 4; natural, 31, 35, 254n25; negative, 11, 12, 30, 60, 68, 75, 81, 95–96, 161, 242n11, 244n40; operations on (*see* arithmetical operations); order among (*see* order among numbers); powers of, 31, 63, 238n17, 238n20, 242n10; Pythagorean conception of, 3, 16, 26, 27, 30–31, 42, 59–60, 68–69, 240n26; rational, 30, 66, 242n18; ratios of (*see* ratios); "real" numbers of modern mathematics, 26, 35–36, 66, 69, 82–83, 119, 231; sequences or series of, 30, 48–50, 68–69, 79, 84, 89; as used in the analysis of conceptual content by Leibniz, 111–112; zero as, 30, 36, 95, 247n8. *See also* arithmetic; arithmetical operations
number systems: binary, 112, 171; decimal, 36, 172; Indian-Arabic, 11–12, 36, 112; Roman, 112

order among numbers, 110; geometric origins of, 65–66, 117, 178, 242n18, 247n2; logical significance of, 114–115, 155, 157, 177, 188–189, 216, 219
order among operations on numbers, 104, 242n17. *See also* arithmetical operations: associative; arithmetical operations: commutative

Pappus of Alexandria, history of geometry of the musical means, 51, 96–97, 244n38; *Collection*, 96, 98; construction of harmonic section in, 98, 246n17
Parmenides, significance for Plato's later philosophy, 27–28, 211
partially ordered sets (posets), 110, 114–115, 189, 222, 247n2, 254n25. *See also* order among numbers
Pascal, Blaise: projective geometry of, 96, 106, 165; theological significance of geometry for, 225
Pascal's theorem, 109, 259n12, 259n14; construed as the "mystic hexagram," 256n1
Paterson, Alan, 10, 36–37, 238n25
Patzig, Günter, 35
Peirce, Benjamin, 84, 177, 245–246n14, 246n26, 253n10
Peirce, Charles Sanders, 177; algebraic logic of, 1, 84, 115, 132, 177, 254n23; importance of order or directionality for, 177, 188, 190, 198, 250n3, 254n25, 255n51, 257n9; irreducibility of continuous to discrete magnitudes for, 242n18; logical similarities to Hegel, 17, 151, 190, 203, 213–219, 229, 256n57, 257n12; logic of relations, 177, 183; notion of abductive inference, 18, 201–203; use of logical quantifiers by, 178–179, 254n26, 254n27
perspective: epistemological considerations concerning, 109, 140; geometric considerations concerning, 98–101, 120–122
Philolaus of Croton, 158; doctrine of the limited and unlimited of, 24–25, 27, 48, 240n15, 240n20
Pinkard, Terry, 5, 258n20
Pippin, Robert B., ix, xiv, 40, 238n30
Plato: alleged "number mysticism of," 3–5; attitude to mathematics of, 11, 25, 29, 61, 69, 123, 243n24, 244n41; cosmology of, xi, 1, 41, 46–49; duality of the one and the indeterminate dyad of the greater and the lesser for, 27, 30, 36–37, 48, 66, 137, 142, 178, 211; importance of Pythagorean mathematics for, 27–28; lecture "On the Good" by, 123; lesson of the "Divided Line" in, 52–56, 57, 71, 241n33; method of collection (*synagoge*) of, 22, 130, 257n7; method of division (*diairesis*) of, 22–23, 29, 31–32, 34, 42, 111, 116, 129, 141, 156, 237n2; "most beautiful bond" of, xiii, 1, 3, 6, 14–15, 42, 46, 50, 57, 71–72, 79, 89, 96, 101, 195; *Parmenides*, 27–28; *Phaedo*, 22; *Phaedrus*, 22; *Philebus*, 22, 27–28, 239n7, 241n28; *Republic*, 25, 27, 28, 51, 52, 78, 161, 239n8, 241n28; role of *paradigmata* for, 28, 211, 258n23; significance of "measure" or "due measure" for, xiii, 16, 21, 23–28, 30, 42, 237n4; *Sophist*, 22, 23, 27, 31, 239–240n11; *Statesman*, 22, 23, 25, 30, 36, 46, 239–240n11; *Theaetetus*, 23–24, 27, 237n13, 244n45; theory of forms in, 27–28, 39, 78, 137, 145; *Timaeus*, xiii, 5, 22, 32, 42, 44–46, 57, 235n4; "unwritten doctrines" interpretation of, 11, 27–29, 66–67, 78, 237n12. *See also* Plato's syllogism
Platonic conceptual pyramid or ladder, 110, 116–117, 122, 140–141, 150, 165–166, 192
Platonic solids, 9–10, 47, 52, 239–240n11, 240n22
Plato's Academy, xiii, 11, 21, 25, 35, 43, 77, 96, 236n1
Plato's syllogism, 1, 11, 15, 36, 40, 43, 58, 60, 71, 80, 143, 147, 149, 151; doctrine of the divided middle term in, xiii, 1, 40, 42, 55–56, 89, 160, 162, 185, 208, 225, 259n9; as structured by the musical means, 14, 16, 32, 47–49, 57, 69, 79, 148, 172, 191–192, 227, 229; three-dimensional nature of, 15, 18, 30, 47, 79, 226, 229, 243n35, 255n50
Playfair, John, 141, 245n13
Plevrakis, Ermylos, 259n2
Ploucquet, Gottfried: critique of idea of universal logical language by, 121–122, 132, 248n19; dispute with Lambert, 17, 115, 121, 235n2; dis-

INDEX 285

tinction between exclusive and comprehensive particularity of, 128, 132, 183, 201, 225, 249n3, 255n40; influence on Hegel's logic of, 128, 131, 183, 225; as logic teacher at Tübingen Seminary, 11, 113, 115, 247n9; use of logical diagrams by, 250–251n5
Plutarch, 239n8
Poincaré, Henri, 118
polarity: in Eschenmayer, 70, 88–89; in projective geometry, 99, 101; in Schelling, 78, 88–89
Poncelet, Jean-Victor, 120, 247n28, 259n13
Popper, Karl, 219
Porphyry's tree, 22, 32, 150, 156, 184
Posch, Thomas, 138
power/*Potenz*/*dynamis*, meanings of, 70, 133, 242n19, 243n27
predication: duality of, 130; as inherence (or "is in" relation), 34, 38, 91, 129, 149, 165; as subsumption (or "said of" relation), 34, 91, 129, 131, 143, 164
principle of duality, xiii; role in Hegel's logic of, xii, 37, 91, 107, 130, 163; role in nineteenth-century algebraic logic of, xii, 166, 171, 173, 180, 184, 225, 253n13, 255n49; role in projective geometry of, xii, 99, 154, 171, 173, 192
principle or law of continuity, 136; Carnot's application of, 93, 136, 165; Kepler's introduction of, 101, 165, 219; Leibniz's application of, 93; role in projective geometry of, 249n12
Proclus, 119, 243n30; account of the history of Greek geometry of, 21, 52, 71, 97, 224, 241n31, 243n23, 243n37; influence on Hegel of, 10, 27, 36, 251n6; presentation of the "musical *tetraktys*" by, 49
projective geometry, xi–xiii, 8–9, 99–101, 106, 118–121, 246n18; idea of points at infinity within, 98, 101, 120, 165, 194, 219; relation of pole to polar within, 99, 101; role of cross-ratio relation within, 8, 16, 80, 96, 100; theological connotations of, 101. *See also* Carnot, Lazare; cross-ratio relation; Desargues, Girard
proportion or analogy: Aristotle's application of, 15; Euclidean-Aristotelian versus Pythagorean-Platonic senses of, 50–51, 240n20; as geometrical double ratio, 1, 14, 58–59, 67; role in Hegel's syllogism of analogy, 203–204; role in Plato's Divided Line, 54; role in Plato's *Timaeus*, 47. *See also* ratios
Protagoras, doctrine of "man is the measure," 23
Pythagoras, 48, 237n6; cult of, 24
Pythagoras's theorem, xiii, 14, 24, 70–71, 237n5
Pythagorean mathematics, 3–4, 11, 16, 24, 26–31, 35, 58–60, 77–79
Pythagorean monas/monad, 59–61, 67, 77; as both point and numerical unit, 29–30, 153; modern abstract reinterpretation of, 36–37, 77, 112, 140; Philolaic-Platonic duality of monas and indeterminate dyad, 27, 36, 48, 211
Pythagorean music theory. *See* music theory: ancient; Archytas of Tarentum
Pythagorean table of contraries, 30–31, 48, 221

quaternions, 84, 236n20, 244n49, 245–246n14

ratios: cross- (*see* cross-ratio relation); direct, 67–68, 72, 149, 150–151; dividing, 73–74, 76, 80, 217, 243n33, 244n39; double (*see* proportion or analogy); epimoric, 49, 239n9; equality of, 50–52, 59, 63; Euclidean-Aristotelian versus Pythagorean-Platonic senses of, 43, 50–51, 72; exponent of, 67–68, 72, 150, 242n19; extension by Eudoxus from numbers to continuous magnitudes, 35, 67, 71, 84; Hegel's treatment of, 67–79; "golden" (*see* Golden Ratio); incommensurable, 135–136, 163, 195, 237n13; infinitesimals as, 92–94, 136; inverse (or invertible), 68–71, 72, 75, 89, 151; as more fundamental than their numerical components, 77, 93, 245n12; π considered as a ratio, 135; of powers, 16, 58, 67, 71–72, 78, 89, 93, 96, 151, 224; Pythagorean conception of, 50, 59, 77, 93, 241n1
Raue, Johannes, 143
redundancy theory of truth, relation to Hegel's duality of judgments, 256n2
Rorty, Richard, ix–x
Rosenkrantz, Karl, 1–2
Russell, Bertrand, xii; advocacy of the arithmetization of geometry by, 242n18; criticisms of MacColl's modal logic by, 174, 181–182; description theory of proper names of, 127, 179; distinguishing of implication from inference, 174, 187, 189, 253n16; early adoption of Frege's conception of judgment, 179; *Principia Mathematica*, 182; role in the development of modern "classical" predicate calculus, 15, 169, 177; theory of material implication by, 174; treatment of role of order in mathematics, 66, 247n2. *See also* modern "classical" predicate calculus

Salamone, Maria Antonietta, 51
Sayre, Kenneth, 27–29, 211, 237n19
Schelling: commentary of Plato's *Timaeus* of, 4; dispute with Eschenmayer, 70, 90, 240n16; evaluation of geometry over arithmetic by, 37, 89, 107; and the philosophy of nature, 4–5, 8, 78–79, 235n4; proximity to Kant's philosophy of mathematics, 16, 62, 245n5; proximity to Spinoza's pantheism of, 4, 78, 87–91, 105, 232; on the relevance of geometry for philosophy for, 89–91; theosophical views of, 4, 5, 8, 225–226, 257n15

Schelling's Constructed Line, 88–90, 139, 141, 151, 212; Hegel's interpretation of, 91–92, 106; indifference point within, 89; as representation of Spinozist absolute, 89

Schröder, Ernst, 179, 181; doctrine of universal logical language in, 252n4; *Vorlesungen über der Algebra der Logik*, 169

Schwikardt, Ferdinand Karl, 7

Sellars, Wilfrid, ix–x, 163; on the "myth of the given," 108

set theory, 109, 242n9, 247n8, 252n13, 253n22, 253n23

Sextus Empiricus, 48

Shorey, Paul, 21–22, 42

Smith, Robin, 43–46, 148, 238n28, 239n10

space: Aristotle on, 118; Hegel on, 124; Leibniz's relational conception of, 119; Newton's absolute conception of, 119, 230–232; as the object of projective geometry, 118

Spinoza, Baruch, use of axiomatic method by, 10–11, 88

Spinozism or pantheism: Baader as critic of, 4, 5, 232; notion of absolute within, 88; Schelling's relation to, 5, 78, 87–90, 105–107

square of opposition: modal, 181, 220–221, 259n8; singular, 157–158, 223–224, 259n8; traditional, 130, 155–156, 157, 188, 200–201, 220, 222, 249n3, 251n7

Steiner, Rudolf, 244n44

Stenzel, Julius, 29, 31

Stevin, Simon, 36, 119

Stoics: conception of possibility by, 128; principle of bivalence of, 159, 251n14; propositional logic of, 128, 155

subcontrariety in geometry, 75; Eudoxus's subcontraries to the Pythagorean means, 73–75, 220; link to harmonic mean, 75, 243n37, 251n10

subcontrariety in logic, 155–156, 158; Blanché's treatment of, 220, 224; Czezowski's treatment of, 224

Swoyer, Chris, 109–111

Szabó, Árpád, 24, 43, 45, 50, 237n7, 239n5, 243n32

Tarski, Alfred, 110

tetraktys, 3–6, 29; layers of significance of, 30, 32, 46–47, 45–47. *See also* musical *tetraktys*

Theaetetus, 52, 236–237n1, 239n11

Theodorus of Cyrene, 24

topology, 245n9, 248n14; links to *analysis situs*, 118, 255n45

Tübingen School of Plato interpretation, 27, 29. *See also* Plato: "unwritten doctrines" interpretation of

vector analysis (or linear algebra), 9–11, 13, 84, 102–204; Clifford's expansion of, 84, 104, 246n25; extension to linear logic, 190; links to projective geometry of, 84; relevance for Peirce's logic, 177

vectors, arithmetical operations on, 102–104; "base vectors" as measures within, 119, 122; Kant's *phora* as, 104

Venn, John, 123, 132, 175; regard for the logics of Ploucquet and Lambert, 175–176; on the semantic reinterpretation of terms in inquiry, 175, 186, 194, 204; *Symbolic Logic*, 175

Wallis, John, 95

"way of ideas," Hegel as critic of, 108

Weiss, Christian Samuel, 102

"witnesses" in intuitionistic logic, 193–194

Wittgenstein, Ludwig, 182, 250n19; *Tractatus Logico-Philosophicus*, 182

Wolff, Michael: linking of Hegel to Grassmann, 11; thesis of importance of Kant's interpretation of negative magnitudes for Hegel, 81, 160

Wood, David, 245n5

Zabarella, Jacobo, 257n12

zero: Indian-Arabic introduction of, 36; as missing in Greek arithmetic, 30, 35–36, 112; modern interpretation of, 247n8; as needed in modern algebra, 112

Zeuthen, Hans Georg, 9

www.ingramcontent.com/pod-product-compliance
Lightning Source LLC
Chambersburg PA
CBHW022038290426
44109CB00014B/904